WAR, POLITICS AND SOCIETY
IN AFGHANISTAN

ANTONIO GIUSTOZZI

War, Politics and Society in Afghanistan

1978-1992

GEORGETOWN UNIVERSITY PRESS/WASHINGTON, D.C.

Georgetown University Press, Washington, D.C. 20007
© 2000 by Antonio Giustozzi. All rights reserved.
Printed in India
ISBN 0-87840-758-8

10 9 8 7 6 5 4 3 2 1   2000

**Cataloging-in-Publication data available from
the Library of Congress**

ACKNOWLEDGEMENTS

There are many people whose advice, assistance and hospitality have alone made this work and the research which preceded it possible. In particular I wish to thank J. Anifi (BBC Monitoring), Mohammed Januf (BBC Tajikistan), Dr S.A. Keshtmand, General Khalil, Farid Mazdak, Juma Khan Sufi, 'Sasha' and Mark Urban (BBC), who all kindly agreed to be interviewed by me; Dr Hassan Sharq for the material he sent me; Mr Paul Bucherer-Dietschi (Stiftung Bibliotheca Afghanica, Liestal), Prof. Yuri Gankovskii (Oriental Institute of the Russian Academy of Sciences), Mr Baghir Moin (BBC Persian Service), Mr Farooq Fardah (Moscow), Dr Ivan Kulikov (Moscow), Mr Kerem Kayi (Berlin) and Prof. V. Naumkin (Oriental Institute of the Russian Academy of Sciences) for their hospitality; Dr V. Plastun (Oriental Institute of the Russian Academy of Sciences), Dr V. Boiko (Barnaul) and Dr Rolf Bindemann (Berlin) for the precious information they provided; Dr Zahir Tanin (BBC Persian Service) and Mr Thomas Ruttig (Berlin) for their invaluable help in organizing my trips, and for their willingness in sharing their knowledge and their own files; Mr Christopher Woodall for reading the manuscript at an earlier stage, and the University of Bologna for providing a two-year bursary. Most of all I wish to thank my supervisor, Prof. F. Halliday, for the advice and help he provided and for putting me into contact with many of the above.

CONTENTS

GLOSSARY

arbab	traditional, notable
bay	khan (in Northern Afghanistan)
Ghund-i Qawmi	Tribal Regiment (one of the government militias)
Harakat-i Inqelab	traditionalist and monarchist mujahidin party
Hizb-i Islami (Hizb)	the most radical Islamist parties among the mujahidin
Hizb-i Islami/Khalis	fundamentalist and pro-*ulema* mujahidin party
Jamiat-i Islami (Jamiat)	moderate Islamist mujahidin party
(Loya) Jirgah	(Great) Assembly
jerib	land unit equal to 0.2 ha.
KhAD	governmental intelligence service, abolished in 1986 and replaced by WAD (Persian acronym)
Khalq	radical faction of the PDPA, in power before the Soviet occupation
khan	tribal leader and big landlord
madrasa	religious high school
Milishia-i Sahard	Border Militia (one of the government militias)
Nasr	nationalist-Islamist Shi'a mujahidin party
Parcham	Moderate faction of the PDPA, brought to power by the Red Army in December 1979 and led by Babrak Karmal
qariadar	rural notable
qazi	Islamic judge
Regional Forces	Tribal Regiments (Territorial forces)

Sarandoy	Ministry of Interior troops
Sepah	an Islamist, strongly pro-Iranian Shi'a mujahidin party
Shura	a traditionalist Shi'a mujahidin party
Territorial Forces	Regional forces (Tribal Regiments)
Tribal Regiments	Territorial forces (Regional forces)
Tribal units	Regional forces + Border Militias
ulema	clergy
Watan (Hizb-i Watan)	Fatherland Party, formerly PDPA

ABBREVIATIONS

AF	*Afghanistan Forum*
AFP	Agence France Press
Afs.	afghanis (the Afghan currency)
AIC MB	*Afghanistan Information Centre Monthly Bullettin*
AN	Academy of Sciences
AP	Associated Press
Bakhtar	Bakhtar News Agency
CC	Central Commitee of PDPA, Central Council of *Watan*
CSM	*Christian Science Monitor*
CTK	Czechoslovak Press Agency
DSP	for service use (closed publication)
DRA	Democratic Republic of Afghanistan
DYOA	Democratic Youth Organization of Afghanistan (the youth organization of PDPA)
FAZ	*Frankfurter Allgemeine Zeitung*
FEER	*Far Eastern Economic Review*
GDR	Revolution Defence Groups (one of the government militias)
IHT	*International Herald Tribune*
INION	Social Sciences Institute of the Academy of Sciences (Moscow)
ION	Institute of the Social Sciences (CPUS, Moscow)
IV	Oriental Institute (Moscow)
KNT	*Kabul (New) Times*
KP	*Komsomol'skaya Pravda*
KPSS	Communist Party of the Soviet Union
KZ	*Kraznaya Zvezda*
LAT	*Los Angeles Times*

LMD	*Le Monde Diplomatique*
MGIMO	Moscow State Institute for the International Relations
MIA	Missing in action
News Bullettin	Embassy of the Democratic Republic of Afghanistan in London
NFF	National Fatherland Front (one of the mass organizations created by the PDPA government)
NT	*New Times*
NWFP	North West Frontier Province (Pakistan)
NYT	*New York Times*
PAP	Polish Press Agency
PDPA	People's Democratic Party of Afghanistan
RA	Radio Afghanistan
RC	Revolutionary Council
RM	Radio Moscow
SAZA	Revolutionary Organization of Afghan Toilers (Sazman-i Inqelab-i Zamatkashan-i Afghanistan)
SR	*Sovetskaya Rossiya*
SZA	Organization of Afghan Toilers (Sazman-i Zamatkashan-i Afghanistan)
TsK	CC
UkSSR	Socialist Federative Republic of Ukraine
WAD	Ministry of National Security (Persian acronym)
WMR	*World Marxist Review*
WP	*Washington Post*
WUFA	Writers' Union for a Free Afghanistan

INTRODUCTION

In many ways, Afghanistan offers a unique opportunity for the study of internal conflicts in both their national and international dimensions. Civil wars in the shadow of the Great Powers have been relatively neglected in scholarly accounts; in particular, the evolution of military and political tactics in the field has rarely been paid the attention it deserves, as it can help the understanding of more general international policies. Due to a particular set of circumstances, a great deal. of sources are today available, to an extent that has rarely been matched in any conflict of the post-Second World War era, for a multi-perspective analysis of the conflict in Afghanistan in 1978-92. Although the Afghan war has been catalogued among the 'forgotten' conflicts, an unprecedented number of 'observers' (journalists, scholars, advisers), often with at least some training in the social sciences, travelled around the country on both sides during the whole period of the conflict. Above all, the Soviet collapse offers new opportunities for information gathering. While archives (those which have not been destroyed) are not yet freely accessible, and will probably not be so for a long time, a sizeable number of individuals involved in the conflict still hold documents and personal diaries or can offer personal reminiscences. Many Afghans of the diaspora are also willing to share their knowledge. It should also be added that much information, which was already available before 1992, has never been exploited, mainly because of excessive distrust towards Soviet and Afghan communist sources. When properly utilized, however, such sources can be very useful. Official and semi-official statistics, for example, have been widely dismissed as mere propaganda, but a large part of them have turned out to be accurate, although they were often manipulated by Afghan and Soviet officials.

One of the outcomes of this situation is that, while the dynamics of the Afghan Resistance and the mutual relationship of its political, social and military aspects, has been analyzed quite satisfactorily, the same cannot be said with regard to the pro-Soviet regime in

1

Kabul. Although many books have been written on the Soviet and Afghan communists' role in the war, they have dealt separately with different aspects – military, political or socio-political – but scarcely any attempts have been made to integrate these aspects in a single analysis. The only real exception so far has been Barnett Rubin's work,[1] which offers the best global analysis so far, covering also the pro-Soviet side, but still leaves out many key points, including the military aspects which is not really examined in depth. The present work attempts to start where Rubin left off. What follows is not a general interpretation of the events in Afghanistan in 1978-92, but rather an exploration of critical themes whose obscurity has so far hampered a full understanding of the dynamics of the conflict.

In order to do this, a full range of sources has been exploited. Afghan and Soviet radio broadcasts have been utilized to a much larger extent than in other analyses and the same applies to printed Soviet and Russian sources; dissertations from the former Soviet Union and East Germany have proved very useful, as well as formerly 'closed' Soviet publications; a number of interviews have been carried out; it has been possible to acquire several formerly secret documents and other documents have been published in the former Soviet Union or in the West since 1991.

When an attempt to evaluate the achievement of Western scholarship in the face of this quantity of sources is made, some conclusions can be drawn. The reconstruction of what happened in 1978-9 and its explanation are today relatively satisfactory. One exception is the dynamic of the anti-communist insurrection in 1978-9, which still remains somewhat obscure, but, due to the scant information available from former Soviet sources in this regard, it is not possible to add much here. The Soviet embassy was mainly relying on information coming from the Afghan armed forces, which were badly demoralized and unwilling to fight, so that they tended to overestimate the size and significance of the rebels' operations. Although the reported clashes probably did take place, it is impossible to estimate reliably their real dimension and impact. Limited armed activity organized by the Islamist parties would not in itself be as meaningful as a real, grass-roots rising. Also because of this, the chronology of the insurrections is still

---

[1] *The Fragmentation of Afghanistan*, Yale University Press, 1995.

subject to controversy. The scarce information coming from the former Soviet side does not always coincide with accounts based on mujahidin sources. The former, for example, puts the date of the revolt in the province of Baghlan as April/May 1979 and of Hazarajat as August 1979, while the latter puts Baghlan in October/November 1978 and Hazarajat in March 1979. While O. Roy maintains that the Durrani tribes of Kandahar province remained quiet until the Soviet arrival, the Soviet embassy sent reports to Moscow of violent clashes in that province as early as May 1979.[2]

The exact chronology of the revolts, however, is not of supreme relevance to the understanding of developments in Afghanistan. The Soviet decision to intervene was influenced more by strife within the ruling party than by the progress of the counter-revolution on the field. The dynamics of intra-PDPA conflicts are quite well known.[3] A point which is still somewhat controversial is the extent of persecution carried out against Parcham by Amin and the Khalqis. Khalq sources admitted 250 killed after September 1978, Parchamis claim 2,000 victims up to the end of 1979, while estimates which appeared in Soviet documents put at 600 the number of PDPA members killed under Amin in September-December 1979 alone. In general, the heavy losses incurred by the party during fighting and in purges seem to have been a decisive factor in the development of the crisis. Kirilienko, as early as March 1979 when the most virulent purges had yet to take place, expressed in front of the Politburo the opinion that the execution of many officers had created a very dangerous situation in the army. Purges added to the bloody disorder in the countryside in depleting the PDPA's ranks. On the whole, 10,000 members

[2] V.A. Merimskii, 'Voina v Afganistane: zapiski uchastika', *Novaya i Noveyashaya Istoriya*, no. 3 (1995); V.G. Safronov, 'Kak eto bylo', *Voenno-istoricheskii Zhurnal*, no. 5 (1990); J.J. Puig, 'La Résistance afghane' in *Afghanistan. La colonisation impossible*, CERF 1984, p. 215; Roy, *Islam and Resistance in Afghanistan*, Cambridge University Press, 1986, p. 103; B. Gromov, *Ogranichennyi kontingent*, Moscow: Progress, 1994, p. 81. The clashes in Kandahar province in 1979 might, on the other hand, have been caused by other tribes in the province.

[3] A. Arnold's works, published in the early 1980s, though biased, turned out to be substantially correct. See *Afghanistan's Two Party Communism*, Hoover Institution, 1983, plus the articles published each year in the *Yearbook on World Communist Affairs*.

of the PDPA appear to have died in 1978-9, while by the end of 1979 6-7,000 of the 18,000 pre-revolution members were no longer in the ranks (they had been either killed or purged). Overall, out of 18,000 original members and a further 28,000 who joined the party between the Revolution and the Soviet occupation, fully half had died, been purged or left the party by the time of the Soviet arrival. In such conditions, the idea that Amin's policies were threatening the survival of the regime was not at all out of place.[4]

Explaining the failure of the reforms is also vital in understanding the developments leading upto and following the Soviet invasion. Although some debate continues, a relative uniformity of opinion has emerged among scholars, that attributes considerable importance to the traditional social structure of the Afghan countryside and to the lack of rural cadres in the ranks of the PDPA. With regard to social structure, the limited degree of modernization of the Afghan countryside, which allowed the survival of local loyalties to rural notables and landlords, has been identified as one fundamental factor in the scant appeal of the Revolution among the peasantry. J.H. Grevemeyer gave an elaborate account of this as early as 1980, describing the patron/client relationship at the root of political life in the Afghan countryside.[5] While others have maintained that the clash has been basically a cultural one, between a Marxist movement and a strongly Islamic rural population,[6] the two points of view are not mutually exclusive. The fact that the

---

[4] R. Anwar, *The Tragedy of Afghanistan*, Verso, 1988, p. 123; interview with Zahir Tanin, London, 8 March 1994; TsK KPSS, 'K sobytiyam v Afganistane, 27-28 dekabrya 1979 g.' in *Sowjetische Geheimdokumente zum Afghanistankrieg (1978-1991)*, VDF, Zurich, 1995, p. 194; Gromov, *Ogranichennyi kontingent*, p. 32; J. Ludwig, 'Einige Probleme der Strategie und Politik der Demokratischen Volkspartei Afghanistans (DVPA) in der nationaldemokratischen Revolution in Afghanistan (1978 bis 1985)', diss., Akademie für Gesellschaftswissenschaften beim ZK der SED, 1986, p. 87.

[5] F. Halliday, 'War and Revolution in Afghanistan', *New Left Review*, 119 (1980); D. Gibbs, 'The peasant as a counter-revolutionary', *Studies in Comparative International Development*, vol. XXI, no. 1, 1986; J.-H. Grevemeyer, 'Afghanistan. Das "Neue Modell einer Revolution" und der dörfliche Widerstand' in *Revolution in Iran und Afghanistan*, Syndakat, 1980.

[6] M.N. Shahrani, 'Introduction: Marxist revolution and Islamic resistance' in Canfield and Shahrani (eds), *Revolutions and Rebellions in Afghanistan*, International Studies Institute, 1984.

reforms were ill-conceived or at least that they needed a much more sophisticated organization to be properly managed is agreed upon by almost everybody. It is also clear that the predominantly urban character of the PDPA, coupled with the policy of absorbing the few rural cadres and potential recruits in the urban bureaucracy after the revolution, condemned the regime to rely on young and unprepared members even in positions of responsibility and in dealing with tensions at the local level. This favoured the emergence of tensions, which in turn eventually ignited the violent confrontation. The weakness of the Afghan state, made only more evident by the overambitious centralization efforts against the tribes, allowed the revolt to spread.[7]

Some former Soviet sources confirm that the cadre policy of the Taraki and Amin regimes was at the origin of the failure in the countryside. At the end of 1979, two-thirds of the 23,000 members of the party were either in the army or bureaucracy, so only the very young and inexperienced were left for work in the rural areas. A Soviet scholar elicited the opinion of the Minister of Tribal Affairs Faiz Mohammed in early 1980, who stated that party cadres in the countryside were seen (and opposed) as '*qaum nishta*', people without clan or tribe.[8]

Soviet sources also confirm a certain relevance of the religious issue. K.M. Tsagolov refers to a village which supported the new regime in the beginning and then joined the counter-revolution when two radical members of the party forbade the population to pray and brought monkeys into the mosque.[9] In fact, the causes of the insurrection were different in different parts of the country.[10] In many villages the first reaction to the revolutionary

[7] F. Ahmed, 'The Khalq failed to comprehend the contradictions of the rural sector', *Merip Reports*, July/August 1980; A. Ghani, 'Gulab: an Afghan schoolteacher' in E.Burke, *Struggle and Survival in the Modern Middle East*, 3rd edn, I.B. Tauris, 1993, p. 348; L. Dupree, 'Red Flag over the Hindukush', *Afghanistan Studies Journal*, vol. 1, no. 2, pp. 117-18.

[8] Gromov, *Ogranichennyi kontingent*, p. 71; Ludwig, 'Einige Probleme', p. 87; I.E. Katkov, 'Tsentral'naya vlast' Afganistana i pushtunskie plemena', diss., Moscow, IV AN SSSR, 1987, p. 172.

[9] D. Gai and V. Snegirev, *Vtorzhenie*, IKPA, Moscow, 1991, p. 197.

[10] The most important text in this regard remains M.N. Shahrani and R. Canfield, *Revolutions and Rebellions in Afghanistan*, Institute of International Studies, Berkeley, CA, 1984.

government was not negative at all, but the inflexibility and in-experience of local officials soon led to open hostility. Elsewhere, the first announcements of the impending land reform led straight to an explosion.[11]

A more confused issue is the impact of the Soviet occupation. The nationalist feelings of many Khalqis and of a large part of the urban middle and upper classes were clearly aroused. With regard to the countryside, little is known. First of all, it is not easy to assess what degree of control the Amin regime still exercised in late 1979. A noted Afghan scholar (H. Kakar) has claimed, presumably basing his statements on Khalqi sources, that at the time of the invasion only four district and two sub-district centres lay outside government control. This is surely an understatement and previously 'closed' Soviet sources reveal that in autumn 1979, in the provinces of Kunar, Nangrahar and Laghman alone, eighteen district and sub-district centres were no longer held by Kabul. Many other sources indicate that many district centres in the Hazarajat were also in the rebels' hands. As early as the summer of 1979 in several provinces only provincial centres were still held by the regime, while many key localities like Khost, Urgun and Asadabad were under siege. In September, thirty district centres out of 185 were in rebel hands. By autumn 1979 rebel formations were active in twenty-five provinces out of twenty-eight, while at the end of the year seventeen provinces were basically under mujahidin control, as well as more than half of the district centres and most of the villages. While some sources claimed that in the autumn some tribes, frightened by the government counter-offensive in Paktia province, began to negotiate with the government, Soviet sources state that other tribes kept hiding in the mountains and were expected to start military operations in spring. The Amin regime was also in trouble because of growing difficulty in managing the transport network around the country; out of 10,000 lorries used to carry goods from the North, only 300–400 were still operational in the autumn of 1979. How this picture

[11] J. Ovesen, 'A local perspective on the incipient resistance in Afghanistan' in Huldt and Jansson (eds), *The Tragedy of Afghanistan*, Croom Helm, 1988; A. Olesen, 'The Saur revolution and the local responses to it' in *Forschungen in und über Afghanistan*, S.W. Breckle and C.M. Naumann (eds), Bibliotheca Afghanica 1983; G. Pedersen, *Afghan Nomads in Transition*, Thames and Hudson, 1994, pp. 224–6.

changed during 1980 is not wholly clear. Western and resistance sources claim that the degree of control exercized by the government fell further and there is no doubt that this did happen at some time between 1980 and 1981, but former Soviet sources are generally evasive or silent about this. One exception is the admission that Lashkargah district was absolutely calm in January 1980 and became infected by mujahidin activities only later.[12]

Surprisingly, developments after 1979 on the Kabul side have not been analyzed with adequate care, although sources are much more abundant. Apart from much cold war rhetoric, the dynamics of the regime have been simplistically subsumed under the rubric of 'sovietization', which spared the analysts much work, while attention was concentrated on the Soviet presence. Some worthwhile insights into the character of the regime and its policies are available,[13] but no full-scale analysis. As an attempt to fill the gap at least partially, Part I of the present work deals with the nature and dynamics of this so-called 'sovietization' and with the degree to which it matched the supposed 'models'.

A number of analyses of military developments are available,[14] but only Mark Urban managed to give an interpretation of Soviet strategies and operational approaches worth the name. Even in this case, the small scale war going on between Afghans was left aside. Part II is dedicated to this matter, with particular attention being paid to the reconstruction of the Afghan Army, a matter which has generally been dismissed by most observers as irrelevant.

Some short essays have been published about various aspects

---

[12] M. Hassan Kakar, *Afghanistan: The Soviet Invasion and the Afghan Response*, University of California Press 1995, p. 125; Yu. Gankovskii, 'Polosa pushtunskikh plemen Afganistana', *Spetsial'nyi Byulleten'* AN SSSR IV, no. 6 (1987), p. 116, n. 15; Gai and Snegirev, *Vtorzhenie*, p. 71; A. Afanas'ev, 'Afganistan: pochemu eto proizoshlo', *Kommunist Vooruzhennikh Sil*, no. 12 (1991), p. 69; A.V. Tchikichev, *Spetnaz en Afghanistan*, CEREDAF 1994, p. 1; J. Ludwig, 'Einige Probleme', p. 93; V. Basov and G.A. Poliakov, *Afganistan: trudnye sud'by revolyutsii*, Znanie, 1988, pp. 30, 34; A. Prokhanov, 'Afghanistan', *International Affairs*, August 1980, p. 16.

[13] O. Roy, *Afghanistan*, and 'Le double code afghan', *Revue Française de Sciences Politiques*, December 1986.

[14] E. O'Ballance, *Wars in Afghanistan*, Brassey, 1993; A. Cordesman and A.R. Wagner, *The Lessons of Recent Wars in the Third World*, vol. III, Westview Press, 1990; D. Isby, *War in a Distant Country*, Arms and Armour Press, London, 1989; M. Urban, *War in Afghanistan*, Macmillan, 1992.

of the pacification policy of the regime,[15] but in general its impact was only recognized in 1990, with little attention being paid to its origins and early development. ·Part III tries to add as much as possible to this key issue. The same also applies to the rise and evolving role of the so-called 'militias', the semi-regular units formed by the government mainly with former mujahidin, whose relevance was also acknowledged belatedly and whose role and characteristics were never fully examined. They are explored in Part IV.

These four points have also been selected because of their mutual links. Other weak spots can be identified in current scholarly production about the pro-Soviet regime in Afghanistan, including the ethnic policies of the Kabul regime and the relative debates within it, but they will not be dealt with here.

NOTE The transliteration system from Cyrillic found in the appendixes of the *Oxford Dictionary of Current English* has been adopted, with the exception that the *ee* and *ee kratkaya* are not distinguished.

---

[15] O. Roy, 'La politique de pacification sur le terrain' in A. Brigot and O. Roy, *La guerre d'Afghanistan*, La Documentation Française, 1985; G. Dorronsoro, 'La politique de pacification en Afghanistan' in G. Chaliand (ed.), *Stratégies de la guerrilla*, Payot, 1994.

Part I. THE LIMITS OF 'SOVIETIZATION'

The solution to the Afghan crisis which the Soviets tried to implement after January 1980 had already been delineated by April 1979, when the aftermath of the Herat revolt was discussed by the Politburo. According to the Soviet leadership, as the mass of the population were not aware of the progressive character of the PDPA program, it was necessary to move step by step, 'in a planned way'. The state apparatus was to be rebuilt, the armed forces reorganized and strengthened. The weakness of the state in the provinces was considered particularly worrying. Clergy and tribal notables were identified as forces with whom it was necessary to make peace, but even the support of social strata which should have been closer to the Revolution needed to be won back (intelligentsia, clerks, petty bourgeoisie, the lowest ranks of the clergy). It was necessary to make peasants understand that it was the Revolution which gave them the land and that, if the government fell, they would lose it. The political base of the regime was to be widened, while maintaining the leading role of the party, whose internal unity had to be restored.[1] In its main features, this was the program President Karmal was expected to put into practice after 27 December 1979. It could be defined as an 'ideological strategy', meaning that it took the shape of a global, thoroughly developed strategy, but within relatively narrow, ideologically defined, limits. It could have been a workable program at the beginning of the Revolution in April 1978, but by the end of 1979 the situation in the country had become much more complicated.

---

[1] 'Vypiska iz protokola N. 149 zasedaniya Politbyuro TsK KPSS ot 12 apreliya 1979 goda' in *Soujetische Geheimdokumente zum Afghanistankrieg, op. cit.*, pp. 90, 94, 96.

1

THE ORIGINAL SOCIAL BASE OF THE 'DEMOCRATIC REPUBLIC' AND ITS TRANSFORMATIONS

The situation in 1980

In the very first period of Soviet intervention a sense of relief prevailed among the Afghan population, as at least the bloody dictatorship of Amin had ended. This was particularly true in the capital,[2] but to some extent it appears also to·have been valid in certain rural areas.[3] However, the situation began to worsen as early as the end of January, with the first, sporadic armed attacks against Soviet troops and a wave of propaganda activism by the opposition forces. By late February 1980 the new regime found itself in almost complete isolation, mainly because of the generalized reaction against the presence of foreign troops in the country, which also took the form of mass demonstrations in Kabul. Armed clashes intensified week after week so that by early 1980 roads were generally under the control of the Resistance, and the government was not even able to pay its provincial employees. The dramatic fall in tax revenue from 280 million Afs. in 1358 (1978/9) to 16 million in 1360 (1981/2), although affecting government revenues only very marginally, shows how government control over the countryside shrank further with respect to 1979. It took Karmal and most of his Soviet supporters some time to accept

[2] S. de Beaurecueil, *Chronique d'un témoin privilégié*, vol. II, CEREDAF, 1993, *passim.*

[3] At least this was the explanation, admittedly not necessarily authentic, given by the first armed groups which abandoned armed rebellion after the Soviet occupation: 'Amin did not leave any freedom, he abused and insulted the faithful' (village of Ouf-Malik, near Mazar-i-Sharif, as cited in E. Mo and V. Pellizzari, *Kabul Kabul*, Vallecchi, 1989, p. 192); 'What our families told us made us understand that Karmal is not like Amin' (*L'Unità* 4 January 1984).

how bad the situation was, as the crisis of February–March 1980 was initially thought to be short lived: the Soviet ambassador in Kabul Tabeev sent Moscow an optimistic message in June 1980, stating that things were going well and the regime was consolidating its position. The crisis that developed during the first half of 1980 even affected the strongholds of the PDPA – mainly the capital Kabul. A great part of later government efforts had therefore to be directed towards winning back some degree of support among these same sectors of society.[4]

While the complex ethnic structure of the country makes a social classification of the groups that proved more receptive (or less indifferent) to the appeal of the Democratic Republic difficult, the most striking element nevertheless is certainly the urban character of the party and particularly its high degree of concentration in the capital. At the end of 1986, the only year for which we have detailed statistics, 69% (111,000) of the party membership was from Kabul. This was even more the case for the youth organization of the party (DYOA), which appears to have worked in the most 'developed' quarters of the capital almost as a Komsomol: here the relevant percentage was 77%.[5]

In tandem with this, the secular intelligentsia surely deserves first place among the social groups that backed the PDPA: these were 'dissatisfied sons of the aristocracy' 'unsatisfied modernizing groups', i.e. mainly officers, teachers and students (according to O. Roy's categorization). In the second half of the 1980s, when the capacity of absorption of the party reached its peak, 76,100 'intellectuals' out of an Afghan intelligentsia of 190,000 were in its ranks, i.e. 40% of their total number. The percentage in fact varied according to the various sectors of the intelligentsia. For example, it was lower than average among teachers: in 1986, 6,691 out of 22,000 were members of the PDPA, i.e. 30%. This figure is surprisingly low if we consider that this professional sector had always been one of the strongholds of the PDPA and that

---

[4] B.R. Rubin, *The Fragmentation of Afghanistan*, Yale University Press, 1995, pp. 122-3, 129; A. Lyakhovskii, *Tragediya i doblest' Afgana*, Moscow: Iskona, 1995, p. 186; Gromov, *Ogranichennyi kontingent*, pp. 117-18.

[5] Yu. Gankovskii, 'O putiakh prekrasheniya grazhdanskoi voiny v Afganistane', *Vostok i Sovremennost*, no. 3 (1993), p. 83; I. Shedrov, *Afghanistan. Molodost' Revolyutsii*, Molodaya Gvardiya, 1982, p. 44.

between 1978 and 1987 the new regime had the opportunity to train 10,000 new teachers. But it should be kept in mind that many former teachers had entered the bureaucracy after the Revolution and many were killed during the 1978-1980 uprisings. Many women had now entered the profession and they were less inclined towards political activism, at least in terms of the PDPA.[6]

Party membership was proportionally much higher among state officials and clerks. If we include the other leftist parties and sympathizers, it appears reasonable to estimate that at least half of the intelligentsia left inside the country had sided with the 'revolutionary' government. It must be noted that a large part of the pre-revolutionary intelligentsia had taken refuge abroad, with defections continuing throughout the whole period of the war. The new regime did its best to replace the fugitives and in fact a quite spectacular social ascent was achieved by groups previously more or less marginal with respect to the real intelligentsia. This process was nevertheless accompanied by a drastic qualitative decline in professional standards; even at the country's main daily paper, *Haqiqat-i Inqilab-i Saur*, most of the journalists had no higher education and lacked any experience. In some cases, particularly where it was difficult or impossible to provide a quick replacement, the situation soon became critical. In 1986 a shortage of 800 judicial personnel was reported despite emergency courses having been established to fill the gaps, and the qualification standard being reputed to have fallen. Although the government claimed throughout the war to have greatly increased the number of physicians in the country, trebling it by 1987, information later released by the Soviets shows that in 1980-5 it hovered around 1,100-1,200 (about 0.7 for every 10,000 inhabitants), one or two hundred less than in 1979. Only later did numbers increase reaching 2,379 by 1988. Yet by 1990 only 100 of those active in 1978 were still in the country, while those trained in shorter courses afterwards were not as well qualified. Furthermore, in 1987, 80%

[6] O. Roy, *Islam and Resistance in Afghanistan*, Cambridge University Press, 1990; M. Centlivres-Demont, 'Afghan women in peace, war, and exile' in *The Politics of Social Transformation in Afghanistan, Iran and Pakistan*, Syracuse University Press, 1994, p. 348; RA, 7 Oct. 1986; N.N. Khakimdzhanov, 'Kurs NDPA na rasshirenie sotsial'noi bazy aprelskoi revolyutsii', *Obshchestvennie nauki v Uzbekistane*, 2 (1988), p. 35; V.R. Krishna Iyer and Vinod Sethi, *The New Afghan Dawn*, Indo-Afghan Friendship Society, 1988, p. 78; Tass, 7 Oct. 1986.

of Afghan physicians were still working in Kabul, while the number of health centres countrywide was down to ninety from 230 in 1978.[7]

The PDPA was also a party of young people. In 1982, 65% of the membership was under thirty. Although recruits in subsequent years were on average older (only 40% of recruits in 1365 (1986/7) were under thirty), the ageing of the party remained quite slow: membership under thirty was still standing at 60% in 1986.[8] The detailed situation at the end of 1983 was as shown in Table 1.

With regard to the generational character of the regime, the role of the Youth Organization (DYOA) deserves special analysis. According to some sources, membership in the DYOA was compulsory for university students, but this is not true. In summer 1980 and in early 1981 only 350 and 400 university students respectively were members of DYOA in Kabul, although in 1981 1,250 more were members of the party. In 1984 only 7% of university students were members of the Youth Organization and even if the percentage had risen to 17% by 1986, it was still considered too low by the party leadership. In 1986 at the Medical Institute the percentage was as low as 3% and at the Teacher Training Institute it was 6%. On the other hand, while it would be excessive to consider the DYOA a Stalinist Komsomol-like organization, pressure was certainly exerted on families and younger students in order to increase its membership. In fact percentages were higher at lower level schools: in Kabul in 1984, 30% of all students were in the DYOA, but while only 7% of university students had joined, 50% had done so in the first eight classes of compulsory education, confirming some attempt at a 'totalitarian' political education of youth. However, such efforts were only half-hearted. In late 1986 the President, Najibullah, complained

---

[7] Z. Tanin, 'To win the confidence of the masses', *WMR*, 1 (1984), p. 52; RA, 19 Oct. 1987; *Narody Azii i Afriki*, no. 6 (1990), p. 136; *Afghan Realities*, no. 69, 16 Nov. 1986, p. 2; Rahim Jan Dardmal, 'Die Herausbildung der sozialistichen Produktionsverhältnisse in der Landwirtschaft Afghanistans', diss., Martin-Luther Universität, Halle-Wittenberg, 1985, p. 83; F. Hoppe, *Kabul '84*, Solidaritätskomitee der DDR, p. 28; *Izvestia*, 16 Oct. 1985; *The cost of freedom* July/Aug. 1990, pp. 6–8; Najibullah, RA 19 July 1988.

[8] RA, 5 July 1983; *Bakhtar*, 27 May 1986; Najibullah, RA, 14 June 1987, CC Plenum.

about the very low levels of DYOA membership in many schools and *lycées*, in some cases less than 5%. – like in the important Balkhi *lycée*, where only ninety students out of 3,200 were DYOA members. Little apparently could be done about those educational establishments where 'the spirit of opposition and anti-Sovietism' was 'almost boasted'. Furthermore, no such attempts at indoctrination were possible in most provinces, where average levels of membership were very low – for example in Takhar only 6%. Lower membership figures for higher education institutes shows how the ideologically conscious membership was in fact much smaller than that claimed. Although the DYOA and PDPA claimed similar numbers of members, in 1984/5 only 50% of PDPA recruits came from the DYOA. In other words, although a significant part of the youth did follow the regime, the majority of DYOA members never joined the party. It can also be noted that immediately before the Saur Revolution, when the party was in no position to push youth into the DYOA, the latter had only 10,000 members as compared to the 18,000 of the PDPA.[9]

As for the countryside, the picture drawn by O. Roy in 1985 with regard to support for the regime is still valid: it relied on more or less proletarianized peasants (in the regions, and in the provinces of Herat, Kandahar, Jallalabad, Pul-i Khumri, Maimana, Laghman, Mazar-i-Sharif, Bagram, Charikar, Shiberghan, Gulbahar, Kunduz, Lashkargah), the smaller Pashtun tribes or the poorest and weakest sectors of the different tribes.[10] A typical example is provided by the 25,000-strong Sabari tribe. It did not take part in the 1978-9 insurrection, but split in the spring of 1981, with a majority leaving for Pakistan and 5,000 'Marxists' openly siding with the government. Although the revolutionary government maintained some degree of support among the majority of the

---

[9] G. Mokrusov, *120 dnei v Kabule*, Moscow, Pravda, 1981, p. 33; 'Postanovlenie politburo TsK NDPA o deyatel'nosti TsK DOMA po dal'neishemu uluchsheniyu organizatsionnoi, politicheskoi i vostitatel'noi raboty sredi molodezhi v svete reshènii...', 17 noyabrya 1984 g.' in *NDPA (sbornik dokumentov)*, Tashkent, 1986, p. 314; Najibullah, RA, 17 May 1986 and 7 Oct. 1986; Politburo Session, RA, 6 July 1985; G.M. Mohsenzada, 'Die Rolle der afghanische Jugend im Kampf für die revolutionäre Umgestaltung Afghanistans', diss., Humboldt University, Berlin, 1985, p. 104.

[10] About the tribes see also M. Olimov, 'Iz zapisok perevodchika', *Vostok*, no. 3 (1991), p. 64.

tribes in the East and South-East of the country, this was generally quite limited. Only among some tribes, like the Shinwari, Mohmand, Jaji, Mangal, Mandi and Ismael Khel, was support more extensive or even, in a few cases, predominant. Among other ethnic groups, it is generally recognized that some of the Uzbek communities in Takhar and Faryab provinces, as well as some Ismaili ones in Baghlan, supported Karmal's government.[11]

We should also add to the list the small 'working class' of only 60,000 individuals in 1978 (and only half in modern factories). This increased during the war to variously 300,000 or 420,000, of which 75,000 were skilled and 60,000 were employed in modern factories. This growth was due to Soviet investment in the industrial sector and possibly also to some manipulation of the statistics. Two-thirds of the factory workers were non-Pashtun, and the Parcham and other non-PDPA leftist groups active among the ethnic minorities exerted some influence among them. This influence is also recognized by sources belonging to the Islamist opposition, although it should be borne in mind that Soviet occupation also stirred up nationalistic or xenophobic reactions among some groups of workers. Near Kandahar, for example, during the summer of 1980, the candidate member of the CC of the PDPA, Bareq Shafii, allegedly saw some workers refusing payments in kind with goods coming from the Soviet Union. According to official statistics, in 1987, 19,300 workers were members of the PDPA (4.6% of all the workers in the country). If we consider the efforts that had been made to attract workers to the party, such a percentage does not look too high, although it should be remembered that many new workers were from a rural background. Such poor results may also have been influenced by the scant regard shown by the government to the working and living conditions of these people. For example, the living conditions of gas field workers have been described as 'very bad' even by Soviet sources and Karmal himself denounced the fact. Similarly to workers, the PDPA also recruited among the more 'proletarian-like' of utility service professions. At AFSOTR (the state bus company), for example, one in seven of the 2,000 employees was in the party.[12]

[11] *International Herald Tribune*, 21 May 1981; M. Hassan Kakar, *Afghanistan: The Soviet Invasion and the Afghan Response*, University of California Press, 1995, p. 126.

[12] *Aziya i Afrika Segodnia*, no. 12, 1988, p. 19; M. Baryalay, 'Indispensable for

Transformations after 1980

The social origins of party supporters lost much of its importance in the face of changes brought about by the seizure of power and by the permanent state of war. The bureaucratization of the party had already started before 1980 – in 1979 a third of the membership worked in the state apparatus – but it had dramatically worsened by 1987, when 82,000 party members were involved in 'the sphere of administration', i.e. almost half of the party. It should be added that the party bureaucracy, as distinct from the state one, also expanded and in 1987 there was one party cadre for every seventy members and one cadre for every 200 DYOA members.[13]

Militarization of the party was another, even more unavoidable consequence (see Table 2). Out of 18,000 members at the time of the Revolution, military men accounted for around 1,400, according to the most trustworthy estimate, equivalent to 7–8% of the total. As 80% of them were officers and 20% NCOs (there were no private soldiers), they could to some extent be considered part of the intelligentsia. The proportion of soldiers could not but undergo a dramatic increase in the years to come. As early as 1983 more than 50% of party members were in the armed forces and the proportion then stabilized around 60-65%.[14] In

victory over counterrevolution', *WMR*, 6 (1985), p. 26; A.V. Loghinov, 'Natsional'ny Vopros v Afganistane', *Rasy i Narody*, 2 (1990), p. 174; Afghanews, vol. 8, no. 1, (1 Jan. 1992), p. 5; AFP, 10 July 1980; N.N. Khakimdzhanov, 'Kurs NDPA na rasshirenie sotsial'noi bazy aprelskoi revolyutsii', *Obshchestvennie nauki v Uzbekistane*, 2 (1988), p. 35; Bradsher, *Afghanistan and the Soviet Union, III unpublished edition*, cap. 10, p. 19; RA 27 March 1985, Karmal; *Sotsialisticheskaya Industriya*, 29 March 1988.

[13] Ludwig, 'Einige Probleme', p. 71; 'National Conference of PDPA on National Reconciliation (18-20 Oct., 1987): Documents', Kabul, *Afghanistan Today*, 1987, p. 58.

[14] Bradsher, *Afghanistan* 3rd edn, from an interview with Yu. Gankovskii, 6 April 1988, cap. 3, p. 19; RA, 22 Nov. 1985; A. Arnold, 'The ephemeral elite' in *The Politics of Social Transformation in Afghanistan, Iran and Pakistan*, p. 51; *Mezhdunarodnyi Ezhegodnik – Politika i Ekonomika* 1987, p. 236; E. Traxler, 'Aufbruch am Hindukusch', *Marxistische Blätter* 3/1987, p. 10; Yu. Gankovskii, 'Vooruzhennye sily respubliki Afganistan', *Vostok i Sovremennost'*, no. 2, 1989. It is actually unclear whether these figures include members of paramilitary forces or not – there are contrasting versions about this. It would seem that the figure given for 1987 does.

addition, by 1988 52,000 of the civilian members of the party (i.e., almost all of them) had also received some military training. If the numbers of bureaucrats and soldiers are combined, it is easy to see that by the mid-1980s few party members did not belong to one or other category. The degree of residual influence of civil society over the party is well shown by Table 3.

At the time of the Revolution, five soldiers were members of the Revolutionary Council, out of a total of thirty-five, while ten more were added in May 1978. When Karmal came to power, his RC was composed of twelve military men out of fifty-seven, a decline which was compensated by their prevalence in the RC Presidium, where they were four out of seven members. In the CC Politburo Karmal had only one military man (Sarwari) among the seven members in 1980 and three out of nine in June 1981, with four more candidates. At the beginning of 1980 soldiers made up 28% of the CC (ten out of thirty-six) and their presence grew only marginally till the end of Karmal's rule, reaching 32%. A sharper increase was registered in the first months of Najibullah's term in power, when their representation rose to 42%. However high such a figure may seem, it is still lower than the proportion of the party rank and file enrolled in the security forces. Anyhow, military men do not seem to have exercized a significant influence over the decision making process – militarization did not come directly to dominate party politics. Rather, it reshaped the nature of the party in the long term.[15]

The countryside

Whatever degree of influence was exerted by the PDPA among the workers, it can be safely said that it was far higher than that enjoyed among the peasantry. According to government sources, in 1980 little more than 5,500 villages were under the control of the government out of as many as 35,500 (see Part III, Ch. 14, Section 2). Very little is known about these villages, even if we can presume that they were mainly located near the main towns and roads. In theory, the 296,000 peasant families who

---

[15] *KZ*, 16 Aug. 1988; Gankovskii, 'Vooruzhennye sily respubliki Afganistan', p. 11; Rubin, *The Fragmentation of Afghanistan*, 1995, p. 128; *FEER*, 25 Jan. 1980; *Aktual'nye problemy afganskoi revolyutsii*, Nauka, Moscow, 1984, p. 432.

benefited from land reform should have constituted the backbone
of the government's social base in the countryside. In reality, as
governmental and Soviet sources were to admit later, during the
'cooperativization movement' innumerable arbitrary acts had been
perpetrated. In fact, it had been in large part a forced process.
Soviet scholars noted that almost half (31,000) of the 64,000 landowners with more than 6 ha. of land still owned more than that
after the reform, while two-thirds of the 900,000 poor and landless
peasants had received nothing. At the same time, many middle
peasants, who were supposed not to be touched by the reforms,
were in fact heavily affected. Furthermore, government sources
tell us that a very large number of these families did not even
begin to farm the land they had received, while others had seen
the land 'taken away' by the old landowners. In reality often the
peasants themselves considered land ownership inviolable and
refused the land assigned to them by the reform.[16]

The same can be said with regard to the cooperatives: 1,145
had been founded prior to the Soviet occupation, but only 20%
of these were functioning. During 1980 the situation actually
worsened, as at the end of 1981 the proportion working normally
was down to 10%. The cooperatives had catalyzed the mujahidin's
hostility and not a single one had been spared from their attacks;
no fewer than 906 had been destroyed. It may therefore be estimated
that the real support for the Democratic Republic in the countryside
came from the 10-20% who were still members of cooperatives
and the 50% who had farmed the land. The two categories overlap
to same extent, as quite a number of peasants who had received
land were in the cooperatives and *vice versa*. Overall a total of
450,000 peasants were touched by at least one of the two aspects
of the reform programs (land distribution and cooperativization).
In sum, DRA supporters numbered less than 200,000 peasants,
probably around 150,000, representing about 12% of the peasantry,
whereas the DRA had aimed to gain the firm backing of at least
900,000 of them (i.e. the poor and the landless).[17] An example

[16] A. Davidov, 'Osnovnye aspekty sotsial'nykh konfliktov v derevne Afganistana',
Spetsial'nyi byulleten' AN SSSR – IV, no. 2 (1987), p. 37.

[17] The figure of 450,000 comprises 300,000 claimed members of the cooperatives
(*Antiimperialistische Bullettin*, no. 7/8, 1980, p. 7) and the estimated half of the
296,000 peasants covered by the land reform who did not join cooperatives.

of a village favourable to the reforms was the village of Shena (Bagram district), one of the first to be shown to foreign visitors. Before the war it was a village of landless peasants and agricultural workers.[18]

Further evidence of the regime's weakness in the countryside is to be found in the number of peasants ('the closest allies of the working class' in Keshtmand's words) who were members of the party in 1980: 3,300 out of a total membership that increased during the year from 25,000 to 55,000. In sum, the DRA's influence in rural areas was limited to an attraction exerted towards the poorest strata of the population and a few weak clans, as is also shown by the influx of Pashtun youths from Pakistan (about 500 until 1985), who had chosen to be educated in Afghanistan or in the USSR.[19]

On the whole, the DRA found itself in a permanent state of siege, with the countryside almost completely beyond government control. To extend its social base was an absolute imperative for Babrak Karmal's government.

This last estimate derives from the statement that half of the 80,000 land-reform peasants actually farming the land in 1987 were members of cooperatives (RA, 14 June 1987).

[18] *NT*, no. 5, (1980); K. Ege, *'Confidence in Kabul: A political solution for Afghanistan'*, unpubl. ms., n.d. [1983], pp. 6-7; *20th anniversary of the People's Democratic Party of Afghanistan. Materials of the jubilee meeting of the PDPA CC, the DRA RC and the Council of Ministers Jan. 10 1985*, p. 23; *Le Monde*, 23 Dec. 1981; M. Saki in W. Bronner, *Afghanistan, Revolution und Konterrevolution*, Marxismus Aktuell, Verlag Marxistische Blätter, 1980; L. Gora, 'Analyse des sozialökonomischen und politischen Entwicklungstandes der Gesellschaft Afghanistans für den Zeitraum von 1973 bis 1978 und der hauptsachlichsten Veränderungen nach der Aprilrevolution von 1978', Diss., Humboldt Universität, Berlin, 1983.

[19] *News Bulletin* (Afghan Embassy, London), 18 May 1987; N. Jawid in T. Amin, *Ethno-national Movements of Pakistan*, Institute of Policy Studies, Peshawar, 1988; *Asiaweek*, 19 June 1986, p. 37; Keshtmand, RA, 26 Feb. 1984.

2

DIFFICULTIES IN THE IMPLEMENT-
ATION OF THE SOCIAL PROGRAM
OF THE REVOLUTION

Female emancipation

From the viewpoint of the PDPA regime and its Soviet patrons, the implementation of social reforms was the key to the extension of its social base. Female emancipation had been a rallying-cry of the regime since the beginning. It cannot be denied that in the main towns women benefited substantially from the new environment, if we leave aside problems deriving from the war. This is particularly true with regard to their employment, as in some professions women were hired in unprecedented numbers. According to Masuma Esmati Wardak, president of the All-Afghanistan Women's Council, 'the war is bringing more women into work, [they are] taking over duties in factories, as police officers and in hospitals.' The Women's Council itself trained women to find jobs in small-scale industries and offices, such as carpet weaving, hairdressing, secretarial and factory work. In the state apparatus as a whole, by the summer of 1988 women accounted for 18.6% of the staff, with the highest proportion in the Ministry of Education, where they formed 43% (1987). Significant numbers also worked in the Ministry of Communications, where they accounted for 15% of the staff, while small numbers of women appeared also in jobs where they had previously been totally absent, like transport, where they now represented 4% of the workforce. According to a Swiss scholar, the number of female teachers in Kabul trebled between 1980 and 1986, while even in a high school in the more conservative Mazar-i-Sharif, in 1990 forty-three out of forty-six teachers were women. Even in industry, the number of working women had quintupled by 1986. Overall, in 1986

270,000 women held jobs, compared to only 5,000 in 1978. Furthermore the regime boasted the presence of 5,000 women (1986) among police and militia (GDR) ranks, while 8,000 more served in the Self Defence groups. The importance of the latter innovation was mainly a matter of propaganda, although women militias are reported by eyewitnesses to have fought bravely in at least two instances: at Urgun (Paktika) in 1983 and at Keranamunyan (Badakhshan) in 1987, when one of the female militias generally branded by critics as a joke resisted for several hours against Commander Massoud's commandos, the most prestigious mujahidin group.

Education for women, according to UN statistics, clearly improved over the pre-revolutionary period. While primary school enrolment rates for males fell from 44% in 1975 to ·27% in 1985, in the same period they rose from 8% to 14% for females. In secondary schools male rates fell from 13% in 1975 to 11% in 1985 and female rates rose from 2% to 5%, while at the universities in 1986 more than half of the 8,800 students were female. In the countryside, however, almost any activity in the field of female emancipation had been frozen since 1979. According to the Education Secretary of the Karmal government, Anahita Ratezbad, the tribes had been promised that women would not have to go to literacy courses without the agreement of the tribal leaders. The promise was maintained: as late as 1987 only 1,917 women were attending literacy courses outside Kabul (including towns) and if we consider that in that year only 2,890 people as a whole attended those courses in the countryside, we can imagine how many women were among them. Even in Shena, the model village already cited, with a twenty-three-member party cell, women rushed inside their homes at the appearance of the first foreigner. Men accepted women's education, but apparently with a 'strong psychological effort' and anyway only ten women out of 5,000 inhabitants attended the courses.[20]

[20] Reuters, 20 June 1989; M. Centlivres-Demont, 'Afghan women in peace, war, and exile' in *The Politics of Social Transformation in Afghanistan, Iran and Pakistan*, pp. 348, 351; *Blatter fur deutsche und internationale Politik*, 1981, p. 1498; Arney, *Afghanistan*, Mandarin Press, 1990, p. 225; V. M. Moghadam, *Modernizing Women*, Lynne Rienner, Boulder, CO, 1993, pp. 224, 239; J. Goodwin, *Caught in the Crossfire*, Macdonald, 1987, p. 140; S. Jamir, *Zum Problem des Analphabetismus in Afghanistan*, LIT Verlag, Hamburg 1990, p. 178; *La Repubblica*, 23 Dec. 1983,

Even in the Ministry of Education no woman held any leading position; and while women made up 10% of PDPA membership, they accounted for only 3.6% in the apparatus. At tribunals the testimony of a woman was still valued at half that of a man. Divorce could still be initiated only by the man, although no longer in the absence of the woman, as happened before the Revolution. Even for girls who belonged to the party or to its social organizations, it was still the father who decided whom they could marry. As far as political representation was concerned, then, the presence of women remained negligible. At elections to local bodies of power in 1986 only 0.4% of those elected were women.[21] One factor clearly working against a fuller implementation of reforms concerning women was their military irrelevance. Even had a large majority of urban women supported the regime, the military balance in the country would have changed little. Besides, other, higher priority reforms, also failed to make much progress.

The literacy campaign

A similar pattern of failure to achieve significant results outside the main towns can also be traced in the case of the literacy campaign. As in primary schools, the government still persevered in inserting the party program and slogans in the curricula, although this time they were combined with the teaching of new techniques, for example in agriculture, or personal hygiene. The Democratic Organization of Afghan Women (later Afghan Women Council) used the campaign to recruit new members. The stated aim was the eradication of illiteracy within ten years, but as is shown in Table 4 the campaign began to decline in pace after 1982, in part because its costs could often not be justified. In fact, at the outset literacy courses had been limited to the main towns and only in 1982 extended to Jowzyan province; other provinces followed only from 1984. In many cases, the help of the *sarandoy*

L'Unità, 7 Jan. 1984; Najibullah, RA, 15 Aug. 1988; Najibullah, II Conf. PDPA, RA, 18 Oct. 1987; LAT, 2 July, 1986; Reuter, 12 Feb. 1986.

[21] Goodwin, *Caught in the Crossfire*, pp. 143-4; M. Centlivres-Demont, 'Afghan women in peace, war, and exile', 1994, p. 353; Najibullah, II Conf. PDPA; RA, 18 Oct. 1987.

(Ministry of Interior Troops) was deemed to be necessary to get the courses started. Even in 1984, although 175 agit-brigades with 7,000 members were created in order to propagandize the courses among the people, enrolment figures were in most cases very low: 11,527 participants in Kabul province, 9,930 in Nangrahar, 3,800 in Badakhshan, 1,900 in Kunduz, and only 117 in Kandahar. Furthermore, the proportion of those who actually obtained the final certificate was also very low: 127 out of 9,000 participants in Balkh province and 318 out of 16,566 in Nangrahar in 1985, so that the number of teachers in the last year of the course was often not much lower than and could even equal the number of students. The literacy skills of most of the other students were in doubt and even Karmal in 1983 privately admitted the untrustworthiness of literacy campaign statistics. As late as 1986, even 20% of party members were still illiterate.

Ordinary (children's) schools were not running well either, as at the end of 1983 only 860 schools out of 3,700 were still open, 130 of which were in Kabul. Although losses among teachers declined after 1978-9, they were still very high. In spring 1983 alone more than 100 were assassinated by the mujahidin in the provinces. Overall, by October 1986 over 2,000 teachers had been killed and 2,000 schools destroyed, while 9,000 teachers had been 'physically assaulted' before the end of 1983. The government later claimed to have greatly expanded the number of students coming from the poorer strata of the population: in 1988, 40% of students came from peasant families, 35% from artisan families and 5% from workers' families, whereas before the Revolution, again according to government claims, 80% had come from well-off families. Whether these statistics are true or not, there is no doubt that even according to official statistics by the mid-eighties only 30% of all children entered primary schools, while the average attendance for compulsory education was 20%. This was an improvement compared to 1983, when only 14.8% of children were registered in schools, but it still left much to be desired. Only in Kabul was schooling complete. Furthermore, most of the schools still in existence were in the open air, with as many as sixty children per class. Finally, in 1989 out of 22,000 teachers only 0.55% had higher education, while 6.1% had incomplete higher education and 40% secondary education; the remainder had either incomplete secondary education or no secondary education at all.

The majority had had no teacher training. As was admitted at the time of the Soviet withdrawal by the then Prime Minister Hassan Sharq, illiteracy was increasing *de facto* because of the destruction of the schools in the provinces.[22]

The land reform

Again, a similar pattern of failure in enacting reforms, notwithstanding their continuous reshaping, is found with regard to the land reform. Initially, grand projects were proclaimed. The distribution of land deeds, designed to give an official and definitive character to the land redistribution and largely neglected under Amin, was planned to begin 'as soon as possible'. While 1,145 cooperatives had been created prior to Soviet occupation, with a total of some 300,000 members and occupying more or less 20% of farm land, it was now envisaged (in accordance with the 1978 plan) to create 3,300 more (in order to achieve a total membership of 1,800,000), 1,400 of which within the current five-year plan. In fact, the situation in the countryside was such that land reform remained completely frozen for more than two years.

In the meanwhile, to appease the peasantry after the occupation, in 1980 the government began to distribute agricultural equipment (including tractors), seeds and fertilizer, imported from Russia and Eastern Europe, free or at subsidised prices. The program intensified in the following years: in 1362 (1983/4) 112,000 tons of chemical fertiliser and 13,000 tons of wheat seeds for sowing were distributed, in 1364 (1985/6) 130,000 tons of fertiliser and 15,000 tons of improved wheat seeds, including 24,000 tons of chemical and

---

[22] Ege, *Confidence in Kabul*, p. 5; V.R. Krishna Iyer/Vinod Sethi, *The New Afghan Dawn*, Indo-Afghan Friendship Society, 1988, p. 77; Basov and G.A. Poliakov, *Afganistan: trudnye sud'by revolyutsii*, p. 48; RA, 7 June 1988; Reuters, 8 Feb. 1986; S.K. Shaniazova, 'Znachenie Aprel'skoi Revolyutsii 1978 g. v razvitii kultury narodov Afganistana 1978-1988' gg. diss., Tashkent 1989, pp. 60-1; E.P. Belozershev, *Narodnoe obrazovanie v respublike Afganistan*, Pedagogika, Moscow, 1988, pp. 49, 50; S. Bazgar, *Afghanistan. La résistance au coeur*, Denoël, 1987, annex 3, p. 191; V.N. Plastun, *Voenno-politicheskaya obstanovka v DRA i polozhenie v NDPA*, 23 July 1986, n.p., p. 4; L.B. Aristova, Yu. V. Bosin, M. Makhkamov and Kh. Khashibekov, 'Mnogonatsional'nyi Afganistan' in *Zapadnaya Aziya*, Nauka, 1993, p. 129; Najibullah, RA, 7 Oct. 1986; PAP, 1 Nov. 1983; Najibullah, RA, 7 Oct. 1986; *FEER*, 29 Dec. 1983; PAP, 2 Nov. 1983.

phosphate fertilisers and 10,000 tons of wheat seeds from the USSR. 1,200 tractors and agricultural machines were imported from the Soviet Union between 1978 and 1982. Credit was offered on a relatively large scale to peasants and 100-120,000 of. them actually received one-year loans each year between 1982 and 1984. Also considerable amounts of money were spent on irrigation, but the overall size of the program was not too impressive when one bears in mind that the development plan of 1361 (1982/3) assigned only 10.4% of available resources to agriculture.

The state also began to lend state land and land abandoned by the 'émigrés' to peasants and landlords, in total 278,000 jeribs; if the owner returned, he only had the right to claim payment of one year's rent. In February-March 1980 measures were taken to find a remedy to the abuses which had taken place place in 1978-9. The main point was the decision to return the land arbitrarily seized during the enforcement of the reform from many middle peasants who, according to the reform decree, should not have been affected. At least some *Khans* were given their land back too, for example in Kama district of Nangrahar province, and they were also allowed to reclaim all the rent owing for the past period. In most cases, however, so as not to hurt the new owners of the land, the former owners were supposed to receive compensation, in place of the original land. This compensation should have been taken from state land, through the mediation of the traditional village councils. It was an apparently wise solution, but as late as 1985 it was still far from having been carried out on a large scale.[23]

[23] S.A. Keshtmand, personal communication, 10 Dec. 1993; RA 12 May 1980 and 6 Feb. 1980; *Anti-imperialistische Bullettin*, no. 7/8, 1980 p. 7; *Mezhdunarodnyi Ezhegodnik – Politika i Ekonomika 1981*; CSM, 28 Dec. 1981; RA, 1 April 1981 and 21 Aug. 1980; *L'Humanité*, 1 March 1985; F. Halliday, 'Report on a visit to Afghanistan 20-27.10.1980', unpubl. typescript, p. 6; Karmal's Speech on 65th Anniversary of Afghanistan's Independence, RA, 16 Aug. 1984; Karmal's Concluding Speech at the Revolutionary Council Session, RA, 2 April 1986; A.D. Davydov, 'Osnovnye izmeneniya v kontsentsii agrarnoi reformy do i posle Aprel'skoi Revolyutsii v Afganistane', in 'Aprel'skaya Revolyutsiya 1978g.', Referatnyi sbornik, AN SSSR i INION, 1982, p. 175; J. Fullerton, 'The Soviet Occupation of Afghanistan, FEER, 1983, p. 166; E. and K.J. Michalski, 'Die revolutionär-demokratisch Umgestaltung der Agrarverhältnisse und die Entwicklung der landwirtschaftlichen Produktion in Afghanistan', *Asien-Afrika-Lateinamerika*, vol. 13, no. 5 (1985), pp. 818-19.

In sum, the government still believed that its political, social and economic aims in the countryside ('deep change in the ways and means of production', the 'economic and cultural development of the farmers and all agricultural workers' etc.) could only be accomplished by 'the step by step implementation of the land reform'. Testifying to the great importance placed on the success of the reform, Karmal himself took the position of President of the Commission for Land Reform, while its provincial presidents were the secretaries of PDPA provincial organizations. It had anyway to accept the fact that substantial changes had to be made to the land reform decree. In August 1981 Amendment no. 1 to Decree no. 8 (Land Reform) was approved, authorizing some categories (mullahs, tribal leaders fighting on the side of the 'Revolution' or at least 'rendering services' to the government, security force officers, modern-minded owners who had mechanized their farms) to own more land than the legal limit and even to receive new land up to it. The legal limit of land ownership was 'unofficially' raised from 10 to 30 jeribs (2 to 6 ha).[24] 'Returnees' were promised the restitution of their land, up to the legal maximum of 30 jeribs. As a Soviet source put it, 'to win the patriotically-minded members of the old exploiting class for the cause of the Revolution, the Revolutionary Council [decided] not to expropriate the surplus land of mullahs and older tribal leaders who took part in the fight against the counter-revolution'. Even mosque land no longer ran any risk of confiscation. Those landowners whose land had already been distributed, would be paid 'a fair value' for it.[25]

Apart from these attempts to adjust the original version of land reform, the first initiatives taken to pursue the reform further (the first 'operational plan' of the 'second phase') came only in November 1981. To this end special bodies were set up within the Ministry

---

[24] This is a controversial point, as according to the version of Decree no. 8 (Land Reform), published in G. Vercellin, *Afghanistan 1973-1978*, Venice, 1979 (the only complete version available in the West) the land ownership limit was fixed at 30 jeribs, while later amendments explicitly referred to a limit of 10 jeribs (see RA, 19 Jan. 1984).

[25] RA, 17 April 1980, 10 Jan. 1984 and 10 Aug. 1981; A.N. Nuristani, 'Zu Rolle der Agrarfrage im revolutionäre Prozess Afghanistans', diss., Hochschule fur Ökonomie, (East) Berlin, 1987, p. 105; A.D. Davydov, *Afghanistan. Voiny moglo ne byt'*, Nauka, Moscow 1993, p. 126..

of Agriculture, numbering 2,600 officials out of 4,000 as a whole.[26] 'A certain number' of operational groups left for the provinces of Balkh, Kunduz, Badakhshan, Baghlan and Kabul to assess the situation and gauge the results of the first phase. It took till the spring of 1983 to complete this work in almost all provinces (twenty-seven out of thirty), even if only two districts (sometimes only one) in each province were really checked. In total, it was possible to assess the situation of 77,800 peasants out of the 296,000 who had received land during the first phase; 53% of them had cultivated the land, 33% had returned it either forcibly or voluntarily and 13% could not farm it because of lack of water. The criteria according to which districts were selected in each province were not stated officially, but certainly they would not have been the most 'difficult' ones; it is thus probable that land reform had been even less successful among the other 218,000 peasants. For example, in the province of Ghazni, one of those where the PDPA was weaker, in the mid-1980s only 300 of the 900 families who had received land during the first phase of the reform were still holding it (33% compared with 53% above); the others had died, abandoned the land or returned it to the former landowners.[27]

The 'second operational plan' of land reform, consisting of 'the solution of the legal problems which arise as a result of the first phase of the land reform', in the resumption of the distribution of land and ownership titles, really only began in March 1982 in some provinces and was later expanded to others. The 'third operational plan', mainly consisting of the formation of cooperatives, began in May of the same year in just three districts of Kabul province, with the establishment of a cooperative in the district of Deh Sabz. A 'fourth operational plan', consisting of the development of infrastructure, including mechanized stations, and the repair of irrigation networks, also began shortly afterwards in the same three districts. In short, the government still expected to put into practice the reform as initially conceived, just taking

---

[26] Keshtmand, RA, 19 Oct. 1987.

[27] S.A. Keshtmand, personal communication, London 10 Dec. 1993; RA, 12 Nov. 1981 and 21 May 1983; *Bakhtar*, 29 Feb. 1984; M. Olimov, 'Iz zapisok perevodchika', *Vostok*, no. 3, (1991) p. 64; Vs. Semenov, 'Zemel'no-vodnaya reforma v Demokraticheskoi Respublike Afganistan', *Mirovaya Ekonomika i Mezhdunarodnye Otnosheniya*, 6/1983, p. 112.

care not to antagonize particular social groups, to avoid arbitrariness and to take account of local conditions. To the extent that land distribution was still going on, it proceeded with great care and the advice of village notables was continuously sought, but rhetoric was still heavily hostile to landowners. According to Prime Minister Keshtmand, the land reform commissions had revealed that many landowners had hidden land, not recording it in the land register. This issue had been neglected during the first phase and it was now obviously necessary to tackle it. Furthermore, expectations regarding the results of the reform were still high: according to Karmal, land reform guaranteed the irreversibility of the Revolution.[28]

In February 1984 Decree no. 8 was amended again, in order to take into account the interests of middle and 'prosperous' peasants, loyal tribal leaders and a section of the landowners. The upper limit of 30 jeribs was now legalized. Furthermore, the land reform was to be 'democratized': while previously the reform had come from above, on the initiative of the state apparatus, the lead was now supposed to be taken by the peasants themselves, who would obviously enjoy the 'support' of operational groups of party cadres and of the state apparatus. Village councils would receive wide powers over land distribution. Finally, the article of Decree no. 8 concerning inheritance was also modified in accordance to Islamic traditions: now peasants were allowed to distribute inherited land even in lots smaller than 5 jeribs, something previously forbidden. Several registration fees were abolished. The formation of cooperatives was still encouraged and the state offered incentives to foster their development, including seeds, fertilizers and credits. Although Karmal appeared by this point a bit disappointed by the achievements of the reform, his idea that the future of the Revolution was dependent on it remained unchallenged: 'The peasants still don't know that the land is theirs, that's why they have to defend the Revolution.' In fact Karmal expected the land reform to drive sizeable numbers of peasants into the village militias, helping to secure Kabul's control over the countryside.[29]

[28] RA, 23 Sept. 1982 and 4 May 1982; *KNT*, 25 May 1983 and 5 Nov. 1984.

[29] RA, 10 Jan. 1984 and 8 Jan. 1984; Basov and Poliakov, *Afghanistan. Trudnye sud'by revolyutsii*, p. 47; *KNT*, 26 June 1984.

Even in 1986 much hope was still officially pinned on the reforms. The plan scheduled to begin that year foresaw further financial and credit measures to stimulate the development of the cooperatives. Karmal still thought that 'the implementation of the process of democratic land and water reform is considered an important factor in increasing agricultural output, assisting the toiling peasants, ensuring social justice, broadening the social base of the Revolution and consolidating state power in the localities'. Open criticism of the reform, now more frequent, was still aimed at its slow and ineffectual implementation. An editorial of the *Haqiqat-i Inqilab-i Saur* of February 1986 for example read: '...there are some shortcomings...which stem from the work of agricultural bodies, land reforms, irrigation and cooperatives. Effort aimed at the elimination of this situation, which is incompatible with the revolutionary process of the society, and genuinely realizing the land policy of the party, should be accelerated.'[30]

With the arrival in power of Najibullah a few months later, however, the approach changed quickly. A Soviet adviser, Kim M. Tsagolov, claims to have twice advised Karmal not to distribute the land free, but rather to sell it, at a symbolic price, in order to overcome religious opposition. Other advisers apparently opposed such an approach and it is obviously impossible to say whether it could have helped if put into practice in 1979-80. It is probable in any case that by 1980 the situation in this regard was already permanently compromised. Najibullah's approach in the end turned out to be more radical. To begin with, government propaganda about the land reform sharply declined. According to a Russian scholar, V. Spolnikov, in mid-1986 the newly-appointed President already considered the reform a substantial failure. While the number of operational groups, charged with the realization of the reform, grew relatively fast after 1983, increasing from thirty-six in that year to 609 in 1363 (1984-5), its actual progress was desperately slow. In some provinces real progress had been made, as in Jowzyan, where as early as October 1983, 20,000 ha. had allegedly been distributed, but in other provinces it was just beginning. In the country as a whole, by late 1986, according to both a Soviet observer and President Najibullah, 30-35% of the

[30] *Obshchestvennye Nauki*, no. 4 (1986), p. 213; RA, 7 Jan. 1986; *Bakhtar*, 14 Feb. 1986.

reform had been carried out, meaning that while 335,000 families had received land, almost 600,000 more were still landless. Only 40,000 new families received land between 1982 and 1986, while we know that many of the 296,000 peasants supposed to have received the land during the first phase had lost it or had returned it or were unable to farm it. A more accurate idea of the situation is probably given by the number of village peasant councils established: there were 423 at the end of 1363 (1984/5), 637 by the summer of 1985 and 1,065 by the summer of 1986, i.e. they existed in less than 5% of all villages. Furthermore, like most of the organizations set up in the villages after the Revolution (cooperatives, councils, committees) they were functioning poorly. Up to October 1987 the land reform commissions had examined the cases of only 1,100 villages out of the maybe 25,000 still inhabited. The comments of the DRA spokesmen were now in sharp contrast with those made at the beginning of the 1980s: Zeray for example admitted explicitly that the reform had failed, as only 25% of the land distributed was actually being farmed. Even those who did not concede total failure, like Prime Minister Keshtmand, openly declared that little had been achieved. 'A joint commission of the PDPA CC and the Council of Ministers under the chairmanship of Comrade Zeray' was then given (apparently in October 1986) the task of 'drawing up a different approach towards distributing land among the peasants and the conditions for the transfer of land to those who have joined the government and also to migrants and to put the land and water reform on a practical, phased and planned footing'. When the 'different approach' was finally defined a few months later, it consisted in bringing the legal maximum up to 100 jeribs of land, from the previous 30, and in guaranteeing immunity to rebel leaders accepting reconciliation with the government. An interesting feature of the new draft was that, although the land given to the peasants was left to them, they were 'authorized to give it back' to the landlords. Basically the new outlook on land reform resembled the one promoted in the 1970s by President Daoud, indeed to some extent it was even more moderate. After 1986 the reform proceeded at a slower pace than ever, apparently more with the aim of achieving reconciliation with armed group leaders than with the claimed one of social justice.[31]

---

[31] *Aziya i Afrika Segodnia*, no. 12, 1988; RA, 8 July 1985; *Bakhtar*, 10 Oct.

For cooperatives too things were difficult. In 1982 their number still stood at 1,217, and only grew to 1,222 in early 1983 and to 1,274 in early 1984, although figures relative to their members 'mysteriously' declined from 300,000 to 183,000 and 193,000 respectively. The government had hoped rapidly to reactivate the large majority of inactive cooperatives, but even in 1983 only 236 were working properly; 308 were active in 1984, with 94,000 members (i.e., 7.8% of all peasant families). It is not difficult to understand why: even when they had not been dismantled or destroyed, they were often besieged by the mujahidin, like in Andkhoi district in 1982, where it was necessary to supply them from the town by means of armoured columns. Dreams of reactivating the other 1,000 or so cooperatives were abandoned shortly afterwards, when it was decided to abolish them.[32]

As Graph 1 shows, the formation of new cooperatives clearly registered a sharp decline in 1986-1987 and then again and even more sharply after 1988, to an almost complete and final stop. As Prime Minister Keshtmand lamented in 1987, 'dynamism in the creation of cooperatives' was diminishing 'every year'. At this point the grandiose plans envisaging the creation of thousands of cooperatives had been given up – the Union of Peasants' Cooperatives and the State Planning Committee now planned the creation of only fifty cooperatives a year, a level which nonetheless was not reached. It should also be observed that many members of cooperatives were no longer real peasants, but rather militiamen: in 1983, of the roughly 50,000 cooperative members remaining after the abolition of the non-operational cooperatives, 6,000 were

---

1983; *Ogoniok*, no. 30 (July 1988); Najibullah, RA, 22 Nov. 1986 and 8 July 1985; *Bakhtar*, 4 Sept. 1986; Najibullah, RA, 13 March 1987; RA, 25 Oct. 1986; RA, 19 Oct. 1987; *Afghanistan Info*, June 1987, p. 21; Najibullah, RA, 22 Nov. 1986, p. 20; V. Korgun, 'The Afghan Revolution: a failed experiment' in D.F. Eickelman (ed.), *Russia's Muslim frontiers*, Indiana University Press, 1993, p. 112; *Afghanistan Info*, Oct. 1987, p. 20; *News Bullettin* (Afghan Embassy, London) 2 June 1987; Tsagolov in *Nezavisimaya Gazeta*, 8 Sept. 1992; Davydov *Afghanistan: voiny moglo ne byt'*, p. 139.

32 *Mezhdunarodnyi Ezhegodnik – Politika i Ekonomika 1982*, p. 223; *Anti-Imperialistische Bullettin*, 4 (1983), p. 21; S. Chakravarty, *Dateline Kabul, an Eyewitness Report on Afghanistan Today*, Eastern Book Centre, 1983, pp. 31-2; Hungarian TV, 29 Dec. 1983; V. Nosatov, 'Afganskii Dnevnik', *Prostor* 11 (1989), p. 122; *LMD*, Sept. 1983, p. 17; Michalski, 'Die revolutionär-demokratisch Umgestaltung der Agrarverhältnisse', p. 815.

enlisted in the GDRs and 9,000 in the self-defence militias. The development of mechanized stations (which were supposed to rent tractors and other machinery to peasants) was also unimpressive: at the beginning of 1986 only nine were in existence (in eight provinces), while only two more were planned. Furthermore, the quality of their work is doubtful, as according to Prime Minister Keshtmand much of their equipment was lying idle because there were no mechanics. Indeed, in 1364 (1985/6) their volume of work declined as compared to the year before. Many tractors used in the Afghan countryside were in fact brought in from Pakistan or had been stolen from state farms. To complete this gloomy picture, state farms too were in bad shape: the 1364 (1985/6) planned production was fulfilled to 59.3%. Service sector cooperatives, which met with greater success due to their non-controversial character, also failed to fulfil the expectations of Kabul, as they were being 'diverted from the objective of strengthening links with and assistance to peasants, participation in the cause of stabilizing prices, supplying the inhabitants with their essential needs and improvements in toilers' welfare, and have been directed mostly towards making profits'. The President of the Cooperatives Union was removed from his position because of this.[33]

[33] RA, 19 Oct. 1987; *Bakhtar*, 4 Feb. 1986; *Anti-Imperialistiche Bullettin* 4 (1983); RA, 2 April 1986; Rubin, *The Fragmentation of Afghanistan*, p. 145; Karmal, RA, 17 Aug. 1985; RA, 2 April 1986.; *LMD*, Sept. 1983, p. 17.

3

THE BUILDING UP OF THE SOCIAL
BASE OF THE SAUR REVOLUTION
AND ITS LIMITS

The expansion of party membership and its limits

The official figures clearly register a growth in PDPA membership, as Graph 2 and Tables 5 and 6 show. It has been debated whether these figures are reliable or not, but formerly secret documents now confirm them. However, while we can accept official figures relative to membership, we cannot do the same with regard to the claim that members were selected according to genuinely 'Leninist' criteria or that, in other terms, the PDPA was a 'vanguard' party. The issue of membership quality, i.e. how many were careerists or opportunists, must be addressed. We know of several purges (apart from those of 1980, 1981 and 1982, probably due to infighting among factions); one in 1984 when 3,000 members were expelled and 6,000 re-admitted and another in 1365 (1986/87) which led to the expulsion from the party of 4,818 members, or 5,967 according to other sources, 478 of whom on corruption charges, 557 because they refused to serve in the army and the others because of 'opportunist' behaviour or the violation of party statute. It would thus seem that some attention was paid to at least certain aspects of membership 'quality'.

To support the view that there existed a degree of commitment among the membership, we should add that to be a party member could involve a very high degree of personal risk, particularly in the provinces, as assassinations of party members were quite common.[34] Table 7 illustrates this. The losses suffered by the party

[34] Ludwig, 'Einige Probleme', p. 143; Najibullah, RA, 11 May 1987; A.A. Lyakhovskii and V. M. Zabrodin, *Tainy afganskoi voiny*, Planeta, 1991, p. 102.

during the war, which amounted to 42,000 up to 1990, are quite substantial, although it seems that more than 10,000 died before 1980.

During their candidate membership, incoming members were screened to some extent at least, as appears from the fact that there were invariably many more new candidate members every year, than the real membership growth would lead one to suppose, so that a significant percentage of members must not have been accepted as full members, although a part of them may have quitted out of disappointment (see also Table 8 and Graph 2).[35]

However, it is clear that the 'ideological quality' of the membership was not very high. The Pakistani intelligence service put the ideologically committed members at 15,000 in 1984-5, while the American scholar Selig Harrison, by estimating the ideologically committed members at 25-35,000 in 1984 and at 40,000 in 1989, was even more optimistic than a Soviet expert, who advanced a figure of 30,000 at the beginning of 1989. Another Soviet scholar spoke of 50,000 'real members' in 1986. A Russian source claimed that in 1989, 32-33% of the PDPA members in Kabul city were 'dead souls', while in 1988 a borough secretary of the party confided to a Soviet specialist that of the 5,000 members under his leadership, he expected only 500 to fight in any attack on Kabul. Among the ranks of the state administration it was 'highly recommended' to join the party if any career advancement was desired and, besides, to hold the party card represented an advantage in many other ways. The complaints of President Najibullah, according to whom the membership, instead of going to the countryside to fight, was hiding in the capital, are a clear indication of the presence of many 'weak' members. Furthermore, factional infighting encouraged the recruitment of relatives, cronies and so on, in order to increase the relative strength of each faction. Soviet sources estimated that after the arrival of the 40th Army, 70% of PDPA members were busy in such feuds, while strains appeared even within the older factions. Parcham, which was initially at a strong numerical disadvantage, in part because of Amin's purges, launched a recruitment drive in order to legitimize its rule. The more than twofold increase in PDPA membership

---

[35] A.P. Zhtnukhin and S.A. Lykoshin, *Zvezda nad gorodam Kabulom*, Moscow, 1990, Molodaya Gvardiya, p. 11; Ludwig, 'Einige Probleme', p. 74.

during 1980 is largely due to this. Membership applications were even presented in lists bearing 150-200 names. In this way, however, even ideologically 'low-quality' members were accepted. Another side effect was the decline in the educational standards of the membership (although the recruitment of soldiers also played an important role) (see Table 9). Some observers also judged as suspect the growth of Najibullah's supporters after his coming to power in 1986. In short, it appears reasonable to estimate the hard core membership of the PDPA at between 15% and 25% of the total, while between 30% and 40% was made up of opportunists and 'dead souls', and between 35% and 45% of partially committed people.[36]

The geographical distribution of party membership remained basically the same throughout the war, but there were some marginal changes, particularly the growth of membership in certain provinces. Jowzyan, Takhar, Helmand, Faryab and Kunduz saw their membership treble or quadruple between 1982 and 1987, while Baghdis registered a record sevenfold growth. In contrast, the rate of growth was considered to be unsatisfactory in the provinces of Kunar, Laghman, Samangan, Ghor, Kandahar, Paktia and Bamyan. The dominance of the capital, however, whose membership also grew three- or fourfold between 1982 and 1987, was not even dented. On the other hand it must be said that numerical growth was no certain guarantee of the good health of the party. It has already been noted how a comparison between recruitment and membership figures shows, even after taking into account war losses and the effects of purges, that considerable numbers were quitting the party each year. A significant outflow was reported in 1980-1, but even later sizeable ones took place in some provinces at least, like Herat in 1984 (see Tables 10 and 11).[37]

[36] *KNT*, 21 June 1987; S. Harrison, 'Afghanistan' in Kornbluh and Klare, *Low Intensity Warfare*, Pantheon, 1988, p. 187; *LMD*, Nov. 1989; *FEER*, 13 April 1989; *RA*, 13 March 1987; *Pravda*, 26 April 1988; Plastun, *Voenno-politicheskaya obstanovka v DRA* p. 7; O. Zharov, 'Cleptsy, navyazyvavshie sebya v povodiri', *Aziya i Afrika Segodnia*, no. 12, (1992), p. 29; V.N. Plastun, *Situatsiya v Afganistane*, lecture given in Moscow in 1988, p. 7; Merimskii, 'Voina v Afganistane: zapiski uchastika', p. 97.

[37] *Babrak's Karmal Speech to the Seventh Plenum of the PDPA, CC*, p. 2; 'Postanovlenie sekretariata TsK NDPA o rabote geratskogo provintsial'nogo komiteta partii po vypolnenyu reshenii XII plenuma TsK NDPA, 10 marta 1984 g.' in

The PDPA thus maintained a relative dynamism in the areas of its original influence and slightly strengthened its presence in Mazar-i-Sharíf. After the coming to power of Najibullah, in 1986, a shift in the balance of power inside the Pashtun component of the party was noted, with the rise of members of the Eastern tribes (based in Nangrahar and Laghman), thanks to numerous promotions of young regional secretaries and area leaders to relevant positions in the CC. Another major shift consisted in the fact that the majority ethnic group, the Pashtun, was losing strength inside the party. Although government statistics differ on this matter, they agree on the general trend (see Tables 12A and 12B). While the composition of the delegates to the II National Conference of the PDPA (1987) still reflected a Pashtun dominance, with 52% belonging to this ethnic group and 44.8% to the minorities, among the rank-and-file the picture was being overturned: in 1989 out of 200,000 members of the party, only 37.7% were still Pashtuns, while Tajiks accounted for 47.7%. This also reflected the growth of the party in the Northern areas, inhabited by the national minorities, while membership stagnated in the Pashtun belt.[38]

The expansion of party structures

Apart from purely numerical growth, the party leadership also took care to expand and strengthen its organization, with some success. If at the end of 1982 PDPA committees were present in 144 districts and sub-districts, by mid-1984 these had increased to 205. In the very sensitive border areas, in the early 1980s fifteen out of fifty-five districts lacked any party primary organization, nineteen had only one and in the remaining twenty-one the party was anyway very weak. In these districts primary organizations grew from 443 in 1982 to 1,331 in 1987 but, as

NDPA (sbornik dokumentov), Tashkent, 'Uzbekistan', 1986, pp. 155-6.

[38] G. Dorronsoro and C. Lobato, 'The militia in Afghanistan', *Central Asian Survey*, vol. 8, no. 4 (1989), p. 96; M. Najibullah, *Taking the Path of National Reconciliation*, Government committee of press and publication, Kabul, 1988, pp. 94-5; J. Newman, 'The future of Northern Afghanistan', *Asian Survey*, vol. XXVIII, no. 7 (July 1988); *Défis Afghans*, no. 19, (July/Nov. 1988); *KNT*, 15 Dec. 1986, 21 Nov. 1987 and 31 Dec. 1989.

Karmal himself said in 1985, party and state organs had 'weak links with the inhabitants' of the tribal areas and decisions taken by the PDPA Central Committee and by the government affecting these regions 'did not have much effect on the state of affairs'. In all the villages, the number of primary organizations rose from 277 in 1362 (1983/4) to 1,160 in 1987, covering 2,000 villages out of maybe 25,000 (see Table 13).[39]

The situation in the provinces and in the countryside, needless to say, was by far the most problematic. Karmal complained that on the rare occasions that members of the party leadership visited the provinces, they did not pay much attention to contacts with the local party cadres and members, not to speak of the common people.[40]

Efforts to improve the situation became more energetic after the coming to power of Najibullah. Towards 1987 it was decided to appoint several secretaries of party village organizations to positions in the CC, in order to encourage members, and a threefold increase in visits by 'leadership personnel' to the provinces was reported in the same period. But even in 1988 in some provinces, for example Nimroz, local administrators did not actually carry out propaganda activities among the population and even leaflets were not distributed. The problem was that the middle level party cadres were generally very reluctant to reside outside the capital: only two provincial party secretaries lived in their respective provinces. In the mid-1980s, of 10,000 officials of the party provincial, district and local organizations, 5,000 resided in the towns and cities.[41]

---

[39] *Bakhtar*, 16 Dec. 1982; *KNT*, 5 May 1984; Najibullah, *Taking the Path of National Reconciliation*, op. cit., p. 97; *News Bullettin*, 18 May 1986; *Documents and Records of the National Conference of the People's Democratic Party of Afghanistan, Kabul, March 14-15, 1982*, p. 42; Najibullah, RA, 13 March 1987; *KNT*, 14 March 1987; RA, 27 March 1985, Karmal; Ludwig, 'Einige Probleme', p. 112. According to a Soviet journalist, in 1988 primary organizations of the Party existed in only 900 villages (*Agitator* no. 17, (1988), pp. 47-9). The two figures are not necessarily incompatible: the first refers probably to the total number of villages where Party members were recorded, the second one to the number of villages where the Party was strong enough to put up local organizations, which required a minimum number of members.

[40] Karmal, 14th plenum CC, RA, 21 Sept. 1984.

[41] *KNT*, 14 March 1987; Najibullah, RA, 11 May 1987; *Voenno-politicheskaya*

In Faryab province in 1982-3 the governor used to tour the province during the winter, when the mujahidin had withdrawn to their villages, in order to meet local notables and to make propaganda among the peasants. He was faced with an over-whelming task, as the party was inactive and the peasants had no idea of what was going on in the country – they believed that Daoud was still in power, his portraits were hanging from the walls. In Nangrahar province in 1980-2 the district of Gushta was considered under complete control by the government, but no party administrator ever visited it over the whole period. In the words of Karmal, 'in dealing with the needs and daily demands of the toilers', the approach of party organs was 'superficial and uninterested'. They did not 'organize work for the solution of problems, which could and should be carried out in the interests of toilers at the local level'. 'With such behaviour', it would have been impossible to 'increase the support of the masses for Revolution and revolutionary sovereignty', rather the masses would have been alienated. 'In work among the masses, superficiality, political fuss, boasting and idle talk' were common.[42]

To raise the quality of the cadres, most of the secretaries of party village organizations were being given some education at party schools inside and outside the country, including the Social Sciences Institute of the PDPA CC, which in 1982 had 2,500 students and by the end of the eighties had given degrees to more than 10,000 PDPA members. 'Party education' began to be implemented 'systematically' during the academic year 1363-4 (1984-5), and in 1985, 4,495 training courses and seminars were held, involving 75,000 members of the party, although most mem-bers, in particular those who had been recently accepted, were still not enrolled in education courses and seminars. Attendance levels of those enrolled seem to have been low. The impact of such courses on the ability to win the raging military-political conflict is dubious. So, although 12,000 members had been trained in Marxism-Leninism by 1985 (4,000 of them abroad), few were

obstanovka v pr. Nimruz na konets febralya 1988g.; Ludwig, 'Einige Probleme', p. 71.

[42] RA, 27 March 1985, Karmal; V. Nosatov, 'Afganskii Dnevnik', *Prostor*, 11 (1989), p. 125; Yu. Gankovskii, 'Polosa pushtunskikh plemen Afganistana', *Spetsial'nyi Byulleten' AN SSSR IV*, no. 6 (1987), p. 116, n. 18.

available for work in the countryside. The organizational department of the PDPA engaged itself in preparing the cadres who had left the villages in the previous years to go back for at least a certain period, a measure that gives an idea of the difficulty in recruiting qualified activists to operate in a rural environment. The social organizations paralleled the effort. The Afghan Women's Council for example sent members to the provinces 'to carry out political, educational and publicity work' there. Since late 1984 it had organized 'peace tents' 'to disseminate the aims of the Revolution' (also by distributing material and offering health services) among women, first in Kabul province, then in Balkh, Takhar, Baghlan and Kunduz.[43]

In many cases the work of the party officials in the provinces encountered objective difficulties, because of totally unsafe conditions. In the province of Ghazni, for example, in the mid-eighties the work of the party district organizers was very problematic. When they went to the main town to attend Provincial Committee meetings, they had to wait up to two or three months until an armoured column or helicopter was available to bring them back. The situation in Zabul province was similar, but elsewhere it could be even worse, as in Uruzgan province, where no army column arrived between 1988 and 1990 and where in 1985 the publication of the local paper *Uruzgan* was suspended because of lack of writing staff. In other cases, something was clearly wrong with party tactics themselves. In Balkh province, notwithstanding the activism of the provincial leadership of the PDPA, which in 1987 earnt a commendation from President Najibullah for having sent activists to thirty villages, and notwithstanding the relatively favourable military situation, peasants and other rural dwellers remained distant from the party: in 1986 only 570 peasants out of 450,000 were members of the PDPA, as were only fifty-two traders and artisans out of 6,000. It should be noted that as late as in 1987 among the provincial committees more successful in recruiting peasants (Badakhshan, Herat, Nangrahar, Jowzyan,

[43] *AIC MB*, no. 60, March 1986, p. 8; *KNT*, 14 March 1987; Arnold, 'The ephemeral elite', p. 58; Karmal, RA, 27 March 1985; Najibullah, RA, 13 March 1987; Karmal, RA, 29-30 July 1982; H. Malik, *Soviet-Pakistan relations and post-Soviet dynamics 1947-1992*, Macmillan 1994, p. 280; Karmal, 15th plenum, RA, 27 March 1985; Ludwig, 'Einige Probleme', p. 145; *Bakhtar*, 18 July 1988, 23 July 1985.

Faryab, Takhar, Baghlan, Kunduz and Baghdis), each of them counting 1,000–2,500 peasant members, Balkh was not included. Yet, the 1986-7 performance was a great improvement on 1983, when the party was totally inactive in the countryside. In other provinces, peasants proved very reluctant to join the party. A few strongholds in Kabul province did not push the total number of peasants in the PDPA provincial organization over 594 in 1987. In the case of Balkh the predominance of small landholding might explain the failure, but even in Laghman province, despite the significant presence of landless peasants, only 179 of them were party members in 1985. Again, Karmal noted the 'serious shortcomings and defects in dealing with people in those areas' where the enemy was not strong enough to cause serious problems, as party men did not organize 'work for the solution of problems', 'political and educational material, placards, propaganda leaflets and pamphlets' were lying in the store-rooms, instead of being distributed, and forms and methods of political work were usually 'monotonous and spiritless', so that in the end the inhabitants had 'very little information about the aims of the party ... and about the measures' being taken.[44]

In sum, the PDPA found it overwhelmingly difficult to expand beyond its traditional, restricted areas of influence (see Map 1), even when conditions were favourable. This weakness prompted the search for new methods of political propaganda in the countryside.

Agitprop

Prior to the summer of 1981 no kind of direct contact existed between the government and villages outside its control. The only propaganda that reached these villages was by radio, and even here the competition, particularly the BBC World Service, was largely dominant.

---

[44] M. Olimov, 'Iz zapisok perevodchika', *Vostok*, no. 3 (1991), p. 63; *KNT*, 14 March 1987 and 2 June 1986; *RA*, 16 July 1985; *KNT*, 8 April 1987; Karmal, 15th Plenum, *RA*, 27 March 1985; A. Podlesnyi, 'Politika Natsional'nogo Primireniya i osobennosti ee provedeniya v yuzhnykh raionakh Afganistana', *Spetsial'nyi Byulleten', IV AN SSSR* no. 2, (1990), pp. 159-60; D.V. Ol'shanskii, *Natsional'noe primerenie*, ION pri TsK KPSS, Moscow, 1988, p. 66; N.S. Leonov, *Likholet'e*, Mezhdunarodnye Otnosheniya, 1994, p. 272.

The first appearance of ideas aimed at overcoming the sharp division between military activity and political work dates back to 1981, when some Soviet political workers and advisers, notably L. I. Shershnev and Kim M. Tsagolov, argued the need to form special agitprop units to carry out political work in the countryside, in coordination with military operations. Shershnev in particular argued that the purely military approach which had dominated till then was only making the situation worse and increasing the hostility of the population. The top military echelons initially opposed such initiatives, as they maintained that the only duty of the armed forces was to wage war.[45]

Although no coordination between agitprop activities and military operations was to emerge for some years, at the beginning of the summer of 1981 the first agitprop detachment was formed, as a result of a decision of the PDPA CC. It was to operate north of Kabul. It had at least been realized that it was necessary to adopt new approaches in dealing with the population, other than purely military ones. This new kind of unit was composed of both Afghans and Soviets. The Soviets were mostly soldiers, whose equipment included tanks, but they also included physicians, mechanics, youth organization advisers and two or three political activists. The Afghans were young artists, party activists, mullahs and the like. This development was in itself an advance, although at the outset the members of the groups were not selected with sufficient care, particularly among the Soviets. Two other groups had been created by the autumn of 1981 and during 1982 more appeared, mainly to be active in Balkh, Parwan and other northern areas. They organized meetings, concerts, individual and collective debates, film shows, the distribution of leaflets, posters, books, consumer goods and medical help in the villages they visited. The speeches were a mix of quotations from the Quran, extracts from PDPA CC documents, quotations from poets, and later also declarations of the *Loya Jirgah*. Atheist propaganda and economic themes were forbidden, while Soviet aid and government reforms were exalted.[46]

---

[45] Gai and Snegirev, *Vtorzhenie*, pp. 195, 203-4, 207-8.
[46] *Babrak's Karmal Speech to the Seventh Plenum of the PDPA, CC*, p. 7; *A Summary of the Babrak Karmal's Report on the Party Tasks Concerning the Intensification of Political Work among the Masses to the Ninth plenum of the PDPA, CC*, p. 27;

Although the start was quite shaky ('The work of these groups does not have a program and the necessary organization and they do not always work effectively'), by the time of the IX Plenum in July 1982 it had been established that their work was having positive effects and that they were being 'of great help' to the party and state. After an experimental period, the agitprop units were given an official status in February 1982 and it was now decided that their numbers and activities would be expanded. Over time, agitprop units were created in each division, brigade and even regiment of the Soviet and Afghan armies and by 1984 at least one *sarandoy* propaganda battalion was in existence. Agitprop units in the Soviet Army always included Afghan agitators. It appears that, as time passed, Afghan-only 'raids', as they were called, became more frequent. Generally groups of fifteen to twenty party activists went to the villages under military escort. The central event of the raid was the distribution of products from the Soviet Union, essentially consumer goods. At the same time a *jirgah* of the village notables was held, in order to explain government policies. Sometimes larger raids were also organized, like the one carried out in 1985 in the Nava and Nadakhi districts of Helmand province which included: two agitprop detachments of the army; representatives of the CC of the PDPA, the political organs of the army, the Women's Organization, the Youth Organization and the National Fatherland Front; mullahs, physicians, the army band and journalists – a total of 170 people. In this way, according to the government, villages inhabited by 30,000 people were visited.[47]

By the time of his removal, Shershnev had managed to launch (January 1986) a radio station named *Khaibargak* (Voice), directly aimed at supporting the agitprop operations in the field; it was later transferred to the Afghan Defence Ministry. But the real

O. Karpenko, 'Iz afganskogo dnevnika', *Zvezda Vostoka*, 12 (1987), p. 179; V.N. Svetikov, *Zharkii mesiats saratan*, DOSAAF 1988, pp. 71, 191, 193-4.

[47] M. Olimov, 'Iz zapisok perevodchika', *Vostok*, no. 3 1991, p. 63: Gai and Snegirev, *Vtorzhenie*, pp. 201-4; *KZ*, 1 April 1983 and 10 July 1985; *Babrak's Karmal Speech to the Seventh Plenum of the PDPA, CC*, p. 7; *A Summary of the Babrak Karmal's Report on the Party Tasks Concerning the Intensification of Political Work among the Masses to the Ninth plenum of the PDPA, CC*, p. 27; Karmal, *RA*, 24 Nov. 1984.

innovation in 1986 was the adoption of combined military operations and agitprop activities. According to this scheme, military offensives were carried out first, then agitprop teams intervened, followed by the establishment of local power bodies, then by the formation of militias and finally by the installation of *sarandoy* garrisons which took care of making a census of the population and distributing ID cards. Generally Soviet troops were withdrawn after a ceremony with the local population. Such combined operations were carried out countrywide, but the main problem with them was that, while military offensives opened up new possibilities for the agitprop effort, these were however limited to the fifteen to twenty days which followed any success achieved on the ground, as afterwards mujahidin would generally stage a comeback. In most cases, the plan could not therefore be carried to its conclusion. Overall, it appears that KhAD and WAD undercover activities were much more effective in getting agreements with the villages.[48]

Up to at least 1985 much of the propaganda effort still consisted of 'separate, scattered and sudden measures', but by the time of the National Reconciliation (see Part III), when the agitprop campaign reached its peak, a large scale effort had been organized. 230 detachments were active with the Afghan armed forces at that time and in the first five months they carried out 3,000 visits to localities. Activity at the time of the withdrawal, when solely-Soviet units made 1,750 visits to localities, was also intense.[49]

Apart from the largest groups which moved in columns, smaller propaganda teams also existed, made up of three to five activists each. In Paktia at the end of 1987 there were six agitprop brigades and sixty of such smaller, local groups, with 306 propagandists, while forty-seven more activists worked among the tribal population. In Kunduz at the beginning of 1987 there were fifty small agit-groups and five medical assistance units.[50]

[48] *Literaturnaya Rossiya*, 21 July 1995; E.G. Nikitenko and N.I.Pikov, 'Razvenchannyi mif', *Voenno-Istoricheskii Zhurnal*, no. 2, 1995, p. 79; *Voina v Afganistane*, Voenizdat, 1991, p. 240.

[49] Karmal, XV plenum, RA, 27 March 1985; RA, 19 May 1987; Najibullah, RA, 14 June 1987, CC Plenum; A.I.Bart, 'Partiino-politicheskaya rabota v voiskakh v usloviakh boevykh deistvii v Afganistane, 1979-1989 gg', diss., Alma Ata, 1990, p. 160.

[50] Ol'shanskii, *Natsional'noe primerenie*, pp. 67-70; *Haqiqat-i Inqilab Saur*, 29 Jan. 1987.

More than propaganda, material help seems to have been welcome. To give an idea of what was being distributed, it will suffice to say that in the first four months of National Reconciliation this included 1,000 tons of wheat, 110 tons of sugar, 73 tons of cooking oil, 100,000 bars of soap, 17,000 pairs of footwear, 23,000 metres of fabric, 6,000 items of clothing and blankets and 32 tons of kerosene. Varennikov claimed that the district of Kishkinakhud in Kandahar province, formerly strongly opposed to Kabul, had been pacified in 1987-8 by Soviet agitprop units, which also built four wells with electric pumps; in the end the notables called a *jirgah* to thank the Soviets. Propaganda efforts were more controversial; in some villages the propagandists would find villagers totally unaware of the situation in the country, and when trying to explain to them the policies of the government, they usually met with unfavourable reactions.[51]

The aim of the propaganda groups was undoubtedly hard to achieve. Overall, in 1981-9 the Soviet forces gave medical assistance to 400,000 Afghans and material aid to over 1,000,000, a small percentage of a rural population of about 8 million. Some idea of the intensity of the operations is given by Table 14.[52]

A particular effort was made in Herat province, which was reckoned to be more vulnerable because of war-weariness among mujahidin and civilians. Here, during 1365 (1986/7), 130 medical groups were active, mainly consisting of Soviets physicians, and 15,000 people were given medical assistance. Nonetheless, even in Herat, military activities remained predominant; indeed, in 1987 they were estimated by Soviet advisers to represent 90% of all government efforts. Furthermore, not all armed services were cooperating as they could have. In 1988, for example, the *sarandoy* were doing little, in contrast with WAD forces.[53]

Often villages were visited by mujahidin propaganda groups soon after and at least on some occasions villagers were fined for having accepted goods from the Soviets or the government. On

---

[51] RA, 19 May 87; Varennikov, *SR*, 16 Feb. 1993; V.N. Svetikov, *Zharkii mesiats saratan*, DOSAAF 1988, p. 69.

[52] Yu. Krasikov, 'Internatsional'naya missiya sovetskogo voina', *Voennyi Vestnik*, no. 10 (1988), p. 5.

[53] *Otchet o komandirovke v pr. Gerat 8-10 noyabrya 1987 g.; Iz otcheta p/i-ka Dashlya o propaganditskoi rabote v pr. Gerat (24 febr.–11 marta 1988 g.).*

the other hand, villagers themselves often did not want to accept aid and continued to see the propagandists as strangers; in the Panjshir in 1987-8, when part of the population had begun to return and was therefore in need of help, local inhabitants refused to be organized by the government forces in any way. Sometimes, in villages visited by agitprop units, people would shut themselves in their houses and refuse any contact with the visitors, who were then forced to withdraw after waiting a few hours. When meetings with villagers were organized, some participants would disrupt them with provocative questions or behaviour. As usual, government efforts were damaged by widespread corruption; Karmal denounced the fact that some of the *gratis* aid from the Soviet Union was not distributed free to the people, as intended, but instead sold in the shops. At the XIX Plenum Najibullah complained that some DYOA activists in Deh Sabz district and in Kabul Province had misappropriated material aid intended for the local population, and cases like this seem to have been plentiful. An obstacle to greater effort was provided by the hostility of Afghan physicians who, apart from being few in numbers, were far from enthusiastic about these measures and rather unwilling to move even to provincial centres, as Prime Minister Sharq admitted in 1988. However, even if not many villages joined the government side as a consequence of the agitprop effort, it may well be that the traditional hostility of the countryside towards Kabul was reduced to some extent. Much also depended on the quality of cadres involved in the propaganda effort. In Samangan province, the success of the Soviet agitprop campaign was in large measure due to the abilities of a Tajik officer of the Red Army, who was well received by the population because he knew the local customs and had 'a respectful attitude' towards the Afghans.[54]

[54] Yu. Krasikov, 'Internatsional'naya missiya sovetskogo voina', *Voennyi Vestnik*, no. 10, 1988, p. 5; *Bakhtar*, 13 April 1987; RA, 7 June 1988; A. Lyakhovskii, *Tragediya i doblest' Afgana*, Iskona, Moscow, 1995, pp. 330-1; L.V. Shebarshin, *Ruka Moskvy*, Tsentr-100, 1992, pp. 178-9; *Sovetskaya Estonia*, 23 Sept. 1987, 26 Sept. 1987; Karmal, RA, 19 May 87; A. Heinamaa, Maija Leppanen, Y. Yurchenko, *The Soldiers' Story*, University of California Press 1994 pp. 113-17; V. Plastun, 'NDPA: voprosy edinstva i soyuznikov na sovremennov etape revolyutsii', *Spetsial'nyi Byulleten' AN IV SSSR* no. 6 (1987), p. 122.

Expansion of the social base

The DRA leadership attempted to enlarge its social base essentially by cultivating the social groups it had been addressing since the outset and by promoting the same policies. As has already been shown, in the countryside the main features of government policy remained land reform and the cooperatives. In general, the PDPA, originally a party of intellectuals, was particularly eager to increase the percentage of members belonging to the 'toiling classes'. While at the time of the Revolution only 5% of the membership was made up of workers and peasants, in the following years 38-47% of new members belonged to these social categories (see Table 15). In some provinces (Baghlan, Takhar, Badakhashan, Balkh, Herat, Nangrahar) the percentage was even higher. As a result, the quota of workers and peasants in the party grew steadily in the first years of the Revolution, then stabilized around 34-35% (see Table 16). It is probable that the leadership would have been best satisfied with 51% which would have justified its claim to be a proletarian party. One of the causes of this limited success is that the villages controlled by the government were exploited by Kabul, particularly for recruits to the armed forces, thanks to the cooperation of party organizations at the village level. Furthermore, workers and peasants were scarcely represented in the institutions. In the Revolutionary Council, for example, up to 1985 out of sixty-seven members only two were workers and one was a peasant. Only after 1985 did the situation improve and in 1986 six peasants were in the Revolutionary Council and twelve workers and seven peasants were members of the Central Committee.[55]

In the end, although the absolute number of peasants in the party ranks in fact grew, from 3,300 in 1980 to 19,200 in 1983,

---

[55] Basov and Poliakov, *Afganistan: trudnye sud'by revolyutsii*, p. 24; Ulyanovsky, 'Afghan revolution', in Bradsher, *Afghanistan and the USSR*, 3rd edn, cap. 9; *Documents and Records of the National Conference of the People's Democratic Party of Afghanistan, Kabul, March 14-15, 1982*, p. 35; *KNT*, 15 Dec. 1982; *Asia and Africa Today*, no. 4 (1984); *RA*, 5 July 1983; *KNT*, 25 July 1985; *Mezhdunarodnyi Ezhegodnik – Politika i Ekonomika 1984*, p. 220; *Mezhdunarodnyi Ezhegodnik – Politika i Ekonomika 1987*, p. 236; *RA*, 6 July 1985 and 14 June 1987; *Bakhtar*, 23 May 1986; *KNT*, 14 March 1987; Ludwig, 'Einige Probleme', p. 98; N.M. Momand, 'Afganistan. Protsess revolyutsionnogo obnovleniya prodolzhaetsya', *Partiinaya Zhizn'*, 1 (1987), p. 78.

24,500 in 1985 (0.66% of all the Afghan peasants) and 35,300 by the spring of 1987, this remained a very small proportion of the rural population, and did not represent an increase as a percentage of party members: 22.58% in 1983, 18.28% in 1985 and 19.6% in 1987. Furthermore, there are good reasons to think that few of these members were activists. At the same time, the percentage of peasants in the ranks of the DYOA declined continuously during the 1980s: 9.9% in 1983, 5.3% in 1985 and 4.0% in 1987. This could mean that whatever expansion the party was achieving in the countryside, it was based on recruitment for patronage rather than ideology. In 1987 Najibullah still asserted the necessity to transform the countryside into the centre of party activities, since the final outcome of the struggle would be decided there and in his opinion everything possible had not yet been done to make the peasants feel linked to the revolutionary government. Overall, also taking into account the influence of the only other party of the pro-Soviet left with a following in the countryside, the Revolutionary Organization of the Afghan Toilers (SAZA), we can estimate that the DRA, even at its strongest, could count on some kind of political support from no more than 10-12% of the peasantry.[56]

The DRA's organized following among women was even weaker. The Democratic Women's Organization grew from 8,300 members in 1360 (1981/2) to a peak strength of 125,000 in 1988 (by which time it had been renamed Afghan Women Council). Peasants and workers were a small minority among them: in 1987 there were 4,506 peasants and 11,401 workers among its 108,931 members, of which only a small minority were also members of the party. At that time this organization was present in 253 villages; although this figure had increased to 359 in 1991, it was still not a very impressive achievement. In provinces like Ghazni, where the influence of the party was weaker, the members of the Council were almost all wives of state and party officers, or teachers from Kabul.[57]

[56] *News Bulletin*, 18 May 1987; N.N. Khakimdzhanov, 'Kurs NDPA na ras-shirenie sotsial'noi bazy aprelskoi revolyutsii', *Obshchestvennie nauki v Uzbekistane*, 2 (1988), p. 35; Khalil Vedad, 'Rol DOMA v sotsial'no-politicheskoi zhizni RA 1978-87 gg.' in *Respublika Afganistan*, Izdatelstvo Fan Uzbekskoi SSR, Tash-kent, 1990, pp. 22, 24, 27; TASS, 2 April 1987.

[57] *KNT*, 2 Dec. 1987 and 13 June 1991; M. Olimov, 'Iz zapisok perevodchika', *Vostok*, no. 3 (1991), p. 66; 'Postanovlenie sekretariata TsK NDPA o rabote

Party militias

Considering the permanent state of war, a vital aspect of the
expansion of the social base of the DRA was naturally represented
by the constitution of armed militias. Of the wide variety of
militias formed by the revolutionary government at various stages,
only those that were ideologically oriented will be dealt with
here. The 'Soldiers of the Revolution' (*Sepayan-i Inqilab*) was
made up of young party and DYOA members who served temporarily (three to six months) and were mainly active in towns,
although they were sometimes dispatched to rural areas, mainly
for propaganda purposes. They were not numerous: when they
were created in 1980 there were barely 200 and even at the
beginning of 1982 those from Kabul (their main recruiting ground)
serving in the provinces numbered only 500.[58] In 1983 1,613
were serving in Kabul, while in the whole period 1980-5 17,700
such 'soldiers' were recruited in the capital, so no more than a
few thousand can have been in service at any given time
countrywide. The 'Revolution Defence Groups' (GDR) were
recruited in considerable numbers also in the villages. The decision
to form such 'Groups' even in the countryside was taken at the
first Agricultural Conference, held in Kabul on 26-27 February
1980 and it was put into practice from the following March,
particularly in the provinces of Laghman, Jallalabad, Kunduz, Balkh
and then, the following year, around Bagram and Charikar, and
finally all around the country. Recruitment to their ranks met
with some response particularly among the middle class youth,
but also among landless peasants, in Kabul and in areas like Baghlan,
Shiberghan, Pul-i-Khumri and Gulbahar. The size of the GDRs
reached appreciable levels only during 1983, according to official
sources. At the beginning of that year more than 1,000 GDRs
existed and their members were '130% more than in 1982'. It
appears that most of them were concentrated in towns, while the
provinces where they were strongest at this stage were Baghlan,
Badakhshan, Herat and Nangrahar. In the countryside, one of

---

tsentral'nogo soveta DOZhA po uluchsheniyu deyatel'nosti zhenskikh organizatsii
v svete trebovanii, 7 iyulya 1984 g.' in *NDPA (sbornik dokumentov)*, Tashkent,
'Uzbekistan', 1986, pp. 299-300; Najibullah, RA, 15 Aug. 1988.

[58] G. Musaelian and A. Sukhoparov, *Ekho razbuzhannykh gor?*, Moskovskii
Rabochi, 1988, p. 48; *Bakhtar*, 24 Feb. 1982.

the preferred recruiting grounds was the cooperatives, 4,710 of whose members were in the GDRs in 1985.[59]

At the end of 1983, 18,000 militiamen were in the GDRs. Government propaganda credited them with operational successes as early as the summer of 1980, particularly in the provinces of Kunduz and Balkh.[60] In reality, the creation of 'revolutionary' militias inevitably clashed with the weakness of the regime in the countryside, worsened by the fracture between the Khalq and Parcham factions of the party. Khalqis often resented the domination of the other (less numerous) faction, which had taken a great deal of power away from them. A French traveller met Khalqi militiamen hostile to the Soviets and sympathetic to some·extent to the mujahidin because of their nationalist feelings. The main argument which kept the militiamen in their place was the salary.[61]

No effort was spared to enlist as many party members as possible into the GDRs, and in some provinces such as Kandahar a high proportion of PDPA members were recruited (60% in 1986). Nevertheless, since at least 1982-3 former 'counter-revolutionaries' were admitted into their ranks – 200 among the GDRs active in Farah province alone – a practice which casts doubts about the existence of any genuine ideological orientation.[62]

At the beginning of 1988 GDR membership numbered 35,000; since National Reconciliation was launched in January 1987, only 2,000 had joined. In other words, their strength had stagnated since 1986. Table 17 confirms that, on the whole, the expansion of the GDRs had almost ceased by the mid 1980s. Not much later the regime's propaganda would totally neglect them. Moreover, it should be pointed out that in no province did the GDRs come

---

[59] Basov and Poliakov, *Afganistan: trudnye sud'by revolyutsii*, p. 39; Z. Tanin, personal communication, 8 March 1994; P. Bonovsky, *Washington's Secret War against Afghanistan*, New York: International Publishers, 1985, pp. 103-4; *KNT*, 24 Jan. 1983; *CTK*, 25 Jan. 1983; *Bakhtar*, 1 May 1985; *Izvestia*, 25 Feb. 1983; Karmal, RA, 8 Dec. 1985.

[60] *KNT*, 7 Dec. 1983; *TASS*, 23 Aug. 1980.

[61] B. Dupaigne in *Le Monde*, 19 Aug. 1980.

[62] *Bakhtar*, 8 Feb. 1988; 'Postanovlenie politburo TsK NDPA o rabote kandargaskogo provintsial'nogo komiteta partii po ukrepleniyu partiinogo edinstva i distsipliny v svete trebovanii XIV plenuma TsK NDPA, 10 oktyabrya 1984 g.' in *NDPA (sbornik dokumentov)*, Tashkent, 'Uzbekistan', 1986, pp. 160; *KNT*, 3 July 1986.

to be present in more then some tens of villages, whereas on the average an Afghan province is made up of 1,100-1,200 villages. As a whole, at the height of their spread, the GDR covered 1,350 villages in all of Afghanistan, i.e. about 6% of those inhabited.[63]

In 1980 the party militias had some impact on the overall situation and Soviet documents refer to the 'not small role' played by them in stabilizing the situation in provinces like Herat, Kandahar and Nangrahar. In some localities their roots may have been real, and some of them were reported to be effective fighting forces, but this was during a transitional phase, when the mujahidin were still badly equipped. Later on GDR capabilities became increasingly stretched, as they were more and more used to 'protect' neighbouring villages and roads. Soon it become clear that the strength of the PDPA and its sympathizers was totally inadequate to face the several thousand increasingly well armed mujahidin groups active in the countryside. If the DRA wanted to find enough support to survive without direct Soviet military help, it would have had to try alternative strategies to the 'ideological' one attempted in the first half of the 1980s, as is illustrated in Part III.[64]

The republic of the notables

Some further qualifications about the nature of this limited support for the party in the countryside are needed. After the first phases of the Saur Revolution some observers noted that the rural structure of the PDPA was prevalently (although not only) based on 'vertical alliances'; particularly during the Amin era membership of the party was mediated through the kin links between its educated members who belonged to the urban bourgeoisie, and the propertied classes of the countryside. State and party officials tended to establish contacts with the landlords, even when the mobilization of poor and landless peasants had been successful.[65] In two of its

[63] *Bakhtar*, 8 Feb. 1988.

[64] *Afghanews*, 1 May 1989, p. 1; Lyakhovskii, *Tragediya i doblest' Afgana*, p. 190.

[65] A. Olesen, 'The Saur Revolution and the local response to it' in *Forschungen in und uber Afghanistan*, S.W. Breckle and C.M. Naumann (eds), pp. 141, 150.

strongholds, the districts of Lashkargah and Girisk (Helmand province), the party had built its social base during the war mainly by mobilizing the most influential members' kin. The main militia leader, Khano, had not been politicized before the war, but was the brother of a locally-well-known party member. The main factor driving recruitment to the party and to the militias was an inextricable mixture of ideology and patronage.[66]

In the same way, in Faryab province, the party structure was very weak and politically paralyzed. The local secretary was very young and was unable to keep the situation under control. The real power lay in the governor's hands, whose personal relationships were the real base of local political power and who enjoyed 'dictatorial power over everything and everybody'.[67]

Therefore the rural notables, instead of being totally opposed to the 'revolutionary' regime, were, rather, divided between supporters and opponents. In Tashkurghan, for example, out of ten notables whose behaviour a French scholar has been able to trace, five sided with the government and it does not seem that their lands were ever affected by the land reform.[68] Traditional notables could even go so far as to join the party, like one notable of the village of Kachkak, near Mazar-i-Sharif, who became a member of the party in 1985. Karmal himself stated in 1985 that 'little attention' was being paid 'to the recruitment of elders, people of influence, ulema and religious leaders in the localities' – more was to be done, but at the same time he complained about the tendency of government officials to 'tie themselves in the circles of their friends' and about the strength of 'clan loyalty, loyalty to material gains, loyalty to family, grouping'. It is doubtful whether it would have been possible to keep the two aspects divided.[69]

The DRA, in the end, wherever it had an influence in the countryside showed a tendency to take the form of a 'Republic of the notables', whether they were 'modern' men of influence

---

[66] G. Dorronsoro in *Afghanistan Info*, no. 33 (April 1993).

[67] J. Anifi (BBC Monitoring), personal communication, 13 Dec. 1993; V. Nosatov, 'V nachale deviatiletnei voiny', *Literaturnyi Kirgizistan*, no. 6 (1989), p. 67.

[68] G. Dorronsoro in *Afghanistan Info*, no. 31, (March 92) p. 17.

[69] *L'Humanité*, 1 March 1985; Karmal at the Plenum, RA, 27 March 1985; Karmal, RA, 26 April 1985; Karmal at 12th Plenum CC, RA, 5 July 1983.

like teachers or traditional ones like *arbabs*. The birth places of important party leaders generally became PDPA strongholds. This is the case for Sourkhaly, Ghazni province, birth village of Taraki, first President of Revolutionary Afghanistan, which throughout the war was a stronghold of pro-government militiamen and the only village in the province to host a party organization worth the name. Qabizan, in the Panjshir, village of birth of Dastagir Panjsheri, an important PDPA leader, was a 'centre of communist activities' before the the the valley fell into mujahidin hands. In Mohmanddara (Nangrahar province), immediately after the Soviet arrival, Jahangir, a Parchami, was named commander of the local militia. He filled the party and state district and provincial bureaucracies with his relatives, while in 1987-8 he managed to be appointed general and elected to the Parliament. When the mujahidin attacked the district in 1988, while other pro-government armed groups melted away, the local militia put up a strong resistance and even some women fought.[70]

Patronage thus played a fundamental role, particularly in attracting economically weaker groups. This does not mean that a social and ideological divide did not cross many villages. In Chehel Dukhtaran, for example, another model village south of Kabul, fifty inhabitants out of 400 did not accept the Revolution, although it had brought education, electricity and mechanical irrigation; they migrated to Pakistan. Another case is a village in Ghor province, where despite the presence of a cooperative, a party cell and the militia, in March 1987 the return of no fewer than fifty 'misguided' inhabitants was announced. The case of the village of Golzar is even more extreme. Western journalists were taken to visit what we should assume to be a 'model' village: in fact 'most people in the village were armed and willing to sing the praises of the Kabul government and the Soviet Union which they said was committed to the welfare of Afghans', but only 250 of the 2,000 inhabitants were still in the village, the others having left, if not to join the mujahidin, either for Kabul or for Pakistan. Furthermore, there were still signs of a pro-mujahidin presence, as slogans painted on walls proclaimed.[71]

[70] *AIC MB*, no. 102 (Sept. 1989), p. 42; Afghanews, 15 May 1991; M.A. Ikram, 'Liberation of Eastern Ningrahar', WUFA, Jan.-March 1989, pp. 35-6, 38.

[71] *The Times*, 23 Jan. 1989; *KNT*, 29 March 1987; Reuters, April 12, 1989.

In many areas, moreover, not only was the party unable to count on locally influential members, it often enlisted elements with a bad reputation among the population. In many other cases administrators from Kabul were sent, who surrounded themselves with cronies in the administrative posts. Particularly harmful was the conduct of certain Pashtun officials, active in the minority-dominated areas like Baghdis, Balkh, Jowzyan, Samangan and Faryab, who at least in the early 1980s, repeating what had been done under Amin, behaved aggressively against local customs and traditions. In these cases the relationship with the local population became one of total estrangement.[72]

---

[72] With regard to Ghazni, see M. Olimov, 'Iz zapisok perevodchika', *Vostok*, no. 3, 1991, p. 66; Lyakhovskii, *Tragediya i doblest' Afgana*, p. 190; *Aktual'nye problemy afganskoi revolyutsii*, p. 580.

4

RELUCTANT CONCESSIONS
AND CO-OPTATIONS

Political approaches

Karmal and his government realized from the beginning that, apart from relying on the resumption of the social reforms, some kind of political overture was needed if some breath was to be given to the beleaguered Democratic Republic. The first initiatives were directed towards reducing the general hostility of the population, creating the image of a more liberal, tolerant and democratic regime than the previous one. In early 1980 Karmal launched a campaign to promote consensus in every quarter: he promised the restoration of the freedoms abolished under Amin, through a new Constitution based on Islam, and ensured that religion would be respected, while maintaining the revolutionary program. Among the various measures taken or proclaimed were the restoration of the old national flag and the adoption of the *Jirgah* (traditional assembly) as representative organ. The gradual nature of the reforms was now stressed. The only substantial measure to be effectively taken was the appointment of non-PDPA members: according to government sources, forty-five out of 103 persons given responsibile positions by the government between January and March 1980 were not members of the party, while according to the calculations of an American observer, the same applies to seventy-eight out of 191 officials named between March and May 1980. Disorder in Kabul in 1980 and the terror and counter-terror campaigns of 1980-1 (anti-government terror attacks caused sixty-three deaths in April 1981 and 201 in May) prevented a relaxing of the political atmosphere in Kabul until early 1983, when finally people were at least able to express their opinions about the government more freely, and within the PDPA open criticism of the leadership was to a certain extent tolerated.[73] On the other hand, the government had not really renounced in the long term what critics called 'sovietization'. In 1982, 651 officials trained in the USSR got positions in the state apparatus, including 266 leading positions, while 359 more had been formed at the Social Sciences Institute of the party, basically ruled by Soviet advisors. At the same time, many workers and specialists, numbering 90,000 by 1986, were also taking Soviet-run courses either in Afghanistan or in the USSR.[74]

The measures discussed above proved to be far too little to calm the population. According to General Varennikov, at least until 1982 the importance of tradition and the supremacy of Islam were acknowledged only verbally – in practice they were ignored. At the same time, slogans in favour of radical social transformations were proclaimed, although conditions were absolutely prohibitive. Some steps forward were made in the following years, but the whole period was characterized by the production of an enormous amount of paper and little concrete undertakings. Resolutions, decrees and directives numbered 17,251 by 22 August 1985. It was estimated that 50-80% of the time of officials at various levels in the capital and in the provinces was wasted in examining paperwork. This would later expose Karmal to the Soviet accusation of having substituted political work at the centre and in the provinces with paper production. In fact, Soviet advisers had been complaining about his inactivity since the very beginning. A month after his arrival in power, a group of them wrote a letter to their own head complaining that Karmal was doing nothing to meet the expectations of the population; they feared a real civil war could begin in two or three months if nothing was done. In reality, it is probable that Karmal, apart from his allegedly limited capabilities (according to Varennikov), either due to his own volition or because of several constraints (which certainly were not lacking), was trying to gain time while hoping that some relief would

[73] *The Guardian*, 12 Nov. 1981; Arnold, 'The ephemeral elite', p. 46; *KNT*, 5 March 1980; Lyakhovskii, *Tragediya i doblest' Afgana*, p. 188; *Hannoverische Allgemeine Zeitung*, 1 July 1983.

[74] Ludwig, 'Einige Probleme', p. 96; B.R. Rubin, *The Fragmentation of Afghanistan*, p. 169.

derive from military operations and from whatever degree of implementation of the reforms could be achieved.[75]

After having waited for some years for results which were not forthcoming and having unobtrusively resisted pressures from his Soviet advisers to take more decisive steps, in October 1985 Karmal had to face Gorbachev's ultimatum. He then decided to launch a new initiative in November 1985, through a public speech ('The Ten Theses') full of conciliatory offers: (1) all national problems should be resolved by political means; (2) the government should become more representative of the various strata and groups and not be monopolized by the PDPA; (3) the private agricultural sector should be encouraged; (4) traders and businessmen should be encouraged; (5) independent organizations of intellectuals should be allowed; (6) tribal self-government should be allowed; (7) the National Fatherland Front should be expanded, but other organizations should also be allowed; (8) Islam should be respected; (9) the armed forces should be consolidated and, when foreign intervention had ceased, the Soviets should leave; (10) a foreign policy of active non-alignment and friendship with the neighbouring countries should be pursued.[76]

The following January the ten theses resulted, among other things, in the inclusion of more 'non-party members, representatives of all the classes, nationalities, tribes' in the leading positions of the administrative organs. The size of the Revolutionary Council, which *de facto* carried out the functions of the Parliament, was increased from sixty-nine to 148 members, in order to provide space for the inclusion of new elements, including non-party ones, who grew from two or three to fifty-eight. Among them, six were peasants, three former counter-revolutionaries, one a land-owner, and nine clerics. At this point, more than 39% of the

---

[75] *Ogoniok*, no. 12, 1989; Yu. Gankovskii, 'O putiakh prekrasheniya grazhdanskoi voiny v Afganistane', *Vostok i Sovremennost* no. 3 (1993), p. 83; *National Conference of PDPA on National Reconciliation (Oct. 18-20, 1987). Documents*, Kabul, Afghanistan Today, 1987, p. 43; Yu. V. Gankovsky, 'The dynamics of Russian-Afghan relations' in M. Mesbahi (ed.), *Russia and the Third World in the post-Soviet era*, University Press of Florida, 1994, p. 360; Gromov, *Ogranichennyi kontingent*, pp. 228-9.

[76] Arnold, 'The ephemeral elite', p. 53-4; S. Harrison and D. Cordovez, *Out of Afghanistan*, Oxford University Press, 1995, pp. 201-3; Gromov, *Ogranichennyi kontingent*, pp. 228-9.

members of the Revolutionary Council were non-PDPA, as against
2.9–4.4% previously. At the end of 1986 Haji Mahammed Cham-
kani, former member of the monarchical parliament, former governor of Paktia, non-PDPA, became President of the Council, a
position to which however very scant powers were assigned. Furthermore, ten non-PDPA ministers joined the government. Although many of these non-party men were already working with
the government previously, they had never held such positions
of high responsibility before. However, as Najibullah would later
say (until 1987 only 'longstanding friends of the Revolution had
joined the leadership organs'), they were basically all sympathizers
of the ruling party. Finally, easier credit and special fiscal terms
were granted to the business world. At a lower level, the space
that the regime was ready to concede to its fellow-travellers was
even broader. Out of 591 members of the Kabul Provincial Council,
for example, only ninety-five were PDPA members.[77]

The government's targets were clearly the professional strata,
who had been leaving the country in large numbers since 1979.
Karmal did not really seem to think that the 'Ten Theses' would
encourage many professionals who had taken refuge abroad to
come back, but he did hope that they would help to keep inside
Afghanistan the new generation of the intelligentsia, which was
then being bred. It appears that in this respect some degree of
success was achieved.[78]

Religious policy

One of the basic policies of the Karmal Government was to
appear respectful of Islam and to establish better relationships with
the clergy. As a French scholar noted, this was actually the only
real, ideological novelty in the PDPA program under Karmal. It
appears that many Khalqi activists were strongly anti-Islamic, or
at least anti-clerical, as the harsh persecutions against the mullahs
which they carried out show eloquently. In fact the PDPA always

[77] *Afghanistan Report*, 22 Jan. 1986; *KZ*, 26 April 1986; Bradsher, *Afghanistan*
3rd unpubl. edn., cap. 10 pp. 5, 8; A. Arnold, *The Fateful Pebble*, Presidio,
1993, p. 157; *TASS* 10 Jan. 1986; R. Kaul, *Democratic Afghanistan – Forever*,
Pulse Publishers, ND, 1987, p. 87; Ludwig, 'Einige Probleme', p. 98; Arnold,
'The ephemeral elite', p. 54.

[78] *The Guardian*, 18 March 1986.

counted some mullahs in its ranks. The most prominent ones figured among the sympathizers of Parcham and SAZA, including some heterodox religious figures,[79] but Khalq had its mullahs too. In Kandahar province, for example, at the time of the Revolution twelve or thirteen mullahs were members of the party and one of them, Maulawi Kabir, was a member of the provincial committee of the party until his assassination in 1981. 'As many as fifteen' pro-government mullahs were assassinated by the opposition under the Khalq regime (1978-9). As soon as Karmal had installed himself in power, some religious notables expressed support for his program, like the Shi'a leader of Mazar-i-Sharif, Garf Abdul Gafar, and a 'renowned' Shi'a *'alim*, S.M. Ali Shah Tavakolli. But there is no doubt that the statement by Maulawi Abdul Aziz Sadeq, leader of the pro-government clergy, that all of the 50,000 Afghan mullahs who supported the government were progressives, while the 5,000 conservatives had left the country, was pure propaganda.[80]

Irrespective of the initial reaction to Karmal's approach, he pursued it further, aiming to improve the Islamic credentials of the regime. In 1981 a law was approved, ensuring state support for pilgrims to Mecca and Kerbala and offering food coupons to the mullahs, who were also granted exemption from land reform and military draft. Furthermore religion was inserted into the school curricula, for a total of three weekly hours, and, it appears, also in the literacy campaign; TV began to broadcast religious programs, one hour every evening. A considerable effort was expended in restoring or building new mosques: 527 by mid-1985, 1,257 by October 1986, 1,749 by the end of 1989. In 1987 Islam was finally proclaimed the state religion. In some localities well

---

[79] For example Maulawi Abdul Wali Hojjat (Minister for Islamic Affairs 1985-6) had been known for his links with Setem-i-Melli: C. Lobato, 'Islam in Kabul', *Central Asian Survey*, vol. 4, no. 4 (1985), p. 114; Maulawi Enyatollah Rashid (Vice Minister), on the contrary, was close to Parcham (C. Lobato, 'Kabul 1980-1986. Un Islam officiel pour légitimer le pouvoir communiste', *Central Asian Survey*, vol. 7, nos. 2-3 (1988), p. 88).

[80] O. Roy, 'The origins of the Afghan Communist Party', *Central Asian Survey*, vol. 7, no. 3 (1988), p. 52; M. Buchhorn, *40 Tage in Kabul*, Beltz Verlag, 1982, p. 33; R. Anwar, *The Tragedy of Afghanistan*, Verso, 1989, p. 150; *Spetsial'nyi Byulleten' IV AN SSSR*, 6 (1987) p. 207; *Aktual'nye problemy afganskoi revolyutsii*, Nauka, Moscow, 1984, p. 575.

known for their Islamic conservatism more was conceded, as for example in Herat, where alcoholic drinks were forbidden.[81]

A great effort was also made towards developing direct contacts with the clergy, aimed at exercising, as critics would put it, control over religious institutions. In 1980 the 'Ulema Society', already in existence at the time of the 'old regime', was reactivated and in June a Department for Islamic Affairs was formed at the Council of Ministers. In April 1981 the 'High Council of Ulema and Mullahs' was formed. Finally, in 1985 the 'Ministry for Islamic Affairs and Religious Interests' was established. Religious tribunals were left in existence alongside the Revolutionary ones, although their number declined sharply compared to the pre-revolutionary period (from 200 to forty).[82]

A certain number of moderate mullahs, a good proportion of them Shi'a, welcomed the government initiatives. Their point of view is exemplified by Maulawi Abdul Shukur (a Sunni from Herat) and by Maulawi Ramatullah, according to whom the points of discordance with the government were limited to some defects in the orthodoxy of the reforms, including the lack of compensation for the landowners in the land reform, the abolition of the repayable loan over the harvest (where the harvest is held as security, as admitted by Islamic law) and the excessively low limitation to the dowry. At least until 1985, the government showed its preference for the promotion of the 'progressive' sector of the clergy. Between 1980 and 1985 about six or seven ulema were admitted to the central state institutions; they were mainly known as leftist elements. In fact, many if not most of the clerics whole-heartedly siding with the government in the first half of the 1980s were rather progressive ones, if not indeed 'heterodox', like Abdul Wali Hojjat, who became Minister of Islamic Affairs in 1985, after having served in government positions since 1972. Of the most prominent nineteen among those assassinated by the mujahidin up to the beginning of 1983, at least nine belonged to this category. In the

[81] C. Mahbub, 'Moralische Aspekte in Islam und deren gegenwärtige ideologische Bedeutung in den Auffassungen fortschrittlicher Geistlicher der DRA', diss., Humboldt Universität, Berlin, p. 89; Centlivres-Demont, 'Afghan women in peace, war, and exile', p. 347; *The Guardian*, 18 March 1986; *Notizie dall'Afghanistan* (Afghan Embassy, Rome), Aug. 1985; *NT*, Oct. 1986, p. 13; *RA*, 13 Dec. 1989; *The Guardian*, 10 Oct. 1988.

[82] C. Lobato, 'Islam in Kabul', p. 113; Mahbub, *ibid.* p. 88.

meanwhile, new generations of progressive mullahs were trained
in the government madrasas. As a whole about ten government
madrasas (with 3,000 students) and ten Quranic schools (with
4,000 students) existed by 1988. Five more madrasas were established by 1991, including a 'female' one. DYOA primary organizations existed in the madrasa, like in any school. In February
1987, furthermore, a university-like Islamic centre was opened
in Kabul; it had 450 students by mid-1988. In ten years, the
regime trained 600 ulema.[83]

The progressive nature of this (largely minority) sector of the
clergy consisted in identifying the principles of the Saur Revolution
with the social principles of Islam, in asserting a substantial secularism
and in supporting equality and social progress, as well as the
literacy campaign. According to Soviet television, 'on Fridays ...
patriotically minded mullahs deliver sermons about what is hap-
pening in the country and about what the Democratic Republic
is doing for the man in the street. They talk to the believers
about the Revolution and how to assist it. For many illiterates,
this is the only place where they can get true information'. The
government came to rely heavily on propaganda in the mosques
and results seem to have been to some extent satisfying, as is
stated in a document with regard to Herat province in 1988. A
certain efficacy is confirmed by the assassination of several hundred
of these mullahs by the mujahidin during the war, including forty-six
ulema up to 1983.[84]

This choice would have anyway shown its limits by the middle
of the 1980s, although the need to attract more clerics onto the

[83] *L'Humanité*, 26 June 1980; Lobato, 'Islam in Kabul', p. 113; *Bakhtar*, 12
Aug. 1986 and 8 May 1987; M.A. Babakhodzhaev, 'NDPA – krupneischaya i
samaya vliyatelnaya sila afganskogo obschestva' in *Respubliķa Afganistan*, Tashkent,
Akademiya Nauk Uzbeskoi SSR, 1990, p. 10; RA, 21 June 1987; *Martyred for
the Cause of Truth: The True Moslems Murdered by the Mujahidin*, Kabul Government
Press; M. Tavus, 'Filosofsko-sotsiologicheskii analiz roli religii i religiozniykh
deyatelei Afganistana v realizatsii politiki natsional'nogo primireniya', diss., Moscow, 1991, p. 123; Hungarian TV, 11 Sept. 1986; L. A. Adamec, *A Biographical
Dictionary of Afghanistan*, Akademische Druck, Graz, 1987, p. 72.

[84] Mahbub, *op. cit., passim*; *Bakhtar* 19 Sept. 1988; K. Atoev, 'Religioznaya
situatsiya v sovremennom Afghanistane' in 'Voprosy teorii i pratiki', p. 218;
Bakhtar, 30 June 1988; *TASS*, 23 July 1988; Soviet TV, 20 Dec 1986; *Iz otcheta
p/i-ka Dashlya o propagandistskoi rabote v pr. Gerat (24 febr.–11 marta 1988 g.*;
Anwar, *The Tragedy of Afghanistan*, p. 150.

government side had already been acknowledged at the VI plenum (mid-1981) of the PDPA CC. First of all, the great majority of the clergy remained hostile to the government, particularly, but not only, in the countryside, sometimes expressing their stand in a spectacular way, as during the July 1980 Conference of Ulema organized by the government, when the climate was of open hostility towards the regime. A mullah who defended the government was repeatedly interrupted and challenged. According to a Western diplomat, at another Islamic meeting at the Kabul Polytechnic, several mullahs criticized the Soviet presence. As late as November 1984 twenty mullahs of Kabul city were removed for criticizing the government. Kabul was finding it difficult to extend the influence of the progressive mullahs beyond Kabul and the main towns, as the Vice-Minister for Religious Affairs Mohammed Sadiqi himself admitted in 1988. The difficulty of penetrating the remotest provinces is also shown by the fact that in 1984 the Department for Islamic Affairs of the Government, according to its president Maulawi A. Wali Hojjat, had not yet been able to find representatives in two of the twenty-eight provinces of the country.[85]

An Indian observer believed that since 1983 the government had begun to gain ground among the clergy, particularly in the non-Pashtun areas, although in 1983 a Soviet journalist listed the areas where the Ulema Councils were particularly active as the Pashtun province of Nangrahar, as well as the mixed one of Herat and the Tajik/Uzbek ones of Jowzyan and Baghlan. The Indian observer's opinion may be partially true, particularly if one recalls that at the First Conference of the Council of the Ulema, held in 1980, only fifty ulema took part, while at the Second in 1984 there were 800. When one considers, however, that the 'particularly' active pro-government clergy of Nangrahar province in 1983 numbered 100 mullahs, as compared to twenty in Kandahar, ten in Zabul, twenty in Paktika, fifty in Paktia and fifty in Kunar – a total of 280 clerics out of 50,000 living in the same areas – it will be realized how relative these considerations are.[86]

[85] AFP, 10 July 1980; *Guardian*, 19 Oct. 1988; *Bangkok Post*, 25 March 1984.

[86] B.S. Gupta, *Afghanistan: Politics, Economics and Society*, Pinter 1986, pp. 65, 130; L. Nikolaev, *Afghanistan between the Past and the Future*, Progress, 1986, p. 90; Tavus, 'Filosofsko-sotsiologicheskii analiz roli religii i religiozniykh deyatelei Afganistana v realizatsii politiki natsional'nogo primireniya', p. 123; Gankovskii,

It appears probable that no real progress was made by Kabul before 1985-6. In 1985, for example, the number of pro-government clergy in Kunar had grown more than fourfold to 205 mullahs and eleven ulema. In 1986 the regime began to claim 11,500 mullahs on its payroll, mounting to 16,000 in 1987 and over 20,000 in 1988. In 1987 the state claimed to subsidize (i.e. to some extent to control) 8,450 mosques out of 15,000. It is no accident that after 1985 Kabul changed its strategy. Between 1985 and 1986 the number of clerics within state institutions grew to fourteen or fifteen, several of whom could boast Al-Azhar in their credentials, while one was a former mujahid. The new pro-government mullahs were mainly non-aligned politically. Twelve mullahs also entered the Revolutionary Council as candidate members. Apart from this group of top individuals, a relatively substantial number of clerics were also getting involved in the various levels of government institutions: 1,400 were members of the National Fatherland Front, the main flanking organization of the regime; 1,092 were engaged in local government; the governor of Balkh province was Maulawi Zarif, imprisoned under Amin.[87] As a result of the first elections for the 'local organs of power' in 1986, 20% of those elected were mullahs. Towards the end of 1986 even sources sympathizing with the mujahidin admitted some success by the regime in co-opting village mullahs in the North. In 1985 the High Council of Ulema and Mullahs was 10,000 strong, but it is difficult to estimate what proportion of the Afghan clergy this represented, given wildly varying estimates of its size ranging from 50,000 to 320,000. What is certain is that the proportion varied considerably from province to province: in 1986 12.5% of the ulema supported the government in Kabul province, while in Kunar province only 6.7% did so. Quite obviously the state found it easier to exercise some control over religious places. In 1987 it 'protected' 16,700 large and small mosques and during the year it came to cover 3,100 more mosques. The total number of mosques has been estimated at 23,000.[88]

'Polosa pushtunskikh plemen Afganistana', p. 115, no. 14.

[87] He appears to have been one of the 'progressives': at least one of his sons was a member of the DYOA (Soviet TV, 20 Dec. 1986).

[88] *NT*, 44 (1986); C. Karp, 'Afghanistan: eight years of Soviet occupation', *Department of State Bullettin*, March 1988, p. 18; *Der Spiegel*, 20 (1988); Lobato,

On the other hand it is also evident that a larger proportion of the clergy was made up of those who where willing to stay neutral or rather were trying to keep a foot in both camps, like the imam of the Kabul Bazar mosque. He both supported the mujahidin and praised the government and resolved controversies by arguing, with regard to women who worked without a veil, that although it was a real problem, economic necessity came first. It is even more difficult to estimate the importance of neutral mullahs than that of pro-government mullahs; as an example we can cite the case of Mazar-i-Sharif, where in 1986 a third of the 370 mullahs received a government salary – the remaining two-thirds, who continued their activity under government control, but without accepting a compromising salary, can be supposed to have been 'neutral'.[89]

It is also important to recall that even as far as the inner affairs of the party were concerned a similar attitude is found. Anti-clericalism was still common in 1982-3, when a party official could only express his amazement with regard to the request ('obviously' refused) by a mullah to be admitted into the party. But such anti-clericalism seems to have died down by the end of 1986, when in the Charasyab district seven mullahs out of fifty were PDPA members. Opening to Islam also meant the establishment of 'prayer leaders' in the army and among the *sarandoy*; since 1986 every regiment of the army had two mosques and two mullahs. At the same time the PDPA leaders were doing their best to show their Islamic credentials, attending mosques and invoking Islam on television. Also Salman Rushdie was condemned for his novel *The Satanic Verses*.[90]

In conclusion, up to 1986 the pro-Soviet regime in Kabul succeeded only to a very limited extent. In fact it consolidated

---

'Kabul 1980-1986', A. Arnold, 'Afghanistan' in *Yearbook on World Communist Affairs, 1989*, p. 461; *The Guardian*, 18 March 1986; Chantal Lobato, *Défis Afghans*, no. 10 Nov. 1986; *KNT*, 10 Aug. 1985; K. Atoev, 'Religioznaya situatsiya v sovremennom Afghanistane' in *Voprosy teorii i pratiki*, pp. 218-19; Gankovskii, 'O putiakh prekrashenyia grazhdanskoi voiny v Afganistane', p. 83; *Voenno-politicheskaya obstanovka v provintsii Kunar po sostoyanie na 1 Maya 1985*; *TASS*, 6 Feb. 1987.

[89] *Le Nouvel Observateur*, 23 Feb. 1989; *Guardian*, 18 March 1986.

[90] Nikolayev, *Afghanistan between the Present and the Future*, p. 89; R. Trask, *Grasping the Nettle of Peace*, Morning Star, 1987, pp. 14-15; *KZ*, 18 June 1988.

its traditional areas of support, particularly in towns, but did not achieve any. sort of breakthrough beyond them. The main new feature, the opening up to the clergy, was pursued only half-heartedly – the real changes in this field too took place after 1986. In such fashion, the survival of the regime could not have been guaranteed without direct Soviet support. The consolidation of the regime's strongholds did play an important role in 1989, after the Red Army withdrew, although the peak of party morale and strength had already passed after 1986, as will be shown later. The main point is, however, that as long as the conflict could be characterized as what a Soviet sociologist called with some justification a war between revolutionary towns and reactionary villages,[91] the PDPA government would always be at a distinct strategic disadvantage. However, while the policy described here was clearly the dominant one in 1980-6, at the same time signs can be noted of an increasing pressure for a real compromise with a society stubbornly resistant to accepting the model of society which the revolutionary government had been trying to impose. Throughout this period concessions were substantially limited, and in any case were not designed to modify the basic assumption that Afghanistan should become something little short of a 'state of socialist orientation' sooner or later. These were the boundaries beyond which the 'ideological strategy' could not develop. A real, strategic reversal would come only with the arrival in power of Najibullah.

---

[91] Ol'shanskii D.V., 'Afganistan. Sud'ba naroda, sud'ba obshchestva', *Sotsiologicheskie issledovaniya*, no. 5 (1988), p. 113.

Part II

THE AFGHAN REGULAR ARMED FORCES: RECONSTRUCTION, REORGANIZATION AND STRUCTURAL LIMITS

5

KARMAL'S 'NEW MODEL ARMY' AND ITS ROLE IN THE WAR

Karmal often spoke of a 'new type of popular armed forces' to be realized in accordance with the social nature of the Revolution, where 'new type' meant basically an increase in the proportion of officers from the lower classes and the intelligentsia and the establishment of a new relationship between them and the rank and file. Before the Revolution 31.5% of the officers came from worker and peasant families and 6.6% from artisan ones, while after some years it was claimed that this share had respectively increased to 70% and 19%, with a further 11% coming from the intelligentsia. Whatever degree of truth was contained in these statistics, little seems to have changed in the actual relationship between officers and troops, which remained bad. According to a Soviet adviser in Afghanistan, Karmal's 'new model army' was in fact meant to be an army personally devoted to him. The low opinion Soviet advisers tended to have of Karmal particularly towards the end of his term in power may to some extent account for this cynical view. There is no doubt, however, that even if no 'new model army' took shape, the Revolution did bring about changes in the military field, although not the ones expected by its supporters.[1]

A KGB officer maintains that the structure and tactics of the Afghan armed forces remained the standard Soviet ones throughout the war and that the 2,000 generals and colonels of the Red Army who worked as advisers in its ranks proved unable to adapt them to local conditions. Undoubtedly, the Soviet occupation had a very heavy impact on the Afghan conduct of the war. Soviet advisers were present down to battalion level and they were involved directly in the fighting, 180 being killed and more than 600 wounded during the period. Even Soviet sources sometimes accuse them of taking the place of their Afghan colleagues, trying mechanically to apply forms and methods learnt in the USSR. In other words, more than giving advice they were giving orders. Moreover, Afghans trained in the USSR rose more and more to prominence during the war, particularly after the reshuffle in March 1985, when some forty senior generals and party officials with military responsibilities were removed from their positions and replaced with others just back from training courses in the USSR. Separate chains of command were retained, but in fact the tactical and operational levels were controlled by a single (Soviet) command structure.[2]

On the other hand, other advisers complain that while advice from the Soviets was verbally accepted, in fact it was generally ignored by the Afghans. A leader of the Pakistani intelligence services stated that intercepted radio communications between

---

[1] Z. Gol', 'Revolyutsionnaya Armiya v natsional'no-demokraticheskoi revolyutsii (na primere Afganistana)', diss., Moscow 1988, p. 123; Gankovskii, 'Vooruzhennye sily respubliki Afganistan', p. 4; S. Krivov, 'Vooruzhennye sily v politicheskoi zhizni Afganistana', *Spetsial'nyi Byulleten' IV AN SSSR*, no. 2 (1990), p. 184; Lyakhovskii and V. Zabrodin, 'Tainy afganskoi voiny', *Armiya*, 9 (1992). pp. 64-5; A. Lyakhovskii, *Tragediya i doblest' Afgana*, p. 180; *Aktual'nye problemy afganskoi revolyutsii*, Moscow, Nauka, 1984, p. 425.

[2] L.V. Shebarshin, *Ruka Moskvy*, Tsentr-100, 1992, p. 192; V.A. Merimskii, 'Voina v Afganistane: zapiski uchastika', *Novaya i Noveyashaya Istoriya*, no. 3 (1995), p. 96; N.I. Marchuk, *Neob"yavlennaya voina v Afganistane*, Luch, 1993, pp. 84-5; E. O'Ballance, *Wars in Afghanistan*, Brassey's, 1993, p. 144; D. Isby, *War in a Distant Country*, Arms and Armour Press, 1989, p. 53.

Afghans and Soviets were often 'mutually hostile'.[3] The following pages will assess to what extent the Afghan armed forces remained linked to the 'Soviet model' and how much innovation can instead be discerned.

Stages of recovery

When the Soviet Army entered the country at the end of 1979, the Afghan armed forces were already in a state of deep crisis. According to the different sources, the army was down to 40-60,000 men, that is to say maybe even less than 50% of the April 1978 level, while the Ministry of Interior troops (*sarandoy*) may have been as few as 8,000, i.e. 40% of levels in 1978. In fact the state of the armed forces was one of justifications of the occupation. The original idea was to occupy the main cities and towns and strategic points, leaving the countryside to the Afghan 'allies'. After six months or so, the Afghan armed forces having recovered and the new regime having consolidated its position, the 40th Army would be able to leave. This project had little contact with reality, as it was naive to think that the Afghan government troops would be able to recover in such a short time span. In fact, quite the opposite happened.[4]

Even today Soviet/Russian sources are quite meagre with information about developments during these early months of their stay in Afghanistan. This may also be a result of an objective difficulty in assessing the messy situation which characterized that period, but a certain reticence to admit the negative impact of the occupation should also be taken into account. So few figures for the army are available for the first half of 1980 (see anyway Table 27) that it is not easy to make comparisons, but there is little doubt that it declined further. The 20th Infantry Division, based in Bagram and covering the North-East of the country, saw three of its regiments virtually disintegrate: the 4th Artillery Regiment, one Infantry Battalion of the 10th Regiment and two

---

[3] Lyakhovskii, *Tragediya i doblest' Afgana*, p. 180; J. M. Strmecki, 'Power Assessment: Measuring Soviet Power in Afghanistan', diss., Georgetown University, 1994, p. 331.

[4] L. Lifschultz, 'Afghanistan: a voice from Moscow', *Monthly Review*, Sept. 1987, interview with N. Simoniya, p. 13.

of the 31st deserted to the mujahidin. The 31st, which was supposed to field 130 officers and 1,300 soldiers when fully manned, was left with only sixty officers and 100 soldiers. Even the 11th Infantry Division was badly shaken and its units could not resume activities until 1982 (see Table 28). A Soviet general admits that after the invasion the situation was much worse, in particular with regard to moral, and that the relationship between the Soviet advisers and at least one part of the Afghan officers worsened too.[5]

None the less, Soviets-only operations were forbidden; at least a token Afghan presence was always required and operational plans had always to be shared with the Afghans, although it soon became clear that they usually ended up in the mujahidin's hands. Until the end of the Soviet presence, details about the participation of Afghan troops in joint operations were agreed upon at the highest levels, usually during meetings between the Afghan leadership and the high-ranking representatives of the 40th Army. Karmal did not neglect to call for the army to take on a more offensive role; yet his Soviet detractors have claimed that he was not ready to go beyond rhetoric, mainly because of his fear of being one day left with only a Khalqi-dominated army.[6]

Many units of the Afghan Army were not capable of running independent operations even at the beginning of 1982, although at that time the Afghan role had increased somewhat with respect to 1980, when for example in Shindand operations were carried out by a Soviet brigade of 5,000 and an Afghan one of just 115 men. In general, joint operations used to see Soviet soldiers march first and Afghans follow, although this did not apparently apply to mopping-up operations. Actually, it seems that as late as autumn 1981 many Afghan soldiers and officers were refusing to take part in military operations. Soviet advisers working with Afghan units could find themselves in very difficult situations, like in Faryab province in 1982 when an Uzbek unit was on the edge of mutiny

---

[5] V.A. Merimskii, 'Voina po zakamu', *Voenno-istoricheskii Zhurnal* no. 11 (1993), p. 36; V.A. Merimskii, 'Voina v Afganistane: zapiski uchastika', *Novaya i Noveyashaya Istoriya* no. 3 (1995), p. 95.

[6] A. Lyakhovskii, 'Na afganskoi vizhzhennoi zemle', *Kommunist Vooruzhennikh Sil*, 19, 1990, pp. 77-8; Col. Ivanov, interviewed in *SR*, 20 Dec. 1989; Meeting of Armed Forces Party Activists Chaired by Karmal, RA, 16 Aug. 1981; Gromov, *Ogranichennyi kontingent*, p. 241.

and the advisers were compelled to accept the payment of a ransom (in weapons and ammunition) to the surrounding group of mujahidin, which was even weaker numerically than the Afghan unit. Before 1982 even self-defense groups organized by trade unions and the youth organization were sometimes to the front, because of the scarcity of available men.[7]

The first independent operation of some relevance was recorded in October 1982 and consisted of a five-day skirmish along the Pakistani border. Even in the role of supporter of larger Soviet forces the army only went beyond battalion and regiment-size operations in 1982, with brigade-size ones; one year later division-size operations were noted. Independent brigade-size operations were not recorded before 1984, division-size ones only in 1985, with a large scale offensive consisting of several regiments in Kunar province.[8]

In April 1985 the 're-organization' of the Afghan armed forces was claimed to have been accomplished, although in fact the Afghan leadership, instigated by the Soviets, continued to seek to improve the performance in large operations. According to the tasks it had been assigned, the Red Army was from the beginning supposed to play only a 'support role' to the Afghan Army, something which in fact took place only after 1985. At that point Afghan forces began to represent the bulk of those involved in most operations. Although figures are far from complete, Table 18 does give an idea of their activity at different times during the war. Overall, the Afghan Army seems to have had an upper limit of about thirty-five for the large scale operations it was able to carry out in a single year. It should be noted that all these military activities affected only a limited part of the country (see Map 2). Even in 1365 (1986/7) and 1366 (1987/8) they covered

[7] *Aktual'nye problemy afganskoi revolyutsii*, Moscow, Nauka, 1984, p. 436; General T.N. Tep-Grigorians, quoted in Harrison and Cordovez, *Out of Afghanistan*, p. 60; V. Nosatov, 'V nachale deviatiletnei voiny', *Literaturnyi Kirgizistan*, no. 6, 1989, p. 76; 'Voina est' voina, i russkikh mnogo', *Posev*, no. 3 (1983), p. 16; J. Fullerton, *The Soviet Occupation of Afghanistan*, FEER, 1983, p. 93; K. Ege, 'Confidence in Kabul: A political solution for Afghanistan', unpubl. typescript, n.d. (1983); B. Gromov, *op. cit.*, p. 137.

[8] O'Ballance, *Wars in Afghanistan*, p. 125; A.H. Cordesman and A.R. Wagner, *The Lessons of Modern Wars*, vol. III, Westview Press, 1990, p. 14.

only sixty-five districts out of 190; in 1366 the Afghan Forces fought in thirty-six of them without Soviet support.[9]

The first experiments in daring all-Afghan offensives (with limited indirect Soviet support) were tried with mixed results in 1986, with the two assaults on Zhawar, in the South-East, close to the border with Pakistan. The first took place in early 1986 and was a failure. Government troops behaved passively and the whole operation risked ending in debacle. The Soviets were forced to commit five battalions to rescue them. The second took place later in the year and was finally a success, with the fall and destruction of Zhawar, although heavy losses were incurred.[10]

The operations around Zhawar, however, did not really have a strategic aim. They were meant to have a psychological impact on the mujahidin and on the Afghan Army itself, showing that it was now able to strike hard everywhere in Afghanistan. Significant long-term results were obtained more through the exercise of constant military pressure, when logistics and geography were favourable. In fact, in the summer of 1986 most Afghan units still limited their activities to mopping-up operations. In December Najibullah explained that the duty was now 'to enhance the readiness of the army to a level that will make it possible for it to carry out independent armed struggle against the armed counter-revolution'.[11] Not much time was left for that.

The impact of military operations

The original strategy seems to have been to cleanse district by district with more or less massive military sweeps, a tactic of

---

[9] 'Kak prinimalos' reshenie', *Voenno-istoricheskii Zhurnal*, no. 7 (1991), p. 43; General T.N. Tep-Grigorians, quoted in Harrison and Cordovez, *Out of Afghanistan*, p. 60; *KZ*, 14 Aug. 1988; E.G. Nikitenko and N.I.Pikov, 'Razvechannii mif. O nepobedimosti plemeni Dzhadran', *Voenno-istoricheskii Zhurnal*, no. 2 (1995), p. 73.

[10] A. Lyakhovskii, 'Na afganskoi vizhzhennoi zemle', *Kommunist Vooruzhennikh Sil*, 20, 1990, p. 54; Ege, 'Confidence in Kabul', p. 2; V.A. Merimskii, 'Voina v Afganistane: zapiski uchastika', p. 111; *KNT*, 22 Dec. 1985; Lyakhovskii, *Tragediya i doblest' Afgana*, p. 301.

[11] Cordesman, *The Lessons*, p. 65; Rubin, *The Fragmentation of Afghanistan*, p. 155.

doubtful appropriateness to guerrilla wars. Sometimes a district was in fact 'liberated', but it was impossible to garrison every village in order to forestall attempts by the mujahidin to infiltrate it anew. This seems to have been the case of Kunar district in Nangrahar province. The Soviet/Afghan forces did succeed in subduing it and then in enrolling militiamen. For some time all of the thirty villages remained under government control, but then the Resistance managed to launch a counter-offensive and to wrest back twenty villages. Most of the militiamen are said to have deserted. Ambitious plans were drafted each year, according to which dramatic successes were expected in the short term (see Part III, Chapter 14, Section 2). Because of this, both Afghan and Soviet forces were distributed throughout Afghanistan in order to crush the enemy in the key areas. The Afghan Army was particularly spread out, so that little opportunity was left for offensive operations of any size. In the early years of the war about half of the army was busy with garrison duties and with the protection of economic assets. Critics among the Soviet adviser corps maintained that it would be wiser to concentrate efforts in a couple of provinces each year, reconstructing state power and reactivating a normal economic life there. While this would in any case have proved difficult to put into practice because of political constraints, at that stage in fact little would have changed, as the army was too demoralized to take action of any sort. The Soviets became increasingly frustrated with the established pattern, but this does not mean that the military effort was totally devoid of influence on the dynamic of the war.[12]

Soviet-Afghan military operations were particularly ineffective before 1983. After that, things began to go somewhat better, in part because the Afghan Army was recovering. Under Soviet pressure, attempts were made at freeing more troops for large-scale offensive operations. Responsibility for the protection of economic assets was transferred to the *sarandoy* in 1985. Roughly at the same time the first signs of fatigue appeared among the population, continuously subjected to reprisals and punishments. In 1984

---

[12] Lyakhovskii, 'Na afganskoi vizhzhennoi zemle', p. 54; Merimskii, 'Voina po zakamu', p. 111; V. Malinkovich, *Afganistan v ogne*, Suchasnist', 1985, p. 94.

Western sources began to report the spread in the countryside of the idea that the war would never end. The 'pacification policy', which will be dealt with in detail in Part III, was also encouraged by the growth of this mood. Relatively often the government succeeded in buying the neutrality of villages near its posts, promising not to bomb them and giving subsidies in exchange for information about the movements of the mujahidin, as in the case of the Turkmen villages around Qaisar.[13]

Behind the large scale resort to violent reprisals lay the conviction that 'the mujahidin are highly receptive to the idea of strength and they immediately submit to an authority or a man who is stronger. [...] A greater strength can attract them on [sic] its side'.[14] In other terms, whatever effect Soviet/Afghan military activities might achieve depended mostly on the sheer display of brute force and on the attrition which derived from it. Yet it appears clear that in some circumstances the actual tactical. outcome of large-scale operations could strongly influence future developments. The psychological impact of successful operations, both on the government's supporters and its opponents, should not be underestimated. In fact, the typical success story in the 'pacification' campaign usually saw a combination of successful military offensives, lasting attrition and skilled political approaches. The most noteworthy example comes from Northern Afghanistan. In mid-1981 the Soviet command elaborated a strategic plan designed to eliminate the mujahidin from the Northern provinces by autumn 1982, a typical, over-ambitious plan of the early years of the war. The outcome was obviously far below expectations, partly because the forces committed were too limited. However, some successes were scored. In fact one of the first lasting defeats inflicted on the mujahidin took place under this plan. In February 1982 (December 1981 according to another source) three to four Soviet and four Afghan battalions destroyed a rebel base in Darzab district, which supplied groups in Faryab, Jowzyan, Balkh and Samangan provinces. As a consequence a certain stabilization was achieved

---

[13] *KNT*, 22 Dec. 1985; *Le Monde*, 28 Dec. 1984; *Afghanistan Info*, Jan.-Feb. 1984, p. 13; J.B. Amstutz, *Afghanistan: the First Five Years of Soviet Occupation*, National Defense University 1986, p. 291.

[14] A. Prokhanov, 'Afghanistan', *International Affairs*, Aug. 1988, p. 20.

in the North, where the level of activity of the mujahidin began to decline. The base was never rebuilt.[15]

The North of the country had not been chosen at random. This was a privileged place for making the most of the advantages that the Soviets and the Afghan Army enjoyed over the mujahidin, thanks to the level terrain and to its distance from the porous borders with Iran and Pakistan, although the Soviets and the Afghan Army never really managed to completely isolate it, having by 1987 and after long efforts only succeeded in cutting one of the three trails from Pakistan, while the second had been made difficult and the third dangerous. With regard to the most important northern province, Balkh, it is worth noting that it was characterized by a relatively conservative mood. According to some journalists who travelled through the region at the beginning of the Soviet occupation, hostility to the newcomers was no less than in the rest of the country. Students, shopkeepers, businessmen and drivers all condemned the Soviet intervention without their opinions being solicited. The countryside must have run out of government control, as was shown by the fact that the supply of lamb had ceased and no more coal was coming from the villages, although it was abundant there. Even *buzkashi*, the traditional Afghan game, was no longer played, as lenders were refusing to furnish the horses needed. As late as 1986, in the whole of the province only 225 of 21,057 students in the literacy courses were women. In short, there is no doubt that Mazar-i-Sharif, one of the most important cities in Afghanistan, although not a conservative fief like Herat or Kandahar, was not a PDPA stronghold like Jallalabad. Even in 1988 almost all the women in the city went around completely veiled, while in Kabul a good half were unveiled. The few women in western clothes were government employees.[16]

The government certainly paid particular attention to this region. A deputy prime minister was assigned to supervize it, while an intensive program of economic development was carried out, one of whose aims was closer economic integration with Soviet Central

[15] Tchikichev A.V., *Spetnaz en Afghanistan*, CEREDAF, 1994, p. 13; Lyakhovskii, *Tragediya i doblest' Afgana*, p. 191; 'Kak prinimalos' reshenie', *Voenno-istoricheskii Zhurnal*, no. 7 (1991), p. 46.

[16] *Journal de Genève*, 10 Nov. 1987; *Guardian*, 8 Feb. 1980; *IHT*, 8 Feb. 1980; *Baltimore Sun*, Jan. 1986; *Guardian*, 18 March 1986; *LMD*, June 1988.

Asia. Even greater care was dedicated to Mazar-i-Sharif, which was subjected to large scale public works. There was also considerable development in social services. Already in 1982 Gerard Chaliand thought that the Northern plains had been pacified, but this was clearly an overstatement. It is probable that the government had succeeded in re-establishing some sort of government infrastructure, as the claimed resumption of tax collection in 1981 shows. On the other hand Red Army documents admit that the local population began to abandon its wait-and-see attitude and join the active resistance on a large scale in March of that year, while the Peshawar parties began to infiltrate the province heavily in the summer. It was simply a gross exaggeration when in 1984 the government claimed to control 90% of the province. A KGB officer remembers that even in the area around Mazar-i-Sharif the initiative was in the hands of the mujahidin in 1983. The government claim that in 1983-4 guerrilla attacks were less frequent is nearer to the truth and in fact it appears that from 1982 the situation improved, at least as far as the security conditions in the city of Mazar-i-Sharif were concerned. In the countryside, the situation was still precarious at best. According to government sources, at the end of the Afghan year 1984/5 the state only controlled eighty-eight villages out of 450 in the province, a percentage only slightly higher than in the rest of the country.[17]

The real crisis of the local resistance seems to have begun in 1985, as the fact that during this year the provincial organization of the PDPA received high praise indicates. This is clearly linked with the death of the top regional commander of the mujahidin, Zabiullah Khan, which unleashed a military crisis among the resistance forces. The inability of the resistance to recover and the beginning of a process of disintegration of Zabiullah's 1,000-strong groups shows that the constant pressure exercised by the government forces had not been in vain. It was a lasting defeat, although the effects of decline were spread over several years. .In January 1986, outside the security belt which extended up to 15 km from

---

[17] Newman J., 'The future of Northern Afghanistan', *Asian Survey*, July 1988; *Nouvelles d'Afghanistan*, June 1985, pp. 9-10; G. Chaliand in *Washington Quarterly*, winter 1982; Gai and Snegirev, *Vtorzhenie*, p. 204; .*Tages-Anzeiger* 11 Sept. 1981; Mo and Pellizzari, *Kabul Kabul*, p. 193; *L'Humanité*, 1 March 1982; N.S. Leonov, *Likholet'e*, Mezhdunarodnye Otnosheniya, 1994, p. 272.

Mazar, conditions were still not safe. Hismatullah Ansari, former mujahidin leader, who went over to the government in 1985 with 350 men, had since that time been unable to visit his village, although it was just 60 miles from the city, as he would have been killed. Even at the beginning of 1989 only half of the sixty-two villages in Balkh district were considered safe for the government forces. Only after the Soviet withdrawal was the area really pacified.[18]

Information for other areas of the North confirms the positive achievements of a combination of military successes, constant pressure and political skills. In the North-eastern province of Baghdis, heavy fighting in the province stopped after 1985, but a large-scale surrender to the government occurred only after Soviet withdrawal, thanks in part to the fact that in May 1989 the top local commander, Nik Mohammed Moalem, had been killed. Another example is provided by Andkhoy district (Faryab province), where in 1986 a Soviet/Afghan offensive smashed local resistance.[19]

Even in the West of the country a similar pattern can be discerned, albeit with a delay of several years. The first successful operation against the mujahidin of Herat province dates from summer 1986 and it caused the local resistance to weaken seriously for the first time. While in 1984 government documents had reported continuing stagnation in the area, with the city centre controlled by the mujahidin at night, now a second safety ring was established around the city and mujahidin morale allegedly plummeted. Many commanders went to Ismail Khan, their regional leader, to express their dissatisfaction. On this point both Soviet and Western sources agree. Factional tensions also contributed to the crisis of the Resistance, which pushed many inhabitants to seek refuge in government-controlled areas. Even such a successful military offensive would have been of little use however, if constant pressure had not been exerted afterwards.[20]

---

[18] Newman, *op. cit.*, p. 736; *Strategic Survey 1985/6*, IISS, London, p. 137; J. Steele, 'Moscow's Kabul campaign', *Merip Reports*, July-Aug. 1986, p. 6; Bonner, *op. cit.* p. 153; *Baltimore Sun*, Jan. 1986; *South*, Feb. 1989, p. 14.

[19] Dorronsoro and Lobato, 'L'Afghanistan un an après le retrait soviétique', *Est et Ouest*, Jan. 1990; AFP, 22 Nov. 1989; M. Urban, *War in Afghanistan*, Macmillan, 1990, p. 196.

[20] M. Urban, ibid., p. 204; *Ogoniok*, no. 12, 1989; *AIC MB 97*, April 1989, p. 17;

Another Western province, Farah, followed the same path: in 1985 a mass offensive defeated Haji Mohammed Anwar, possibly the most powerful mujahidin leader in the province. Mujahidin activity thus grew weaker in the plain areas of the North (which was also isolated from the borders) and the West, where operations with the typical, Soviet-style large mechanized forces were more practicable, while it maintained its full strength in the East (which also enjoyed the advantage of easy communications with Pakistan) and in the North-East, where the terrain is more rugged. Provinces where there was little Soviet/Kabul military pressure rarely experienced any wave of agreements with the government, even when the latter offered substantial economic benefits. During the National Reconciliation, for example, not a single village signed agreements with the government in Bamyan, Uruzgan and Kapisa provinces, where the government had little presence.[21]

However, without Soviet support the government's ability to carry out large operations was limited. Some were carried out even after the Soviet withdrawal, notably in Herat province and around Kabul and Jallalabad, but with limited results. The availability of Red Army units as a reserve had been a powerful boost, which was now lost. On the other hand, since the war experience had demonstrated the supremacy of attrition warfare over decisive, World-War-II style operations, offensive operations were not deemed to be particularly necessary. After withdrawal the attrition strategy was carried out mainly by means of the militias, while the large scale operations of the regular army were mainly limited to counter-offensives.

Organizational developments

The coordination of counter-guerrilla activities in such a large and rugged country was in itself a difficult task. The high degree of internal disorganization of the Afghan armed forces in 1980,

'Postanovlenie sekretariata TsK NDPA o rabote geratskogo provintsial'nogo komiteta partii po vypolnenyu reshenii XII plenuma TsK NDPA, 10 marta 1984 g.' in *NDPA (sbornik dokumentov)*, Tashkent, 'Uzbekistan', 1986, p. 157; Kasperavichius, *Nachal'niku politotdela-zamestitelyu glavnogo voennogo sovetnika v DRA po politicheskoi chasti, General-Leitenantu Aunapu E.M.*, Oct. 1986.

[21] A. Bonner, *Among the Afghans*, Duke University Press, Durham, NC, 1987, p. 317; *KNT*, 21 Oct. 1987.

coupled with low morale, made it an impossible one. At that time infantry divisions were just paper entities; the different subunits did not have any contact among each other and no contact existed between them and the divisional command either. A thorough reorganization was needed; it began in July 1980, when the III Plenum decided to divide the country into eight zones, whose leaders would be responsible before the CC for the coordination of all military, political and economic activities within each zone. The leader himself was always a member of the CC and he presided over a commission composed of the provincial governors and a Soviet adviser. Political and military tactics were supposed to be adapted to the particular needs of each zone. These zones did not have a real operational role; they seem to have been inspired by the model of the Soviet Military Districts, having more to do with recruitment, mobilization and the collection of supplies. The closest thing to a regional operational HQ was represented by the Army Corps, three of which were created and placed in charge of all the units subordinated to the Ministry of Defence in their area. Such networks came to cover most of the country only with the creation of the 4th Army Corps in Herat in 1987, the 5th in Parwan in 1989 (downgraded to operation group status in 1991), the 6th in Kunduz in 1990 and four Operation Groups, with leaner support and staff structures, in 1987-90 (Sarobi, Khost, Parwan, North).[22]

A further, small improvement took place when the Border Troops were transferred from the Ministry of Tribes and Frontiers to the Defence Ministry in 1983, reducing from four to three the number of ministries involved with the organization of regular troops.[23]

A more effective initiative was taken in 1983, when the XII Plenum decided to create headquarters at the various levels (ranging from the centre to the districts and sub-districts), where military,

[22] Merimskii, 'Voina po zakamu', p. 36; Ludwig, 'Einige Probleme', p. 98; M. Hassan Kakar, *Afghanistan: the Soviet Invasion and the Afghan Response*, University of California Press, 1995, p. 193; Cordesman, *Lessons*, p. 39; Mark Urban, telephone interview, London, 19 May 1995; Lyakhovskii, *Tragediya i doblest' Afgana*, p. 337; A. Davis, *Jane's Intelligence Review*, 1 March 1993; Najibullah, *Bakhtar*, 22 Sept. 1989.

[23] D. Isby, *War in a Distant Country*, Arms and Armour Press, 1989, p. 89.

economic and party officials would coordinate their activities. One of the main duties would be the coordination of army, *sarandoy*, KhAD and militia activities. The decision was implemented slowly, and in September 1984 such headquarters did not yet exist in most districts and subdistricts. Although some HQs (Kabul, Jowzyan, Badakhshan) were praised by Karmal for their effectiveness, in general 'the organization and co-ordination of their activity' was 'blunt and weak'. Moreover, no organ existed in the capital 'to exercise permanent administration and provide urgent leadership to the lower headquarters and to bring about a permanent coordination in the activity of ministries and offices in the solution of the problems of localities'. Some members of the HQs made 'privileged claims for themselves and for their departments and establishments' and guarded 'their independence with jealousy', inflicting damage on the activity of the HQ. Once again Karmal blamed the 'bureaucratic approach', the 'indifference' and the 'weak leadership by the party committees' for these shortcomings.[24]

Whatever successes some HQs might have achieved, coordination between the different armed services does not seem to have been among them. In February 1984 Karmal 'gave instructions to armed forces' commanders to bring the principle of joint effort to the accomplishment of their activities'. The need for such coordination was strongly felt, particularly in Herat province, where military activity was quite intense and the landscape was quite suitable for large, coordinated operations. While Karmal continued to complain about its absence, he also claimed in his ten theses of November 1985 that efforts to build 'an integrated system and a defence complex, consisting of armed forces, police, KhAD, Revolution Defence Groups, militia, Soldiers of the Revolution, self-defence and tribesmen' were underway.[25]

1986 was characterized by faster progress towards a greater

[24] Ludwig, 'Einige Probleme', p. 98; Karmal, XIV plenum CC, RA, 21 Sept. 1984; B. Karmal's Speech at the 13th Plenum of the PDPA, CC March 1984, pp. 28, 29.

[25] Karmal, 12 Jan. 1984, RA, 11 Feb. 1984; 'Postanovlenie sekretariata TsK NDPA o rabote geratskogo provintsial'nogo komiteta partii po vypolnenyu reshenii XII plenuma TsK NDPA, 10 marta 1984 g.' in *NDPA (sbornik dokumentov)*, Tashkent, 'Uzbekistan', 1986, p. 159; *Speech of B. Karmal*, 1365, p. 14; *Babrak Karmal's Theses, Declaration of DRA RC*, Kabul, Nov. 1985, p. 20.

degree of cooperation, as 'serious measures' were finally taken 'towards securing joint efforts by the DRA armed forces'. Already in January of that year a joint all-services operation under the command of the 17th Infantry Division HQ had been carried out in Herat province. A further step in this direction was the creation in 1986 of 'defence councils' at the provincial and zonal levels. They were composed of zonal/provincial military leaders, provincial governors and superior officers. Later the zonal Defence Councils were disbanded, enhancing the 'responsibility and independence of the provinces' defence councils'.[26]

A department of the Ministry of Defence was put in charge of co-ordinating 'the work of the army, the local self-defence forces and the border tribal units', while a more concrete achievement was represented by the creation of the Ministry of National Security (WAD) in 1986. Given its peculiar nature, KhAD had already played a role in organizing 'joint efforts' with the army and *sarandoy*. The first step in this direction was made in April 1982, when an internal directive was issued to KhAD's officers, stating the need to strengthen cooperation and exchange of information between organs and units of KhAD and the *sarandoy*. The new ministry exerted a certain amount of operational control over forces belonging to other ministries, in particular over many *sarandoy* units, apparently including the Provincial Commands. Operational power was now in the hands of joint WAD/*sarandoy* provincial commands and the *sarandoy* operational battalions were more closely linked with the WAD's network of agents.[27]

In mid-1987, finally, it was decided to subordinate Border Troops and operational units of WAD and *sarandoy* to the area commanders of the army. In this way divisional HQs became territorial ones, commanding all the armed forces in their assigned sector. Many divisional commands were thus given a real function

---

[26] Najibullah, RA, 21 July 1986; M. Urban, *War in Afghanistan*, p. 188; *KZ*, 27 Nov. 1988; Najibullah, Second Nation-wide PDPA Conference, RA, 18 Oct. 1987.

[27] Gen. Nabi Azimi, Defence Minister's First Deputy, Hungarian TV, Sept. 1986; Karmal's speech to KhAD personnel meeting, RA, 23 May 1982; O. V. Starodubova, 'Moral'no-politicheskii potentsial vooruzhennikh sil Afganistana', diss., Tashkent, 1991, p. 86; Isby, *War in a Distant Country*, p. 88; Cordesman, *Lessons*, p. 60; M. Urban, *War in Afghanistan*, p. 183.

for the first time, as their sub-units had rarely (if ever) operated together as a whole; at this point they had little to do with their original purpose, as they were not even supposed to act as operational entities. Units theoretically belonging to one division could in reality operate at the orders of another HQ, if they were located within its area of responsibility. According to one source, brigades replaced some regiments, exercising the same functions as the divisional HQ, i.e. being 'composites of all the units in their area of operations'. The situation could still be quite messy in many circumstances, like Khost in autumn 1989, when the 4,400 men of the garrison were divided into thirty units belonging to WAD, army, Border Guard and *sarandoy*, some of them counting as few as between thirty and fifty men. Moreover, the Supreme Command continued to enjoy authority only over the troops on the Ministry of Defence roll, coordination being at the regional level alone.[28]

Factional infighting within the party was probably responsible for the inability to create effective, nationwide coordination, as the existence of three armed forces was part of a checks and balances system. It is worth noting that Najibullah, who personally agreed to give the Supreme Command 'guidance of all military operations, became resolutely opposed to such proposals (coming from Soviet advisers) after Defence Minister Tanai's attempted coup in 1990. It added to the paradoxical character of the situation that WAD and the Interior Ministry were only concerned with administrative, training and logistical matters and did not exercise any leadership over the activity of their units. Only the Special Guard, created in 1988 within the framework of WAD but largely independent of it, had its own military command, although this too was not able to direct its operations on a daily basis.[29]

[28] A. Lyakhovskii, *Tragediya i doblest' Afgana*, p. 337; D. Isby, *War in a Distant Country*, p. 84; M.A. Gareev, *Moya poslednyaya voina*, Moscow, Nisan, 1996, pp. 258, 102.

[29] M.A. Gareev, *Moya poslednyaya voina*, pp. 214, 202, 284; *KP*, 29 June 1991.

6

THE POLITICAL SHORTCOMINGS
OF THE ARMED FORCES
AND THE PARTY RESPONSE

Factional infighting

One of the biggest problems the Soviets and the Karmal regime had to face was internal to the regime. The PDPA had split a few months after the Saur Revolution into its two traditional wings, Khalq and Parcham. At first, the Soviet leadership did not react to the exclusion from power of Parcham, although its more moderate approach probably suited Soviet interests in Afghanistan best. It was only in late 1979, as Khalq itself was torn apart by internal rivalries and the Soviets were getting ready for intervention, that they brought Parchami leaders in exile out of oblivion. Once Parchamis had been brought back to .power by the Soviets, the latters' aim was to pacify the PDPA, offering Khalqis a share of power. But the conflict was not going to subside. While the initial intention had been to purge only the staunchest supporters of Amin, the Parchamis could not resist launching a wide purge of Khalqi officers in the army. This was what the Khalqis had been expecting and many had already abandoned their units, further jeopardizing whatever battle readiness the army still possessed. At the same time they were not willing to abandon their ideological positions; in some military bases Khalqi slogans remained on display. It is not clear to what extent Karmal himself was involved in the purge among middle and lower echelon officers, but he was certainly responsible for giving the highest positions in the hierarchy to Parchamis, allegedly without even obtaining the approval of his Defence Minister. Around the middle of 1981 Parchamis controlled twenty-nine heads of political department out of fifty; by the beginning of 1982 twenty-three provincial commanders out of twenty-nine belonged to this faction. In the end the Soviets were forced to intervene, if nothing else because of the destructive effects of the purge (the Khalqis making up 90% of the officer corps at the end of 1979). The purge was actually stopped after a visit to Karmal by Sokolov, the top Soviet military adviser. But at this point the Parchamis were already dominant in the upper levels and did not give up discriminating against their Khalqi subordinates. As a result, Khalqis in the army behaved passively, sabotaging the initiatives of the centre and sometimes even cooperating with the rebels or deserting.[30]

On the other hand the policy of Parchamization did manage to reduce the Khalqi supremacy in the army, but only marginally and in the commanding positions. One source puts Khalqis at 64-65% of party strength in the army in spring 1980. In 1982, among the army delegates at the National Conference of the party 70% were Khalqis. Little reduction was experienced later, with Khalqis still at 65-70% of party membership in the army in 1983 and declining slightly only later, accounting for 60% in 1991. The reduction was mainly achieved by transferring as many Khalqis as possible to the *sarandoy*, where by 1983 75-80% of party members were Khalqis. On the contrary, it was decided to reserve KhAD to Parchamis, who in fact accounted for 90% of the PDPA members there. The transfers from the army were partially offset, at least in the early days, by the fact that some radical Parchami officials in the civil administration used to send Khalqis as 'volunteers' to the army, in order to get rid of them, largely undermining the efforts to increase the Parcham share there.[31]

The idea was evidently to separate as much as possible the two factions, striking a balance of forces among the different services of the armed forces. The last flare-ups of Parchamization were apparently seen in some internal party elections in Herat province in July 1983, which were overwhelmingly won by

[30] Lyakhovskii, 'Na afganskoi vizhzhennoi zemle', p. 54; Halliday, 'Report on a visit to Afghanistan 20-27.10.1980', p. 7; A. Qader quoted in Merimskii, 'Voina v Afganistane: zapiski uchastika', p. 111; *Aktual'nye problemy afganskoi revolyutsii*, p. 434; Yu. Gankovskii, 'Vooruzhennye sily respubliki Afganistan'.

[31] *Aktual'nye problemy afganskoi revolyutsii*, p. 427, 440, 435; Lyakhovskii, *Tragediya i doblest' Afgana*, p. 265; AFP, 10 July, 1991.

Parchamis. A KGB officer visiting Afghanistan at that time expressed the opinion that it was impossible to create even a single effective Afghan Army unit because of factional infighting. Other sources state that the conflict showed a certain tendency to subside after that year, at least within the army, although it was never exinguished. In October 1985, for example, the Logar 'clique' – allegedly a group of extremist Khalqis – took control of the Logar province *sarandoy*, pushing ahead reform in the brutal way which had characterized the first phase of the Revolution, i.e. expropriating the land of the Wardak, Ormud and Ahmadzai tribes and clashing with tribal customs. Their behaviour was claimed to have been the cause of a particularly bad situation in the province.[32] In the end it was the Soviet presence that kept the conflict within certain limits, avoiding if nothing else the disintegration of the party and the armed forces. The activities of the latter were nonetheless heavily affected. In 1983 a Soviet specialist, having carried out an enquiry among the Afghan Army rank and file, reported that factional infighting within the officer corps was having further demoralizing effects on the troops.[33] Fissures became very evident again as soon as the 40th Army left.

At that time Khalqis occupied 137 command positions out of 310 in the army, the remaining ones going essentially to Parchamis. While a certain balance existed in the distribution of Defence Deputy-Ministers, seventeen out of thirty-five being Khalqis, the Parchamis controlled the most sensitive positions in the army itself, counting on the loyalty of four out of five Army Corps' commanders and fifteen out of twenty Division commanders.[34]

The first signal of fissure was the reemergence of one extremist faction of the Khalq at the end of the '80s and beginning of the 1990s (the so-called Zhargounists, after the name of a Khalqi leader killed in 1979). Around the end of 1989 or the beginning of 1990 they numbered 350-500 followers among the top echelons

---

[32] L.V. Shebarshin, *Ruka Moskvy*, p. 184; *Aktual'nye problemy afganskoi revolyutsii*, p. 442; I.E. Katkov, 'Tsentral'naya vlast' Afganistana i pushtunskie plemena', diss., Moscow, IV AN SSSR, 1987, pp. 163-4.

[33] V. Plastun, 'Gorkii urok', *Aziya i Afrika Segodnia*, part II, 2/93, p. 26.

[34] M.A. Gareev, *Moya poslednyaya voina*, Moscow, Nisan, 1996, pp. 109-10.

of the army alone. The culmination of this escalating trend, after
a lull due to the fierce 1988-9 confrontation with the mujahidin,
was Defence Minister Tanai's coup attempt in 1990. Obviously
such rivalries also played a role in Najibullah's final demise, but
by then the traditional Khalq-Parcham conflict had been finally
supplanted by more complicated, trans-factional ones, which had
been forming over the years. As early as 1987, according to one
of the Khalq leaders, Panjsheri, there were 200 groups and factions
within the party, including the emergence of at least one faction
of Karmalites. The PDPA could not do much to cure its internal
illness, nor did the Soviet advisers manage to treat much more
than the symptoms.[35]

Desertions

It did not take long for the Soviet advisers in Afghanistan to
realize that the other great symptom of ideological weakness in
the Afghan Army was the high desertion rate. In 1980 its effects
were intensified by low levels of recruitment, particularly in the
first part of the year. Table 19 clearly shows that desertions remained
at very high levels till the end of the war. It is true that, as a
percentage of the total strength of the armed forces, their incidence
was halved between 1981 and 1988. However, if we look at the
army itself, little changed over the whole period. For example,
the 14th Infantry Division, based in Ghazni, recorded in 1363
(1984/5) alone 1,640 desertions from an average staff of 2,500.[36]

   The causes for such a high level of desertions are quite clear.
Although ideological motives might have played some role, the
average deserter was more interested in avoiding the war altogether,
rather than joining the other side. The level of desertions has
been reported to have been higher when commanders announced
forthcoming operations, during the peak of winter (barracks being
very cold) and during summer (work being needed in the fields).
The highest level of desertions (reaching at times 60-80%) appears
to have been among Border Troops, who were active in areas

[35] Starodubova, *Moral'no-politicheskii*, p. 97; V. Korgun, 'Natsional'noe primirenie
i vnutripoliticheskaya situatsiya v 1988 g.', *Spetsial'nyi Byulleten' AN SSSR – IV*,
no. 2, (1990), p. 60.

[36] M. Olimov, 'Iz zapisok perevodchika', *Vostok*, no. 3 (1991), p. 60.

that were both 'hot' and close to the borders. The nearest thing to active opposition to the regime that had a (statistically) significant impact on the proclivity to desertion was membership of one of the Pashtun 'rebel' tribes, i.e. those more strongly involved in insurgency. This also partially explains the generous offers made to the tribes with regard to recruitment (see Part IV, Chapter 18). Finally, desertions were less common when troops were deployed in areas peopled by other ethnic groups.[37]

The non-political character of most desertions is confirmed by the low sensitivity of the desertion rate to the overall political situation. Official sources claimed that desertions went down by 30% after the completion of the Soviet withdrawal,[38] but the final figure (see Table 19) shows that the overall rate for 1989 was quite normal. The figure for 1991 is clearly influenced by the regime's difficulties in supplying its troops with pay and food.

Desertions from the *sarandoy* were much fewer. That most of these troops were deployed very close to their place of origin, that their salary was higher and that they were allegedly subject to a harder selection process must all have played a role. It appears that forced recruitment was less common among the *sarandoy*.[39] It is also important to consider that after 1981 many *sarandoy* recruits were in fact reservists who had only just been demobilised from the army. As they had not deserted from the army previously, they had no incentive to do so now that the conditions of service were better. Table 20 gives some idea of how *sarandoy* were recruited in larger numbers in the provinces; army recruits came from the cities, mainly Kabul.

Soviet advisers were unable to propose significant measures to tackle this problem directly, apart from increasing the strength of party organizations in the armed forces. The idea of holding families responsible for the desertion of their relatives seems to have been the only one that went beyond ideological and patriotic rhetoric. With time, the army learnt to avoid as much as possible those

---

[37] *Otchet o komandirovke v pr. Baghlan, 15-18 dekabrya 1987 g.*; V.N. Plastun, 'Voenno-politicheskaya obstanovka v DRA i polozhenie v NDPA', 23 July 1986, unpubl., p. 3; A.A. Kotenev, 'Natsional'no-etnicheskii faktor v vooruzhennoi bor'be s kontrrevolyutsei v DRA', diss., 1983, IV AN SSSR, p. 154.

[38] *Izvestia*, 7 Aug. 1989.

[39] Starodubova, *Moral'no-politicheskii potentsial*, p. 57; Ludwig, 'Einige Probleme' p. 107.

activities that might trigger desertions; often simply sending units the size of a battalion out on a mission might mean the disappearance of most of the rank and file.[40] The defensive posture adopted after the Soviet withdrawal owed much to such considerations and it can be noted how the year 1985, when comparatively few operations were carried out, was actually characterized by a relatively low level of desertions.

Even the widespread presence of party primary organizations was not always enough to avoid the desertion of whole units. In the first half of a relatively quiet year like 1987 at least one whole *sarandoy* battalion and part of a regiment crossed over, as well as a whole army battalion. Mass desertions from elite units also continued to take place, as in May 1989 when half of a detachment of 400 from the 15th Tank and the 37th Assault Brigades deserted on its way to the battlefield of Jallalabad. Even more impressive is the case of a new Armoured Brigade, formed on the Amu Darya with personnel trained in the USSR, which saw 243 of its 370 men desert during the transfer to Kabul. During the critical phase of the general onslaught which accompanied and followed the Soviet withdrawal, mass desertions caused sever trouble in Kunduz and Teluqan among others.[41]

The Soviets and the regime succeeded – in keeping the number of desertions among officers relatively low (see Table 21). Apart from 1989, where the high level suggests a possible mistake, officers showed little inclination to desert.[42] According to personnel charts, there should have been about one officer to every ten soldiers; yet because officers' ranks were more nearly complete than soldiers', officers represented more than 9% of the total manpower.

The party and the armed forces

In the eyes of the Soviet advisers and of the Afghan government, the strengthening of party control over the armed forces, down to the smallest unit, was of the highest importance. As early as

[40] Shebarshin, *Ruka Moskvy*, p. 204; Gareev, *Moya poslednyaya voina*, p. 198.

[41] Lyakhovskii and V.M. Zabrodin, *Tainy afganskoi voiny*, p. 120, 188; Gareev, *Moya poslednyaya voina*, pp. 196, 197.

[42] O'Ballance, *Wars in Afghanistan*, pp. 106-7.

June 1979 Amin had sent 1,500 party instructors to the army to improve PDPA's strength there, with a resulting 50% increase by the end of his stay in power. After his fall the program was continued with renewed energy. It was the obvious way to fight desertions and to improve the combat capability of the army. From a quantitative point of view, it did succeed. Table 22 shows a quite dramatic improvement. Even in percentage terms progress was remarkable (see Table 23). As late as 1987, at the II National Conference of the PDPA, in order to increase party dominance further, it was decided to send party members into the armed forces and 3,000 actually joined the army in 1988. In 1989 600 more activists were sent.[43]

It is also important to note the success in terms of the creation of primary organizations within the armed forces (see Table 24), as each organization generally corresponded to one unit. In 1981 they were present only in one third of the units and the following year the army political chief, Brigadier Gol Aqa, was fired because of the slow progress in this sensitive field. His successor, Brigadier Yasin Sadeqi, did a better job. By the end of 1984, 86% of the companies and batteries had party organizations. Although success was not total (in autumn 1987, 527 units still had no party organization), it was a great achievement indeed.[44]

Some doubts however exist about the qualitative aspect of this effort. The party military press, for example, according to a defector, had only a limited readership. In 1984-5 the daily *Haqiqat-i Sarbaz* had a circulation of only 2,000, while the army magazine sold 7,000 copies. Even more interesting is the level of desertions among party and particularly DYOA members. Figures are not plentiful, but some partial ones can still give an idea. In 1362 (1983/4) a 'high number' of party members deserted from the armed forces in Herat and went over to the enemy. Overall more than 1,100 members of DYOA deserted from the army and the *sarandoy* in 1362 and the first half of 1363. This meant a desertion rate seven or eight times lower than the overall one – a good

[43] Ludwig, 'Einige Probleme', p. 74; S. Krivov, *op. cit.*, *Spetsial'nyi Byulleten' IV AN SSSR*, no. 2 (1990), p. 187-8.

[44] M. Urban, *War in Afghanistan*, p. 106; Brig.-Gen. Sadeqi Interviewed by *KZ*, 25 Dec. 1984; *National Conference of PDPA on National Reconciliation (Oct. 18-20, 1987). Documents*, Kabul: Afghanistan Today, 1987, p. 34.

achievement if one considers that DYOA members were recruited less selectively than party ones. It is difficult to say whether the quantitative expansion of PDPA and DYOA later on changed the situation, i.e. if it diluted the 'ideological quality' of the membership. A sixth of the deserters from the 20th Infantry Division in November 1987 were DYOA members, not very far from the percentage of DYOA members in the army, but the statistical sample is too small to allow any serious conclusion.[45]

More important than the mere quantitative growth of the party was the establishment of a network of political workers in the armed forces. At the time of the Soviet arrival, only 18-20% of positions for political cadres were filled. An intensive program was put together with the armed forces organizing one-month courses, and the Social Sciences Institute of the party three-month ones. By 1984 the Social Sciences Institute had trained 1,200 members of the armed forces. In September 1987, in order to raise the quality of such cadres, an 'Armed Forces Military-Political University' was opened. Overall results can be seen in Table 26.[46]

This well-known tool of political control seems to have worked to some extent – it is claimed that during the coup attempted by Defence Minister Tanai, no political worker took his side. But again there are doubts. The political consciousness of some political officers did not go unquestioned, particularly at the platoon level, where they were generally illiterate. A high number of desertions was reported even among the graduates of the Social Sciences Institute of the party.[47]

---

[45] *Afghan Realities*, no. 31 (16 April 1985), p. 2; 'Postanovlenie sekretariata TsK NDPA o rabote geratskogo provintsial'nogo komiteta partii po vypolnenyu reshenii XII plenuma TsK NDPA, 10 marta 1984 g.' in *NDPA (sbornik dokumentov)*, Tashkent, 'Uzbekistan', 1986, pp. 155-6; 'Postanovlenie politburo TsK NDPA o deyatel'nosti TsK DOMA po dal'neishemu uluchsheniyu organizatsionnoi, politicheskoi i vostitatel'noi raboty sredi molodezhi v svete reshenii..., 17 noyabrya 1984 g.' in *NDPA (sbornik dokumentov), op. cit.*, p. 316; *Otchet o komandirovke v pr. Baghlan, 15-18 dekabrya 1987 g.*

[46] T. Gaidar, *Pod afganskim nebom*, Sovetskaya Rossiya, 1981, p. 52; Ludwig, 'Einige Probleme', p. 108; RA, 24 Sept. 1987.

[47] Starodubova, *Moral'no-politicheskii potentsial*, p. 157; *Otchet o komandirovke v pr. Baghlan, 15-18 dekabrya 1987 g.*; Hakim, *Nedostatki (negativnye yavleniya) v rabote voenno-politicheskogo uchilisha"*, 10.10.87g.

7

QUANTATIVE EFFORTS TO BUILD UP
THE ARMED FORCES AND THEIR LIMITS

Recruitment

If it was difficult to prevent people from deserting, in the long
term it proved relatively easier to recruit them. It was still possible
to flee across the borders to avoid the draft, but sizeable numbers
remained in Afghanistan. In fact, the flow of people from the
countryside to the capital increased the pool of human resources
available to the armed forces. The January 1980 call up however
was an abysmal failure, as only 875 men out of 59,000 turned
out (see Table 25 and Graph 3). After some rhetorical attempts
to persuade youths to do their duty and early recourse to pressganging, a number of measures were taken by the Politburo in 1981,
including the lowering of the draft age from twenty-two to twenty,
the fixing of the duration of service at two and a half years
(previously two years) and the mobilization (August) of fourteen
classes of reservists for one year. In February 1981 measures were
also taken to encourage enrolment in the *sarandoy* of soldiers
demobilized from the army. However, recruitment in 1981 improved
only slightly, as a mere 8,000 of the 130,000 called up in October
are thought to have turned out. New measures had to be taken
and in April 1982 the minimum age was lowered further to nineteen
and in July the length of service was increased to three years, a
move not welcomed by the troops. The latter decree was enforced
apparently in the summer of 1983 and may have been responsible
in part for the record number of desertions that year (see Table
19). Furthermore, after 1982 demobilised soldiers were compelled
to join the *sarandoy*, while in August of that year reservists began
to be recalled for a two-year period, instead of one year as before.[48]

[48] *Aktual'nye problemy afganskoi revolyutsii*, pp. 430, 433, 436, 437; Gankovskii,
'Vooruzhennye sily respubliki Afganistan', p. 13; O'Ballance, *Wars in Afghanistan*,

In April 1983, in an effort to dynamize the provincial recruitment officers, 'some secretaries of the PDPA Central Committee, vice-chairmen of the Council of Ministers and also heads and commanders of the ranks and units of the Ministry of Defence were sent to the zones'. The local state administration was also involved in the recruitment efforts, previously reserved to the army and *sarandoy*.[49] Exemptions, particularly for students, were continuously reduced throughout this period.

This policy increasingly encountered resistance from the population. When exemptions for government employees and businessmen were abolished in August 1981 and they were included among the recalled reservists, the state and party apparatus was badly shaken. Traders, officials and clerks began to flee to Pakistan, causing such concern that Interior Minister Gulabzoi was forced to come out against the measure. In September the government was forced to exempt PDPA and social organization cadres, local administrators, certain categories of workers, drivers, state employees and some categories of traders. Some hints of. a new tendency towards a greater realism seemed to appear at this point, as estimates of available reserves were drastically reduced from 450,000 to 85,000. Furthermore, worried about how the population might react, the government never even dared to introduce I.D. cards among the general population, as Soviet advisers were suggesting. Soon, however, the government made another blunder. In October 1982 Defence Minister Qader revoked, under pressure from the Soviets, the exemption from recruitment of border tribes, like the Shinwari, Jaji and Mohmand, and the relatively wide support the regime had been building among them was put at stake. Roads to Kabul were blocked in protest and in the end the government had to step down.[50]

---

p. 127; *NYT*, 24 Dec. 1981.

[49] S.A. Keshtmand, *RA*, 26 June 1983.

[50] *Aktual'nye problemy afganskoi revolyutsii*, p. 431; Eliza Van Hollen, 'Afghanistan. Two years of Soviet occupation', *Department of State Bulletin*, vol. 82, no. 2060, p. 22; N.S. Leonov, *Likholet'e*, Mezhdunarodnye Otnosheniya, 1994, pp. 270-1; J. M. Strmecki, 'Power Assessment: Measuring Soviet Power in Afghanistan', diss., Georgetown University, 1994, p. 330; Rubin, *The Fragmentation of Afghanistan*, p. 132; Gareev, *Moya poslednyaya voina*, p. 206. I.D. cards were introduced only in some rural areas.

Things were made worse by the fact that recruitment officials often misbehaved in their drive to meet the quotas for their region. According to one U.S. source, they might ignore documentation proving exemption status or even draft obviously under-age boys. A Soviet General confirms that they often destroyed documents in order to recruit people already demobilised from the army.[51]

Lack of enthusiasm for military service was not limited to the general population; in fact, draft avoidance was common even within the PDPA. Not only party and state staff, but even relatives of higher cadres and 'people with influence' generally managed to avoid conscription, causing resentment among the population. Karmal protested against this practice as early as December 1980, but no actual measure was taken until the XVIII Plenum in May 1986. In the end Najibullah tackled it by decree in November 1986, but the problem was still a cause for debate in May 1987, in part because even when such people were drafted, they served in the military bureaucracy in Kabul, where they continued to wear civilian clothes and travelled to work in the official cars of their powerful relatives.[52]

Bureaucratic difficulties also slowed down any increase in recruitment. The civilian administration did not join the effort until at least the mid-1980s, forcing the army to devote considerable resources to this task and possibly to over-rely on forced recruitment. In 1983-4, properly equipped recruitment centres existed only in Kabul, Nangrahar, Balkh, Herat and Kunduz, while in three more provinces prisons were used; military commissariats for recruitment were available in only twelve provinces. Further criticism targeted the 'bureaucratic' approach of the commissariats and the lack of cooperation between them and other party and state organs. In

[51] J. M. Strnecki, 'Power Assessment', p. 305; Merimskii, 'Voina v Afganistane: zapiski uchastika', p. 112.

[52] Karmal, RA, 4 Dec. 1980; Rubin, *The fragmentation of Afghanistan*, p. 156; RA, 19 May 1987, text of broadcast made by Mohammad Rafi, member of the Politburo of the PDPA Central Committee and DRA Minister of Defence; A. Lyakhovskii, 'Na afganskoi vizhzhennoi zemle', *Kommunist Vooruzhennikh Sil*, 21, 1990, p. 62.

this context, the Military Commissar for Kandahar Province was removed because of his low performance.[53]

By 1984 it must have become apparent that the pay-off from a policy of increasingly stringent measures was limited indeed. Graph 3 shows how recruitment stagnated in 1983-4, while desertions increased. From 1985, emphasis began to be placed on various (mainly economic) incentives to make military service less unattractive. The option for voluntary, financially rewarded, two-year terms of service was successfully introduced; many who feared that they would in any case be drafted, decided therefore to volunteer. Efforts were made to improve the living conditions of the soldiers. Finally, in February 1987 length of service was reduced back to two years for everybody, with positive effects as is shown in Graph 3.

Recruitment in the countryside improved somewhat in the second half of the 1980s, also thanks to the provinces. In 1988, 50% of the troops had been recruited among peasants. Such a figure compares unfavourably to the 90% of peasants who made up the army in 1978, but was probably a marked improvement on the early 1980s. On the other hand a crisis followed in 1988, as the abandonment of many positions to the mujahidin caused the recruitment area to shrink. In order to recover, in 1989 many exemptions from recruitment (because of age, job and people already demobilized) were cancelled.[54]

Recruitment was dependent on the extension of the area under government control. Kabul was never able to supply much more than 40,000 recruits per year, the rest coming from the provinces. Table 25 also documents how the government persisted in drawing up unrealistic plans for recruitment, which called for provinces almost completely outside the government's reach to contribute

[53] B. Karmal's Speech at the 13th Plenum of the PDPA, CC March 1984, pp. 17-18; 'Zapis' besedy zamestitelya zaveduyushego Mezhdunarodnym otdelom TsK KPSS t. Ul'yanovskogo R.A. s chlenom Politbyuro TsK NDPA, zamestitelem Predsedatelya Soveta Ministrov DRA t. M. Rafi', Kabul, 18 Oct. 1984, unpubl. document, p. 4; Ludwig, 'Einige Probleme', p. 108; Karmal, XV plenum, RA, 27 March 1985; Speech of B. Karmal, 1365, p. 14.

[54] Rubin, *The Fragmentation of Afghanistan*, pp. 132, 156-7; Najibullah, RA, 7 Oct. 1986; Lyakhovskii, *Tragediya i doblest' Afgana*, p. 429; *AFP*, 21 Feb. 1989; Krivov, 'Vooruzhennye sily v politicheskoi zhizni Afganistana', p. 184.

to the draft in a measure proportionate to their population. Only Kabul usually managed to fulfil the plans or almost do so.[55]

Levels of manpower

The improvement in recruitment allowed the regime to build up its military strength, although not as much as it would have liked. Table 27 shows such improvements. It should be borne in mind that figures cannot always easily be related to an exact time span; furthermore actual manpower must have varied depending on how long had elapsed since the last batch of recruits had arrived. Najibullah himself once stated that nobody was sure about the actual figures, not even the competent ministries. One cause of uncertainty was the fact that officers would sometime inflate the quantity of troops under their command and then pocket the surplus wages.[56] Still, there is no doubt that a significant increase took place, even if it was far from fulfilling the expectations of the government and of its Soviet supporters. During the war the personnel charts of the armed forces were continuously expanded, so that the goal of reaching full-strength looked even more distant after ten years of effort. Table 30 shows growth in the number of active divisions and brigades, while Table 29 illustrates the same process with regard to planned manpower. Even according to the somewhat inflated government figures (Table 27), the 1982 army personnel chart full-strength level was not reached until the late 1980s or early 90s. Unfortunately by then the army was supposed to have 90,000 more men. Table 29 shows how the completion levels of the armed forces charts actually declined over time. One possible explanation for an otherwise irrational policy lies in the pressures coming from the Soviet side, which continually demanded an increase in the size of Afghan military forces (see Table 31 for a record of the creation of new units). As in many other fields of its activity, the Kabul government took decisions which it did not and could not fulfil, trying to gain time from the increasingly irritated Soviet advisers. Also, this expansion meant the multiplication of the number of officers, making it possible

---

55 Najibullah, RA, 14 June 1987, CC Plenum.

56 Starodubova, pp. 57-8; Gareev, *Moya poslednyaya voina*, p. 203.

to reward many party members and factional supporters. In 1983 a supply branch in Kabul was reported by a defector to count twenty brigadier-generals out of 400 men.[57]

[57] J. B. Amstutz, *Afghanistan: the First Five Years of Soviet Occupation*, National Defense University, 1986, p. 183.

8

ATTEMPTS TO ADDRESS THE STRATEGIC PROBLEMS

Police operations

Although the *sarandoy* did not figure as prominently as the army in press reports about the war, they nevertheless played a·sensitive role in charge of most small towns and villages. Their strategic relevance should not be underestimated, precisely because the Afghan war was mainly fought at village level. The *sarandoy* had become largely unable to control the countryside before the Soviet invasion and the situation worsened dramatically in early 1980. At the end of 1979 *sarandoy* units in some provinces were only 10% complete, while the local organs of state power were abandoned to their own devices, unable even to communicate with the centre, because links had been cut by the mujahidin. In one district of Nangrahar province the only garrison left was a remnant of the local *sarandoy* contingent, i.e. eleven men, for a population of 80,000. On 28 December 1979 there were only fifty-eight sarandoy instead of 560 in the whole of Baghlan province.[58] Although army troops were also deployed in the province, in most districts only *sarandoy* were present. Some reinforcements were apparently sent to Baghlan at the beginning of 1980, but the government hold was still precarious at best, as one can judge:[59]

---

[58] Gankovskii, 'Vooruzhennye sily respubliki Afganistan', Merimskii, 'Voina po zakamu', p. 36; T. Gaidar, *Pod afganskim nebom*, Sovetskaya Rossiya, 1981, p. 37.

[59] *Svedeniya o sostave 'Yader' dlya formirovaniya i ukrepleniya vlasti v zone Severo-Vostok po sostoyanyu na ..... 1980 goda.*

Doshi district 70 *sarandoy*, Nahrin district 9, Pul-i-Khumri 65, Dakhonami 18, Khindjan 15.'

This may well help to explain why many district centres fell to the mujahidin in the first few months of 1980. Musa Qala district, in Helmand Province, was taken by the Mullah Nasim group, who had already occupied it briefly in 1979. This second time all those who were linked to the PDPA were massacred. Internal government sources estimate that 2,000 party members or supporters and their relatives lost their lives. The same Mullah Nasim also conquered Sangin district, Helmand Province, with similar effects. This time 600 people are estimated to have perished, while the six schools, the *lycée* and the hospital were burnt down. It would only be won back by the government in early 1988. Another large scale massacre of government supporters took place among the Sangokhel section of the Shinwari tribe, which had strongly supported Amin. Even where developments were not so dramatic, Karmal's government and the presence of the Soviet Army were not welcome. Also in early 1980, the population of Qaysar district in Faryab province refused to acknowledge the new government, to pay taxes and to be drafted into the armed forces. Attempts at bringing the locals back on to the government side failed: some officials, sent there to discuss such a possibility, were assassinated. A detachment of the army tried to take the town back by force, but was repulsed by the mujahidin.[60]

The re-establishment of a reasonably efficient gendarmerie/police force was therefore one of the most urgent strategic tasks of the new Karmal government in 1980, particularly because the Red Army could not be expected to fulfil the *sarandoy's* duties as well as the army's. Table 27 shows how *sarandoy* manpower increased much more rapidly than the army's in the first years after the Soviet arrival. At the end of August 1980 the Politburo decided to raise the quota of recruits for the *sarandoy* to 30%, although the army still had priority. Recruitment of volunteers was given particular emphasis and in 1981 the CC decided that 15,000 of them were needed to fill the ranks of the *sarandoy*

---

[60] *Voenno-politicheskaya obstanovka v pr. Gil'mend (Uezdy Kadzhani, Sangin i Musa Kala) na konets febralya 1988g.*; V. Nosatov, 'Afganskii dnevnik', *Prostor*, no. 4 (1989), p. 127; M. Hassan Kakar, *Afghanistan: The Soviet Invasion and the Afghan Response*, University of California Press 1995, p. 178.

operational battalions. In fact the *sarandoy* probably had a higher percentage of volunteers than any other service, as they numbered 24,000 out of a total manpower of 77,000 in 1984, although at the same time some of the local garrisons were partially composed of former mujahidin.[61]

The ability to carry out the most basic duties was achieved by 1983-1984. By then Kabul and the other main towns were reasonably policed and the *sarandoy* also provided garrisons for towns and villages, although the troops 'protecting' the latter were generally difficult to distinguish from the local militias. Around the mid-1980s they garrisoned 67% of the districts and 19% of the population centres. Furthermore, they had been taking over the protection of economic assets from the army, covering about 2,000 of them in 1985 and 2,700 by 1988. In fact by 1988 their role in the protection of the economy began to decline, as the need to gather as many regular troops as possible made it advisable to substitute them with self-defence militia whenever possible; by August 1988 120 *sarandoy* posts had been taken over by the militias.[62]

The *sarandoy* were also charged with anti-guerrilla operational tasks. As early as April 1979 a special section against 'political banditism' was created. This was organized into motorized companies to be dispatched to the provinces; their personnel charts amounted to 4,000 men. Their initial achievements were disappointing, but the mobile units multiplied over the subsequent years, reaching the level of six regiments and fifty battalions by 1984. In many provinces special battalions were also formed for column escort duties; elsewhere mountain battalions were established.[63]

As early as 1984 there were talks of enhancing the 'combat readiness' of the garrison units of the *sarandoy*, in order to have them also carrying out offensive operations. The process of actually transforming these *sarandoy* units into something more similar to

[61] *Aktual'nye problemy afganskoi revolyutsii*, pp. 402, 437; Gankovskii, 'Vooruzhennye sily respubliki Afganistan', p. 14; O. Karpenko, 'Iz afganskogo dnevnika', *Zvezda Vostoka*, 12/1987, p. 185.

[62] Karmal's Speech to Sarandoy Party Activists' Meeting, RA, 20 Oct. 1982; KP, 2 July 1988; Yu. Gankovskii, 'Vooruzhennye sily respubliki Afganistan', p. 14; Karmal, RA, 20 Dec. 1985; KZ, 16 Aug. 1988.

[63] *Aktual'nye problemy afganskoi revolyutsii*, p. 401; Gankovskii, 'Vooruzhennye sily respubliki Afganistan', p. 14.

a proper army began in 1986 and it led to the creation of at least two divisions and several brigades (see Table 28).[64]

Intelligence operations

The Afghan intelligence service (KhAD) was pretty weak in early 1980, numbering just a few thousand (Table 27). Intelligence gathering was very thin and state organs were unable to provide a detailed map of the insurgency (see Chapter 9). KhAD had little presence in the provinces, as for example it had only twenty-eight men in a key province like Baghlan. It is hard to imagine a more important asset than intelligence reports in a counter-insurgency campaign and KhAD was soon given large resources, particularly after Andropov's ascent to power. Up to 600 KGB advisers helped shape the expansion of KhAD. Its annual budget is said to have risen from 36 million Afs. in 1982/3 to more than 8,000 million in 1985/6. Incidentally even the Intelligence Department of the Interior Ministry is said to have experienced a twelvefold increase in professional staff in the 1980-6 period. In January 1986 KhAD was upgraded to a Ministry (WAD), while previously it had only been a department of the Prime Minister's office. Its role kept growing, up to the point where it assumed charge of the security of whole administrative areas, like Kabul and the Kabul-Hairatan road.[65]

By late 1982 almost the entire country was covered by KhAD's network and in some areas this net was already quite tight, as for example has been reported with regard to the North of the country. Judging by the availability of information in Soviet reports, by 1983 KhAD was able to put together a fairly detailed picture of the Resistance. In the summer of that year it deployed 1,300 agents in the mujahidin units, 1,226 along the communication lines, 714 in the underground political organizations and twenty-eight in Pakistan. Mujahidin commanders reported an increase in the threat to caravans and other targets, like the commanders

---

[64] Karmal, RA, 24 Nov. 1984; Najibullah, RA, 1 Oct. 1986.

[65] *Svedeniya o sostave 'Yader' dlya formirovaniya i ukrepleniya vlasti v zone 'Severo-Vostok' po sostoyanyu na.....1980 goda*; J. M. Strmecki, 'Power Assessment', p. 294; Kriyov, *op. cit.*, *Spetsial'nyi Byulleten' IV AN SSSR* no. 2, 1990, p. 183; *Afghanistan 1989-1995*, Beiheft zur *Allgemeinen Schweizerischen Militarzeitschrift*, 5/1996, p. 9.

themselves. KhAD also played an important role in bringing rebel groups on to the government side and in a whole range of other counter-insurgency measures, including the reported creation of fake mujahidin units in order to alienate the civilians from 'genuine' resistance forces. The expansion of KhAD's size is reported in Table 27.[66]

KhAD/WAD tasks included those of a political police, which led it to arrest 150,000 people before 1990, while 8,006 were executed between 1980 and 1988,[67] but it also carried out genuinely military activities. Its armed units were given the task of safeguarding key military positions, including airports, from threats such as mass desertions. In at least some cases these units managed to prevent the fall of important positions to the enemy. On average several hundred such troops were present in each province and accounted for most of the KhAD strength in them. Overall its impact on the military balance grew dramatically in the second half of the 1980s, as is clear from Table 30.

Special operations battalions and other units were also set up. At first, presumably in the early 1980s, three special battalions were formed. By 1986 thirty mobile units with 12,000 men were in existence, making a considerable contribution to the counter-insurgency effort.[68] Later two full divisions were created, both garrisoned in Kabul. Finally it should be remembered that the Special Guard was part of WAD.

Porous borders

Apart from garrisoning towns and villages, performing column escort duties, running small counter-insurgency operations in areas where the mujahidin were weaker and supporting big operations carried out by the 40th Army, the Afghan armed forces also took on the task (jointly with the Soviets) of making the borders less permeable to infiltration. Initially this was supposed to be the

[66] Leonov, *Likholet'e*, p. 270; Strmecki, 'Power Assessment', pp. 297-8, 323; J. Fullerton, *The Soviet Occupation of Afghanistan*, Hong Kong, 1983, p. 125.

[67] Rubin, *The Fragmentation of Afghanistan*, p. 137.

[68] *Informatsionnyi byulleten' po materialam XX plenuma TsK NDPA*, Kabul, 1986, p. 1; F. Halliday, *Political change and regime survival in Afghanistan, 1978-1992*, ESRC End of Award Report, 1995, p. 11.

Afghans' job, as the Soviets did not want to commit themselves to operations too close to the border. To this end in 1980 it was decided to create the Border Guard. A small border guard, numbering only 1,200, had existed for a long time, but it was occupied with customs duties only. The new one was meant to be a real fighting force. It began to materialize in 1981, when it reached a strength of 8,000. At this size, even when the border militias were added, it was far from representing a threat to the rebels, considering that about 100 supply routes existed. Since at that time its personnel charts were only 25-35% complete, a decision was taken to increase its share of recruits and bring its completion level to 70%. At the same time the minefields at the borders, laid first in July 1980, were extended. The porosity of the border was in any case unaffected, as in 1984 ten of the twenty-five main roads along the border with Pakistan, all the roads along the border with Iran and all the caravan tracks were under mujahidin control. At this point the Red Army was forced to commit itself on a large scale.[69]

At the beginning of 1984 the 'Zaves' plan was adopted. Its aim was to close off the infiltration routes. To this end the Red Army devoted eleven Motorized Infantry, three Reconnaissance and eight Spetnaz Battalions, as well one Spetnaz and eleven Reconnaissance Companies and sixty Reconnaissance Platoons. They were intended to conduct 180 ambushes every day; in fact they never went beyond thirty to forty per day at best, with the average nationwide being thirteen to fourteen over May-September 1984 and sixteen to seventeen over the winter of 1984/5. It should be noted that the figure was higher before the plan was actually started, with eighteen to nineteen ambushes prepared daily over the period May-September 1983. Whereas the Border Guard displayed a level of commitment, other Afghan units deployed close to the border continued to behave passively. Caravans were reported to have passed close (10-30 km.) to army posts without any measures being taken. Still more minefields were laid, but to be effective they needed to be constantly renewed; in the case of Kunar province, those laid in December 1984 were neutralized by the mujahidin within one month, although not before the

[69] Lyakhovskii, *Tragediya i doblest' Afgana*, p. 189; Ludwig, 'Einige Probleme', p. 120, n. 1.

loss of 150 men's lives. Later the rebels reportedly used animals or prisoners to clear the mines.[70]

In the spring of 1985 Spetnaz forces were increased to two full brigades, covering 60% of the border with Iran and Pakistan. Some Spetnaz battalions were indeed effective, managing to attack one or two caravans every month, but overall the military authorities themselves estimated (optimistically) that only 12–15% of caravans were intercepted. Actually, it was estimated that to seal the border effectively 80,000 men would be necessary, pratically the whole of the 'limited contingent'. At best, the Afghan Border Troops defended their positions without really closing the border; in mitigation, they were still badly understrength, lacked transport equipment and were paid many months in arrears.[71]

In 1984, government statistics claimed the destruction of 160 caravans out of 230 spotted crossing the border in the period January-October (i.e., sixteen per month), while the Soviets succeeded in ambushing fifty-two to fifty-three caravans each month in May-September 1983 and thirty-six to thirty-seven in May-September 1984. Even assuming that these figures are correct and all these caravans were really destroyed or heavily damaged, the actual number crossing into Afghanistan was certainly much higher. One American scholar estimates it at 20,000 every year (i.e., 1,600-1,700 each month) and on the basis of his interviews with mujahidin commanders he puts the number of those attacked at 3% of the total. According to his figures, only half of those attacked suffered casualties. It is worth noting that, if the figure of 20,000 is correct, government and mujahidin claims of losses more or less coincide. During the winter of 1984/5, 198 caravans were 'destroyed' by the Soviets alone, according to internal documents (sixty-six per month), a significant improvement, but still a very small proportion of the total (see Table 32).[72]

In mid-1986 Najibullah, who deemed 'the most fundamental

[70] Lyakhovskii, *Tragediya i doblest' Afgana*, pp. 288-9, 237; A.V. Tchikichev, *Spetnaz en Afghanistan*, CEREDAF 1994, p. 29.

[71] Gromov, *Ogranichennyi kontingent*, pp. 199, 219; Lyakhovskii, *Tragediya i doblest' Afgana*, p. 239; Tchikichev, *Spetnaz en Afghanistan*, p. 17; Ludwig, 'Einige Probleme', p. 112.

[72] Ludwig, 'Einige Probleme', p. 104; Strmecki, *Power Assessment*, p. 457; Lyakhovskii, *Tragediya i doblest' Afgana*, pp. 288-9.

task of the present moment' was 'sealing the borders', decided to bring the Border Guards to full strength, and they reached 30,000 in 1987 (see Table 27). Yet troops were not numerous enough to cover the border and in spring 1987 a new system was adopted. The idea was to seize control of the mountain heights in order to monitor the routes. The mujahidin were left to stockpile supplies in their bases, which were then attacked by the air forces, whose role was thereby increased. In this way in 1987 the government could claim to control seventy-four of the ninety-nine routes and indeed several sources recognize that infiltration was harder at this time, particularly into the North and West of the country.[73]

In 1366 (1987/8) the anti-caravan activity of the government troops peaked at about thirty ambushes every day, while Soviet participation declined somewhat, to twelve to thirteen each day. In the second half of 1988 the monthly rate of caravan interceptions by the Soviet forces was a respectable 69.5, bearing in mind that the border protection system was being dismantled. The first part of the year seems to have been even better, with a peak in February when 132 caravans were intercepted. Yet this quantitative increase hides the fact that many of the intercepted caravans were only slightly damaged by the attacks. In 1987, for example, 1,000 caravans were 'intercepted' by the Soviet forces (eighty-five each month), but the number actually destroyed was much smaller. The overwhelming majority of the caravans eliminated were victims of the Spetnaz, which claimed 131 of them in the first half of the year. A further 128 were intercepted by other Soviet ground units, whose ability to really crush them was certainly inferior. In the whole of 1987 it can therefore be estimated that not much fewer than 500 caravans were attacked from the sky alone; all reports confirm the ineffectiveness of this sort of attack.[74]

After 1988 the government capability to stem the flow of supplies to the mujahidin declined sharply. While in the single month of October 1988 100 caravans were sighted (a precondition for their

[73] Najibullah, RA, 10 July 1986; Lyakhovskii, *Tragediya i doblest' Afgana*, Lyakhovskii and Zabrodin, *Tainy afganskoi voiny*, p. 100.

[74] *KZ*, 14 Aug. 1988; Gromov, *Ogranichennyi kontingent*, p. 323; *KZ*, 11 March 1988; Lyakhovskii, *Tragediya i doblest' Afgana*, pp. 341, 355-6.

interception), in the first six months of 1989 only 270 were spotted.[75]

Strategic reserve

One important limit to the offensive capacity of the regime was the difficulty in massing forces for offensive operations. Kabul was committed to defend at least its historical strongholds, even if they were in a strategically hopeless situation. The most obvious case is the town of Khost, in Paktia province. Isolated from the main highways, very close to the Pakistani border, surrounded by pro-mujahidin tribes, Khost was the refuge of the pro-government clans of Southern Paktia. As long as the 40th Army was available, it was possible to organize rescue operations in order to resupply it and break the siege, as happened at the end of 1987. Although in that instance the Soviets had only a support role, that role was none the less of fundamental importance. Once the Red Army was gone, Khost became off limits for the government supply columns. A whole division (the 25th) was tied down there for the whole of the war, relying only on air supplies, and its fall, with the loss of around 10,000 government troops and militiamen, could not be averted.[76]

The withdrawal of the Red Army made the creation of a strategic reserve absolutely necessary. Some Soviet sources state that the Najibullah government did not really believe till the very end that the Red Army would be withdrawn, so that the steps recommended by the advisers were taken late and implemented slowly. In fact, the presence of the Red Army had shaped the Afghan armed forces to a point that no Afghan garrison had any tank or artillery reserve (or indeed any sort of reserve at all). The situation was made worse by the disappointing draft of 1988, whose consequences for the army were exacerbated by the priority given to the Special Guard and the *sarandoy*, so that its recruitment plan was only 18% completed.[77]

Measures were taken, especially in the area bordering Pakistan,

[75] Lyakhovskii, 'Na afganskoi vizhzhennoi zemle', p. 58; Gareev, *Moya poslednyaya voina*, p. 184.

[76] Lyakhovskii, *Tragediya i doblest' Afgana*, p. 561.

[77] Lyakhovskii, 'Na afganskoi vizhzhennoi zemle', p. 59; Gareev, *Moya poslednyaya voina*, pp. 200, 103.

to withdraw troops from non-decisive or indefensible positions and mass them around a few strongholds, like Nangrahar and Kandahar, and along the key communication lines. The Border Guards abandoned their positions and joined those of the army. In this way easy victories were denied to the mujahidin and the morale of the government troops was not endangered further. It was envisaged that the mujahidin thrust would exhaust itself in two or three months and the armed forces would then be able to mount local counter-offensives. In Najibullah's words, each provincial centre should be transformed into a 'military fortress' capable not just of defending itself, but also of launching attacks. Some Western military analysts think that this strategic redeployement was not radical enough and some of the districts and provincial centres which the government wanted to keep did in fact fall into the mujahidin's hands. Furthermore, the local counter-offensives were not always very effective. Overall, however, the strategy did work.[78]

In Najibullah's eyes it was even more important to guarantee government control over the key sections of the road network till May 1989, when the mujahidin onslaught was expected to die down. The Soviet air bridge to Kabul could only cover a fraction of what was required: between the end of the Soviet presence (15 February 1989) and the end of 1989, 48,434 vehicles transported 340,000 tons of goods to Kabul from Hairatan, while only 71,027 tons were carried by 5,280 flights. Soviet observers and Najibullah himself were unsure whether the Afghans could have done the job by themselves. Gromov openly stated that the regime was vulnerable in its communications with the North. It was estimated that 4-5,000 more men were needed in order to ensure the protection of the Hairatan-Kabul highway. Several scenarios for the participation of Soviet troops were considered, such as deploying a division of 12,000 men on the Hairatan-Kabul road having supply columns escorted by Soviet troops or leaving some Soviet troops in hot spots along the northern highway.[79]

[78] Lyakhovskii, *Tragediya i doblest' Afgana*, pp. 374-5; Lyakhovskii, 'Na afganskoi vizhzhennoi zemle', p. 64; RA, 1 Sept. 1988; J. Hill, 'Afghanistan in 1988: year of the Mujahidin', *Armed Forces Journal International*, March 1989.

[79] Gareev, *Moya poslednyaya voina*, p. 209; TsK KPSS, 'O rabochem vizite Ministra oborony SSSR v Respubliku Afganistan', in *Soujetische Geheimdokumente*,

The situation was undoubtedly worrying. Up to 1989 an average of forty-five lorries a month had been destroyed nationwide by the mujahidin in the war of the roads, which meant that by April 1983 14% of the government means of transport had been destroyed. In 1367 (1988/9) twelve to thirteen had been lost each month on the Kabul-Hairatan highway alone; the corresponding figure for the period March-June 1989 was sixty-nine, with a loss to the state of 5,000 tons of goods (as against 11,000 during the whole of 1367).[80]

A possible solution to this problem was the formation of the Special Guard in March 1988. Its main aim was to 'defend and ensure the safety of ... Kabul City and also to react promptly to changes in the situation in other parts of the country', around the key cities and the highways. At least initially, recruitment was voluntary and was carried out among experienced troops. About twenty soldiers 'in the new Guards uniform' were sent to the provinces with the task of agitating for recruitment into the Guards. Later it was claimed only that the majority of guardsmen were volunteers. Significantly, its first military activities in late 1988 and early 1989 were reported along the Salang highway north of Kabul, in Kunduz and along the Kabul-Jallalabad and Jallalabad-Torkham highways and were claimed as 'remarkable successes'. It was supposed to be an elite unit, although observers were surprised by the heterogeneity of the troops: males and females as young as seventeen and as old as forty-five were allowed to volunteer (but apparently even these wide limits were sometimes not respected) and they came from a wide variety of units, including WAD. It is not surprising that 'the uniforms did not match' and that they were often 'out of step' when marching. However these troops were paid a salary twice as big as other units and this may have propped up its morale. In the end, the Guards' battle performance was definitely better than that of the average Afghan Army unit and they at least managed to keep the main highways

pp. 506, 508; TsK KPSS, 'O meropriyatiyakh v svyazi s predstoyashim vyvodom sovetskikh voisk iz Afganistana', 23 Jan. 1989, in *ibid.*, pp. 466, 468, 470, 472, 474, 476; A. Borovik, *Echshe raz pro voinu*, Mezhdunarodnye Otnosheniya, 1990, p. 222.

[80] Najibullah, RA, 20-21 July 1989 and RA, 15 April 1989; J. Fullerton, 'The Soviet Occupation of Afghanistan', *Far Eastern Economic Review*, 1983, p. 53.

open, although they were not suitable for much else.[81] Initially its strength was projected at 16,000, but it is not certain whether it ever reached this level (see Table 27).

Furthermore, some other units were utilized *de facto* by the Supreme Command as *de facto* reserves, in particular the 53rd Infantry Division, the most combative of the whole army. Yet the strength of available strategic reserves remained well below that needed till the end of the war; and when offensives became necessary, it remained common practice to regroup units from different provinces and to dispatch them wherever needed. This happened in 1987 in Arghandab district (Kandahar province), when the Afghan armed forces committed five battalions from the 7th Infantry Division, five from the 15th, two from the 7th Tank Brigade, two from the 466th Commandos Regiment, two from the 38th Commandos Brigade, two from the 21st Motorized Infantry Brigade, two from the 1st *Sarandoy* Operational Regiment, one from the 93rd Operational Regiment, plus some independent WAD and *sarandoy* operational battalions – 'a complicated and difficult system'.[82]

[81] *Defense and Foreign Affairs Strategic Policy*, June 1992; Lt.-Gen. Mohammad Afzal Ludin, Commander of the Guard, interviewed in *KZ*, 4 Aug. 1988; *AP*, Feb. 3, 1989; *Bakhtar*, 9 Jan. 1989; Rubin, *The Fragmentation of Afghanistan*, p. 157.

[82] Gareev, *Moya poslednyaya voina*, pp. 308, 200; Lyakhovskii, *Tragediya i doblest' afgana*, p. 340.

9

(IN-)EFFECTIVENESS OF THE
AFGHAN ARMED FORCES

Morale and professionalism

The low morale of the troops was clearly an obstacle to the counter-insurgency effort. Officers treated their soldiers with contempt and corporal punishment was still in use. Furthermore, the officers sometimes lived in Kabul and other cities, leaving the troops to fight on their own in the countryside. According to deserters' reports on arrival in Pakistan, training was bad, as it had been cut from three years before the war to two after the Revolution (in theory – in practice it could be as short as three months) for officers and from three to four months to one to two (in practice as short as a single week) for private soldiers. Efforts were made to improve living conditions, which at the outset were quite poor. The Defence Minister in 1987 claimed as a success the fact that most soldiers now had 'bunk beds' and 'mattresses, bed sheets, pillows and blankets'. The most important devices for improving morale turned out to be salary increases and access to the food and fuel coupon system. As early as January 1981 salaries were doubled, but the real improvement took place in 1987, when they increased seven- to eightfold for ordinary soldiers and doubled for junior officers.[83]

Further increases took place; in 1367 (1988/9) alone the plan was to increase them five- or tenfold. An improvement in armed forces morale after the Soviet withdrawal has been widely reported;

---

[83] V. Nosatov, 'V nachale deviatiletnei voiny', *Literaturnyi Kirgizistan*, no. 6 (1989), p. 66; Gareev, *Moya poslednyaya voina*, p. 207; RA, 19 May 1987; Arnold, *The Fateful Pebble*, Presidio, 1992, p. 128; RA, 19 May 1987; Najibullah, RA, 28 June 1987; Amstutz, *Afghanistan: the First Five Years of Soviet Occupation*, p. 187.

it really seems that officers at least were now more pugnacious. However, as late as 1990 the number of soldiers surrendering to the mujahidin was estimated by the Soviet advisers themselves to be three times greater than the number of mujahidin surrendering to the armed forces. A minority of the troops did fight to the last man, as in Tarin Kot in 1990, when out of a garrison of maybe 500, sixty soldiers and some WAD troops resisted in the airport refusing to give up even after the surrender of the governor. In other cases, however, even large garrisons displayed a negligible level of combativeness, as in Kunduz in 1988, where 4,500 soldiers ran away or deserted in the face of 1,100 mujahidin. The same happened in Teluqan and Khanabad, which were occupied by the mujahidin without a fight.[84]

The real problem lay in the fact that to the ordinary Afghan soldier it was difficult to imagine why he should fight for a Revolution which had only meant trouble for him and his family, as some of them openly declared to a Soviet General in the summer of 1979. The elite units, which were more favourable to the party, ended up overstretched by too many commitments. Pilots in the Air Force were flying as many as five or six sorties a day. As is shown in Table 33 losses were heavy (considering that the Afghan Air Force counted about 300 planes and helicopters in 1988), particularly after the Soviet withdrawal, and the average crew could not have hoped to last very long. Although desertions remained low (seven pilots went over to the mujahidin in 1989), the effectiveness of the Air Force was severely hampered.[85]

Yet losses cannot explain the ground forces' poor performance, as in fact they were not particularly severe. A total of 70,000 government troops were killed between 1979 and 1988,[86] a serious but not unsustainable yearly loss rate of 7,000. Pakistani intelligence sources confirm this figure (see Table 34). Nor were losses of equipment very high (see Table 36). Table 35 shows how the

[84] *AF*, vol. 16, no. 3, (1988) p. 35; Gareev, *Moya poslednyaya voina*, p. 198; *AFP*, 4 Oct. 1990; Lyakhovskii, *Tragediya i doblest' Afgana*, pp. 401, 403.

[85] Merimskii, 'Voina v Afganistane: zapiski uchastika', p. 79; Gareev, *Moya poslednyaya voina*, pp. 201, 208; *Iz besed ruzh. sostava RA s Shevarnadze. VPO v RA avgust 1988 g.*

[86] *Guardian*, 27 Feb. 1989.

monthly casualty rates of the army were, except in 1989, relatively limited.

The unpopularity of the regime among the rank and file is only partially attributable to an ideological opposition. Such opposition was in any case broad enough to allow room for infiltration attempts by the mujahidin. In 1980, five such attempts were uncovered; in 1987, 300. *Hizb-i Islami* appears to have been the most active here: in 1981, 400 of its members in the armed forces were arrested, including seventeen army officers, four KhAD members and fourty-seven military schools' students.[87] It is furthermore known that many high-ranking officers, as well as top leaders of the party, had contacts with the opposition, as became evident in April 1992.

Apart from infiltration proper, low morale also meant a willingness to trade with the mujahidin which could extend up to the delivery of weapons, where the 5th and 7th Border Brigades appear to have been involved in 1990.[88]

Even the relationship with the general population was far from good. At the end of a counter-insurgency operation the troops often looted the civilian population. *Sarandoy* and DYOA militias appear to have been the most despised by the population for their arrogant behaviour and their habit of taking goods without paying for them. KhAD/WAD troops seem to have been better appreciated.[89] In the countryside, the practice of bombing the villages was usual.

Another great shortcoming was the chronic incompleteness of the armed forces' personnel charts. As is evident from Table 38, the real problem was the combat units, which were much more undermanned then the staff and the services. Moreover, units based in areas of greater mujahidin activity were even weaker than average. Soviet advisers complained in particular about the lack of specialists like tankmen and artillerymen. Training more specialists was no easy task. Volunteers were scarce and even when plenty were available, their quality was abysmally low, as

[87] N.I Marchuk, *Neob''yavlennaya voina v Afganistane*, p. 121; Lyakhovskii, *Tragediya i doblest' Afgana*, p. 249.

[88] Gareev, *Moya poslednyaya voina*, p. 103.

[89] *Ibid.*, p. 25; Mohammed Januf, personal communication, London, 23 Feb. 1995.

one might expect given the fact that 60% of the troops were illiterate. In autumn 1990 a Soviet medical commission arrived in Kabul in order to select sixty trainees for the Soviet flying schools. Out of 2,500 candidates, only fifty-three were accepted, as the others were either sick or illiterate. Great effort had been invested in training Afghans in the USSR since the very beginning, so by August 1988 the ranks of the *sarandoy* counted 16,000 men trained in the USSR, while 2,000 more were attending similar courses at that time, together with 1,000 men from the Ministry of Defence.[90]

Even so, in August 1988, 350 tanks, 150 BMP and 350 BTR did not have any crew, 6,000 vehicles had no driver and 760 guns and 1,000 mortars had no gunners. These figures for equipment look impressive, but in reality the Afghan Army already operated with huge quantities of military hardware (see Table 37). More operational tanks would anyway have been of limited use, as they could only be effective on the highway network, in defense of Kabul and Jallalabad and in the flat areas of the North and West. Already at the beginning of the war the Soviet Command had come to the conclusion that its thirty-nine tank battalions in Afghanistan were in large part useless and their number was reduced to seventeen. The only specialists the Afghan Army would have really benefited from were technicians, as a lot of equipment was often not in working condition. The situation had been much worse in the early years – like 1984 when only 20% of the armoured vehicles were operational – but in some sensitive areas it was still worrying. In the isolated garrison of Khost during the autumn of 1989 only four M/30 guns out of eighteen were serviceable. After the Soviet withdrawal, some installations, including the airport, could not work because of a lack of trained personnel.[91]

The real problem was the extreme weakness of infantry units, which in fact were even weaker than the statistics demonstrate. It has already been observed that some officers kept fictitious

[90] Lyakhovskii, *Tragediya i doblest' Afgana*, p. 554; Gankovskii, 'Vooruzhennye sily respubliki Afganistan', p. 14; Lyakhovskii and Zabrodin, *Tainy afganskoi voiny*, p. 189; *KP*, 29 June 1991; *Iz besed ruzh. sostava RA s Shevarnadze. VPO v RA. avgust 1988 g.*

[91] Lyakhovskii, *Tragediya i doblest' Afgana*, p. 476; Gankovskii, 'Vooruzhennye sily respubliki Afganistan', Gai and Snegirev, *Vtorzhenie*, p. 148; Gareev, *Moya poslednyaya voina*, p. 258; *KP*, 29 June 1991.

soldiers on the roll, in order to pocket the salary. Moreover statistics tended to reflect the situation at the time of peaks in manpower availability, not taking into account the 400-700 desertions which each division experienced each year. So in practice in 1988 most divisions could only field 200-300 infantrymen, rarely 500, battalions twenty or thirty and companies five to seven.[92]

Najibullah promoted attempts to 'resolutely transfer healthy soldiers from non-combat units to combat units', as 'the Ministries of Defence, State Security and Interior are full of extra officers and soldiers'. He also proposed to pay extra money to combat units for each combat operation they carried out. Attempts were made to transfer troops from the services to the combat units, but generally they never stayed more than two to three months. Among the consequences of the low morale of the army, reconaissance became particularly weak, since to send out small units was to risk seeing them disintegrate through desertions. Radio interceptions were widely used, but were not effective enough.[93]

Officers were in better supply, but at the price of a qualitative decline. In 1983 they were 96% complete, but only 26% of them had received complete training and 43% had not received any training at all. In 1980 many low rank officers had been promoted to command positions. During the whole course of the war many NCOs were promoted to officers; 800 in 1982 alone and 1,050 in 1365 (1986/87). This represents a very high percentage of the whole officer corps, which numbered 10,000 in 1988 (plus 5,000 platoon commanders). This also caused a terrible shortage of NCOs, particularly experienced ones, as generally they were all promoted to officer rank after three years of service.[94]

Other practices contributed to lower the quality of the officer corps, like the habit of appointing to higher positions those who were removed because of some mistake. Even in such an extreme

---

[92] *Aktual'nye problemy afganskoi revolyutsii*, p. 436; Lyakhovskii, *Tragediya i doblest' Afgana*, p. 480.

[93] Gareev, *Moya poslednyaya voina*, pp. 203, 202; Najibullah, PDPA CC plenum, RA, 23 Oct. 1988.

[94] Merimskii, 'Voina v Afganistane: zapiski uchastika', p. 112; Yu. Gankovskii, 'Vooruzhennye sily respubliki Afganistan'; RA, 19 May 1987; *Iz besed ruzh. sostava RA s Shevarnadze. VPO v RA avgust 1988 g.*; Gareev, *Moya poslednyaya voina*, p. 204.

case as the fall of Khost, in 1991, Najibullah's representatives in the town managed to return to Kabul unharmed, basically by trading surrender for their own personal safety. They were removed from their positions, but were not punished. This aroused strong protests within the party. At a lower level, in 1990 alone 10,000 cadres were tranferred within the Interior Ministry because of demands which had nothing to do with service tasks.[95]

Equipment

The Afghan regime undoubtedly received plenty of military support from Moscow, but of a type that was quite unbalanced. Weapons systems, while not very up to date, were certainly overabundant (See Table 39).

On the eve of withdrawal, the Afghan leadership was asked by the Soviets what it needed and all its requests were satisfied. Basically the armed forces were re-equipped as if they were full-strength. In 1990 the Afghans requested military help for a further 6.4 billion rubles, but 'only' 2.2 billion were granted (see Table 40 for the evolution of Soviet help over time). Requests for more advanced weapons, like MiG-29 fighters and T-72 tanks, were turned down after some debate, while 45 Mi-35 helicopters were delivered in 1989-90.[96]

Other supplies were often scarce. Plans agreed with the Soviet Union for the creation of three-month strategic reserves over the winter 1989/90 were fulfilled to only 50-60% with regard to food, 25-30% for fuel and 10-20% for ammunition. As early as mid-1988 the Ministry of Interior was complaining about a shortage of ammunition for its troops.[97]

[95] Karmal's Speech to Top Armed Forces' Administration Board, RA, 21 Aug. 1982; KP, 29 June 1991; Starodubova, Moral'no-politicheskii potentsial, p. 61.

[96] A. Vassiliev, Russian Policy in the Middle East: from Messianism to Pragmatism, Ithaca Press, 1993, p. 281; Gareev, Moya poslednyaya voina, p. 310; TsK KPSS, 'Po voprosu rassmotreniya pros'b Presidenta Respubliki Afganistan', 5 Oct. 1989, in Sowjetische Geheimdokumente, p. 716.

[97] Gareev, Moya poslednyaya voina, p. 211; Iz besed ruzh. sostava RA s Shevarnadze. VPO v RA avgust 1988 g.

The overall strategic balance

It remains to be ascertained how many fighting men the Kabul regime could effectively field. In 1990, 35,000 men were busy in Kabul making the central apparatus work, so they should be discounted. The army could count on 50,000 fighting men in 1986-7 and on 75,000 in 1988, the latter figure apparently including the Border Guard. A higher percentage of the *sarandoy* was actually made up of armed men, as their logistics system was leaner. Their mobile units seem to have numbered about 25,000; garrison and village troops perhaps twice as many. WAD, including the Special (National) Guard, had around 40,000 fighting men. So at the time of the Soviet withdrawal the total regular fighting force was about 190,000 (which matches the figures ranging between 160-200,000 given by Soviet witnesses and observers) plus as many as 100,000 actually fighting militiamen (the official figure for militiamen being 200,000).[98] A comparable figure for 1986 might be 145,000 and for 1983, 100-110,000 regular fighting troops, but at this period about 73,000 fighting troops from the Red Army should be added.

When these figures are compared to mujahidin strength levels (see Ch. 14 and Table 47), it would appear that a certain quantitative balance of forces existed in 1989. But the mujahidin's arsenal was improving faster than the government's. By the end of 1982 some Western sources estimated that the mujahidin had already received between 5,000 and 7,000 heavy and squad weapons and 100-150,000 individual weapons. In 1983-4 they received 10,000 tons of supplies each year, which rose dramatically to 50,000 in 1985 and to 65,000 in 1987. Figures for 1988-9 were certainly higher, as intelligence sources estimated that in the first half of 1989 alone they received 400 anti-tank missiles, eighty-five guns, 450 mortars, 275 recoilless guns, 140 anti-aircraft missile launchers, 900 machine guns, 850-900 RPG and 8,600 light weapons. These quantities may still seem small in comparison to what Kabul was receiving, but the mujahidin enjoyed the tremendous advantage

---

[98] Gareev, *Moya poslednyaya voina*, p. 200; Lyakhovskii and Zabrodin, *Tainy afganskoi voiny*, p. 187; *Iz besed ruzh. sostava RA s Shevarnadze. VPO v RA avgust 1988 g.*; Soviet 'expert' interviewed in *Jane's Defence Weekly*, 23 April 1988; Rubin, *The Fragmentation of Afghanistan*, p. 155; Ambassador Egorychev interviewed in Vassiliev, *Russian policy in the Middle East*, p. 281.

of not being constrained by the heavy logistics of a regular army. Furthermore, their supplies were better suited to the kind of war to be fought in most of the Afghan countryside (see Table 41). According to Soviet sources, in some regions (Jallalabad, Khost, Gardez, Ghazni) the mujahidin were equipped with more heavy munitions than the army."[99]

The mujahidin also enjoyed large training facilities in Pakistan; Soviet sources estimated that about 60% of the rebels operating in Nangrahar province in 1988 had been trained there. Further from the Pakistani border the figure must have been lower, but columns of newly trained mujahidin were sent as far as the Soviet border. Pakistani refugee camps provided a safe haven where large numbers of reservists (estimated by intelligence at 50,000 in 1990, while 20,000 more were in Iran) were available to support the military effort of the mujahidin, particularly in the border provinces. For most of the war only 5-8% of the mujahidin operated from Pakistan,[100] but most of these reserves were activated during the 1988-9 general onslaught, when the number of mujahidin crossing the border from Pakistan peaked (monthly rates):[101] 1980-2, 2,000; 1985, 1,700; 1986-7, 2,000 (plus 1,250 from Iran); May-Oct. 1988, 3,600; Jan.-Feb. 1989, 10,000.

While the military proficiency of the mujahidin will not be discussed here in detail, it is worth noting that they were never able to seize any garrison with more than a few hundred defenders (unless the garrison went over to them) and even that quite exceptionally, although in some circumstances the balance of forces was hugely in their favour.[102] The 700-strong garrison of Qalat, completely isolated, was attacked in the summer of 1988 by 7,000

---

[99] P. Schweizer, *Victory. The Reagan Administration's Secret Strategy that Hastened the Collapse of the Soviet Union*, Atlantic Monthly Press, 1995, p. 251; Strmecki, *Power Assessment*, p. 457; Gareev, *Moya poslednyaya voina*, pp. 184, 209; P. Franceschi, *Guerre en Afghanistan*, Paris, La Table Ronde, 1984, p. 156.

[100] A. Olinik, 'Zarnitsy nad gindukushem', *Kommunist Vooruzhennykh sil*, no. 8, 1988, p. 77; Gareev, *Moya poslednyaya voina*, pp. 185-6; V.G. Safronov, 'Kak eto bylo', *Voenno-istoricheskii Zhurnal* no. 5 (1990), p. 69.

[101] *Aktual'nye problemy afganskoi revolyutsii*, p. 429; Gareev, *Moya poslednyaya voina*, p. 98; Lyakhovskii, 'Na afganskoi vizhzhennoi zemle', p. 58; Gromov, *Ogranichennyi kontingent*, p. 297; Reuters, 20 Jan. 1986.

[102] A. Giustozzi, 'La resistenza afghana: rivolta tradizionalista e movimenti politici moderni', *Rivista di Storia Contemporanea*, no. 1 (1991), pp. 110-11.

mujahidin, who failed in the end to take it. Many similar examples are available. The rebels, on the other hand, managed to impose a heavy toll on the columns travelling along the highways and were more than a match for the understrength and demoralised infantry fighting for Kabul. The low losses of tanks suffered by the army suggests that the main reason preventing the government from routing the mujahidin at least in the flat areas of the country was the lack of infantry support, which could have made the most of the armoured thrusts. Only a few infantry units, generally belonging to or coming from the militias, were able to fight the mujahidin on their own ground.

There are no reliable sources on mujahidin losses. The only approximation comes from Pakistan's intelligence, which puts them at about 90,000 (including 56,000 killed) over 1980-9. This figure is probably underestimated, as it does not take into account losses from independent mujahidin groups, which made up a third of the total, although they were on average far less active than the politically aligned ones. The estimated number of wounded (17,065) must also be much lower than the real one. On the other hand, government and Red Army statistics are even less accurate, as they were calculated in a deductive way: a certain amount of ammunition expended corresponded to a fixed number of mujahidin killed.[103] A more useful estimate can be provided by statistics about the number of weapons recovered by the armed forces (see Table 42), that point at 300-800 losses every month. Certainly not all recovered weapons were taken from dead mujahidin; on the other hand many weapons belonging to dead mujahidin may have been carried away by their fellow rebels. Extrapolating from these figures, it can be estimated that at best the armed forces were never able to inflict more than 12,000 or so losses each year on the mujahidin even in the most successful periods. This might amount to as little as 3% of the total manpower of the armed opposition groups. A tentative estimate for total mujahidin losses in 1980-92 may be in the 150-180,000 range, with maybe half of them killed. In general, the inconclusive character of the military confrontation is confirmed by figures on both sides' losses.

[103] Leonov, *Likholet'e*, p. 265; K. Matinuddin, *Power Struggle in the Hindu Kush*, Lahore, Wajidalis, p. 169.

10

PERVERSE EFFECTS ON THE ARMY OF THE TRANSFORMATIONS CAUSED BY THE WAR

The many shortcomings which have been examined in the previous chapters deprived Kabul's regular forces of several of their potential advantages over the mujahidin, such as nationwide coordination. However, the Afghan armed forces did play a role in the war, although not a decisive one. Soviet advisers pushed the Afghans to emulate their own army model, but the latter proved unable to match this satisfactorily. Some of the features advocated by the advisers were to prove useful to the survival of the regime, like the strengthening of party organizations and political control over the army or the creation of a reasonably efficient intelligence service. Others, like overstuffing the Afghan units with armour and heavy guns, were aimed in the wrong direction.

The Afghan regular forces also introduced changes to the Soviet model in accommodation to the needs of the war. Their structural limits were such, however, that at most they might have reached a condition which enabled them not to lose the war. Attempts at winning it did grow in sophistication from the first large-scale conventional offensives to the border sealing strategy, but were still far wide of the mark. A purely political solution would not have proved realistic either, as the mujahidin would not have accepted a compromise unless seriously challenged militarily. The only conceivable way out of the dilemma was the creation of militia units which could confront the enemy on its own ground (see Part IV), and at the same time present a 'political' response to mujahidin power in the countryside. The rise of the militias from 1987 changed the basic role of the army. It was now supposed to provide a central reserve for large scale offensives and counter-offensives and, locally, to guarantee the protection of the main

116

strategic centres and towns, while at the same time counter-balancing the spread of the militias, which in most cases were not easily controlled by the central power. The latter task proved particularly difficult to fulfil (see Part IV). In fact, by 1988-9 the regular forces were confined to merely defensive activities; almost all operations were counter-offensives, few initiatives were taken.

The most important structural develoment was the greater degree of independence vested in regional army commanders, so they could run the war according to the basic features of their area. A Soviet 'expert' stated that Afghan units were organized in such a way that 'the troops were personally loyal to their officer' and would follow him 'regardless of the political context'. This may well have proved helpful on the battleground, but it gave an excessive margin of manoeuvre to an officer corps which was badly factionalized. Most commanders, even in the WAD and in the *sarandoy*, surrounded themselves with their own acolytes and did not communicate with other commanders of the security forces, let alone the local population.[104]

One of the stated aims of the Saur Revolution was the end of ethnic discrimination against minorities. The army was largely Pashtun-dominated in 1978 and the situation cannot have improved by the end of 1979, as Amin's supporters were overwhelmingly Pashtuns. After Karmal's advent to power, something began to be done about this. In the army discrimination began to lose its importance, although it never disappeared. Tajiks benefited particularly and in the end they were the only ethnic group to be over-represented in the army (see Table 43). In 1985 there were more Tajiks (48%) than Pashtuns (45%) in the military schools, indicating a long term trend. The fact that most Pashtun areas were beyond government recruitment efforts certainly helps to explain this development, but it is still true that other minorities living in the same regions as the Tajiks did not experience any such improvement.[105]

Whether the rise of the Tajiks was a positive development or not may depend on one's subjective point of view. It is however

---

[104] *Jane's Defence Weekly* April 23, 1988; *Otchet o komandirovke v pr. Baghlan, 15-18 dekabrya 1987 g.*

[105] *Aktual'nye problemy afganskoi revolyutsii*, p. 434; Starodubova, *Moral'no-politicheskii potentsial*, p. 104.

beyond doubt that the ethnic policy of the regime, in the context of the civil war, did play a role in an ethnic 'awakening' which rose to particular prominence in the final period of the war and which, in the end, ran out of Kabul's control. A Soviet military historian stated that the presence of Uzbeks and Tajiks in the Soviet contingent (particularly strong in the first years of the war) played a negative role, as it exacerbated the nationalistic or xenophobic feelings of Pashtuns. The preference diplayed by Soviet advisers for Tajik and Uzbek interpreters had a similar effect. Reports of an ethnic dimension in the spiral of violence between mujahidin groups and government troops date back to as early as 1982. In the summer of that year Uzbek troops in Faryab province made a reprisal against Pashtun nomads because of a bloody attack against an Uzbek village by a Pashtun group, which in turn was taking revenge for a massacre perpetrated by an Uzbek group against a Pashtun village. Things worsened in the latter part of the war, when it became very difficult to transfer military units consisting of Northeners to the South; mass desertions of such troops took place in 1991, when units from the 18th Infantry Division (Mazar-i-Sharif) were transferred to Gardez. The transfer of Uzbek units from the 53rd Infantry Division to Khost in 1991 did not cause them to desert, but did trigger a negative reaction on the Pashtun side. Worse still, in 1990, several ethnic clashes took place among units of the armed forces in the provinces of Kabul, Balkh, Baghlan and Herat. As a consequence of Defence Minister Tanai's attempted coup in 1990, Najibullah promoted some non-Pashtuns to high positions in the armed forces structure. In late 1991 he tried to reverse this policy, but it was too late.[106]

---

[106] V.G. Safronov, 'Kak eto bylo', *Voenno-istoricheskii Zhurnal*, no. 5 (1990), p. 69; *Literaturnaya Rossiya*, 21 July 1995; V. Nosatov, 'V nachale deviatiletnei voiny', *Literaturnyi Kirgizistan*, no. 6 (1989), p. 75; Lyakhovskii, *Tragediya i doblest' Afgana*, pp. 566, 562; Starodubova, *Moral'no-politicheskii potentsial*, p. 105.

Part III

THE 'PACIFICATION POLICY' 1980-1991

Parts I and II make it clear that the traditional Soviet approach to the consolidation of allied, ideologically close regimes was not working in Afghanistan. It is also clear that Soviet advisers and Afghan leaders gradually became aware of the limits of their strategy. Parts III and IV will deal with the attempt to elaborate an alternative approach.

'Pacification' is the term which has often been used in Western writings about Afghanistan (mainly French) to describe the policies developed in the context of a search for this 'alternative approach'. The term, probably not the most appropriate one, as it will appear from Part IV, is accepted here for the sake of convenience. Basically, this term is used here to indicate the attempt to co-opt the armed opposition in the countryside, striking deals with single commanders or single villages.

The aim of this policy changed over time. Initially mainly a tactical and auxiliary (and maybe temporary) device to calm the situation in specific areas, it developed into a long term strategy, which would eventually re-shape the nature of the regime itself. The original 'ideological strategy' was thus replaced by a 'flexible strategy', which attempted to create a balanced mix of policies aimed at ensuring the survival of the regime after Soviet withdrawal and at giving it a shape that was better suited to the actual Afghan environment. Some relative local successes during the early 1980s led to the upgrading of the whole policy. By the time of the Soviet withdrawal, therefore, the criteria for success had changed, becoming much more demanding. Nobody ever expected that all the 'counter-revolutionary groups' would join the regime, but the stabilization of the military-political situation in all the key areas of the country was deemed to be a realistic target.

119

11

THE EARLY APPROACHES

The first strategic and tactical elaborations

The first traces of a 'pacification' approach to the Afghan crisis date right back to January 1980, when a group of Soviet specialists led by V. Safronchuk tried to put together a policy including contacts with some mujahidin which resembled the later National Reconciliation. It appears that it was the urban uprising of February 22 that put an end to this attempt, although it is quite probable that opposition to it pre-existed among both the Soviet advisers and the PDPA leadership.[1] It is likely, however, that the 'contacts' with the armed opposition were intended to be at the higher levels of political leadership. At that time, indeed, neither the Karmal government nor the Soviets had the skills or the ground knowledge to deal successfully with the grassroots resistance movement. The ability to do so developed only gradually, out of the field work carried out in the first years of the war.

In the confused situation in 1980, the new government decided, together with its advisers, that the best way to recover the countryside was to implant or maintain 'cells' (i.e. local administrative units and party groups) in the largest possible number of districts, in order to extend 'people's power'. The hope was that their presence would spread out the influence of the 'revolutionary' regime, attracting the collaboration of the local population, by virtue of the obvious advantages offered by the combination of social reforms and a soft approach to the Islamic issue. It took some time to implement this policy, first because many districts had been lost and had to be reconquered, and second because the Democratic Republic was unable to appoint governors and officials

---

[1] Rubin, *The Fragmentation of Afghanistan*, p. 135.

to the most remote places before the beginning of 1983. In reality 'people's power' in most districts remained limited to the district administrative centre or little more, as is shown in the last chapter of this Part. Later, a number of Soviet and Russian commentators were particularly critical towards this policy, in part on military-strategic grounds, but it is difficult to say whether it had really been a total mistake (see Chapter 5). To some extent at least, it allowed the government to maintain a symbolic presence in large areas of the country and it may indeed have inclined part of the rural population and rebel groups to seek some form of cooperation with the state, particularly after the very first, chaotic period of the Soviet occupation.[2]

Propaganda activity was not at all easy to carry out in the climate of hostility and violence which dominated the Afghan countryside. One obvious and safe method was to intensify radio broadcasts in the various Afghan languages. Immediately after the April 1978 Revolution the total broadcasting time of central Kabul radio was raised from twenty hours a week to 31.5, rising slowly to forty hours by August 1983. At the end of the Karmal period this was further increased to 51.30 hours and it was planned to bring the total to 105 hours within the five-year plan. The propaganda content, however, did not match what some Soviet advisers considered to be appropriate. In early 1987, for example, one Soviet scholar complained that only 9% of broadcast material was aimed at workers and peasants. This shortcoming probably did not affect the performance of Kabul radio as much as its poor competitiveness with regard to foreign stations in Dari and Pashto, like the most popular among them, the BBC. The situation was even less promising in the provinces. Although in 1985 Karmal had pressed for a higher degree of urgency to be given to the expansion of the local radio network, in 1988 the Paktia provincial radio station was still broadcasting only two hours a day.[3]

It was partly because of the lack of feasible alternatives, therefore,

---

[2] Abdul Samad Qaumi, Director-general of DRA Department of Local Organs of State Administration, RA, 12 March 1983; General Varennikov, interviewed in *Ogoniok*, no. 12 (1989).

[3] *Bakhtar*, 4 Dec. 1986; *Neues Deutschland*, 11 Aug. 1983; Karmal, XV plenum, RA, 27 March 1985; D.V. Ql'shanskii, *Natsional'noe primerenie*, ION pri TsK KPSS, Moscow, 1988, pp. 66, 68.

that during the first years of the war the Kabul government and the Soviets basically relied on military operations to defeat the 'counter-revolution'. They adopted a wait-and-see approach with regard to politics, hoping that the end of Amin's regime would persuade most rebels to cease hostilities. Although some top military officers in the Red Army (Sokolov, Akhromeev, Varennikov) already realized during 1980 that no purely military victory was achievable (they even managed to persuade Defence Minister Us-tinov to propose a withdrawal from Afghanistan in early 1981), military activities were actually not completely ineffective, as pointed out in Part II. It was no accident that the earliest groups of militiamen were formed around government posts, where military pressure was stronger. After a while, a ring of pro-government villages were formed around the post and then, thanks to the pressure of the population on mujahidin commanders, cease-fire agreements with the neighbouring area followed. The physical shape of the territory was also influential: these protective circles were generally thicker in the plains and in the large valleys.[4]

War weariness among the population and the mujahidin, how-ever, turned out to be really significant only when combined with active measures aimed at winning the 'hearts and minds' of the population. The need for elaborate tactics, if any expansion of government influence in the countryside was to be achieved, soon became self-evident. As a result of the political and, one might say, 'cultural' unpreparedness of the leading circles in Kabul and of the Soviet adviser corps, the first concrete attempts to deal directly with the mujahidin took the shape of pragmatic tactics, developed thanks to continued exposure to the widely varying regional circumstances, with the aim of weakening the enemy at the local level and/or of gaining some breathing space. Initially, since the Karmal government was too weak to be accepted by many as a negotiating partner, the 40th Army did most of the work. While a number of military operations, aimed at the destruc-tion of the most active mujahidin groups, were organized each year, most of the time Soviet units tried instead to establish *a modus vivendi* with local groups, theoretically in the expectation

---

[4] *Est et Ouest*, Nov. 1985, pp. 15, 16; Yu. Gankovsky, 'Afghanistan: from intervention to national reconciliation', *Iranian Journal of International Affairs*, vol. IV, no. 1 (1992), p. 134.

that the government would take business into its own hands once it had consolidated its grip. Sometimes, however, Soviet units were more interested in making life easier for themselves and agreements were reached at the cost of Kabul's troops. In Samangan province, for example, guerrillas were convinced not to attack Soviet troops anymore and even to assume the task of guarding the pipeline from the USSR in the mountains, in exchange for flour and oil. While relations with the Soviets became so warm that mujahidin even went to visit the regimental base, attacks against government units continued.[5]

According to the report of a Spetnaz officer, it did not take long for the Soviets to realize that the mujahidin had two reasons to cooperate with the Red Army and the government: tensions between different clans and the desire of certain tribes to live in peace with the Russians, whose great military strength (or, more appropriately, destructive power) they feared. The latter tribes in particular favoured agreements with the KGB or with the GRU, to whom they would pass information about the movements of mujahidin caravans in their territory. Sometimes, officers in command of Spetnaz units were welcomed as their equals by tribal notables. Significantly, some of these tribes or local groups refused outright to have similar contacts with Kabul.[6]

Even in Herat province where, thanks to fierce conflict among mujahidin groups, for the first time two groups were brought over to the government side, early contacts were generally the conclusion of a long and tricky process. Every Red Army commander was responsible for his own zone and was given detailed information about the presence of mujahidin. The first step was to distinguish the orientations of the different groups. Even a simple contact with the Soviets was a guarantee that attacks against the mujahidin group would not be carried out immediately. Furthermore, the group would be given medicines and food. Some sort of 'informative contact', i.e. involving collaborators with the intelligence service, existed in practically every group of the region, so whenever it was reported that a certain rebel commander was

[5] A. Heinamaa, Maija Leppanen, Y. Yurchenko, *The Soldiers' Story*, University of California Press, 1994, pp. 113-17.

[6] Tchikichev, *Spetnaz en Afghanistan*, p. 63; Gromov, *Ogranichennyi kontingent*, pp. 142-4.

wavering, he would immediately be sent some help, without waiting for his answer to a proposal to deal. Once a meeting was agreed upon, negotiations would start at the lowest level and then they would move upwards step by step, to the highest levels of authority considered suitable by the Supreme Command.[7]

This kind of relationship developed in every region of the country, at first 'illegally', then with the full sanction and approval of the 40th Army command. Particular care was devoted to the road to Termez, but cooperation was also quite well developed with groups North and East of Kabul, on the road to Jallalabad, in Herat and in the Sarobi area. On the other hand, relationships were difficult with groups operating South and West of Kabul and it came to be very hard to stabilize the situation in Bagram and around the airport, though after a while some progress was recorded here too. In conclusion, some improvements were registered from winter 1981/2, as communications between Kabul and Paktia and Laghman became easier and transports were not hindered as happened during the previous year. According to General Gromov, in nine years of war not a single mujahidin unit refused to sign a ceasefire of at least some duration.[8]

These tactics were progressively adopted and refined by the government in the course of the war and became a constant part of its activities up to 1992, as many of the examples which follow will show.

The most obvious opportunity for the government to intervene was provided by strains among mujahidin groups, when it could attempt to bring one of the conflicting factions onto its side. Often it was a matter of blood feuds; for example M. Pohly cites the case of a 100-strong mujahidin group which went over to the government because its leader had been assassinated by another group. Sometimes the pattern was repeated on a much larger scale: in Ghor province, during National Reconciliation, the bulk of Harakat-i Inqilab mujahidin entered the government militias in order to fight more effectively against their local rivals of Hizb-i Islami. One of the Harakat commanders who took this opportunity was Ibrahim Beg of Tagai Timur, who went over to the government in the summer of 1989 and who, during the war, had lost 250

---

[7] Gromov, *Ogranichennyi kontingent*, p. 142-4.

[8] *Ibid.*, pp. 264-6; *Tages Anzeiger Magazin*, 17 July 1982.

men fighting against his mujahidin rivals and only twelve against the Soviets. He declared to journalists that he had accepted Kabul's offer because, since the Soviets had left, the government was no longer infidel and, moreover, because weapons supplies from Pakistan had dried up.[9]

But it was not necessarily a matter of rival groups aiming to improve their military position in the conflict against rivals within the 'Resistance'. Many villages also accepted deals with the government, in order to escape from continuous internecine warfare waged by neighbouring armed groups. In 1986, for example, in a Northern area, 3,000 Uzbek families, alienated by the 'fratricidal' war between two mujahidin parties, Jamiat and Hizb, went over to the government and formed militias. Even in Kajaki district (Helmand province) the arrival of Soviet troops was welcomed by part of the population in 1988, as a consequence of the ferocious conflicts between mujahidin which had shaken the region.[10]

Often local rivalries had an ethnic flavour. In fact it was in the ethnically mixed areas that the government was particularly successful. In the Pashtun villages in Daulatabad. district (Faryab province), for example, many enrolled in the militias because of their hatred for the traditional ethnic rivals. The Kabul government tried to profit from tensions between Uzbeks and Pashtuns throughout the whole of Faryab province and an analogous reason must be behind the case of the Turkmens in the Marochaq area (Baghdis province), who formed a militia after the Soviet invasion.[11]

Violence and abuse carried out by mujahidin against the civilian population was obviously a blessing for the government, which usually hurried to exploit the resentment it aroused. In much the same way as government repression had been one of the causes which had led so many Afghans to hate the Democratic Republic, similar behaviour by resistance groups (even if relatively less fierce on the whole) achieved the opposite effect. As early as 1980, in

[9] M. Pohly, *Krieg und Widerstand in Afghanistan*, Das Arabische Buch, 1992, p. 365; *AIC MB*, Oct. 1989, p. 19; N. Danziger, *Danziger's Adventures*, HarperCollins, 1992, p. 208-10.

[10] Pohly, *Krieg*, p. 382; Urban, *War in Afghanistan*, p. 240.

[11] *Afghanistan Info*, Jan.-Feb. 1984, p. 13; *AIC MB* Oct. 1989, p. 10, and Sept. 1984.

Kunduz province, a bloody punitive expedition by Jamiat caused the population of a whole valley to go over to the government and to form what became the strongest group of militiamen in the province. In 1981 one of the party publications of Jamiat recognized that episodes of abuses against civilians were discouraging potential supporters. Throughout the war, Islamist parties were often responsible for pushing many villages towards Kabul with their abuses. This sort of problem increased when collaboration with the government and the occupiers became more common. In 1984 a flight of part of the population from Kunar province because of excessive taxation from the mujahidin was reported. Refugees arriving in Pakistan from Afghanistan reported that the Resistance was losing its prestige in several regions. In 1985, according to some sources, the assembly of Afghan refugees in Isfahan decided that it was better to deal with the government in Kabul, rather than tolerate Iranian repression. A pro-mujahidin mullah reported to a Western traveller that in the second half of the 1980s many 'neutral' Afghans were killed by mujahidin in the Nazian valley south of Jallalabad, since the fact that their villages were not bombed by the air force was deemed sufficient proof that they were 'collaborationists'. Finally (but the list could continue) the case of the town of Kunduz can be cited, where as early as 1987 it was reported that refugees leaving the province were not fleeing to escape government bombings, but mujahidin infighting. The town was briefly occupied by the mujahidin during the initial phase of the Soviet withdrawal, in 1988. According to Soviet secret documents based on intelligence sources, because of the violence committed by the mujahidin on that occasion the population, who had welcomed them like heroes, became hostile. As a result, some neighbouring commanders, like Mulham Dasseghi, accepted reconciliation with the government. The violence has been confirmed by 'private Western aid workers'.[12]

It is not at all surprising that KhAD was involved in such

---

[12] Pohly, *Krieg*, pp. 381, 382, 425; V. Spolnikov, *Afganistan: islamskaya oppositsiya*, Moscow: Nauka, 1990, p. 78; O'Ballance, *Wars in Afghanistan*, pp. 126, 132; *Le Monde*, 28 Dec. 1984; *Journal de Genève*, 10 Nov. 1987; *L'Unità*, 5 Feb. 1989; Lyakhovskii, *Tragediya i doblest' Afgana*, p. 404; Steven R. Galster and Jochen Hippler, 'Report from Afghanistan', *Middle East Report*, May-June 1989, p. 39; R. Schultheis, *Night Letters: Inside Wartime Afghanistan*, Orion Books, New York, 1992, pp. 97-8.

activities, especially where Kabul's influence was slight and an open approach would be too dangerous. KhAD's influence was in fact proportionally higher when the party was weak and/or divided, as in Faryab province in the early 1980s. According to information from the Resistance, KhAD members tended to work in their original regions, utilizing ethnic, tribal and kin solidarity. Their role was particularly important when the aim was to strengthen the traditional segmentation of Afghan society in antagonist solidarity groups, in order to divide the Resistance. Allegedly the Clans and Tribes Department of the Ministry for Tribal and Frontier Affairs was led by the same man who was in charge of the equivalent department of KhAD. A typical example of the pattern followed by KhAD is given by one case reported from Zabul province in May 1984. Two 'major figures' in the local administration contacted local tribal chiefs to propose a ceasefire agreement. It is not clear whether the practice of taking hostages among the notables was common, but in this case four tribal elders from the local population were kept at the provincial centre in order to ensure the safety of the KhAD agents who were meeting with the chiefs. The latter were offered regular salaries and the cessation of bombings in their tribal areas in exchange for putting an end to ambushes against convoys and attacks on Afghan army posts. On this occasion, after the KhAD members returned to the capital and the hostages were released, the tribal chiefs turned down the offer, and regime aircrafts resumed air strikes soon thereafter, but in other instances conditions were often created for the establishment of ceasefires with local armed groups, which were then turned against their neighbours, without demanding any ideological accomodation. Only later these groups might be transformed into openly pro-government militias. Finally, once the area was more or less cleansed of mujahidin, the state apparatus was progressively reintroduced. A ceremony marked the side-switching, with the former mujahidin grouping together to form a circle and laying down their weapons to symbolize the end of their opposition to the government. They would then take their weapons back to 'defend the Revolution'. KhAD's role was a key one particularly when 'informal' agreements were negotiated. Such accords were necessary where the government was not strong enough to support militias openly. By the end of 1983 'dozens and dozens' of such agreements had been signed, and they covered 10,000 mujahidin by May 1988. KhAD's activities were also directed at the general population, with the dissemination of arguments like 'an end to the war', 'the state is no longer communist' and, after Soviet withdrawal, 'there are no more Soviets', 'peace among Afghans'.[13]

Soon the government also realized that the ambition of many local and regional mujahidin commanders to expand their own power base offered great opportunities to gain some influence in the countryside. In particular, it was discovered that it was much easier to attract the leaders of hierarchically structured tribes (*rutwali*) on this basis. Furthermore, they were much more capable of changing the attitude of the members of their tribe. On the other hand, the closer the tribal structure was to 'democratic' (in the form of the *qawm*), as the border tribes of the East were to a considerable extent, the more government efforts tended to be useless, since even when the notable was drawn onto Kabul's side, his followers could perfectly well chose another notable and continue their fight against the regime. So in some cases tribal authorities ('elders') would hamper government attempts to form effective militias even among pro-Kabul clans, simply to safeguard tribal traditions. Among the Tani, for example, the formation of a Border Militia regiment in spring 1984 was rendered useless by the intervention of the elders, who collected the weapons given by the government to the militiamen and redistributed them among all the tribesmen, including pro-mujahidin ones. In other cases, tribal authorities would strike agreements with Kabul even when facing strong opposition from their own tribesmen.[14]

Yet another quite obvious way of influencing life in the

---

[13] O. Roy in *Le Monde*, 17 Nov. 1983; G. Dorronsoro and C. Lobato, 'The militia in Afghanistan', *Central Asian Survey*, no. 4 (1989), p. 101; *Est et Ouest* Nov. 1985, pp. 15, 16; V. Nosatov, 'Afganskii Dnevnik', *Prostor*, 11 (1989), p. 121; O. Roy, 'La politique de pacification sur le terrain' in A. Brigot, O. Roy, *La guerre d'Afghanistan*, La Documentation Française, 1985, p. 66; Strmecki, 'Power Assessment', p. 322–3; Amstutz, *Afghanistan: The First Five Years of Soviet Occupation*, p. 292; *L'Humanité*, 24 May 1988.

[14] I.E. Katkov, 'Tsentral'naya vlast' Afganistana i pushtunskie plemena', diss., Moscow, IV AN SSSR, 1987, p. 182; H. Taniwal and A.Y. Nuristani, 'Pashtun tribes and the Afghan Resistance', *WUFA*, vol. 1, no. 1, (1985) p. 48; Selig S. Harrison, 'A breakthrough in Afghanistan?', *Foreign Policy*, no. 51 (1983), p. 12.

countryside was the economic lever. As a Soviet scholar noted, the relationship between a tribe and the state or other political organization was always based on material interests. This was probably one of the reasons behind the establishment, from 1983, of a national power grid which, in accordance with Lenin's dictum, would make it possible to reward with electricity those villages that agreed to enter the network of government-sponsored local councils. A glimpse of direct economic support to agriculture has already been given in Part I, but the government also resorted to more sophisticated tactics. Particularly in Northern Afghanistan, 'the struggle over food versus commercial crops had become a key issues in the battle for social control'. Reports from some provinces tell of 'peasants being pressurized by the government to produce cash crops and by the resistance subsistence crops'. The outcome was not particularly encouraging for the government, as in 1986 the distribution of 2,000 tons of seed only led to the production of 14,000 tons of cotton, while in the 1970s peasants were given 65-80 tons of seed to produce 40-50,000 tons of cotton. The government also kept raising the purchase price of cotton and other commercial crops up to 1991 to encourage production. In other cases, massive purchases of wheat at high prices were carried out by government authorities, as reported from Kunduz, Balkh and Badakhshan provinces in 1982 and from Helmand province in 1985, in order to raise prices for the mujahidin and to reduce the availability of food during winter, but such efforts met scant success. Preventive purchases of pack animals for transport were also reported in the Eastern provinces. One problem in exercizing economic pressure on the countryside lay in the fact that economic conditions for peasants were better in some zones outside Kabul's control than in areas controlled by the government, to such an extent that the latter areas imported goods from the former ones, which in turn had received their supplies from Pakistan. Only where devastation had been really large-scale, as in Herat province, or where famines had been raging, as in Faryab in autumn/winter 1989/90, or where support was coupled with a certain strategic superiority on the part of the government, which made widespread reprisals redundant, like in Balkh province, could economic support tip the balance in the war for the hearts and minds of the people. Faryab province was a particularly successful case, as the shipment of many tons of wheat brought a large number of mujahidin onto the government side. These policies, however, were very expensive in the long run and increased the vulnerability of the state to supply crises. As Najibullah stated in mid-1987, the distribution of food to the localities actually caused a decline in production, as wheat was being transferred to regions 'which previously not only maintained themselves, but sold their surplus products'.[15]

Tribal policy

The traditional border tribe policy of Afghan governments gave the Karmal regime a ready instrument to exploit in order to relieve the situation in the border areas, where armed opposition was more active in the early phase of the war. Even Amin appears to have tried such an approach in late 1979, meeting with some success, according to some sources. An early attempt by Karmal to send delegations to the provinces achieved few results as most of the delegations could not reach their destinations. Governors were instructed to summon local notables and explain the approach of the new government to them, also with little success. In April 1980 the PDPA Central Committee stressed the importance of the 'traditional policy of peace and cooperation of the Afghan state with the border tribes'. The tribes were to be helped economically, their traditions would be respected and a *jirgah* of tribal representatives would be created within the forthcoming National Fatherland Front (see Chapter 12). The Basic Principles of the DRA attributed a 'patriotic role' to the tribal chiefs and notables in keeping peace in the tribal areas and announced the establishment of the *Loya Jirgah* (the traditional tribal council) as a state institution.[16] It took quite a long time however, to put all these projects into practice. In the course of 1980 the Ministry of Tribal and Frontier

---

[15] Rubin, *The Fragmentation of Afghanistan*, pp. 145, 173; 'Sekretnye dokumkenty iz osobykh papok', *Voprosy Istorii*, no. 3 (1993), p. 25; Danziger, *Danziger's Adventures*, p. 197; *Chicago Tribune*, 22 Feb. 1990; Katkov, *Tsentral'naya vlast'*, p. 176; O'Ballance, *Wars in Afghanistan*, p. 130; Strmecki, 'Power Assessment', p. 374; Reuters, Sept. 18, 1986; Najibullah, CC Plenum on 10 June, RA, 14 June 1987; Fullerton, *The Soviet Occupation of Afghanistan*, p. 171.

[16] *NT*, 52 (1986), M. Hassan Kakar, *Afghanistan: the Soviet Invasion and the Afghan Response*, p. 127; *Aktual'nye problemy afganskoi revolyutsii*, pp. 565-6; B. Male, *Revolutionary Afghanistan*, Croom Helm 1982, p. 196.

Affairs launched a new wave of initiatives designed to raise the priority given to tribal policy. The organization of the Ministry was based on three main agencies at Jallalabad, Kandahar and Khost and several less important departments in Asmar, Asadabad, Torkham, Lashkargah, Spin Boldak. The area of main interest to the government appears clearly to have been made up of Kunar, Nangrahar, Paktia and Kandahar provinces. Each tribal zone was led by a deputy-minister, reportedly given full authority to spend money and do whatever necessary to pacify the local groups. At the outset, the activities of the Ministry were heavily hampered by the scarcity of human and financial resources. The Ministry could in fact count on barely 100 cadres, some of which were suspected of cooperating with the mujahidin. There was not even enough money to pay the officials, let alone rewarding notables and tribal leaders for their cooperation. Financial problems were resolved after a while, but problems of coordination among the activities of the Ministry remained, in much the same way as conflicts of competence with other ministries and organs of the state (Defence, Interior, Transport, Commerce, Finance, KhAD). Although more personnel became available later, the quality was still deemed insufficient at the end of 1985, when Karmal asserted the need to appoint 'a number of experienced cadres from the party and government machinery who are from the tribal regions or from the tribes themselves and possess a profound knowledge of tribal issues, in order to strengthen [the Ministry]'. And obviously, as in any other field of activity of the DRA, 'representatives of the Ministry of Nationalities and Tribal Affairs in the localities' were accused by Karmal of working 'in most cases' 'inactively and slowly'. This policy culminated in 1986 with the enactemnent of a law that sanctioned the traditional rights of the tribes.[17]

The start looked quite promising. According to the judgement of a Pakistani (North West Frontier Province – NWFP) politician, the very fact that ministers were receiving tribesmen played a positive role, stimulating their sense of self-importance. Some of the tribes which were fighting against the government at the end of 1979 stopped doing so the following year. During 1980 the

---

[17] A. Rasul Amin, 'Stealthy sovietisation of Afghanistan', *Central Asian Survey*, vol. 3, no. 1, 1984, p. 59; *Aktual'nye problemy afganskoi revolyutsii*, p. 569; Karmal, RA, 20 Dec. 1985; Karmal, XV plenum, RA, 27 March 1985.

Minister of Tribal and Frontier affairs, Faiz Mohammed, who had already occupied this position under Daoud, succeeded in striking a deal with some clans of the Shinwari, Mohmand and Tani tribes, according to which they would supply 7,000 militiamen, and then also with sections of the Mangal and Zazay tribes, thanks to their estrangement from the fundamentalists. More generally, thanks to his activities during the summer of 1980 the confrontation between the state and tribes subsided somewhat, but Faiz was later assassinated during a similar attempt with the Jadran tribe. His successor Suleiman Laeq continued his policy, assisted by the fact that by the end of 1981 the government had finally come to the conclusion that the tribal problem could only be resolved in the framework of a long-term compromise and that no purely military solution was within reach. In December 1981 a new policy with regard to the tribes was announced (significantly by Najibullah) at the plenum of the CC. After 1982, following more than a year of virtual stasis, discussions with tribal notables began to yield better results, basically thanks to the readiness of the state to sign agreements according to which all state activity in the tribal areas would be regulated and planned. The tribes were asked not to carry out armed action against the state, to deny support and passage over their territories to the mujahidin and to guarantee the safety of government convoys. The state offered in exchange to deliver various kinds of goods, to open schools and health centres, build mosques and not to interfere with local traditions. Minister Laeq also favoured the re-establishment of bazaars in the tribal areas, in order to attract the tribes, which 'could not do without' them.[18]

So Laeq succeeded in establishing a good relationship with elders particularly in Nangrahar province, while negotiations with notables from Nuristan after 1983 may have played a role in a later agreement with Sarwar Nuristani, a warlord who controlled part of the region. The new approach paved the way for agreements with clans of the Jaji, Safi and Mangal tribes, and 'basis was laid' for 'further progress' with tribes in Kunar and Helmand. Laeq

[18] *Asiaweek*, 29 June 1986, p. 37; Observer News Service, 31 Dec. 1980; T. Gaidar, *Pod afganskim nebom*, Sovetskaya Rossiya, 1981, p. 61; Hyman, *Afghanistan under Soviet domination*, Macmillan, 1984, p. 191; Hassan Kakar, *Afghanistan: the Soviet invasion*, p. 193; *Aktual'nye problemy afganskoi revolyutsii*, pp. 567, 570, 571, 572; Leonov, *Likholet'e*, pp. 270-1.

himself survived at least one attempt on his life during his activities in the tribal areas of Laghman province.[19]

Notwithstanding all the problems it. had to face, the Ministry engaged in considerable activity. In 1983 all hotels in Kabul were reported to be under its control and were filled with its 'guests' from the tribal areas. In 1361 (1983/4) 700 meetings were held with tribal authorities in the whole of Afghanistan and by 1983 Laeq could claim, to a KGB general, that he had won over to his side not less than 5,000 tribal notables. The quality of their support, however, is questionable. In reality, government documents themselves stated that the number of tribal notables the government could seriously rely on was much lower, about 500 altogether: in the province of Kandahar 80; Zabul 20; Paktika 50; Paktia 100; Nangrahar 150 and Kunar 100.[20]

The basic logic of tribal policy was that in general Pashtun tribes were more amenable than other sectors of the population to the government's attempts to 'buy' their support, and this was a sound judgement, although at least from 1981 the same policy began to be applied countrywide. But it was also true that most of those tribal groups which agreed to establish contacts with the government maintained their independence and, as Najibullah put it, wanted 'to keep their feet in two camps'. Faiz Mohammed was fully aware of the impossibility of bringing the frontier tribes permanently onto his side, as he declared to a Soviet interlocutor as early as April 1980, but he also knew that similar attempts by the Islamist parties were going to fail too. It was rather a matter of gaining better positions than the Islamist rivals in the game of manipulating the tribal interests. At the XII Plenum of the CC (July 1983) Karmal explicitly asserted his intention to utilize traditions in order to stabilize the Revolution, but without being enslaved by them. By the end of the year, party cadres were receiving instructions to establish as solid as possible contacts with

---

[19] K. Ege, *Confidence in Kabul. A political solution for Afghanistan*, unpubli. ms., n.d. (1983), p. 3; *Tages-Anzeiger*, 28 Dec. 1981; *Aktual'nye problemy afganskoi revolyutsii*, p. 572.

[20] Yu. Gankovskii, 'Polosa pushtunskikh plemen Afganistana', *Spetsial'nyi Byulleten' AN SSSR IV* no. 6 (1987), pp. 110, 115 n. 14; Leonov, *Likholet'e*, pp. 270-1; A. J. Khalil, 'My impressions of Afghanistan's visit', *Central Asia*, no. 13 (1983), pp. 193-4.

notables and clergymen and to consult them regularly, in order to 'canalize' their influence towards the 'revolutionary state'.[21]

If the tribal population as a whole was not very sensitive to political arguments, the nomadic part of it was even less so. Nomads seemed to think that the new government did not differ much from previous ones. They had been exempted from conscription (provided they formed border militias) and were given veterinary clinics and mobile schools, although a propaganda campaign in favour of sedentarization was also promoted by Kabul.[22]

Apart from the guarantee that the customs and traditions of the nomads, as much as their 'existing traditional tribal, commercial, economic, cultural and family relations and also the migration routes' would be respected, measures taken in order to please the tribes included the digging and construction of artesian wells for irrigation, improvement in veterinary services, organization of health centres and construction of schools. Goods were supposed 'in the first instance to be distributed justly among tribal inhabitants who are actively co-operating with the DRA, and the families of those who defend the gains of the Saur Revolution with arms'.[23]

Although some successes were recorded in 1980 and in 1982, as has been shown, the overall pace of tribal policy was disappointing. The flux of local groups going over to Kabul seems not to have been totally insignificant in some areas, as for example the plains of Kunar province, where according to a journalist (sympathetic to the government) in 1980 twelve Mohmand and three Safi leaders had taken such a step. Still in 1985 Karmal asked for 'serious attention' to be paid 'to establishing, expanding and strengthening relations with tribal leaders and elders, mullahs and clergy of the border regions', as earlier attempts had not been successful enough.[24]

One factor which diminished the attraction of Kabul's tribal

---

[21] RA, 22 Nov. 1986; Mahbub, 'Moralische Aspekte im Islam', p. 48; Katkov, *Tsentral'naya vlast'*, p. 175; S. Bazgar, *Afghanistan. La résistance au coeur*, Paris: Denoël, 1987, annex 3, p. 191.

[22] G. Pedersen, 'Is there a future for the nomads of Afghanistan?', *WUFA*, vol. 3, no. 4 (1988), p. 77.

[23] Karmal, 15th plenum PDPA–CC, RA, 27 March 1985.

[24] *L'Humanité*, 3 July 1980, 3 Jan. 1981; Karmal, XV CC Plenum, RA, 27 March 1985.

policy was the counter-measures put into effect by the mujahidin. For example in summer 1982 a Mangal notable, Din Gol' Mangal, was kidnapped in Pakistan and asked to cease his collaboration with the government. He was executed after his refusal. But another obstacle lay within the government itself. Factional in-fighting and disagreements within the Afghan state made the con-duct of a unified strategy impossible. A Soviet scholar complained in 1984 that some Parchami leaders favoured the use of force against the tribes, in order to get rid of them once and for all, and they therefore did their best to undermine the activities of the Ministry and the prestige of Minister Laeq himself. Certainly, the dispatching of vital goods to the tribes was often interrupted. Tribal headmen complained that these actions weakened their authority and hence the prospects of 'pacification' they supported. Karmal himself often complained about this: the goods destined for the tribes often did not go farther then the provincial centre, or were sold on the black market. It was decided that it was necessary to take effective measures in the border provinces, to be implemented as soon as possible. Special attention was to be paid to the issue of the provision and mobilization of transport vehicles, including tribal transport, to the transfer of goods to the border regions, and to the transportation of tribal products to Kabul and other regions of the country. Karmal also proposed the formation of an operational group of 'responsible officials possessing authority and sufficient power to enable them to resolve most of the cases directly in the localities'. But one year later the new President Najibullah was still complaining that the governmen-tal departments had violated the protocols with the tribes. In some cases it was the Red Army that caused trouble, as with the Zazay in 1981, when it entered the tribal territories, violating the accords and causing the militias to rebel.[25]

In short, the poor results obtained in the first period were due to the realization by some group leaders that the Democratic

---

[25] *PAP*, 28 Jan. 1981; *Neues Deutschland*, 17 April 1981; Karmal, XV plenum CC –PDPA, RA, 27 March 1985; Yu. Gankovskii, 'O putiakh prekrasheniya grazhdanskoi voiny v Afganistane', *Vostok i Sovremennost'* no. 3 (1993) p. 84; Karmal at the XV plenum PDPA –CC, quoted in Ludwig, 'Einige Probleme', p. 112; RA, 30 March 1986, 22 Nov. 1986; Hassan Kakar, *Afghanistan: the Soviet invasion*, p. 176; *Aktual'nye problemy afganskoi revolyutsii*, pp. 568-9, 572; Karmal, RA, 20 Dec. 1985.

Republic would not fall quickly. Also the less bloody character of the new regime (compared to Amin's) contributed to some extent. Some of the most 'opportunist' (or least ideologized) elements of the opposition took a way opposite to the one taken at the same time by other more nationalistic or xenophobic sectors of the population. In the end the Soviet invasion had two contrasting effects: on one side it pushed many into active opposition, on the other, it made a short-term fall of the Karmal regime unrealistic. The more the Democratic Republic consolidated itself, the more its credibility as an alternative choice for discontented or battle-shy mujahidin groups gained strength. The general breakdown of state power in 1979 and early 1980 had encouraged many local groups to assert their independence but, as at least a shadow of state power was re-established, together with the capacity to conduct reprisals and to distribute resources, some of them chose to accept deals.

12

THE FIRST POLITICAL STRATEGY
OF 'PACIFICATION'

The local organs of power

The first development of the tribal policy, in the direction of an attempt to stabilize as much as possible the relationship with the border tribes, took the form of the institutionalization of the *jirgah*, the traditional tribal assembly, and its adoption in the whole of the country, i.e. even outside the tribal areas, as a sort of local council. Amin had already organized *jirgahs* of tribal notables and many *jirgahs* had been held in 1979 and 1980 by the rebellious tribes, often sponsored by the traditionalist opposition parties, which hoped to use them to check the advance of the Islamist parties, but it is not clear where the government took its inspiration from.

The first *jirgahs* were held by the government as temporary gatherings of notables as early as 1360 (1981/2), with a total of 150 in that year, although they were soon recognized as not very effective. In 1981 a draft Law of the Local Organs of State Power had been submitted, but it took until June 1984 to have it approved, after a 'deep debate'. It established permanent local *jirgahs*, to act as local administration councils down to the village level and to be elected by the population. These *jirgahs* were to become the highest state organs in their respective areas and matters as important as conscription would (according to the law) be left to their decisions. The PDPA, the National Fatherland Front (see next section) and the other cooperative, social and political organizations had the right to appoint candidates to become people's representatives for local *jirgahs*; an election by the population (by show of hands) would then follow. Once elected, the *jirgahs* would perform their activities on the basis of the 'consistent party line', toward the consolidation of the gains of the Saur Revolution and 'the abolition of the remnants of the feudalistic and pre-feudalistic relations'. Their duties included cooperation in the implementation of the social reforms and of the literacy campaign and helping with conscription. The stated aim was to 'valorize the *jirgah* as pillar of the new articulation of the local powers', i.e. transform it into an institutional link with the central power. With an ambiguous formulation, the law guaranteed 'the right of broad participation by all true patriots ... and credible social personalities of all nationalities, tribes and clans'. The government apparently put much hope in this new institution and as early as in February 1984 the first sixty-three graduates of the Faculty of Local Organs of the State Power (part of the Institute of Social Sciences of the PDPA CC) received their diplomas. The faculty had been created two years earlier.[26]

A large-scale *jirgah* campaign was launched in 1985, after long planning which had begun no later than early 1983, in order to spread throughout the country the idea that the government respected traditions and allowed a measure of local self-government. The two main events were the *Loya Jirgahs* held in Kabul in April (bringing together representatives from all around Afghanistan) and September 1985 (gathering the border tribes), with the participation of 1,796 people in the first case and 3,700 (mainly NWFP Pashtuns) in the second one; they were the culmination of the previous campaign for the election of local councils. By no means all the participants were tribal notables – at the *jirgah* held in April they amounted to 25.4% of the total, plus another 11% who were clerics, while 130 representatives of the 'old regime' and thirty-eight militia commanders were also there. In the September *jirgah* notables were much more heavily represented, making up 60% of the participants, with the clergy accounting for a further 10%. It is difficult to say how much influence these initiatives may have had, but the mujahidin were undoubtedly irritated and a wave of assassinations of 'collaborationists' was trigged. In parallel and in connection to the *Loya Jirgah* organized in Kabul, the

[26] *KNT*, 12 Feb. 1984; 'Draft of the law on the local organs of state power and administration', *Bakhtar*, 30 Sept. 1981; *KNT*, 3 and 4 Oct. 1981; A. Rasul Amin; 'Local organs of Soviet pattern in Afghanistan', *WUFA*, vol. 1, no. 4 (1986), pp. 61-2; *L'Unità*, 4 Jan. 1984; 'DRA Revolutionary Council Statement on Sowr Revolution', *RA*, 13 Nov. 1985; *Bakhtar*, 22 Feb. 1984; *Aktual'nye problemy afganskoi revolyutsii*, p. 571.

government tried to organize permanent *jirgahs* in as many localities as possible. The tribal *jirgahs* were supposed to represent each tribe and eighty-eight of them were organized in 1985-6 in the Frontier Areas, with 500 'trustworthy' tribal representatives taking part. Every town had his own *jirgah*, while the village ones soon numbered in the hundreds.[27]

Once the form of elections is considered, 'broad participation' and democracy appear mere rhetorical concepts. In the August 1985 elections for the local *jirgah* of Kabul city, out of 466 candidates, 413 were elected unanimously, forty-eight by a majority and five were rejected. This appears to have been the foremost display of democracy in local elections. Just outside the capital, in the province of Kabul, all of the 591 candidates were elected unanimously. Participation in the vote was 90.3% and votes against were only 0.22%.[28]

In fact the role of the *jirgahs* was merely consultative. In Karmal's words 'tribal leaders and members of permanent *jirgahs* ... should be attracted, through active co-operation with revolutionary power based on common interests, to solve local problems and deal with the needs of the inhabitants.' He also maintained that where this was achieved, 'the people also begin to co-operate actively with the government. The party and state organs thereby strengthen their influence on the tribal masses'. A limited improvement in the capacity of the government to recruit local clans was indeed noted by some observers in 1984, but once again Kabul found it difficult to implement the policies it had devised. Even the start was quite slow, as by July 1986 *jirgahs* had been created in only 1,300 residential localities. Furthermore, as President Najibullah would admit later, 'the expansion of central and local organs has been implemented mainly by including members of the intelligentsia, whereas the representatives of private investors, traders, peasants, small landowners and nomads have been forgotten or their representation is very small'. Out of 14,000 people elected

---

[27] Karmal, RA, 15 March 1983; M. Baryalay, 'National Traditions serve the revolution', *WMR*, 4 (1986) p. 90; B. Kh. Umarov, 'Stanovlenie i tendentsii razvitiya politiki natsional'nogo primireniya v Afganistane', Tashkent, diss., 1990, pp. 50-1; A. Sadat, *Afghanistan: Land of Jirgahs*, Kabul, 1986, p. 26.

[28] Ludwig, 'Einige Probleme', p. 103; M. Baryalay, 'National Traditions serve the revolution', *WMR*, 4 (1986), p. 92.

to the local *jirgahs*, no less than 2,500 were teachers and 4,338 were members of the intelligentsia as a whole. Karmal himself complained that among the 'shortcomings and deficiencies in the work with the frontier tribes' was also to be added the fact that the consultative *jirgahs* were not regularly held. At one point in summer 1986 it was admitted that new local councils had not yet been converted into 'genuine organs'.[29]

Furthermore, the majority of the local notables were not very eager to support the formation of such organs, even when they favoured contacts with the government, particularly as these councils were associated with the implementation of the socio-economic reforms, albeit in a sweetened form. One additional, but serious shortcoming, lay in the fact that, in Najibullah's words, the local organs had no real power with regard to serious problems, due to the sabotage of the local party officers, who did not want to lose their power.[30]

It is noteworthy that while plans to restructure the local administration on a *jirgah* basis were being drafted, a different trend was going on at the level of the provincial administration. Traditionally in Afghanistan local power had been concentrated in the hands of the provincial governors, but after the Revolution this power was transferred into the hands of the party organs. These transformations had been resisted not just by peasants, who continued to deal with governors for the majority of their requests and complaints, but also by many governors, as is reported for example by a Soviet interpreter about the governor of Ghazni province in 1983-4 and admitted by Karmal himself in late 1984. Apparently Karmal accentuated such a policy from early 1982 and provincial party secretaries 'were supreme'.[31]

[29] Karmal, XV plenum CC, RA, 27 March 1985; Karmal, RA, 8 July 1986; Najibullah, 20th plenum, RA, 22 Nov. 1986; Najibullah, RA, 7 Oct. 1986; RA, 4 Oct. 1986; Karmal, *Speech at the 17th Plenum of the PDPA – CC, March 1986*, p. 15; *Bakhtar*, 12 July 1986.

[30] *Aktual'nye problemy afganskoi revolyutsii*, p. 574; Najibullah at the XIX Plenum CC-PDPA (July 1986), quoted in V. Plastun, 'NDPA: voprosy edinstva i soyuznikov na sovremennom etape revolyutsii', *Spetsial'nyi Byulleten' IV AN SSSR*, no. 6 (1987), pp. 129-30.

[31] M. Olimov, 'Iz zapisok perevodchika', *Vostok* no. 3, p. 61 (1991); Hassan Kakar, *Afghanistan: the Soviet invasion*, p. 197; Karmal, XIV Plenum CC, RA, 21 Sept. 1984.

Soon, in any case, the process was reversed. The governors' authority was increased by the decision to let them appoint district and subdistrict governors (in consultation with provincial party committees), while 'provincial headquarters' headed by governors were established. The autonomy of the provincial authorities was also increased by the approval of local state budgets. Governors were supposed to 'take into serious consideration the decisions and resolutions of the party and state leadership and the leadership of the party committees and act in accordance with their decisions', so that 'complete unison' could be achieved. The position of provincial governors became stronger in later years, when 'provincial party secretaries and commanders of the armed forces' units and police and provincial heads of state security were not only supposed to work closely with, but also to 'obey' them.[32]

The latter measure was allegedly enacted on the recommendation of Soviet advisers who in 1987-8 pressed for the strengthening of the power structure, including the Presidency, district governorship and village headship. This appears to have had positive effects, particularly when the governor was a locally-influential figure, as happened in later years in Herat and Kandahar (see Ch. 13, Section 3) and, according to Soviet claims, also (but to a lesser extent) in Nangrahar, Uruzgan and Helmand. With regard to Nangrahar province, a high-ranking officer in the KGB reported that the governor Wakil Azam Shinwari appeared much more in touch with the situation than the party secretary, who was only able to talk about propaganda activities and meetings. In most provinces, the governors proved unable to use the new powers entrusted to them effectively, and the management of the reform came under criticism by Soviet observers after the withdrawal, since although governors had become the 'real lords' of their provinces, they kept on relying on the centre (and the Red Army) to rid them of the mujahidin.[33]

Another aspect of the utilization of local government structures

---

[32] Keshtmand, RA, 26 June 1983; Najibullah, Plenum CC PDPA, RA, 23 Oct. 1988.

[33] Lyakhovskii, 'Na afganskoi vizhzhennoi zemle', p. 63; Merimskii, 'Voina v Afganistane: zapiski uchastika', p. 110; Lyakhovskii, *Tragediya i doblest' Afgana*, p. 356; Shebarshin, *Ruka Moskvy*, p. 188-9.

in the 'pacification' effort was the creation and upgrading of administrative units, clearly aimed at manipulating local interests. Several new sub-districts were created, as for example in Kabul province Goldara (Shakardara district) in 1983 and Musa'i (Charasiab district) in 1986. Other sub-districts were upgraded to districts, like Kaldar (Samangan province) in 1983. In 1983 Khost major district was directly subordinated to the General Department of Local Organs, thereby severing it from Paktia province. Even two new provinces were created, Sar-i Pul in 1988 and Nuristan a few months later.[34]

The *jirgah* reforms represented the extension of the tribal policy to the whole country. In this regard, the Ministry for Tribal and Frontier Affairs in May 1981 became the Ministry of Nationalities and Tribes, with directorates for nationalities and for tribes, the latter being in charge of dealing with local groups and communities all over the country.[35]

The National Fatherland Front

The first properly political attempt to find a solution to the condition of isolation in which the government found itself came in 1981. On 18 July 1981, an amnesty for counter-revolutionaries who laid down their weapons was declared – a *de facto* official acknowledgement of the impossibility of uprooting the rebellion solely by force (in fact an unofficial amnesty appears to have been in force even earlier). The main innovation was the creation of the 'National Fatherland Front' (NFF), a pro-PDPA mass organization, aimed at gathering the support of those ready to cooperate with the government but who did not share its ideological outlook. The idea of a 'broad national front' had in fact been launched by Karmal as early as March 1980, but, given the difficult situation, the campaign in favour of the Front only began in January 1981, with a wave of 'spontaneous' demonstrations. The first real step towards its formation was the establishment of a tribal *jirgah* in Kabul in May 1981, within the framework of the Ministry for Tribal and Frontier Affairs, which then expressed its support for the establishment of the Front (later it became one of the collective

[34] RA, 7 Feb. 1986; RA, 3 April 1988; RA, 14 March 1983.

[35] Rubin, *The Fragmentation of Afghanistan*, p. 134.

members of the Front). The inaugural congress was finally held in June 1981, after having been announced first for March, then for April and finally for May. It actually lasted just one day instead of the four originally foreseen. It took time for the Front to take root: the first Provincial Committees were formed from November 1981, while the first local NFF *jirgah* (nothing to do with the administrative *jirgahs*) was established in a village in Kabul province in December. In reality the first two years of activity of the NFF were not fruitful at all. It seems to have acquired real significance only after 1983, partly because its activities were slowed down by an assassination campaign against its senior members, twenty-seven of them being killed within one month of the founding congress.[36]

The Front was responsible for appointing mosque Imams, for local administration appointments, for the distribution of free assistance from the Soviet Union and so on. The President of the NFF, Saleh Mohammad Zeray, a prominent PDPA personality, maintained that he worked 'in strict cooperation with the tribal leaders'. In fact the PDPA enjoyed a position of absolute dominance within the NFF, where it held all of the key positions. The NFF was soon said to total 700,000 members, who later became 1,000,000, but in fact the vast majority were members of pre-existing affiliated organizations, like the Women's Democratic Council of Afghanistan, the Democratic Youth Organization of Afghanistan and the trade unions, all of them controlled by the PDPA. The real measure of the strength of the Front was given by individual members, who were much fewer in number: 67,000 in 1984. In 1986, at their peak, there were 112,209, not an insignificant amount but less than the PDPA itself. In May 1985, in an attempt to give the Front a boost, a new president was appointed, Abdul Rahim Hatif, a non-party trader personally close to his predecessor. This move may have had a limited pay-off,

[36] RA, 10 March 1980; *Bakhtar*, 14 Jan. 1981; RA, 20 May 1981; E. van Hollen, 'Afghanistan 18 months of Soviet occupation', Department of State Bulletin no. 2055, (Oct. 1981), p. 64; RA, 19 Nov. 1981; *Bakhtar*, 2 Dec. 1981; *Est et Ouest*, Nov. 1985, pp. 15, 16; *Aktual'nye problemy afganskoi revolyutsii*, p. 568; Cymkin T.M., 'Aftermath of the Saur coup: insurgency and counter-insurgency in Afghanistan', *Fletcher Forum*, summer 1982, p. 291.

as in 1985-6 for the first time a significant number of personalities enjoying a 'good muslim' image joined the Kabul regime.[37] The degree of NFF success in the countryside appears somewhat controversial. It represented only 295 villages in 1984 and 922 at the height of its expansion, in 1986, which meant that only 20% of its councils were active in the villages. However, most councils in the urban areas did little more than gather the members of the 'social organizations', so rural dwellers were a more significant percentage among individual members, although their absolute numbers were still far below expectations. In 1988 the pattern of membership was as follows: peasants 54.5%, small landlords 3%, workers 9%, artisans 13% and the intelligentsia 11%.

The initial aim of the government was to co-opt Pashtun notables, particularly from the frontier tribes. Instrumental in this was its first President Zeray who belonged to the Durrani tribe from Kandahar, while the leading circle in 1982 was made up of three Pashtuns, one Tajik and one Uzbek. The National Committee was more balanced, as its composition (ninety-six members) was 45.8% Pashtun, 35.4% Tajik, 5.2% Uzbek, 5.2% Hazara, 3.1% Turkmen and 5.1% other. In reality, whatever influence it acquired in rural areas, it was mainly concentrated in Northern areas, as is evident from Tables 44 and 45. The ethnic breakdown of individual membership (1988) confirms this, as Pashtuns accounted for only 30.4%, compared to 40% Tajiks, 13.5% Uzbeks, 7.7% Hazaras and 3.5% Turkmens. According to a French scholar, notables from the tribal areas found it easier and safer to escape to Pakistan, rather than siding with the government. Also the South-West (Nimroz, Farah, Helmand provinces) was reported to have shown some results, as well as the Kohistan and the Nuristan regions.[38]

---

[37] Najibullah, RA, 18 June 1986; Saleh Mohammad Zeary, *Neues Deutschland*, 28 Aug. 1981; Ludwig, 'Einige Probleme', p. 126; *Afghanistan Report*, 27 June 1986; Rubin, *The Fragmentation of Afghanistan*, p. 135; Chantal Lobato in *Defis Afghans*, no. 10 (Nov. 1986); 'Postanovlenie politburo TsK NDPA o dal'neishem povishenii roli NOF DRA v dele splocheniya patrioticheskikh sil strany', 26 sentyabrya 1984 g.' in *NDPA (sbornik dokumentov)*, Tashkent, 'Uzbekistan', 1986, p. 305.

[38] RA, 18 Oct. 1987; G. Dorronsoro, 'La politique de pacification en Afghanistan' in G. Chaliand (ed.), *Stratégies de la guerrilla*, Payot, 1994, pp. 457-8; CEREDAF, *Chronique des Evènements 1984-1985*, p. 20; AFP, 16 Sept. 1984; *Est et Ouest*,

In some local environments the NFF performed relatively satis-factorily in recruiting militias to oppose the mujahidin. In Sholgara district, for example, where the NFF enjoyed one of its first successes, the main resistance party (Jamiat-i Islami) was able to field 300 armed men at the beginning of 1984. The militias were formed here in January 1984, when Ismatullah Khan, a 'rich but illiterate landlord and clan leader', who claimed to be on bad terms with Jamiat because he had accepted the land reform before escaping to Pakistan in April 1979, made peace with the government and entered the NFF. He brought 340 men, 120 of them armed. Thanks to government support, he could rapidly field a 250-strong militia group.[39]

In itself the message conveyed by the Front in the countryside was very simple and easy to understand. It has been reported that the villagers in the southern part of Balkh province in 1985 knew that they could prevent their villages from being bombed by joining the NFF. Sometimes this kind of approach did succeed and agreements were negotiated with village elders, where a stop in the bombings was traded with a cut in the village ties to the Resistance. Then Resistance sources would charge 'some traditional leaders' with letting themselves be bought off, thanks to the 'naivity' of the peasants.[40]

In the end, however, the activity of the NFF over several years was disappointing. After 1987 its decline in the government's strategy appeared evident. At the Second PDPA Conference 'an alliance of various political forces in the NFF' was proposed, together with the transformation of the NFF into an 'independent institution', influential over the villages, but nothing came of it. President Najibullah himself declared in October 1987 that 'the

Jan. 1987; *Nouvelles d'Afghanistan*, July 1981 p. 8; J.J. Puig in *Est et Ouest*, Jan. 1987, p. 6; *L'Humanité* 24 May 1988; 'Postanovlenie politburo TsK NDPA o dal'neishem povishenii roli NOF DRA v dele splocheniya patrioticheskikh sil strany, 26 sentyabrya 1984 g.' in *NDPA (sbornik dokumentov)*, Tashkent, 'Uzbekistan', 1986, p. 305, 311; I.G. Maidan, *Problemy sotsial'noi bazy Aprelskoi Revolyutsii i politiki natsional'nogo primirenie v Afganistane*, Kiev, 1988, p. 28; *Aktual'nye problemy afganskoi revolyutsii*, pp. 604-5.

[39] *Journal de Genève*, 8 March 1984; J. Steele, 'Moscow's Kabul campaign', *Merip Reports*, July/Aug. 1986, p. 6.

[40] Rubin, *The Fragmentation of Afghanistan*, p. 143; *Journal de Genève*, 8 March 1984.

activities of the NFF are still largely characterized by formalism and only big cities are under its influence' and that 'this organization was considered as an integral part of the party and as lacking political independence'. The PDPA CC Plenum complained about the delay in the training of the cadres and about the fact that some positions had been given to inexperienced, uneducated and work-shy people. Its limited cooperation with the social organizations which composed it was also criticized. Its decline was also numerical. In 1988 a limited fall was recorded, with the total of individual members standing at 106,000, but in the following two years the decline quickened and at the beginning of 1990, shortly before its disbandment amid criticism of inactivity, only 72,665 individual members were left.[41]

The NFF policy clearly had advantages over the tribal policy, as has been pointed out, because it was not so easily reversible and its achievements were more durable. Unsurprisingly, it was not very popular among the border tribes. Elsewhere, a number of notables, who would never have accepted any contact with the party, now welcomed this non-ideological approach. On the other hand such a policy was heavily dependent on the military achievements of the Soviet and Afghan armies and even more so on the establishment of solid militias, otherwise the notables would often be forced to seek refuge in the towns, losing their rural clients, as indeed happened in many instances. The main shortcoming of the NFF was its limited impact on the creation of militias; it also failed in the more general aim of mobilizing society behind the regime. In 1984, for example, the Kabul NFF 'convinced' 500 youths to join the armed forces, a negligible fraction of the numbers from the capital actually drafted and the situation was not much different in 1986, the peak year of its activities, when in the whole of Afghanistan it recruited 3,685 people to the armed forces, 795 to the Self Defence groups and 1,300 to the GDRs. In the same year the literacy courses organized by the Front counted 17,000 participants, a small proportion of the whole effort.[42]

[41] TASS, 20 Oct. 1987; RA, 18 Oct. 1987; *KNT*, 5 March 1990; I.G. Maidan, *Problemy sotsial'noi bazy Aprelskoi Revolyutsii i politiki natsional'nogo primirenie v Afganistane*, Kiev, 1988, pp. 31, 28.

[42] O. Roy in *Défis Afghan*, no. 10 (Nov. 1986); G. Dorronsoro, 'La politique

Achievements and further initiatives

1983 was the first year to record what the Soviet foreign minister (and also admitted by sources close to the Resistance) in a secret document called a 'consolidation' of the Afghan regime, although Gromyko himself admitted that the situation was still 'complicated'. In fact, while the government may have begun to pacify some areas of the countryside, its ability to control the situation there was still very limited. In 1983 the Afghan state was able to collect only 34,000 tons of wheat. Some 'Soviet sources', although disputing the Western assumption that the regime would have been immediately overrun by the mujahidin in the event of Soviet withdrawal, privately admitted some doubts about its viability, even when foreign support to the Resistance had ceased.[43]

There were some talks among notables in the refugee camps in Pakistan about the possibility of convening a *Loya Jirgah* in order to negotiate with Karmal's government, but nothing came of it. Inside Afghanistan the main yardstick for the expansion of government influence was provided by the surrender of armed groups. How the government dealt with them before the creation of the Regional Forces in 1983 (see Part IV) is not clear. The claim that 200 commanders with 21,000 rebels had laid down their weapons by March 1983 does not seem credible, and at most it may refer to the number of able-bodied men under the leaders' command and not to those actually armed. In fact in July 1982 Karmal had claimed that 'hundreds' of mujahidin had surrendered to the government. Whatever the numbers, most of them still enjoyed an ambiguous status, as they did not seem to have joined the government, but had only signed preliminary protocols. At this stage, certainly, they were only receiving ammunition, and no weapons, in exchange. Discussions with the apparently very promising figure of 56,000 more mujahidin were

---

de pacification en Afghanistan' in Chaliand (ed.), *Stratégies de la guerrilla*, p. 458; S.K. Shaniyazova, 'Znachenie Aprel'skoi Revolyutsii 1978 g. v razvitii kultury narodov Afganistana 1978-1988 gg', diss., Tashkent 1989, p. 55; Maidan, *Problemy sotsial'noi bazy Aprelskoi Revolyutsii*, pp. 29, 30.

[43] A. Gromiko, in 'Zasedanie Politbyuro TsK KPSS 10 marta 1983 goda' in *Soujetische Geheimdokumente*, p. 408; Ludwig, 'Einige Probleme', p. 120; Harrison, 'A breakthrough in Afghanistan?', p. 14.

going on at the beginning of 1983, but it is clear that most of them did not join the government afterwards. In March 1983, as a propaganda operation, a *jirgah* of former counter-revolutionary chiefs, that had gone over to the government or agreed ceasefires with it or were just carrying on discussions, was held in Kabul. According to government claims, this event marked the start of a massive surrender of mujahidin. In fact, at the end of October 1983, Karmal claimed again that 'hundreds' had come over, which suggests a more limited achievement. Overall, out of the 598 mujahidin groups which signed ceasefire agreements in 1982-3, only eleven tribal battalions and three companies were formed. R. Anwar's estimate of 2-3,000 real, armed mujahidin having surrendered by the end of 1983 looks realistic.[44]

The groups which made peace were mainly small ones. Results with larger ones and particularly with those that were more militarily effective were still poor, although great hopes did exist in this regard too. It appears that, faced with the unprecedented efforts made by Kabul in the year following the March 1983 *jirgah*, many groups did agree at least to temporary truces with the government and the Soviets. According to a Kabul internal source, by March 1984 such agreements had been reached with 900 units (numbering 100,000 men, many in fact not armed), while contacts with 460 other groups (numbering 50,000) were being held. Baghlan and Parwan appear to have been the provinces most affected. In the latter, according to a Western traveller, most of the groups went over to the government or signed ceasefires. Again, the government failed to keep pace and was unable to transform the wave of truces into a really significant number of defections from the enemy's side – in March 1985 Karmal talked once more about 'hundreds' of surrendering mujahidin. A typical example was the ceasefire with commander Massoud (the most renowned opposition

---

[44] Harrison, 'A breakthrough in Afghanistan?', p. 16; Keshtmand, personal communication, 10 Dec. 1993; B. Sen Gupta, *Afghanistan. Politics, Economics and Society*, Pinter, 1986, p. 124; *News Bulletin*, April 1984; P. Bonovsky, *Washington's Secret War against Afghanistan*, International Publications, 1985, p. 165; *KNT*, 1 Nov. 1983; 'Karmal's Id al-Fitr Speech', *Bakhtar*, 21 July 1982; A.A. Kotenev, 'Natsional'no-etnicheskii faktor v vooruzhennoi bor'be s kontrrevolyutsei v DRA', diss., 1983, IV AN SSSR, p. 122; R. Anwar, *The Tragedy of Afghanistan*, Verso, 1989, p. 217; V.A. Merimskii, 'V boyakh s modzhakhedami', *Voenno-istoricheskii Zhurnal* no. 8 (1994), p. 42.

commander) in 1982-3: this agreement did not lead to a reconciliation at all, contrary to what the Soviets appear to have expected.[45]

In 1984 the pace of 'pacification' seemed to slow down, notwithstanding an influx of members of the Shura traditionalist party from the Hazarajat, where it was losing a civil war with the pro-Iranian Nasr and Sepah parties. A desire for a separate peace with the government was also reported from some regions like Paktia, but the military weakness of the government there allowed the mujahidin to react: warning attacks against militias were stepped up. The difficulty of transforming truce agreements into real peace accords may have been the cause behind the decline of the propaganda campaign about repenting mujahidin, which was scaled down with respect to the previous year; the government appeared to have lost part of its regained self-confidence.[46]

The reason why the results of 1984-5 were still considerably below expectations appears to have been the fact that what had been offered to the rebels up to then looked to many of them like little more than an honourable surrender. On the other hand, to give more would have meant to call into question the very meaning of the Revolution itself, and maybe even the idea of 'modernizing' the country. Nonetheless, the policy of small steps continued in 1985, albeit in a climate of growing tension between the Karmal government and the Soviets. While the participation of local notables, clergymen and other personalities had already been given a positive role in some regulations enacted in 1984 concerning discussions with mujahidin commanders willing to make peace with the government, in 1985 Karmal acknowledged the need to 'establish firm and durable relations with the *qariadars* (local notables) and to recognize their authority. They were to be made 'active' and to help in resolving urgent problems. This apparently implied transferring some power from party cadres to notables. The only act of caution would be to keep the old feudal lord from taking control of the local organs, by means of elections

---

[45] Roy in *Le Monde*, 17 Nov. 1983; Karmal, 15th plenum CC – PDPA, *RA*, 27 March 1985; J.J. Puig, quoted in Amstutz, *Afghanistan: The First Five Years of Soviet Occupation*, p. 148 and *ibid.*, p. 267.

[46] *Nouvelles d'Afghanistan*, Dec. 1986 p. 16; Coldren, 'Afghanistan in 1984', *Asian Survey*, Feb. 1985, p. 241; V. Plastun, 'Gorkii urok', *Aziya i Afrika Segodnia*, 1/93, p. 10.

by all members of the village. Overall, however, in the words of a Russian adviser, this was only a 'practical step', from a 'revolutionary point of view', a backward but necessary one, if the party did not want to continue to be 'too far ahead of the people'.[47]

Although it is not clear whether Karmal's project was in any way reflected in the actual policy of the government, some improvements were claimed in 1985-1986. In 1985 Afghan and Soviet sources announced a growing number of defections among mujahidin, and several Western sources accepted these claims. The defection to the government of Firdaus Khan Mohmand, an important leader of Hizb-i Islami in Nangrahar, dates from 1985. A wave of defections was also reported among other tribes like Khugiani, Shinwari and Durrani.[48]

One year later these reports were further substantiated. According to *Asiaweek*, militias at the border with Pakistan were growing and they were being recruited even from inside Pakistan. For example the militia leader Ismatullah Muslim recruited members of the Achekzai tribe, who then continued to live in the refugee camps and to receive rations. An American journalist, back from a trip inside Afghanistan in the summer of 1986, reported that in many villages the inhabitants became nervous when mujahidin approached the village and then forced them to leave, while in some places the population refused to cooperate. *The Economist* informed its readers that the population was cooperating with the government to a greater degree, forming militias and giving information, and also in some cases asking the rebels to leave. Again, a greater number of neutral villages and more cooperation from the population only marginally increased the government's ability to run the countryside: in 1986 still only 40,000 tons of wheat were collected by the state, out of a total agricultural production of 2,800,000 tons.[49]

---

[47] *Mainstream*, 12 Jan. 1985; 'Polozhenie o poryadke vedeniya peregovorov s predstavitelyami vooruzhennikh otryadov plemen i kontrrevolyutsionnykh band po skloneniyu ikh k perekhodu na storonu gosudarstvennoi vlasti, 30 dekabrya 1984 g.' in *NDPA (sbornik dokumentov)*, Tashkent, 'Uzbekistan', 1986, p. 418; Reuters, 24 Jan. 1986.

[48] *News Bulletin*, 2 Dec. 1985; *KZ*, 6 Jan. 1985; Keshtmand, Personal communication, 10 Dec. 1993; *Foreign Report*, 1 Aug. 1985; IISS, *Strategic Survey, 1985/6*, p. 134; Pohly, *op. cit.*, p. 320.

[49] *Asiaweek*, 29 June 1986; *The Muslim*, 13 Aug. 1986; *The Economist*, 25 Oct.

On the whole, the government's early 'pacification policy' was based on the assumption, shared by some Western observers, that a basic feature of the Afghan situation consisted in the neutrality of a significant part of the population. This was the thinking of a Soviet diplomat, who in 1981 asserted that future developments would be determined by the behaviour of the many who remained neutral in the conflict. Apparently the same concept was reiterated by Karmal in private conversations to Western observers. It can in general be accepted that many armed groups had not consolidated a profound, ideological hostility to the regime, so that to some extent it was not totally inappropriate to consider them as equidistant between Kabul and the 'real' mujahidin, i.e. those ideologically aligned to the Resistance parties. One authoritative Soviet source stated that out of 6,000 mujahidin groups, one third were not affiliated to any of the Iran- or Pakistan-based parties. In terms of the general population, in April 1988 Soviet sources estimated that while 25-30% supported the government and another 30% were in favour of the opposition, no less than 40-45% declared themselves neutral.[50]

The term 'neutral' was also used to mean that many villages, although totally independent of the government, did not support (at least not as a whole and not openly) any armed mujahidin group. Although sparse references to 'neutrality' agreements are found in the Western literature on the war, government and Soviet sources seem to have used the term extensively only from 1986 onward. At this time the government classified as 'neutral' those villages whose notables promised not to allow military operations to be carried out on their territory, nor the concentration of mujahidin forces, nor the establishment of weapon and ammunition depots, while at the same time not allowing the deployment of government armed units or the establishment of local organs of power either. In exchange the government would not bomb or attack them. While agreements of similar substance are found right throughout the war, it is not clear when and if a specific, codified policy of offering such special status to villages

---

1986; Lyakhovskii, *Tragediya i doblest' Afgana*, p. 333.

[50] *Guardian*, 11 Nov. 1981; N.I Marchuk, *Neob"yavlennaya voina v Afganistane*, Luch, 1993, p. 113; Yu. Gankowski, quoted in J.-C. Kipp, 'Afghanistan: après la guerre', *Politique Internationale*, Aug. 1989, p. 393.

came into being, but reports about 'neutral' villages abound for late 1986. At the beginning of 1987, fifty such villages existed in Kandahar province alone, while around the same period a Western traveller reported the existence of many such villages in Ghazni province. Other examples of Western travellers encountering neutral villages exist (for example A. Bonner) and some Western observers, including O. Roy, admitted the neutral stance of a section of the population. Although what we could call the 'neutralization policy' probably existed since the beginning, an intensification apparently took place after the arrival in power of Najibullah. Ghazni province, probably by virtue of the low-level presence of radical mujahidin parties outside restricted areas, proved to be particularly inclined towards such 'neutralizations' and by the end of 1987 they covered 728 villages, probably a record level in the whole of Afghanistan. Attempts at further expanding their number met with serious problems.. As early as August 1983 a group of village headmen, travelling to meet the regional commander of the Soviet-Afghan forces, with the aim of agreeing to a ceasefire in order to harvest the crops, were assassinated by the mujahidin. Small resistance commanders were occasionally assassinated for agreeing even temporary cease-fires with the Soviets. Even when they did go quite to such extremes, the mujahidin did not always comply with the requests of the village authorities and the armed forces often hit those villages when attacking mujahidin units in their neighbourhoods.[51]

Meanwhile the government became for the first time the object of open criticism from Moscow. In October 1985, M. Gorbachev talked of 'distortions and negative aspects in PDPA practices' and recommended measures to correct the situation and to strengthen the armed forces, in view of a Soviet withdrawal. Karmal's answer came in December 1985, when he spoke of an operation to be launched in two phases, in order to install state power in the majority of villages and in all districts; the two

[51] *CSM*, Dec. 22, 1986; A. Bonner, *Among the Afghans*, Duke University Press, 1987, pp. 119-20; O. Roy in *IHT*, 7 Oct. 1986, Coldren, 'Afghanistan in 1985', *Asian Survey*, Feb. 1986 p. 241; *RA*, 26 Dec. 1987; A. Podlesnyi, 'Politika Natsional'nogo Primireniya i osobennosti ee provedeniya v yuzhnykh raionakh Afganistana', *Spetsial'nyi Byulleten' IV AN SSSR* no. 2 (1990), pp. 158-9; O'-Ballance, *Wars in Afghanistan*, pp. 126, 132.

phases were to last two and four months respectively. These aims look so ambitious (in fact they recall the plans approved in 1980-1, see Ch. 14, Section 1), that it seems appropriate to agree with the commentary of a Soviet adviser: they were only cosmetic measures, just to placate Moscow.[52]

---

[52] Lyakhovskii, 'Na afganskoi vizhzhennoi zemle', p. 56; *KNT*, 22 Dec. 1985; A. Arnold, 'The ephemeral elite' in *The Politics of Social Transformation in Afghanistan, Iran and Pakistan*, p. 54.

13

NATIONAL RECONCILIATION

Najibullah: continuity and discontinuity

The reasons behind the replacement of Karmal with Najibullah will not be examined in detail here, suffice it to say that the latter was basically recognized as a much more active and dynamic man than his predecessor. Knowing what the Soviets wanted to hear, he advanced his own candidature proposing an ambitious program of 'National Reconciliation': to earn the support of the peasant masses for the state (in fact Karmal too had always claimed to be seeking this); to compromise with the opposition forces; to open discussions with the King. The Afghan politburo appears to have opposed such measures, but the Soviets were pleased, to the point that they apparently overstated Najibullah's aims. In late 1986 UN mediator Cordovez was told by Soviet negotiators that Najibullah would establish a new government with 'nothing Marxist about it – lots of landlords'. In fact, thanks to divisions within the Soviet government with regard to the policy to be followed in Afghanistan, Najibullah always maintained some room for manoeuvre to pursue his own policy.[53]

At first Najibullah advanced decisively along the path that Karmal had outlined, but only partially put into practice, in his last year of leadership. Assessing the first few months of his leadership, the CPSU CC appreciated the increased activity of the party organs, the development of new forms and methods of propaganda and the improvement of the army's performance. However, he soon

---

[53] 'Sekretnye dokumenty iz osobykh papok: Afghanistan', *Voprosy Istorii*, no. 3 (1993), pp. 23-4; G.M. Kornienko, 'The Afghan endeavor: Perplexities of the military incursion and withdrawal', *Journal of South Asian and Middle Eastern Studies*, vol. XVII, no. 2 (winter 1994); Rubin, *The Search for Peace in Afghanistan*, pp. 78-9.

moved beyond this. In November 1986 a new Constitution was approved (a draft version was first submitted in April 1980); it cancelled the absolute power of veto that the President had previously enjoyed. Introducing it, Najibullah talked about the need for real power-sharing. On 13 July 1987 the denomination *Democratic* Republic of Afghanistan was abandoned. The Revolutionary Council (the legislative and representative organ up to June 1988) whose members were picked by the party leadership, was replaced by an elective National Assembly (*Jirgah-i Melli*). The 'socialist' character of the PDPA was now denied more strongly than before. In 1990 Tahir Enayat, rector of Kabul University, took charge of explaining that all of the members of the party were Muslims and that Marxism had been abandoned. In 1989 a new non-party Minister for Higher Education began to work on the 'de-sovietization' of the universities. Government monopolies on fuel and sugar transportation were lifted and the state allowed private traders to take part in food distribution in the cities, previously a monopoly too, although in this case rather than a concession it was more a request for help, as the government expected trouble in feeding the people during the winter. Kabul's mayor, Abdul Hakim Misaq, even said that traffickers in stolen goods would not be prosecuted as long as they got the pilfered goods to market.[54]

At the time of withdrawal, Gorbachev's envoy Vorontsov managed to obtain the PDPA's agreement to offer the opposition the positions of President of Gossoviet (state planning organ), President of the Council of Ministers, Ministers of Defence, State Security, Communications, Finance, presidencies of banks and that of the Supreme Court. On the other hand, it wanted to hang on to the positions of vice-minister or deputy-chief in all of these institutions which, in addition to the preponderance of the party in the bureaucracy, would have given the PDPA a fair degree of control over the entire state machinery. It also wanted to keep all the provincial governor positions. Furthermore, the willingness of the government really to concede all those positions

---

[54] Gromov, *Ogranichennyi kontingent*, p. 230; RA, 16 April 1980; *NT*, no. 52 (1986), p. 22; Mahbub, *Moralische Aspekte*, no. 232 and part II, p. 48; *NYT*, 7 Dec. 1988; Rubin, *The Fragmentation of Afghanistan*, p. 167; AP, Jan. 15, 1990.

is doubtful. For good measure, the offer of the Ministry of Defence and the Ministry of State Security was not made public in Afghanistan.[55]

It would seem that a large part of the intelligentsia, whether sympathizing with the regime or not, took this overture seriously and began to express itself more openly. Hopes, however, cooled on 18 February 1989, when the state of emergency was proclaimed and 1,700 'intellectuals' were arrested. In such a situation the exodus of academics and intellectuals could not but continue. All media, including the few small independent publications that had emerged mainly in 1990, were still subject to tight supervision and the latter were forced to close down in November 1991.[56]

Even party members took Najibullah's initiative seriously, which according to him caused 'panic and pessimism' and met with strong opposition from them and many Soviet advisers too. At the II National Conference of the party, the delegates from the radical wing were a majority, maybe as much as 60%. According to a Soviet source, a bitter debate broke out within the party (end 1987) between those who feared an 'islamization' of the political life of the country and those who wanted to give the Constitution an even stronger 'Islamic character'. In fact Najibullah had met opposition to the National Reconciliation policy particularly from Karmalists ever since he first put it forward to the higher party echelons in April/May 1986. In general, many party members feared the 'sell out' of the Revolution, or rather, as cynics (and Najibullah himself) would put it, the sharing out with the opposition of the already unplentiful state resources and positions in the bureaucracy. This is why he faced strong opposition within the party, from 'internal enemies' who were 'making a hue and cry and claiming that we are retreating and undermining the gains of the [Saur] Revolution'. Some factions apparently even publicly proclaimed anti-Soviet slogans, as they correctly identified the Soviet Union as the source of the new policy – Najibullah himself talked of a provocation organized in some girls' schools in June 1986. So Najibullah had to reassure the party by underlining that

---

[55] *National Reconciliation in Practice*, Afghanistan Today Publishers, 1987, pp. 46-7; Gromov, *Ograničennyi kontingent*, p. 232.

[56] M. Amin, former philosophy teacher in Kabul, interviewed in *Journal de Genève*, 17/18 Feb. 1990; *US Dept. of State Dispatch*, 1 Feb., 1991, '1990 Human Rights Report: Afghanistan'.

'reconciliation' would not be with 'reactionary mullahs' or with all 'feudals', but only with those 'who have recognized the new reality' and wish to 'repent their crimes' and 'prove their loyalty to the homeland', although he was in fact holding discussions with whoever was available. Newspapers claimed that 'there are issues which are of sacred essence for the party members. [...] We will not retreat even an inch from the achievements of the April Revolution. [...] Those who come to us should officially recognize the leading role of the PDPA.'

Najibullah failed to convince many, and the Geneva agreements sparked a new wave of criticism and protests. According to Soviet documents, in Jowzyan province alone two new factions appeared within the party, named *Kor* and *Kozha*, which opposed the agreements. The polemic went on till the October 1988 Plenum of the party, on the eve of which Najibullah cracked down on the internal opposition, arresting more than 300 people, including several prominent Karmalists. He tried to achieve reconciliation shortly afterwards and the impending general onslaught from the mujahidin helped dampen the conflict for a while, but tensions continued to surface from time to time. In January 1989 the President of the Senate, not a member of the PDPA but an 'intellectual of the revolutionary left', criticized Najibullah's inclination to negotiate at any cost and declared his opposition to the transformation of the PDPA into a new party. A factor in keeping tensions alive was the divergence of feelings and opinions about the expected general offensive of the Resistance and how to meet it, as some provincial leaders of the party and of the state feared that the local armed forces would be unable to stand up to the onslaught (for example, in Helmand province), while others, particularly a number of army officers, displayed considerable self-confidence and favoured a tougher line in dealing with the mujahidin, as was shown in January 1989 by a petition signed by as many as 700 officers.[57]

---

[57] Bradsher, *Afghanistan and the USSR, III unpublished edition*, chap. 10 p. 11; RA 18 Oct. 1987; *Pravda*, 17 Oct. 1987; Shebarshin, *Ruka Moskvy*, p. 189; V. Korgun, 'Natsional'noe primirenie i vnutripoliticheskaya situatsiya v 1988 g.', *Spetsial'nyi Byulleten' AN SSSR – IV*, n. 2, 1990, p. 60; Najibullah, *Bakhtar*, 14 May 1986, RA, 10 July 1986 and RA, 11 May 1987; Lyakhovskii, *Tragediya i doblest' Afgana*, p. 318; *O khode realizatsii politiki natsional'nogo primireniya" 26.04.88*, p. 2; Rubin, *The fragmentation of Afghanistan*, p. 150-1; AFP, 25 Oct. 1988 and

Yet the policy of 'moving to the centre' reached its peak only between spring and summer 1990. As early as February 1982 Andropov had asked Karmal to offer prominent government positions to non-PDPA members, but Karmal did not agree. Najibullah, although not taking Vorontsov's advice to share power too seriously, at least moved some steps in that direction. In May a new government took office and officially only twelve ministers out of thirty-six belonged to the party (but the twelve were still the key ones). In reality, some non-PDPA ministers, like M.A. Gafur Rahim, Minister of Water and Energy Resources, and F.M. Terin, Minister for Returnees Affairs, were deemed not to be members only because Najibullah had decided that way – they both held a PDPA card. Fazel Haq Khaleqyar, a notable from the age of the monarchy and governor of Herat, was named Prime Minister. In fact, apart from Mohammed Hakim, Minister of Finance, who had some contacts with the Royal Family, all the other ministers were far from having any contact with the opposition. In conclusion, it is doubtful whether the presence of many non-party men had any impact on the population; as a Soviet source stated, many of them did not represent anybody. In July, at the II Congress of the party, the PDPA was renamed Hizb-i Watan (Fatherland Party) and it adopted a platform in which all of the members were requested to be Muslim and favourable to National Reconciliation. The new statute of the party required members to live in accordance with the Shariat, while the seventy other duties now listed were quite different from the previous ones. At the Congress, Najibullah never referred to the 'April Revolution' and defined the events of April 1978 as a 'rising of army officers, with the support of the popular masses'. He also declared that the entry of Soviet troops into Afghanistan had not furthered national interests, although he went on to laud Soviet help after the withdrawal.[58]

The mass organizations around the party moved along similar lines. The DYOA, for example, announced its renunciation of

---

3 Jan. 1989; Starodubova, 'Moral'no-politicheskii potentsial', p. 92; *Bakhtar*, 20 Sept. 1990.

[58] Lyakhovskii, 'Na afganskoi vizhzhennoi zemle', p. 65; S. Harrison and D. Cordovez, *Out of Afghanistan*, Oxford University Press, 1995, p. 94; M.A. Gareev, *Moya poslednyaya voina*, Nisan, Moscow, 1996, p. 159, 160; *KP*, 13 June 1990; *Izvestia* 29 June 1990.

'some principles borrowed from the Komsomol'. The Constitution was modified again and Afghanistan became an Islamic State. No reference to the privileged role of the party was any longer made. At this point the political overhaul of Najibullah was essentially complete; only small adjustments of purely symbolic value followed – for example, in 1991 female television presenters and announcers began to cover their heads.[59]

The attempt to attract the clergy to the government side continued, but without dramatic innovations. According to official figures, between March and October 1989 twenty mullahs and ulema abandoned active opposition to go over to the regime. Undoubtedly hostile elements were still present even among the mullahs operating within government-controlled areas. In March 1989, for example, the imam from Pol-i Kheshti mosque in Kabul was arrested for having criticized President Najibullah: 'As you did nothing for your Creator, you cannot do anything for his creatures'. Nonetheless the regime inclined towards greater tolerance of such elements; the imam was in fact released seven months later, with the acknowledgement that it had been a mistake.[60]

Since 1986 changes also appeared in the field of human rights. Fewer civilians were killed in 1986 – 10,000 to 12,000 deaths were reported compared with 37,000 for the preceding year, according to a UN report. The estimate by Amnesty International

[59] *Pravda*, 25 June 1990; *KP*, 12 June 1990; *Afghanews*, 15 April 1991.

[60] N.N. Khakimdzhanov, 'Kurs NDPA na rasshirenie sotsial'noi bazy aprelskoi revolyutsii', *Obshchestvennie nauki v Uzbekistane*, 2 (1988), p. 36; AFP, 10 July 1980; G. Bensi, *Allah contro Gorbaciov*, Trento, Reverdito, 1988, p. 278; *Guardian*, 19 Oct. 1988; *AF*, June 1984; Sen Gupta, *Afghanistan: Politics*, pp. 65, 130; L. Nikolayev, *Afghanistan between the Past and the Future*, Moscow: Progress, 1986, p. 90; *NT*, no. 44 (1986); C. Karp, 'Afghanistan: eight years of Soviet occupation', *Department of State Bulletin*, March 1988, p. 18; *Der Spiegel* no. 20, 1988; C. Lobato, 'Kaboul 1980-1986: un Islam officiel pour légitimer le pouvoir Communiste', *Central Asian Survey*, no. 2/3 (1988); M.A. Babakhodzhaev, 'NDPA –krupneishaya i samaya vliyatelnaya sila afganskogo obschestva' in *Respublika Afganistan*, Tashkent, Akademiya Nauk Uzbeskoi SSR, 1990, p. 10; A. Arnold, 'Afghanistan' in *Yearbook in International Communist Affairs*, Hoover Institution, Stanford, 1989, p. 461; *The Guardian*, 18 March 1986; *Défis afghans*, no. 10 (Nov. 1986); TASS, 25 Dec. 1987; *KNT*, 10 Aug. 1985, 10 Feb. 1988, 8 Nov. 1989; Asia Watch, *Afghanistan: The forgotten war*, Human Rights Watch, pp. 76-7.

for 1987 was 14,000. Since 1987 the number of political prisoners began to decline, while reports about the use of torture went down substantially. It would appear that at least up to 1988, government ('central bodies') efforts to 'bring the human rights situation into line with its international obligations' could not always be implemented in places away from the centre 'wherever people have a free hand'. After 1988 conditions of detention in Pol-i-Charkhi prison were reported to have improved somewhat. However, up to the last months of the regime, these conditions were very bad by any standard and in trials by special security courts 'procedural guarantees of the accused [were] not in conformity with international human rights standards'. Finally from 1990 the government fully cooperated with international organizations in an attempt to alleviate the economic, social and cultural consequences of the conflict; the ICRC was allowed to visit some persons detained by the government. The death penalty now followed 'a more regulated procedure and [appeared] to be less arbitrary than before'. Improvement of conditions in Pol-i-Charkhi prison continued after the Soviet withdrawal and finally in July 1991 Najibullah convened a commission on prison reform, which then held regular meetings, but still the whole judicial system stayed more under the control of the Ministry of Security than under that of the Ministry of Justice. In late 1991 the UN assessed the human rights situation as 'satisfactory', but to a too large extent dependent 'on the principal structures of the government which are not subject to sufficient controls through a system of checks and balances'.[61]

Najibullah seemed to realize the need to abandon strict one-party rule, mainly for reasons of international politics, although the wish to win over more members of the educated middle class may have played a role. A certain degree of political pluralism was in fact created in 1987. Karmal had already repeated in 1985 his old promise (December 1979) to allow other parties into legal existence. In fact as late as 1986 the merging of some small leftist

[61] Ermacora report, Reuters, 11 Nov. 1986; Amnesty International, *1988 report*; *CSM*, 25 Nov. 1987; Ermacora, Reuters, 2 March, 1988; Ermacora, Reuters, 15 March 1988; Ermacora, *AP*, Nov. 17, 1988; Ermacora, Reuters, 21 Feb. 1989; Ermacora, Reuters, 15 Nov. 1990; AFP, 17 Sept., 1991; AFP, 15 Nov. 1991; *Kyodo News Service*, 5 Jan., 1992; *US Dept. of State Dispatch*, 1 Feb., 1991, *1990 Human Rights Report: Afghanistan*.

parties took place, with 1,000 members joining the PDPA, in continuation of a process begun in 1980, while others were being pressured to do the same. In mid-1987 a law on political parties was finally approved: to be legalized, political parties were requested not to carry out armed actions against the state and other political parties, to support the policy of National Reconciliation, to oppose colonialism, neo-colonialism, imperialism, Zionism, racial discrimination, apartheid and fascism. According to Najibullah, only the most extremist part of the opposition would not have been included in the future coalition government. Other parties were not obliged to share PDPA positions on theory and tactics, but they had to agree on the common aims of a ceasefire and of the 'strengthening of the historical friendship with the USSR'. All this culminated in the parliamentary election of April 1988, when the opposition was granted the right to be present in the Parliament. According to the official version, at least two or three candidates (sometimes as many as six or eight) fought for each seat. It is impossible to verify whether this was true or not, but figures seem to indicate precise modalities with regard to the distribution of seats: in the Chamber of Deputies the PDPA got 46 seats, its allies 69, the 'pacific opposition' 69, while 50 seats were reserved for the armed opposition, which obviously refused the offer. It appears that in many of the constituencies reserved for the pacific opposition (usually located in places where the government was weak) very few electors actually bothered to exercise their rights. For example, in a by-election (the cause of the delay is unknown) in October 1988 for the constituency of Gomal-Sawrobi-Bamal (Paktia), the deputy of the 'opposition' was elected with 500 votes.[62]

While several small parties from the centre and the left, including some dummies created by WAD for propaganda purposes, registered under the new law, over the whole 1987-92 period the only active armed party of the opposition to strike a deal with the government (in May 1990) was Hizbollah, a small Shi'a party, not to be confused with the party of the same name based in Iran. This Hizbollah was founded in 1965 or 1978 (depending on different sources) by Maulawi Abdul Halim Raqim, from Faryab

---

[62] *Pravda*, 29 June 1987; *Guardian*, 18 March 1986; RA, 18 Oct. 1987; *Bakhtar*, 7 July 1987; *Das Parlament*, 27 Oct. 1989; V.V. Basov/G.A. Poliakov, 'Afganistan: trudnye sud'by revolyutsii', p. 57; RA, 25 Oct. 1988.

province. In 1980 it was in the official list of the parties based in Pakistan. At that time it would have counted on 500 members. When in spring 1988 discussions with the government started, it claimed to have more than 3,000 armed men in the Centre and in the North of the country, and particularly in Jaghori district (Ghazni province). At the time of the 'reconciliation', its president was Hujat ul Islam Shaikh Ali. It was a centrist party, that during the war had maintained a good relationship with the Shi'a traditionalist party, the Shura. In November 1990 a protocol of cooperation with the Watan was signed. It actually seems that the government also offered a legal status to at least the Jamiat-i Islami in early 1989, in exchange for a ceasefire, but it is doubtful whether Najibullah really expected such a proposal to be accepted.[63]

To revitalize this unconvincing multiparty system, in September 1990 a new constitutional amendment, allowing any group of 300 people to form a political party and to contest elections, was introduced, but disillusion with Najibullah's democracy had already gone too far. A member of the Peasants' Justice Party, one of the PDPA satellite parties, said that some leading Watan party members would oppose the move, because they had ruled for so long that they would not agree to coexist and compete with new parties unless these joined the regime. A former member of SZA (Sazman-i Zamatkashan-i Afghanestan, Organization of Afghan Toilers), a leftist party allied to the PDPA-Watan, complained: 'It is another cosmetic strategy of the government and even if they were sincere, the old guard will not allow any sort of liberty to the new entrants into our political field.' The general idea was that the legal parties were tolerated only after the PDPA had ensured they would toe the party line.[64]

In short the development of a true multi-party system never figured among Najibullah's plans. The assessment of a Soviet scholar, according to whom Najibullah's goal was to be an 'absolute dictator with no opposition', may be excessive, but Najibullah does seem to have at least aimed at models like the semi-one party regimes of the Third World, such as Egypt, where opposition serves to

---

[63] *Bakhtar*, 2 May 1990; *AIC MB*, no. 50 (May 1985), pp. 4-5; *KNT*, 27 March 1988; Keshtmand, personal communication, London 10 Dec. 1993; *Bakhtar*, 21 Nov. 1990; *AF*, 2 (1996), pp. 28-9.

[64] AFP, 14 Sept. 1990.

legitimize the government while guaranteeing a somewhat larger degree of freedom for the urban intelligentsia. According to ·a telegram by Vorontsov, dated October 1986, Najibullah never had any intention of really making agreements with 'fundamentalists, aristocrats and feudals', in other words with the Peshawar parties. Still even these limited aims met several obstacles. Prime Minister Sharq (1988-1989), the first one since the Revolution not to be a member of the PDPA (although still a leftist), found himself quite unable to rule effectively, because the PDPA members did not recognize his authority, which they could outflank through party channels.[65]

National Reconciliation in the countryside

If National Reconciliation was largely a fiction in terms of relationships between the government and the opposition parties, an assessment of its impact on the Afghan countryside is more ambivalent. Since his first speeches, the new President placed National Reconciliation at the core of his policies, although stressing at the same time its continuity with Karmal's ten theses. Operational from 15 January 1987 onward, it was aimed at 'representatives of the refugees, moderate forces, monarchists, the three parties (nationalists), commanders of the second-category groups, political personalities of past regimes, influential and famous spiritual leaders', and 'special sections of tribes and armed opposition groups inside the country'. A unilateral, temporary ceasefire was proclaimed, while armed opposition groups were invited to lay down their weapons. The minimum requirement of the armed groups was to guarantee the security of their own area and lead a 'peaceful life', which corresponded to the old 'neutralization policy', now subsumed within the National Reconciliation. Those who made peace were guaranteed land ownership, 'free choice of work in the area of transport, industry, trade and agriculture', the writing off of past taxes, allowances for the disabled and the families of martyrs. Moreover 'arms and ammunition [would] not be taken away from them'. With regard to other concessions and conditions, the government also declared itself ready 'to consider separately in talks with the

---

[65] Gromov, *Ogranichennyi kontingent*, p. 231; AFP, 8 May 1990; B. Rubin, *The Search for Peace in Afghanistan*, p. 167.

commanders and group leaders inside the country all proposals and demands put forward by them'. More general economic and practical benefits were offered, such as the dispatching of health groups and agricultural experts, medicines, fertilizers, seeds and consumers goods, exemption from taxes for one year and salaries for village heads and imams. Further advantages were available, including the granting of the right to transport and sell primary goods in the localities. Finally, the former mujahidin could enroll in the militias, where they would be paid at least 4,000 to 10,000 Afs per month (1989) and given land holdings.[66]

On the ground the work would be carried out by 'reconciliation commissions'. 'Credible personalities, elders, ulema and religious leaders, social personalities and the representatives of the party and state organisations as well as neutral and opposition personalities' would be included in the commissions. They were to be led by the chairmen of the NFF councils or 'other personalities acceptable and credible to all'. These extraordinary commissions would then have formed and convened peace *jirgas*, whose duty was to approve a protocol on reconciliation with the single armed group. Afterwards the protocol would have been handed to the provincial extraordinary commission for approval before becoming legal. Next a ceasefire would be enforced, a joint administration would be formed and the ceasefire consolidated, finally the ground for local elections would be gradually prepared. The state would allow the villages to choose their own administrators at least to some degree, depending on whether the village had been totally out of government control or not. In this regard various kinds of solutions were devised: opposition representatives could be elected to the existing local councils; 'coalition' organs could be formed preserving the autonomy of the former rebel commander; or 'old administrative organizations' (i.e. autochthonous village councils) would stay the same while being renamed as organs of state power. A relatively large recourse was actually made to 'coalition administrations' and these ruled 600 villages by October 1987 and 1,500 two years later. In these cases almost 100% of the village heads were non-party.

[66] Najibullah, RA, 24 May 1986; Najibullah, CC Plenum, RA, 14 June 1987; *Pravda*, 16 April 1989; Najibullah, RA, 10 July 1989; *KNT*, 4 Jan. 1987; *National Reconciliation*, pp. 20-3; Rubin, *The Fragmentation of Afghanistan*, p. 175; AFP, 22 Nov. 1989.

In January 1988 Suleiman Laeq proposed free local elections, even allowing local commanders to be elected as village heads, but that was too much for Najibullah, who probably wanted to keep some degree of control over the process. At higher levels, i.e. district councils, the process was much slower. The formation of similar coalition organs of power in three districts of Balkh province (Balkh, Shutela and Kaldar) in 1989 was still deemed a sort of experimental process. The state also offered to withdraw regular army units from areas where 'reconciliation' was particularly successful and later claimed to have done this in Nimroz, Farah, Bamyan, Ghor and Uruzgan provinces, although in reality in the last three provinces National Reconciliation had achieved nothing at all. In Bamyan, Ghor and Uruzgan the government had little presence anyway, so the mujahidin had little incentive for striking deals with Kabul. By withdrawing whatever little regular forces it had there, while at the same time pursuing dialogue with local groups, Kabul encouraged the local armed units to pursue their internecine feuds, which later might allow a government comeback to support one of the warring factions, as happened in Ghor province from 1989 onwards.[67]

The launch of National Reconciliation was accompanied by a very large display of propaganda. Apart from relying on propaganda teams and on the good offices of pro-government notables who as before were trying to propagate the idea that the government was more tolerant and ready to make peace, a cleverly devised show was put into motion. Exceptionally good achievements were announced in the first two or three months of the campaign and this led many observers, including some Soviet ones, to dismiss the whole affair as a joke. Mir Abdul Ahad Mirzad, former director of Bakhtar press agency internal services, declared after his defection that the regime inflated figures of surrendering mujahidin. It appears clear that a large degree of manipulation was indeed involved.

---

[67] Najibullah, CC Plenum, RA, 1 Jan. 1987; *National Reconciliation*, pp. 45, 49–50; *News Bulletin*, 13 Nov. 1989; Umarov B. Kh., 'Stanovlenie i tendentsii razvitiya politiki natsional'nogo primireniya v Afganistane', Autoreferat dissertatsii, Tashkent, 1990, p. 15; Lyakhovskii, *Tragediya i doblest' Afgana*, p. 357; *Kommunist Tadzhikistana*, 24 Aug. 1989; *Comrade Najib's Speech at the Plenum of PDPA*, CC Jauza 1366 (June 1987), p. 16; Najibullah, *Afghanistan Taking the Path of National Reconciliation*, Government Committee of Press and Publication, 1987, p. 124.

Although the figures given by the government in this period may well have reflected the real number of 'able-bodied men' signing protocols, many groups had in fact already struck secret agreements with the government in previous years. The new policy was to bring into the open these agreements all at once in order to impress observers and create a 'momentum'.[68]

This is also shown by the fact that, apart from the groups already in contact with the government, most of the Resistance commanders completely ignored the National Reconciliation at first and many of them actually stepped up their attacks. In the period between 1 January and 24 April 1987, attacks by the mujahidin were more numerous than during the same period in 1986 (Table 46).

Despite the fact that the main target of the propaganda drive was international opinion, in line with the new approach inaugurated in October 1986 with the withdrawal of six Soviet regiments, the operation seems to have worked to some extent even within Afghanistan. The BBC correspondent for Afghanistan at that time, G. Arney, reports that in the refugee camps a rush to change Pakistani rupees for afghanis and a massive sale of possessions took place. Privately, even Resistance officials were critical of the complete refusal by the Peshawar parties of Najibullah's offers and admitted that he had seized the political initiative. Later, Najibullah's move troubled even the military forces of the mujahidin. During government operations along the border in autumn 1987, the Resistance parties were reported to have needed a firm stand in order to send some restive mujahidin to the battlefront. While by spring 1987 the wave of mujahidin going over to the government had been exhausted, a few months later the flow increased again. Even Resistance sources admit that the government was successful in establishing contacts with all political groups in the country, even in remote regions like Hazarajat. Soviet documents report that in the spring of 1988 in Herat province even groups classified as 'irreconcilable' entered discussions with the government. Elsewhere, as in Laghman

[68] V. Korgun, 'Natsional'noe primirenie i vnutripoliticheskaya situatsiya v 1988 g.', *Spetsial'nyi Byulleten' AN SSSR – IV*, no. 2, 1990, p. 56-7; *AIC MB*, 99, June 1989; Zahir Tanin, personal interview, London, 16 June 1995; *L'Humanité*, 1 March 1985, 25 Feb. 1987.

province, intelligence sources reported that notables favoured acceptance of the government offers, but could not from fear of mujahidin reprisals. In fact assassinations of notables who were having contacts with Kabul did take place as in Zabul province in 1988, when two notables of the Tuki tribe were executed. Even when the population criticized the activities of the PDPA and of the state, it did not oppose 'reconciliation'. Soviet sources maintain that by the beginning of the Red Army withdrawal (May 1988) out of 6,000 armed groups, 3,000 were still 'waiting for a good opportunity', 1,500 were holding negotiations with the government, 700 had already ceased to fight and 100 had entered the militias.[69]

Was the National Reconciliation such a radical departure from Karmal's policies? To a large extent the underlying concepts stayed the same. The Minister for Tribal and Frontier Affairs S. Laeq in October 1981 reportedly reproached a group of headmen from Logar, who were complaining about the military operations being carried out in their region and the fact that the supplies they had been promised had not materialized: 'If you really want to live in peace, cooperate with us, expel the rebels from your region, and pay your taxes, for which you will be granted local autonomy.' During 1982 a similar approach was unofficially advanced by several Soviet diplomats and specialists as the key to the 'pacification' of Afghanistan, together with some sharing of power at the central level, although at that time the idea was to put it into force only after the conclusion of a UN-sponsored agreement. In spring 1984 Karmal gave the autonomy approach an almost official status, announcing to an American interviewer his future policy, based on the appeal to tribal self-interest. Participation in the local organs of power would bring economic benefits and political rewards, while a boycott would be met with reprisals. Once the administrative bodies were chosen, the landlords who had taken refuge in

---

[69] *L'Humanité*, 25 Feb. 1987; M.M. Pashkevich, *Afganistan: voina glazami kombata*, Voennoe Izd., 1991, p. 28; Zahir Tanin, personal interview, London, 26 June 1995; G. Arney, *Afghanistan*, Mandarin Press, 1990, pp. 196-7; *Journal de Genève*, 10 Nov. 1987; O. Sarin and L. Dvoretsky, *The Afghan Syndrome*, Presidio Press, 1993, p. 134; *O khode realizatsii politiki natsional'nogo primireniya* 26.04.88, pp. 4, 5; *Obstanovka v provintsii Laghman, 6.02.88 g.*; K. B. Harpviken, 'Political Mobilisation among the Hazara of Afghanistan: 1978-1992', diss., Dept. of Sociology, University of Oslo, 1995, p. 96.

Pakistan would have to come back, otherwise their land holdings would be given away. Karmal also declared his readiness to renounce fielding party candidates below the district/subdistrict level, giving *de facto* local autonomy to the villages. With the ten theses of late 1985 he finally appeared to be willing to put this policy into practice even before reaching any agreement for the Soviet withdrawal, but he was replaced a few months later.[70]

In 1989 Ibrahim Beg, a freshly 'pacified' regional commander of Haraqat-i Inqilab near Chakhcharan (Ghor province), when asked whether females would be allowed to attend the schools, diplomatically answered 'we will see later', while the party-faithful interpreter was filled with rage. This might look like an abrupt departure from previous policies, but in fact even before the launch of the National Reconciliation, at the beginning of 1986, in a model village like Tochta, which hosted a cooperative 15 km. from Mazar-i Sharif, no woman could be seen by any visitor. Although three literacy courses had been activated, no woman was taking part in them. The President of the cooperative, 'Mr Aslam', claimed not to have forbidden his wife to attend them, she was just very busy at home. Early in 1985 in another model village, Onaba in the Panjshir, where the party had ten members, women would run away when males were in sight. In short, most of what Najibullah was throwing away was *the dreams* of 'modernizing' the Afghan countryside, rather than the reality.[71]

Even the land reform is a typical example of this. The extraordinary commissions for reconciliation were authorised, 'should the need arise', to 'temporarily' suspend the work of the operational land and water reform groups. While Najibullah as late as March 1987 voiced a point of view which essentially repeated what Karmal had said in the past ('when explanations are given in a simple and ordinary way, the need for revolutionary transformations will not run counter to Islamic traditions and the peasants' interests'), in fact the new land reform decree of mid-1987 fixed such a high ceiling (100 jeribs instead of 30), that the number of families

---

[70] Hassan Kakar, *Afghanistan: the Soviet Invasion*, p. 235; S. Harrison in *WP*, 13 May 1984; Harrison, 'A breakthrough in Afghanistan?', p. 12.

[71] Danziger, *op. cit.*, 1992, pp. 208-10; *Baltimore Sun*, Jan. 1986; *L'Humanité* 2 (March 1985).

exceeding it was actually very small. The real rationale for this change was hidden behind justifications in terms of class analysis (the old decree 'exerted pressure on the medium-sized peasants') and of economic opportunity ('we were unable to supply' peasants, who had also been given pieces of land that were too small, with seeds, fertilizers, water, equipment, etc., and respect had to be paid to 'objective economic laws'), but it was really a matter of 'objective and political necessity': 'fixing the maximum size of land ownership at 30 jeribs artificially destroyed the size of land useful for normal farming as well as *traditional relationships*' (my emphasis). Even landlords would be allowed to participate in the distribution of barren land, so that they could 'use it and increase agricultural production' up to the limit of 100 jeribs, while no restriction in the unit size of land ownership would affect those 'who [had] an important role in the fulfilment of the National Reconciliation policy and [had] played a major part in ending the war'. Although the land reform commissions were still reported to be active in 1988, as early as 1987 the land reform had got almost completely stuck, as detailed in Part I. In 1989 Najibullah officially condemned the choice of granting the cooperatives a privilege as a model of agricultural development: together with the state farms their production only amounted to 1% of the whole and had been given an absolutely disproportionate government priority. On the contrary, he lamented that the traditional sector of landownership had been virtually abandoned to its own devices. The reform was officially abandoned in 1990 when every mention of reforms in agriculture was removed from the new Constitution and the inviolability of property was declared.

In 1990 the limitation of ceremonial expenses (bride price), one of the other driving factors in the 1978-9 revolt, was abolished too. The literacy program had been drastically reduced; in the last six months of 1986 only 7,000 persons received the final certificate.[72]

According to S.A. Keshtmand, then Prime Minister, the main push towards 'reconciliation' was economic: fertilizers, seeds, water control. Again this was no novelty, although quantities may have been larger. There are several reports that economic support was instrumental in bridging the gap between the government and

---

[72] Keshtmand, *Bakhtar*, 30 Jan. 1987.

some rural communities, as in Kol Mohammed village, in Balkh province and close to the Soviet border, where the availability of electricity and other forms of aid convinced the locals, including the armed group operating from the village, to switch sides and join Kabul. In Herat province, for example, the population was reported by Soviet intelligence to have welcomed initiatives like the digging of wells and the asphalting of roads, particularly as they came after years of widespread destruction, although at that time no school, hospital or mosque was being built. Repair of roads became particularly important from 1365 (1986/7) onward, when 70% of the state's civilian budget was devoted to it.[73]

While it is often difficult to distinguish it from previous policies, National Reconciliation did represent a shift from the conception of 'pacification' as an auxiliary policy (the creation of a revolutionary social base remaining the final aim) to one where it was the means to gain a new legitimacy for the government. Karmal still viewed the formation of local *jirgahs* as a means to increase the 'influence of party committees', under whose leadership the whole process would be realised. In Baryalai's words, the basic aim remained to 'acclimatize' and 'root' 'internationalism' in the national soil, although what he called some 'serious objective difficulties' in the 'internationalist education of the masses' were being encountered. In the beginning at least, Najibullah too hoped to be able to train a significant number of propagandists 'able to work among small groups of the people and travel from one village to another', 'armed with the principles of the theory and knowledge of revolution' and 'familiar with the forms and methods of the specific political and propaganda work among the peasants in the villages', but in reality most of the 'propagandists' were 'carrying out formulative [sic] work in the villages without previous preparation or any specific guidance'. Najibullah did not wait till the party was ready to conquer the countryside (which might have meant waiting forever) and he did dare to pursue the policy even if the party structures and potential were not developed enough to carry the burden of the whole operation. A Soviet scholar in

---

[73] S.A. Keshtmand, personal communication, London, 10 Dec. 1993; Inter Press Service, 21 May 1988; *O khode realizatsii politiki natsional'nogo primireniya 26.04.88*, p. 5; *Otchet o komandirovke v pr. Gerat 8-10 noyabrya 1987 g.*; Reuters, 24 Jan. 1986.

1984 noted how the DRA could not accept a long term compromise with the tribes, as the British had done, because of the revolutionary nature of the regime. He interpreted Karmal's strategy of co-opting tribal notables into the local organs and of offering them salaries as a way of incorporating them into the state structure. Their enrolment in the NFF was seen as a key factor in the process. With National Reconciliation instead, although it was never openly stated, the NFF was no longer supposed to play a key role in dealing with opponents who had repented. In fact very little was heard of the NFF after 15 January 1987. While Karmal talked of utilizing traditions in order to stabilize the Revolution, in early 1988 Soviet advisers interpreted Najibullah's policy as a compromise aimed at unifying the 'new social structure' with 'traditional forms of social life'. In fact in the end the 'traditional forms' (or rather what was left of them after being reshaped by the war) played a dominant role in the compromise. A Soviet scholar in early 1987 forecast that the PDPA might consolidate its power by extending concessions in the field of local autonomy. This is exactly what increasingly happened after 1987. The would-be pro-government warlords were now much more readily offered self-rule, without any real supervision of their area. Such favourable conditions had been rather exceptional earlier. In Najibullah's own words, since 'true patriots and long-standing friends of the Revolution' had 'already joined the leadership organs', it was now necessary to attract into 'the leading organs' those 'who are still neutral but who want to serve their people sincerely'. Although obviously 'nobody wanted the election to the local councils and *jirgas* of those who looked at our banner and life with contempt', it was necessary to 'accept this fact because elections are continuing in the country's villages where the situation is not normal'. 'In this regard our skill in compromising on small and trivial matters in order to achieve victory for the main cause, the struggle for peace, will play its part.' In other terms, Najibullah was now determined to accept the reality of the country: 'national reconciliation is a precise calculation of the present national and tribal structure of our society'. People like rebel leader Abdul Hakim, commanding 2,000 mujahidin in Herat province, went over to the government (in 1990) partly because of material support from the government, but mainly thanks to the fact that Kabul had 'corrected its mistakes', recognizing the limits to its authority and

avoiding interfering with local affairs. He clearly stated that this
ruled out the existence of schools for females and the enforcement
of the land reform. Had the government tried to interfere once
more, he would have had no problem in taking up arms again.[74]

It is impossible to specify in detail what was left of the role
of the NFF, but figures relative to the composition of the local
organs of state power show to what extent the government was
now willing to surrender its political control in the countryside
and rely on more indirect means, like patronage. Traditionally,
it used to consider as 'under complete control' villages where a
party organization existed and had a leading role. In Helmand
province, for example, at the end of 1986 100 out of 333 villages
under government control were also under party (i.e. complete)
control. In November 1985, 57% of representatives elected to
the local organs of power belonged to the PDPA, proof that few
villages outside the couple of thousand pro-PDPA ones were
taking part in the election of local bodies. In the first phase of
the 1986 local elections (winter), apparently carried out in provinces
where the government was stronger, but including villages were
the party was weak or absent, this percentage went down to
40.8%. In the second phase (summer 1986), held in provinces
where the government had less support, it fell further to 32.47%.
In the local elections held in 1987, finally, only 10.4% of those
elected belonged to PDPA. Furthermore, by 1988, 26% of those
elected to the local bodies were former opposers or 'returnees'.
Overall, while 65% of villages lay outside party control in February
1987, this had risen to 76% by December 1987. National Reconciliation added relatively little from the theoretical point of view,
but intensified this process to such an extent that manipulation
of local groups came to overshadow the development of relatively
genuine, ideological support.[75]

---

[74] Karmal, XV plenum PDPA – CC, RA, 27 March 1985; Najibullah, RA,
13 March 1987; Najibullah, XX plenum PDPA – CC, RA, 22 Nov. 1986;
Najibullah, RA, 11 May 1987; *FAZ*, 18 July 1990; *Aktual'nye problemy afganskoi
revolyutsii*, p. 575; L. Lifschultz, 'Afghanistan: a voice from Moscow', *Monthly
Review*, Sept. 1987, interview with N. Simoniya, p. 17; M. Baryalai, 'Indispensable
for victory over counterrevolution', *WMR*, no. 6 (1985); D.V. Ol'shanskii,
'Afganistan: sud'ba naroda, sud'ba obshchestva', *Sotsiologicheskie issledovaniya*, no.
5 (1988), p. 108.

[75] *KNT*, 25 Nov. 1985, 11 Feb. 1986, 6 July 1986; *News Bulletin*, 29 March

The new trend was also strong at levels higher than the village. Under Karmal districts or subdistricts might be 'reactivated with the cooperation of the local notables', like Charkunt subdistrict in 1984, but Najibullah went farther. He made much more room for non-party men in local administrations; in late 1987 eleven provincial governors (Baghlan, Helmand, Faryab, Bamyan, Ghazni, Zabul, Paktia, Kandahar, Farah, Wardak, Herat) out of thirty were non-party, generally 'influential figures', former parliament members, clerics or former army officers. By spring 1988 the number of non-party governors had grown to sixteen, while at the same time more than half of the district governors were not members of the PDPA either. In reality most of these new governors were linked to the regime in some way, or were in any case not from the opposition, but by October 1987 former mujahidin had been appointed governors in fourteen districts and four provinces, including such an important one as Baghlan. At the end of 1987 and the beginning of 1988 the Soviets tried to push for more positions to be offered to armed opponents, asking for the liquidation of 'people's power' in areas where the population did not cooperate. But the resistance exerted within the PDPA on this matter was at its strongest, as governors were one of the most important components of state power. In order to appease the Soviets, in March 1988 the government decided to give local notables control over seventeen districts occupied by force of arms, where no cooperation with the population had been won. In May 1988, moreover, Najibullah managed to appoint as governor of Nangrahar province Wakil Azam, a Shinwari tribal chief with influence over six districts. He had been a member of Hizb-i Islami for years, but, irritated by the growing influence of the mullahs, had clashed with Hekmatyar, the party leader. In a Shinwari *jirgah* he openly declared that, if Hekmatyar did not accept tribal traditions he would go over to the government. When he actually did so, the population did not appear to think that he had surrendered, but rather that power and authority would in this way be returned to the Shinwari tribe. Pro-government notables were evidently strengthened by this development and a

1988; RA, 10 Dec. 1987; A. Podlesnyi, 'Politika Natsional'nogo Primireniya i osobennosti ee provedeniya v yuzhnykh raionakh Afganistana', *Spetsial'nyi Byulleten' IV AN SSSR*, no. 2 (1990), pp. 158-9.

Shinwari *jirgah*, gathering 300 of them, dared to take strongly worded resolutions in the wake of the Soviet withdrawal, condemning the anti-Kabul activities of 'some' members of the tribe and asking their relatives to convince them to go back to their respective villages. The disobedient ones were to be deprived of their land. Furthermore, Shinwari militiamen who deserted were threatened with a fine of 500,000 Afs and the loss of their properties. Nangrahar became the second important province to be ruled by a former mujahidin.[76]

A similar pattern was followed in Kaldar subdistrict, Balkh province. As early as spring 1984 a Swiss journalist reported strong tensions between the most activist mujahidin groups and certain villages that wanted a compromise with the government, out of fear of reprisals. These strains must have worsened in the following years, until the top political leader of the Resistance in the subdistrict, Teka Baba, came out in favour of negotiations with Kabul, in contrast with the radicals. In 1987, after the launch of the National Reconciliation, a dialogue with the authorities was activated and this culminated in the signing of a protocol. Teka Baba became president of the district, previously almost completely controlled by the mujahidin.[77]

In at least some cases the new governors were able men, like Herat governor Khaleqyar, who became very popular in the West of the country, succeeding in attracting many commanders in Herat, Farah and Baghdis provinces. In a similar way, Tashkurghan district governor Jamil Rahman, whose father was a local *bay*, was able to use his social and kin relationships in order to reach agreements with several local commanders.[78]

Clearly Najibullah's strategy at the outset was far from completely

---

[76] *National Reconciliation in Practice*, pp. 43-5; *KNT*, 14 March 1984, 24 March 1988; M.A. Babakhodzhaev, 'NDPA – krupneischaya i samaya vliyatelnaya sila afganskogo obschestva' in *Respublika Afganistan*, Tashkent, Akademiya Nauk Uzbeskoi SSR, 1990, p. 15; *AIC MB*, 110, May 1990, pp. 6-7; Arney, *Afghanistan*, p. 244; Lyakhovskii, *Tragediya i doblest' Afgana*, pp. 356, 374; Lyakhovskii, 'Na afganskoi vizhzhennoi zemle', p. 59; S. Mukherjee, 'Evolution of the polity in Afghanistan during the last decade' in V.D. Chopra (ed.), *Afghanistan: Geneva Accords and After*, Patriot, New Delhi, 1988, p. 153.

[77] *Journal de Genève*, 9 March 1984; *KNT*, 12 March 1988.

[78] Dorronsoro in *Afghanistan Info*, no. 31 (March 1992), p. 18.

developed or clear – he just chose to intensify old policies. In one of his first speeches as leader (May 1986), Najibullah declared that the main weakness of the party and regime lay in the tactical and practical sphere, whereas strategy was 'profound' and theory 'comprehensive'. In other words, at the very beginning of his term in power Najibullah did not think of making major strategic modifications. A French observer noted that the National Reconciliation was more a political experience than a political project. Its contents, its substance, its application and the instruments needed were defined day by day, although with a 'very remarkable tenacity and political competence'. The only fixed point was that, unlike Karmal, he was ready to sacrifice the Revolution's ideological dogmas to any extent the situation might require. He in fact pursued this path to the point where the tactics and practices of the National Reconciliation eventually outpaced and pushed into a corner the 'profound' strategy and the 'comprehensive' theory. As has already been pointed out, many people, particularly in the armed forces, were opposed to concessions to the Resistance, even to the relatively limited extent to which they had been carried out. At the end of 1990, for example, after more than one year free of military operations by mujahidin in Balkh province, the army felt that the mujahidin were so weak as to be unable to hamper army activities, which were then resumed, including forced recruitment. In retaliation, the mujahidin bombed the fertilizer plant in Mazar-i Sharif. According to Prime Minister Khaleqyar, some generals considered the government policies too soft. Such problems had already been experienced in the past, as for example in 1982 with Sayyid Jagran, the Shura commander in control of Jaghori district (Ghazni province), who had expressed his readiness for talks with the state about the cessation of hostilities, but then changed his mind after provocative raids by the government air force. Ethnic animosities might have played a role in such incidents.[79]

Although the National Reconciliation did have a significant impact in some important provinces like Herat or Baghlan, it

[79] Najibullah, RA, 18 Aug. 1987; *KNT*, 4 Dec. 1986; A. Borovik, *Afghanistan. La guerra nascosta*, Leonardo, 1990, p. 139; *Link*, 30 Dec. 1990; Najibullah, *Bakhtar*, 14 May 1986; J.-J. Puig, 'Après le retrait soviétique en Afghanistan' in *Approches polémologiques*, dir. D. Hermant, D. Bigo, FEDN 1991, p. 241; Lyakhovskii, *Tragediya i doblest' Afgana*, p. 224.

barely affected the Pashtun belt from Kunar to Helmand. In Paktia province, for example, at the end of 1987 still only seven main tribal leaders out of forty-three were loyal to the government.[80]

Impact of the Soviet withdrawal

From the point of view of 'pacification' in the countryside the most important turning point was the departure of the Soviet Army. In itself this fact is somewhat paradoxical, as the withdrawal was clearly conceived in terms of international policy, rather than in order to influence the Afghan internal situation. Since 1986 the Soviets had been trying to play down their role in Afghanistan and to let the indigenous 'communists' do most of the work. By mid-1987 the Soviets claimed to be no longer present in ten provinces, by November 1987 two more had been vacated and still another one by January 1988. In fact this was mainly propaganda, as Soviets troops had never been present in more than twenty-one provinces out of thirty. The point anyway is that the Soviets now wanted their Afghan comrades to stand on their own feet and were trying to boost their image, as well as their performance. Unfortunately, the pace of improvement was not fast enough to guarantee the easy survival of the Kabul regime. There had been widespread reports of panic within the party as Soviets troops were leaving the country, and the Afghan population in general did not expect the PDPA regime to last for long. This is also apparent from the developments of the National Reconciliation in the countryside. The pace of 'reconciliations' fell dramatically in late 1988 and remained low until spring 1989 (see Graph 4). Indeed in 1988-9 the government lost many of the positions it had recovered in 1987-8, particularly in the most remote provinces. In Badakhshan, for example, Kabul had by 1984 greatly expanded its control over hundreds of villages in low-lying areas, but, as only 10% of them were solidly under the government's influence (i.e. covered by party organizations), in 1988 Kabul rapidly lost 240 villages, about 40% of those it controlled. Things must have been no better in the southern 'Pashtun belt'; Kunar province, where the regime had enjoyed a certain degree of control, was

[80] V. Plastun, 'Pushtuny i ikh rol' v politicheskoj zhizni', *Aziya i Afrika Segodnya*, no. 11 (1995), p. 52.

completely lost, and a sizeable number of villages were also lost in the border areas of Nangrahar province. Soviet sources claim that the Afghan government had not believed in the reality of the Soviet withdrawal and the measures recommended to face the mujahidin had been delayed till the last minute. Actually, according to A. Borovik, many party and state functionaries did not want the Soviets to leave at all. Najibullah himself seems not to have been totally confident in his chances. First of all he managed to foil Soviet plans to start the withdrawal in April 1987 and then the decision to remove the 40th Army from Afghanistan in 1988 was forced upon him. In January 1989 he reportedly asked the Soviets to send a 3,000-5,000-strong brigade back to Kandahar, to help relieve the besieged town and again in March he requested intervention of the Soviet Air Force at Jallalabad, where a key battle was raging.[81]

What happened was that the spectacular Soviet withdrawal could not but offer an unprecedented chance for the spontaneous and contemporary mobilization of a large part of the otherwise fragmented Resistance forces. A general assault on government posts and garrisons occurred in much of the country, particularly in the Pashtun areas, putting a heavy strain on Kabul's resources. Najibullah's government survived, but the price paid was high, as in many areas the government presence was wiped out or at least reduced to insignificance. This development was clearly bound to hamper any future prospects for the country-wide success of the National Reconciliation effort. On the other hand, the general population seems to have approved of the Soviet withdrawal from the start, in some districts (like Kulangar in Laghman province and Nava in Helmand) even exerting open pressure on the

[81] Najibullah, *Afghanistan Taking the Path of National Reconciliation*, Government Committee of Press and Publication, 1988, p. 116; RM, 16 Nov. 1987; Najibullah, RA, 22 Jan. 1988; 'Kak prinimalos' reshenie', *Voenno-istoricheskii Zhurnal*, 1991 -7, p. 43; V.P. Polianenko, adviser to President Najibullah, *op. cit.* in Lyakhovskii and V.M. Zabrodin, *Tainy afganskoi voiny*, p. 126; A. Tschernajew, *Die letzen Jahre einer Weltmacht*, Deutsche Verlags-Anstalt, Stuttgart, 1993, pp. 235, 237; 'Postanovlenie sekretariata TsK NDPA o rabote badakh-shanskogo provintsial'nogo partiinogo komiteta po vypolneniyu postanovleniya politburo TsK NDPA ot 17.9.1361, 30 dekabrya 1984 g.' in *NDPA (sbornik dokumentov)*, Tashkent, 'Uzbekistan', 1986, p. 259; A. Lyakhovskii, 'Na afganskoi vizhzhennoi zemle', p. 59; Rubin, *The Search for Peace in Afghanistan*, pp. 81, 84; *Ogoniok*, no. 30 (1988).

mujahidin to stop the war, and at least in Helmand province even the pro-Resistance clergy were reported by the intelligence to have invited the mujahidin to suspend hostilities after the Soviet withdrawal. After all, this was what many local notables had been asking for since 1980 in order to re-establish links with the central power, as some of them had told the governor of Balkh province in June of that year and as was repeated in 1987 by 200 commanders in Kandahar province, who were turning down Kabul's offers. But the number of mujahidin groups willing to strike agreements with Kabul fell dramatically in the second half of 1988 and in the first half of 1989. As Najibullah lamented, 'nobody wants to discuss things with the government any more'. In some provinces, like Baghlan, the mere announcement of the Soviet withdrawal, at the end of 1987, was enough to break the pace of the 're-conciliation' process. Many commanders had considered unacceptable any 'reconciliation' with the government prior to Soviet withdrawal, but once the withdrawal actually took place, as is reported by intelligence sources (for example in Laghman province), many of them adopted a wait-and-see stance, since it would not have made any sense to join a government that might crumble at any time. In September 1988 intelligence sources quantified at 300 units with 12,000 mujahidin those who assumed a non-belligerent stance, in the whole of the country. Many others resumed or continued armed activities, eager to join what they thought to be the victorious side or just attracted by the prospect of booty.[82]

The positive potential implications of the withdrawal were only fulfilled a few months after its completion, once the regime had survived the mujahidin onslaught. The government could now benefit from the favourable fall-out from the departure of the occupiers. A Soviet observer described the process this way: 'The moment our troops leave, [...] groups of local mujahidin with diverse leanings but consolidated by the struggle against our troops – the 'infidels' – instantly fall apart and begin competing with one another, if not militarily, then at least politically and economically.

[82] *O khode realizatsii politiki natsional'nogo primireniya"* 26.04.88, p. 3; Hassan Kakar, *Afghanistan: the Soviet Invasion*, p. 127; Lyakhovskii, *Tragediya i doblest' Afgana*, pp. 455, 418; *Otchet o komandirovke v pr. Baghlan, 15-18 dekabrya 1987 g.*; Podlesnyi, 'Politika Natsional'nogo Primireniya', p. 163; *Obstanovka v provintsii Laghman, 6.02.88 g.*.

They start fighting over who gets the best land, over water sources or control over gorges and mountain passes. [...] These groups need arbitration and get it from Kabul officials, the militia and security troops.'[83]

A similar point of view has also been expressed by some French scholars sympathetic to the Resistance. The alliance between Islamists and the rural population after the withdrawal showed a tendency to weaken, since for the peasants the jihad had ended the exact moment that the Soviet troops left the country. 'Reconciliation' accords were now assuming a new dimension. The motivation to fight was gone. The same explanation was given by former group-leaders to Western journalists, as exemplified by Hasaudin's account given to the British traveller Nick Danziger: in his view, the mujahidin should no longer kill soldiers since they were Afghans too. The French scholar O. Roy recognized that many small commanders had negotiated local agreements with Kabul. In short, the two sides were now 'all the same'. In the Tashqurghan area, for example, the different mujahidin groups broke up the united front which they had formed against the Soviet/Afghan forces, in order to strike separate agreements with the government and to fight each other.[84]

President Najibullah was quick to exploit the new situation. In May 1989 he had a new law on the local organs of state power enacted, which placed on a legal basis the removal of any limit on the size of landholdings of the commanders who joined the state and furthermore allowed them to appoint district, subdistrict and provincial governors, executives, prosecutors, judges and civil servants in their own regions. The National Reconciliation was now even more attractive.[85]

Thanks to the change in the general mood and to Najibullah's attractive offer, the government was able to make significant

[83] A. Prokhanov, 'Afghanistan', *International Affairs* (Moscow), Aug. 1988, p. 21.

[84] Dorronsoro and Lobato, 'L'Afghanistan un an après le retrait soviétique', *Est et Ouest*, Jan. 1990; Majiruh in *LAT*, 30 April 1990; Danziger, *op. cit.*, 1992, pp. 200-1; Roy in *AF*, Sept. 1989, p. 21; Arney, *Afghanistan, op. cit.*, p. 198; G. Dorronsoro, 'La politique de pacification en Afghanistan' in G. Chaliand (ed.), *Stratégies*, pp. 459-64.

[85] RA, 20 May 1989; RA, 27 March 1989.

progress in recovering a kind of legitimacy in several regions, as for example in the provinces of Ghazni and Baghlan. Baghlan in particular had already shown signs of improvement after a former mujahidin leader, Sultan Mohammed, had been appointed governor in 1987. When the Ismaili leader Naderi (see Part IV) took up his position, the process became much more intense and Naderi was able to claim at the end of 1990 that 75% of the groups were no longer fighting against the government. Throughout Afghanistan and in Pakistan, some mujahidin commanders now refused to fight, since they preferred Najibullah to such resistance hard-liners as Hekmatyar. Some World Peace Council members, after visiting Afghanistan, went so far as to say that in general Afghan citizens had a good opinion of their government and of its 'pacification' policy. This however seems an overstatement, even if in relation to the main urban centres alone. In reality, the mood of the population towards the possibility of striking a peace with the government varied from area to area. In 1990, for example, in one of the resistance strongholds, the small province of Logar, in each district different feelings were dominant. In Baraki, people were talking about the war as of something in a remote past and soldiers' wives now chatted with mujahidin's wives. In Kharwar the jihad was still officially on, but without any concrete combat activity, since the population was preventing the mujahidin from attacking the government troops. Only in Kalangar was fighting still actually taking place, partly because the district was dominated by Hizb-i Islami radicals, but the government had strengthened its positions there too.[86]

In Balkh province several districts were still quite unsafe for the government in 1988, but by the autumn of 1989 mujahidin activity had fallen to negligible levels.[87] Elsewhere, as in Nangrahar province, since the Peshawar parties and the Pakistani Intelligence were in better control, the mujahidin remained very active.

The case of Kandahar province is particularly striking. It had been 'the most difficult province' for the government: about a third of all weapons sent into Afghanistan from Pakistan were reported to have ended up there. Every column travelling along

---

[86] *Est et Ouest*, Jan. 1990 p. 11; *Link*, 30 Dec. 1990; *LAT*, 30 April 1990; *The Nation*, 12 June 1989; *Nouvelles d'Afghanistan*, no. 50 (Dec. 1990), pp. 15-16.

[87] AP, 3 Oct. 1989.

the Kandahar-Herat road was attacked and suffered losses. In 1982 in the whole province just a single school was open. One year later the number of schools increased to twenty-seven, but the near totality of the rural areas and part of the city itself were still under the control of the mujahidin. Notwithstanding great Soviet/Afghan efforts, the situation was even worse in 1984, when not a single village in the province had a party organization and recruitment in the party was 40% lower than the year before, with a particularly big fall among workers and peasants. At the beginning of 1986 Kabul had managed to reactivate eleven out of twelve district/subdistrict centres, proof of the willingness to expand its influence as much as possible, but in six of them government forces controlled only the administrative centre. In 1987 out of the thirty-seven members of the Provincial Commission for National Reconciliation, three were assassinated, five wounded and sixteen ran away. Even when the authorities managed to set up local commissions, it was only a formality – often the members of these commissions did not even know that they had been appointed to such a position. Although a military offensive seems to have effectively eliminated the mujahidin from the city, the rural areas were still utterly beyond Kabul's reach. Ismatullah Muslim was still the only mujahidin commander to have joined the government (see Part IV).[88]

The situation only changed when Brigadier Olumi was appointed governor in 1988. From the outset he stated openly that he would use his kinship ties to seek an agreement with the population. He was respected for observing the traditional norms of behaviour of the Pashtuns, and was also known for his scant affection for the Soviet Union.[89]

He was successful: after one year of Olumi's rule, the population of the city rose from 50,000 to 150,000 souls (according to official claims), approaching its pre-war level, while the number of shops

[88] *Izvestia*, 22 March 1983; *Pravda*, 12 Jan. 1986; Varennikov interviewed in *Ogoniok*, no. 12, 1989; 'Postanovlenie politburo TsK NDPA o rabote kandagarskogo provintsial'nogo komiteta partii po ukrepleniyu partiinogo edinstva i distsipliny v svete trebovanii XIV plenuma TsK NDPA, 10 otkyabrya 1984 g.' in *NDPA (sbornik dokumentov)*, Tashkent, 'Uzbekistan', 1986, p. 162; Podlesnyi, 'Politika Natsioanal'nogo Primireniya', pp. 163, 160-1.

[89] *Journal de Genève*, 24 Aug. 1988; Lyakhovskii, *Tragediya i doblest' Afgana*, pp. 556-7.

had doubled and supplies were finally regular. That Olumi's policy was causing trouble for the Resistance is supported by the statement of an important mujahidin leader of the province, Mullah Malang, who in 1989 made a British journalist aware of his preoccupation with the anarchy reigning among the mujahidin: if the Peshawar 'government' did not react, the jihad would really be over and many commanders might switch sides. In fact the number of 'pacified' groups was never particularly high. By mid-November 1989 only ten groups of 30-100 men each had signed protocols, but a much larger number (90 per cent according to official sources) was holding discussions with the government and observing a *de facto* ceasefire. According to Olumi only thirty-four groups were still active and Soviet documents confirm that mujahidin operations in the area were reduced practically to nothing during the three years of his rule. Olumi also aimed at building up the militias; new recruits were offered 18,000 Afs every month, plus coupons and rations in such a quantity as to satisfy everyday needs. By 1990 the population seemed to have come to consider him as 'the unchallenged strength and reliability [that] Afghans traditionally demand to settle disputes and deliver favours' and it was speculated that Olumi-backed candidates could have won any hypothetical elections.[90]

Whenever the Resistance parties tried to mount offensives against the city garrison, Olumi succeeded in keeping them divided, whether by offering them money (as mujahidin sources allege) or by appealing to the citizens, who would mobilize and leave for the countryside in order to persuade the commanders not to attack. A total 'pacification' would have been very difficult to achieve, in part because such Resistance parties as the two Hizb-i Islami were made up of Ghilzai Pashtuns, with whom the Durrani Olumi could not establish strong links, however by 1991 the mujahidin from the surrounding areas were sending their children to government controlled schools and Najibullah was able to claim that more than 80% of the Kandahar mujahidin had ceased to fight. At this point Olumi was so popular, that apparently Najibullah

[90] *KZ*, 23 May 1989; TASS, 2 Nov. 1989; C. Lamb, *Waiting for Allah*, Penguin, 1992, p. 252; AFP, 16 Nov. 1989; Inter Press Service, Feb. 26, 1990; Lyakhovskii, *Tragediya i doblest' Afgana*, pp. 556-7.

was beginning to fear him, particularly because of his contacts with the opposition. Olumi already had enemies, both at the centre, like Tanai's hard line faction in the party and armed forces, and in Kandahar, among the local party and WAD officers. But Najibullah's distrust was potentially much more dangerous; in 1990 Olumi was sent to the USSR for several months for 'medical treatment', but this caused a destabilization of the situation in the region, as many mujahidin groups, which had stayed neutral under Olumi, returned to active opposition. Najibullah had to bring him back to Kandahar, but with his death in April 1991 the situation became unstable again.[91]

Something similar happened in Herat province. Fazel Haq Khaleqyar was appointed governor in 1987. Although a non-party man, as a minister in the 'revolutionary' governments of the eighties he always shared the orthodox rhetoric: 'an undeclared war unleashed by the imperialist forces and by the regional reactionary countries'. Yet he had maintained contacts outside PDPA circles.[92]

Herat too was a resistance stronghold, although here the situation was not as bad as in Kandahar. Cases of 'reconciliation' had been recorded throughout the war. The first two important ones had related to Sher Agha and Turan Rasool. The former deserted Haraqat-i Inqilab in 1981 in East Herat with 800 men (see Part IV, Ch. 16), the latter left Hizb-i Islami in 1983 in Guzara district. In 1983 the flow of 'reconciliations' became significant, with twenty-two groups in the first five months. At this point anyway it was still evident that Herat province was largely dominated by the mujahidin and the city itself was frequently partially occupied by them. What little was left of the state-party apparatus was under constant pressure. In 1982 for example sixty PDPA activists were assassinated, though this was not as bad as 1980, when 106 were killed in the February-June period alone, but still a strikingly bad record.[93]

---

[91] Dorronsoro, 'La politique de pacification en Afghanistan', pp. 465-7; *KP*, 29 June 1991; Rubin, *The Fragmentation of Afghanistan*, p. 169; TASS, 19 Feb. 1991; Gareev, *Moya poslednyaya voina*, p. 306; Lyakhovskii, *Tragediya i doblest' Afgana*, pp. 556-7, 566.

[92] *Pravda*, 6 Feb. 1986.

[93] *Free Afghanistan*, Summer 1986; *NT*, no. 12 (1985), p. 28; *Izvestia*, 27 May 1983; *L'Humanité*, 23 June 1980; *NT*, no. 17 (1983).

It was only Khaleqyar's arrival that really turned the tables. Both Soviet and Western sources recognized his success in manipulating traditional *jirgahs* and striking deals with clan leaders and notables. Herat city and the immediate surroundings were soon under government control and in late 1989 it was clear to many observers that the government was gaining ground. 35,000 militiamen were already there (including self-defence groups) and more recruits were arriving from the Western part of the province. The population did not identify itself with the jihad anymore and sometimes even accused the mujahidin commanders of being 'parasites'. The economic situation was very hard, while the central power now accepted the traditional forms of exercising power (i.e., the role of the notables) and therefore was no longer perceived as a menace by the peasants.[94]

The authority of the mujahidin top commander, Ismael Khan, was defied within his own party, Jamiat-i Islami, partly because traditional elites were not happy about his meritocratic attitudes. In 1990 a wave of 'reconciliations' took place in the East of the province, particularly in Pashtun Zarghoun district. A large scale government offensive in spring 1991 reportedly damaged the 'reconciliation' policy, but at this time the whole of Najibullah's tribal/ethnic operation was already showing signs of crisis on its own.[95]

Soviet General Varennikov also claimed that similar results were achieved by governor Shah Nazar in Helmand province.[96]

According to the Soviet Ambassador Vorontsov, in July 1989 three quarters of the mujahidin were negotiating ceasefire agreements and in mid-1990 Najibullah claimed that 'two-thirds of the commanders of the armed opposition groups are either at the stage of talks with the government or have given up the fratricidal war having perceived [its] futility'. According to Najibullah's assistant, Farid Zarif, by this point the situation was very different to six months before, when the other side had been 'prisoner of

---

[94] *Ogoniok'*, no. 12 (1989); *The Herald*, Dec. 1989; *Independent* 22 Sept. 1989; Inter Press Service, 26 Feb., 1990; *Afghanistan Info*, no. 26 (1989), pp. 8-9; C. Lobato in *Journal de Genève*, 27 Dec. 1989.

[95] Dorronsoro, 'La politique de pacification en Afghanistan' pp. 467-8.

[96] *Ogoniok*, no. 12 (1989).

a mental block' which was forbidding any contact with the government. In fact it appears that the real turning point was represented by the battle of Jallalabad, whose day-by-day developments were broadcast to the Afghan countryside by international radio services (mainly the BBC). This must have given many mujahidin the impression that the regime was not going to crumble and Graph 4 shows that the number of 'reconciliations' rose again just after Kabul's victory there. As the Pakistani political leader Abdul Wali Khan (National Awami Party) noted, Jallalabad changed the attitude towards the war of many mujahidin commanders, who then requested peace talks with Najibullah.[97]

Some observers also claimed in 1990 that Najibullah, thanks to his charisma, his ability to communicate and co-opt former mujahidin leaders and regional notables, might have won a national election if one had been held. This was also the opinion of Mohammed Ashgar, leader of the legal opposition National Salvation Society: 'The reason Najibullah would win an election is that his party is well-organized, the army is with the party, and internal security is with the army.' In other words, 'might is right'. Najibullah now appeared to many people as a man of peace. It is certainly true that 1990 was Najibullah's 'annus mirabilis', as he was even able to recover some districts which had been in mujahidin hands for years, sometimes for the whole of the war, like Mohammed Agha (Logar), Pashtoon Zarghoun (Herat), and Khani Charbak.[98]

---

[97] Lamb, *Waiting*, p. 250; TASS, 18 Dec. 1989; Najibullah, RA, 27 June 1990.
[98] Inter Press Service, Feb. 26, 1990; Gareev, *Moya poslednyaya voina*, p. 155.

14

OVERALL CONSIDERATIONS ON THE POLICY OF 'PACIFICATION'

Achievements

It has already been noted that Western observers dismissed National Reconciliation in 1987 as a government trick. A prominent Soviet political adviser in Afghanistan, Kim M. Tsagolov, also heavily criticized it, on the grounds that the underlying idea at its base was totally outdated by the time the initiative was launched. The very fact that it was announced by the PDPA government meant that defeat was guaranteed – the only way would have been to have it proclaimed by a 'third force', for example the clergy. According to Tsagolov, given the way it was actually done, it could achieve nothing. There may be some truth in what Tsagolov said and possibly Najibullah himself realized it later, when he told a group of ulema (1990): 'You initiated the policy of National Reconciliation and laid the cornerstone for peace and prosperity', trying to attribute to the ulema a role they never had in reality.[99] When attempting to assess the National Reconciliation and its later developments, however, it should be taken into account that Najibullah's aims were not the same as those of the Soviet government, let alone those of Western observers. The Soviet leadership, or at least an important faction within it, was mainly interested in gaining international credit from the operation, although Foreign Minister Shevarnadze appears to have tried to guarantee some degree of survivability of the regime, and the Soviet government made it clear that it would only support a government led by Najibullah, who in this way was guaranteed some room to manoeuvre. Unlike many in the Soviet leadership, Najibullah was

[99] *Literaturnaya Gazeta*, 8 Sept. 1992; Rubin, *The Fragmentation of Afghanistan*, p. 165.

aware of the fact that a power-sharing agreement with the mujahidin would not work and he tried with considerable success to manipulate different factions in the Soviet government in order to pursue his own policy. His idea was to pacify as many armed opposition groups as possible, giving away much of government power at the local level, but at the same time consolidating his grip on the central state. This strategy obviously satisfied Najibullah's personal interests, but it also made sense from the point of view of the survival of the Afghan state.[100]

To what extent was Najibullah successful? Undoubtedly, with the Soviet withdrawal and the mujahidin defeat at Jallalabad, fighting subsided throughout the country. Government sources in autumn 1989 claimed that 70-80% of the mujahidin commanders were not fighting anymore (although many had no real written agreements with the government) and this evaluation was shared by the London-based International Institute for Strategic Studies. These statistics can be better understood if one takes into account the fact that only in very specific circumstances (basically just in 1989) had a majority of the mujahidin been actively fighting the government at any one given time. It is true, however, that intelligence reports about mujahidin operations pointed to a decline in the number of active mujahidin from 85,000 at the time of the general onslaught of 1989 to little more than 50,000 in late 1989 and 1990 (see Table 47). This was certainly good news for Najibullah, but the long term problem was to sign protocols with the group leaders, in order to stabilize the situation. Official sources claimed in May 1989 that 20% of rebel commanders had made peace with Kabul; if this figure is correct, by the end of Najibullah's regime the total would be as high as 40%. The real difficulty in assessing these figures lies in establishing how many mujahidin did in fact exist. Table 47 shows what intelligence sources were reporting. The Afghan and Soviet intelligence systems were obviously constantly busy trying to put together as accurate a picture as possible, particularly after 1983, when their network was finally complete. Even mujahidin sources admit that from 1983 KhAD possessed a quite detailed and exact picture of the Resistance. In

---

[100] TsK KPSS, 'O rabochem vizite Ministra oborony SSSR v Respubliku Afganistan' in *Soujetische Geheimdokumente* p. 500.

1981-3 they relied mainly on radio monitoring, obviously not as effective a device as real informers, while figures for 1980 were basically guesses, since the mujahidin were not yet using radios on a large scale at that time. Statistics usually made a distinction between active and inactive mujahidin, while a third figure, the total number of mujahidin, was sometimes given, with different services (KhAD/WAD, GRU, KGB) using their own criteria of classification. 'Active' mujahidin seem to have been those engaged in some sort of continuous warfare against the government; 'inactive' ones probably engaged in such activities only rarely, while the third figure included also many other groups thought to be hostile to the government, but for a variety of reasons, including geographical ones, who had not carried out armed attacks for some time.[101]

In reality, however, the number of men mobilized in any sort of non-government militias or armed formations in·the Afghan countryside was larger than that shown in Table 47. Table 48 shows KGB estimates for 1983. These figures also included clans and tribes living in the Pakistani border areas, so they overestimate by about 150,000 for our purpose. In the beginning, only a minority of the remaining 600,000 were armed at all, often with antiquated weapons. Both the absolute number of mobilized men and the proportion that were actually armed grew in later years, maybe reaching the figures of respectively 900,000 and 400,000 by 1990-1. It can be estimated that as many as two-thirds of these men never or hardly ever fired a shot against Soviet or Kabul troops, sometimes just because of their geographical location, while on average during the war only a third of the remaining third (i.e., a ninth of the total) exerted a constant military pressure on Kabul. These figures do, however, give some idea of the background against which the Kabul leadership was working.

Table 49 shows how many 'mujahidin' (in the broadest sense of the word, i.e. members of non-government militias) went over to the government or respected ceasefire agreements or just held negotiations at different times during the war.

Comparing Tables 49, 50 and 51, we can estimate that by the end of the war more than a quarter of non-government armed

[101] TASS 8 Sept. 1989; *Bakhtar*, 16 Jan. 1990; IISS, *Strategic Survey 1989/90* p. 159; *News Bulletin*, 13 June 1989; Chah Bazgar, *La Résistance au coeur*, Denoel, 1987, annexe 2; Gromov, *Ogranichennyi kontingent*, p. 152.

groups had signed 'reconciliation' agreements with the government, while another 40% had signed ceasefires. About 12% of the 'mujahidin' strength consisted of really 'irreconcilable' groups. While a lot of wishful thinking was going on in Afghanistan and especially abroad about 'elections' being instrumental in reaching a peace agreement, Najibullah was doing his best to win the only 'elections' that really mattered in war-ravaged Afghanistan, i.e. the allegiance of armed group leaders. Even when, as in most cases, their loyalty was doubtful, they were successfully detached from the opposition parties. Graph 4 shows that although some success was registered in 1987, as compared to previous years, the real breakthrough took place only between the second half of 1989 and the end of 1990.

In terms of territory, Najibullah's achievements are more controversial, as is shown with great clarity by Table 50. Apart from source P, which tries to take into account factors other than territory, government/Soviet sources seem to agree on the fact that during the course of the war there was no significant expansion in the government-controlled area. Indeed, figures oscillate according to seasons and other contingent events like military operations and so on. In this regard, Varennikov's statement, that the mujahidin parties (meaning the Pashawar ones) actually controlled only 20-30% of the territory might at first seem to be a wild understatement, but it no longer appears in this light if one recalls that Afghanistan is made up mainly of mountains and deserts. Varennikov' successor, Gareev, stated that 35-40% of the country, consisting of mountains and desert, was nobody's land. Column P above refers in fact to 'useful' Afghanistan. The figures given in the table below are, however, of some relevance, as they also reveal the degree to which mujahidin caravans could enjoy free movement inside Afghanistan. More concrete figures are, however, needed if the impact of the 'pacification' policy is to be assessed.[102]

This may also be the case for statistics on the control exercized over single districts and subdistricts. The government claimed it had 'freed' 206 districts/subdistricts out of 286 in May 1983, 214 in 1987 and 216 in March 1988, but this obviously only applied

---

[102] Varennikov interviewed in *KZ*, 23 May 1989; Gareev, *Moya poslednyaya voina*, p. 193.

to the administrative centres. Reality was much more complex and not so reassuring,[103] as is apparent from Table 52.

When seasonal fluctuations are taken into account, different sources are less incompatible. Another Russian source stated that during the Red Army involvement, the government never controlled more than 40-50 districts/subdistricts. In short, apart from a limited number of districts where it had been stronger from the beginning, the government was unable to consolidate whatever broadening-out had been achieved. In terms of population, Kabul's estimate was that in 1986-7 4.5-5 million people lived under government control (2 million of them in the countryside), which seems fair. Some other sources estimated that in 1989 7,000,000 Afghans were living under government control, which looks a rather optimistic assessment. Among this mass of people, some had stronger interests in supporting the regime. This was certainly true of the more than 250,000 families that were receiving government food and fuel coupons in 1983, which often had a decisive role in keeping the beneficiaries out of the everyday struggle to earn something to live on. The figure had grown to 340,000 by 1988 and it increased much faster afterwards, reaching 450,000 in 1990 and 550,000 in 1992. Most of the coupons were distributed in Kabul, 230,000 in 1989 alone. In 1990 80% of the population of the city benefited from them. Coupons played an indirect role in the National Reconciliation, as many members of mujahidin units had relatives in the capital or in other cities and the emergence there of a social climate that was more favourable to the government does seem to have influenced the behaviour of several armed groups. In general, the number of Afghans on the Kabul 'payroll' was estimated at 350,000 (including soldiers) in 1982 and their number increased afterwards, as the state claimed to be creating 40,000 new jobs each year. In 1987 181,000 civilians were working in the state sector. In 1988 700,000 people were receiving salaries, coupons or rations from the government, out of a total workforce of 3,000,000. Ideology and patronage managed to bind to the regime a sizeable section of the civilian population, which also proved able to withstand considerable losses during the war without collapsing, although civilian victims of the government/Soviet

[103] *Asia and Africa Today*, June 1989, p. 21; TASS, 18 Oct. 1987; *KNT*, 24 March 1988; K. Nayar, *Report on Afghanistan*, 1981, p. 147.

policy of reprisals were at least two or three times more numerous. One official source puts total casualties on the government side between 1978 and 1988 at 243,900, including 35,700 women and 20,000 children. This figure seems high, since after 70,000 soldiers and 42,000 party members are subtracted, at least 130,000 non-party civilians are left. Even if we take into account the fact that many thousands were killed during the insurrections in 1978-1980, that executions of collaborators and 'spies' were widely reported throughout the war and that towns and cities, particularly Kabul, were repeatedly bombed with rockets and mortars which again killed several thousands, the figure still looks somewhat inflated. Another Soviet source claims that 45,000 civilians were killed by mujahidin between 1980 and 1988, which is a more acceptable figure.[104]

If an assessment of the overall influence of the government is hard to make, it is possible to take as an example a single Afghan province, Kunar, neither a government stronghold nor one of its black spots. When in October 1988 the province fell to the mujahidin, some 5,000 people fled to nearby Nangrahar province; it is reasonable to suppose that these were the strongest government supporters, totally compromised and in peril of their lives. At the time of the following elections of 12 March 1990, organized by the Resistance parties, some 60,000 inhabitants were excluded from the electoral lists, because of their participation in pro-government militias or simply because of collaborationism. If we consider that the population numbered around 300,000, including children and women, mostly not allowed to vote, we can estimate that in such an 'average' province the government at the apex of its influence counted on some form of support or cooperation from a large

---

[104] Arney, *Afghanistan*, p. 176; S. Harrison, 'Afghanistan' in Kornbluhand Klare (eds), *Low Intensity Warfare*, Pantheon Books, 1987, p. 187; N.M.Momand, 'Afganistan: protsess revolyutsionnogo obnovleniya prodolzhaetsya', *Partinaya Zhizhn*, I (1987), p. 78; Yu. Gankovskii, interviewed in *Aziya i Afrika Segodnia*, no. 6 (1993), Gareev, *Moya poslednyaya voina*, pp. 193, 113; Rubin, *The Fragmentation of Afghanistan*, pp. 161, 170; *Pravda*, 17 Sept. 1990; Ludwig, 'Einige Probleme', p. 97; *National reconciliation in practice*, p. 67; Yu. Krasikov, 'Internatsional'naya missiya sovetskogo voina', *Voennyi Vestnik*, no. 10 (1988), p. 6; Najibullah, *Bakhtar*, 9 June 1988.

part of the population, as much as 50%.[105]

Regional diversity also has its importance, as a relatively stagnant situation nationwide may have sometimes hidden important developments in single provinces. Map 3 gives some idea for the early period, while Table 52 adds more details.

The following is an approximate chronology of the 'pacification' process, attempting to delimit the years in which it took place in each province:

1982	Jowzyan	1985	Balkh	1987-8	Kunduz
1983	Farah	1986-91	Herat	1987-91	Takhar
1983	Nimroz	1987	Faryab	1988	Kandahar
1983-8	Badakhshan	1987	Samangan	1988	Ghazni
1985-90	Baghdis	1987	Baghlan	1989	Ghor

We can see from this just how many provinces were significantly affected by the 'pacification' process in any given year:

1982	1983	1984	1985	1986	1987	1988	1989	1990	1991
1	4	4	6	7	12	12	13	13	11

Admittedly this is very rough, as it tells us nothing of the intensity of the process within every single province (see, however, Table 52), but it does give us an idea of its breadth. In fact the 'pacification', however slow, was relatively widespread after 1987; only the Eastern and Central (Hazarajat) parts of the country were not significantly affected.

Solidity and limits of the 'pacification' policy

It has already been noted that the Soviets expected to 'consolidate' the situation in Afghanistan in about six months and then to leave. They were soon to realize that such optimistic evaluations were misplaced, but it took time before they could accept how intricate the situation was. Vladimir Kryuchkov is reported to have predicted the final defeat of the counter-revolution by the summer of 1981. Indeed, in 1982 a new plan for the 'definitive'

---

[105] *Bulletin CEREDAF*, 58 March 1990, p. 3; TASS, 5 Nov. 1988.

liquidation of armed groups in Afghan territory was prepared. Once again, the stress was on military efforts, although it is reported that many Soviet cadres and specialists, like some Afghan politicians, already had doubts about the plan's chances of success. One Soviet adviser, while visiting an Uzbek village in northern Afghanistan, asked some peasants what the Revolution had brought them, and they had no answer but death and misery.[106]

When they were not busy planning megalomaniac enterprises like those above, the PDPA were preparing plans to extend government influence throughout the countryside. For January and February 1981, the idea was to wrest the control of twenty-four districts from the mujahidin, but ambitions soon had to be scaled down to reality. In the whole of 1362 (1983/4), the plan was to 'free' nine districts and to broaden state control in another thirteen, thus bringing 1,257 villages under their control. At the end of the year the government was able to claim that the plan had been 80% fulfilled. In the following year, 1363 (1984/5), thirteen districts and 1,431 villages were to be freed, extending Kabul's influence over thirty-six districts. In fact statistics reported that 1,252 villages were freed in 1363. We do not know about plans for other years, but similar achievements were claimed: in 1362 (1983/4) 1,819 villages were freed, in 1364 (1985/6) 1,535, in 1365 (1986/7) 1,319. But this was essentially the outcome of military offensives; it was impossible to garrison all these villages permanently, unless local militias were recruited. To form 'local organs of power' and militias in each village was the real aim of the government, but in the end it could fulfil its plans only in a fraction of the villages. For example in 1365 'state power' was established in only 294 villages of seventeen different provinces. The other villages conquered in 1365 were bound to be lost again soon. Even when the government's representative went to the newly 'freed' villages, they stayed just a short time. So, while 6,200 villages were 'conquered' by the government between 1980 and 1986, in the same period the number of those under its control only grew by 1,750. In 1980, 5,515 villages were under Kabul control, 7,265 at the start of the National Reconciliation.

[106] Hassan Kakar, *Afghanistan: the Soviet Invasion*, p. 192; Shebarshin, *Ruka Moskvy*, p. 183; Gareev, *Moya poslednyaya voina*, p. 22.

Developments during 1980 are unclear, but thereafter the government managed to extend its influence to 250-300 villages every
year, i.e. just 1% of the total number of villages in the country.
By late 1984, when large scale Soviet offensives actually ceased,
the physical limits of military 'pacification' had been reached,
with about 7,000 villages under government control (as claimed
by Najibullah in September of that year). The two following
years, when relatively timid attempts were made to shift the emphasis of the 'pacification' effort in a political direction, it was
shown that more was needed to achieve significant progress.[107]

Did the policy of National Reconciliation succeed in this regard?
Certainly the number of villages co-opted by the government
grew at an unprecedented pace. In the first nine months, 1,596
villages joined the government and the number had grown to
4,000 by the beginning of the Soviet withdrawal. At that time
the total number of pro-Kabul villages had risen to over 10,000,
while the government claimed it was able to take its activities
(agitprop, elections) for short periods of time to another 5,000,
which it did not control permanently.[108]

There was no real guarantee that villages that struck agreements
with the government would necessarily keep them, but chances
were higher than when villages were conquered by brute force.
In fact within the first months of the withdrawal several hundred
had already been lost due to mujahidin counter-offensives and to
redeployments of the army, which was getting ready for the expected

---

[107] Ludwig, 'Einige Probleme', p. 104; V. Plastun, 'Gorkii urok', *Aziya i Afrika
Segodnia*, vol. I (1993), p. 10; *KNT*, 21 Oct. 1987; V. Sherbakov, 'Po dolgu
internatsionalistov', *Voennyi Vestnik*, 3, 1987, p. 16; *NT*, 2 (1988), 30 (1987),
p. 12; *KNT*, 1 July 1987; *Rabochnaya Tribuna*, 29 Dec. 1990; Lyakhovskii,
Tragediya i doblest' Afgana, p. 179; *Voina v Afganistane*, Voenizdat, 1991, p. 320;
Gareev, *Moya poslednyaya voina*, p. 24; Selig S. Harrison, 'Containment and the
Soviet Union in Afghanistan' in T.L. Deibel and J.L. Gaddis (eds), *Containment:
Concept· and Policy*, NDU, Washington, 1986, p. 468. The total number of
villages is 35,500, but about 10,000 were destroyed or abandoned during the
war. These statistics on the number of villages controlled by the government
seem to refer to inhabited villages. In May 1988 the total number of villages
(inhabited or not) under government control was given by the government as
13,000 (*L'Humanité*, 24 May 1988).

[108] Umarov, 'Stanovlenie i tendentsii razvitiya politiki' p. 104; Abdul Rahim
Hatif, *Link*, 24 April 1988; *Bakhtar*, 4 July 1988.

general mujahidin offensive after the Soviet withdrawal. Many militias melted away as soon as the army left and hundreds of pro-government village headmen had to flee. By autumn 1989 only 6,100 villages were still under government control, as against 15,240 that were outside it.[109]

The problem of the quality of the 'pacification' process was certainly a serious one. Pro-resistance propaganda often claimed that many 'militiamen' only joined the government to get weapons and ammunition, which they would then turn on the government troops themselves. This may have happened sometimes, but the real reason for the apparent duplicity of many militias was more a matter of opportunism. If it is true that many 'reconciliations' were due to the fact that 'mujahidin·are receptive to strength', then a shifting balance could lead some militiamen to reconsider once again their allegiance. Cases are cited where mujahidin groups went over to the government, formed militias, then deserted, then made peace with the government again. Soviet advisers, on the other hand, were perfectly aware of the fact that commanders accepted the 'pacification' mainly in order to avoid bombings, gather strength and means, receive help from the state and, most of all, wait for future developments. A number of mujahidin commanders were clearly playing their own game and sometimes 'reconciliation' was just an expedient to enhance one's own stand in face of the Resistance organizations. In Tashqurgahn, for example, a commander of Harakat-i Inqilab was expelled by the local mujahidin council for carrying out an unauthorized attack. He was left no choice but to cross over and to become a government militia leader, then after a few months he deserted and was welcomed back by the mujahidin. In another case, a Hizb-i Islami commander in Dahar-i Sabz went over to the government in a strategic valley and blocked the passage to mujahidin; as agreed with the government, but not to those belonging to Hizb. For the government, the challenge was to provide the conditions whereby commanders would have found it convenient to stay on its side. In some cases links with certain groups proved to be surprisingly lasting. In March 1991, for example, Prime Minister Khaleqyar met militia

---

[109] Gareev, *Moya poslednyaya voina*, p. 193.

commanders from Uruzgan, a province where at that time no government presence was left.[110]

Few statistics were released after the Soviet withdrawal, but it appears clear that the number of pro-government villages began to rise again from summer 1989 and for the whole of 1990, although at a somewhat slower pace. For example, between 21 September and 21 December 1989, 165 villages came under government 'control'. Yet there were limits inherent in the 'reconciliation' policy. Particularly in areas where the government relied on local strains among mujahidin groups to bring some of them onto its side, as a reaction the local groups opposed to the pro-government ones would eventually strengthen their allegiance to the Resistance. In Balkh district, for example, at the beginning of 1989 an agreement with a group aroused the envy of another unit, which first attacked the group and then the town itself.[111]

Furthermore, Najibullah found it difficult to promote the development of the links established with the pacified villages into anything more then a very superficial allegiance. In November 1986 he complained that in Kabul province only one supposedly pro-government village out of every three actually voted in the local elections. Shortly later he complained that people elected to the local councils were making no effort on behalf of the Democratic Republic. Even the connection between the NFF and the local *jirgahs* was weak.[112]

Another potentially dangerous side-effect lay in that the continuous effort to establish contacts with the mujahidin was double-edged. Sometimes the local truces, which were supposed to lead sooner or later to a 'reconciliation', developed into quite ambiguous relationships. In 1988 a Western journalist visited a village where the government had a presence, but the mujahidin were in fact in control. The 'few government officials' there had a 'tacit agreement with the guerrillas': the mujahidin did not touch them, and

---

[110] KNT, 31 March 1988; RA, 14 May 1988; AIC MB, no. 92 (Nov. 1988); RA, 10 March 1991; Journal de Genève, 26 April 1991; M. Pohly, op. cit., p. 381; Gareev, Moya poslednyaya voina, p. 193; Lyakhovskii, Tragediya i doblest Afgana, p. 330.

[111] Najibullah, RA, 27 Dec. 1989; Roy, Le Monde, 17 Nov. 1983; South, Feb. 1989, p. 14.

[112] KNT, 5 Nov. 1986, 23 Nov. 1986; Najibullah, RA, 6 March 1988.

they pretended the guerrillas did not exist. 'But over the last year the guerrillas have started to flex their muscles: local vehicles are allowed into the village; anything else is attacked or turned back.' This was not limited to more or less isolated villages. According to a British traveller, in 1990 the administration in Mazar-i Sharif was anxious to please the Resistance. Several officials asked for letters in order to be able to demonstrate one day that they did not annoy people connected to the Resistance. In Mazar officials shared the same social environment with landlords and old aristocrats. Worse still, according to some Soviet sources the Interior Minister Gulabzoi established contacts of his own with the Peshawar party leaders Khalis and Gailani and agreed the establishment, under the cover of the National Reconciliation, of unauthorized 'coalition organs of power' between representatives of the Interior Ministry and the opposition in several population centres. The 'pacification' strategy, which to be 'flexible' needed a great degree of agility, risked stretching the fragile structure of the Kabul regime beyond its limits and beyond President Najibullah's capacity to compensate for such fragility with his manoevering skills.[113]

Furthermore, the fragility of the regime was exacerbated by the negative impact of National Reconciliation on the morale of the armed forces and party members. The alleged increase in desertions does not seem to have been very marked (see Part II), but it appears true that party members grew more indifferent to the political fight (Tsagolov) and, consequently, 'some parts of the state apparatus' (particularly in the localities) lowered the intensity of their fight against the armed opposition. An increase in sabotage was also reported.[114]

All this would play a role in the fall of Najibullah in 1992.

[113] *CSM*, 7 Dec. 1988; L. Palmer, *Adventures in Afghanistan*, Octagon Press, 1990, pp. 148, 153, 155-6; V. Korgun, 'Natsional'noe primirenie i vnutripoliticheskaya situatsiya v 1988 g.', *Spetsial'nyi Byulleten' AN SSSR – IV*, no. 2 (1990), p. 61.

[114] Lyakhovskii, *Tragediya i doblest' Afgana*, pp. 345-7, 342; *Izvestya*, 23 Dec. 1988.

Part IV
THE ROLE OF THE MILITIAS

15

ORIGINS OF THE MILITIA SYSTEM

By the term 'militia' we mean irregular or semi-regular formations, generally local or regional in character, semi-trained or not trained at all, subject to a less formal discipline than the regular armed forces, often not even wearing uniforms, often (but not always) supplied with fewer and worse quality weapons and equipment. The main advantage of the creation of such formations laid in their easier recruitment, in the possibility of mobilizing large numbers in a short time and particularly, in the case of village ones, in their cheapness.

Militias in Afghanistan were not invented by the pro-Soviet regime. A sort of militia existed in Afghanistan even before the Saur Revolution, although it was reduced to a mere historical relic by the end of the Doud regime. In the nineteenth century it had consisted of irregular formations making up a third of the army and recruited through their leaders, rather than individually like regular troops. It was resumed on a large scale for the first time by Taraki, who formed large units mainly in Paktia and in the Eastern provinces. The same pattern was pursued by Amin, who from spring 1979 began to distribute weapons to the Kharoti, his own tribe. Later in 1979 weapons were distributed to a number of other Pashtun tribes. The numerical strength of these militias, many of which appear to have been mainly tribal groups with little cadre structure, is difficult to estimate, but it may have been quite considerable. General Zaplatin claimed in 1989 that Amin had 250-300,000 men under arms just before the Soviet invasion. As no more than 80-90,000 can have been regular troops, it should be assumed that the remaining 160-200,000 were militiamen. When Karmal came to power, he was confronted with the existence of these potentially hostile armed groups. A number of militias were disbanded, but others continued to exist, though maintaining an uneasy relationship with Kabul. Some militia leaders just continued to work for Kabul as they always had done, with the difference that more resources now became available. Ghulam Khan Kharok-hel, for example, inherited his job as militia commander from his ancestors who had served under the kings and Daoud for eighty-five years. In April 1978 he commanded a fifty-man militia near Kabul; he served under Taraki, under Amin and then under Karmal, before deserting in 1984. At the time of his desertion he claimed (with some exaggeration) to have 2,000 men in his ranks, with 1,000 more soon to be armed. He was later accused of having maintained contacts with KhAD even after his desertion. In Paktia the government continued to supply the militias and pay them for some time, but the latter tended to act independently, disregarding orders from the Parchamis. So payments were stopped and the militias were asked to return the weapons, but they refused to comply. It is not clear how militias generally reacted to the Soviet occupation, although in Ghazni province, where the majority of the population was made up of Ghilzai Pashtuns, like Khalq itself, only a few militia units were reported to be in existence in the following years. In Kunduz province many militiamen recruited by Amin among his fellow tribesmen allegedly deserted to Hizb-i Islami, whose leader belonged to the same tribe as Amin. Overall, the small number of militiamen available in 1980 (see Table 53) points to the dissolution or disarmament of most older militias.[1]

---

[1] Interview with Farid Mazdak, Berlin, 31 March 1996; Dorronsoro, 'La politique de pacification en Afghanistan', p. 454; F. Halliday, 'Report on a visit to Afghanistan 20-27.10.1980', unpubli. typescript, p. 13; *Afghan Realities*, no. 22 (1-15 Sept. 1984), p. 1; A.A. Stahel and P. Bucherer, *Afghanistan 1986/7*, Schweizerisches Afghanistan-Archiv, 1987, p. 18; Hassan Kakar, *Afghanistan: The Soviet Invasion and the Afghan response*, p. 175; Dorronsoro and Lobato, 'The militias in Afghanistan', 4, p. 102 (quoting Raja Anwar); *Rodina*, no. (1989), p. 15, cited in *25 let PDPA*, Moscow, It. ON pri TsK KPSS, 1990, p. 43.

The situation in 1980 must in any case have been quite confused. The earliest statistics available date back to 1981, when militias 'patrolling the border' were claimed to number 3,000 men (see Table 53), spread along 55-60% of the frontier (Kunar, Nangrahar, Paktia and Paktika). Several militias were already in existence at that time, like the 'Revolution Defence Groups' (*Geruh az defa-i Inqilab* – GDR) and the 'Soldiers of the Revolution' (*Sepayan-i Inqilab* – see Part I, Ch. 3, Section 5), and others were created later, like the Self-Defence Groups (*Geru-ye Defa-ye Khodi*), at the beginning of 1983 which were non-ideological, part-time units strictly limited to the protection of work places and villages. Although their status is not clear, the Interior Ministry also had militia units among its ranks, recruited along criteria analogous to those used by the Regional Forces. Certainly many of its units did not differ very much from the Regional Forces, as they were deployed in their own villages, did not usually take part in operations outside them and did not wear uniforms. Even the GDRs and the Self-Defence Groups were not expected to play an active role in the war, being largely charged with protecting villages or propaganda duties, although the former were sometimes brought to the front to make up for the shortage of manpower in the army or used in active operations. In 1987, for example, the GDRs' main activity consisted in repelling 2,707 attacks against their villages, but they also carried out 281 independent operations (i.e., attacks against the mujahidin) and 209 joint ones.[2] Anyway, although the distinction is somewhat blurred, our attention will be focused mainly on the two most important militias, the *Milishia-i Sahard* or border militia, to which the above figure refers, and the *Ghund-i Qawmi* or Tribal Regiments, also called Regional/Territorial Forces. In fact the latter were already something more than a militia in the strict sense, receiving a salary higher than the regular forces and in some cases even receiving heavy weapons.

The decree regulating the activities of the *Milishia* was approved in June 1982, after the failed attempt to introduce recruitment into the regular armed forces for tribal youth, but such formations were probably operative from 1980 onward. Originally they may have been linked to the Ministry of Tribes and Nationalities, which had always had a military department and remained the

[2] *Bakhtar*, 8 Feb. 1988; PAP, 28 Jan. 1981; *Neues Deutschland*, 17 April 1981.

main source of their recruitment, but the 1982 decree assigned them to the Defence Ministry. Later they were fully integrated into the Border Guard 'in the general, national system of border protection and defence'.[3]

The Regional (or Territorial) Forces also appeared in some primitive form as early as 1359 (1980/.1), when at least one small group of mujahidin rallied to the regime in Dasht-i Qala district of Kunduz province and established a militia there. It really began to take shape, however, in 1982 when the first large formation of mujahidin joined, with the enrolment of Abdul Ghafar Pahlawan and 1,000 of his mujahidin in Jowzyan and Faryab provinces. The March 1983 *jirgah* in Kabul sanctioned the creation of the Regional Forces and the first regiments were formally organized. A directorate/department of Regional Forces, led by a vice-minister, was created at the Ministry of Defence in order to take care of them. The corresponding decree, finally establishing a framework for the conduct of such 'tribal units', was approved in December 1984.[4]

While the border *milishia* had the specific duty of closing the mujahidin's infiltration routes, the regional units were expected to exercise control over the countryside, to hamper the movement of rebel groups and to carry out recruitment, their troops being drawn from the local population. The final aim was to create 'a structure based on the traditional principles of defence of the state of Afghanistan and residential areas of the tribal people', in order to cover as much as possible of the countryside, utilizing sectors of the rural population which would otherwise have rejected service in the regular army. Najibullah justified this choice by claiming that 'one third of all forces in the regular army during the reign of Ahmad Shah were local volunteers'.[5]

Even in the Amin years most militias were 'officered and supervised' by army officers, generally Khalqis from the same

---

[3] Khan A.H., 'The Militias in Afghanistan', *Central Asia*, no. 31 (winter 1992), pp. 63, 69, 71; Karmal, 15th plenum, RA, 27 March 1985.

[4] *KNT*, 10 July 1988; *News Bulletin*, 2 Feb. 1988; *Sel'skaya Zhizn'*, 25 Feb. 1988.

[5] Strmecki, 'Power Assessment', p. 324; *Comrade Najib's Speech at the Plenum of PDPA, CC Jauza 1366* (June 1987), p. 30.

area. A more thoroughly developed organization was put in place by Karmal's government. Theoretically, the commanders were chosen by the Ministry from a list of candidates presented by tribal notables and group commanders. In practice, it was always the group leader, most often a former mujahidin commander, who was appointed and received military rank and his unit became a company, a battalion, a regiment or (later) a brigade and even a division. The unit was in many cases subordinated to a military unit, forming the fourth (or fifth, sixth and so on) battalion of a regiment or (rarely) the fourth regiment of a brigade, but in several cases it remained independent. In general, the commanders of regular army units in the area were in charge of the completion of the personnel charts and of the training of cadres. Regiment and battalion field commanders and regiment, battalion and company political officers, service commanders and KhAD representatives were taken from the regular forces, while platoon and smaller unit commanders were selected by the group leader, now transformed into regiment or battalion commander. Army officers provided training.[6]

Border militias were subjected to less strict controls by the Regular Forces. Formally they were dependent on the Deputy Commander on Militia Affairs of the Border Guard and, at the local level, on the commanders of each brigade of the Border Guard. Each unit counted regular officers in its ranks, but they only acted as 'advisers' for combat education and training and political affairs. The selection as unit commander of the group leader who had agreed the establishment of the unit with the Ministry was automatic, although still subject to the approval of the Ministry.[7]

The role of KhAD in recruiting and managing the militias grew over time. Militias like the Revolution Defence Groups were trained by KhAD and *sarandoy*, while the creation of militias was the job of the three 'security ministries', of the party and

---

[6] Hassan Kakar, *Afghanistan: the Soviet Invasion*, p. 175; 'Ukaz prezidiuma revolyutsionnogo soveta DRA, 30 dekabrya 1984 g., O Prinyatii Polozheniya o territorial'nykh voiskakh Vooruzhennikh Sil Demokraticheskoi Respubliki Afganistan' in *NDPA (sbornik dokumentov)*, Tashkent, 'Uzbekistan', 1986, pp. 406, 412; *KNT*, 29 March 1984.

[7] Khan, 'The Militias in Afghanistan', pp. 63, 69, 71.

NFF, of the local organs of power and practically of any willing notable or 'man of importance'. In Mazar-i Sharif, for example, a 680-strong tribal regiment was set up by the 'well-known' Afghan businessman Rasul Barat, under the command of Barat's military aide, Capt. Sepahi Bahaoddin, who 'served for twenty-two years in various sub-units of the Afghan gendarmerie'.[8]

A certain number of militia units, logically the most combative and mobile ones, enjoyed a special status and cooperated more closely with KhAD. Some sources call them '*opratifi*' battalions, a term used mainly for *sarandoy* and KhAD mobile units. Apparently terms like 'war units' were also used, as in the case of the Border Militia regiment in Herat province, which was organized into seven battalions plus a 'reserve' or 'war unit' – practically a special forces battalion, better equipped than the others and available to operate in 'any part of the country'. This particular one was also sent to Jallalabad. Such battalions were occasionally mobilized by KhAD for special operations. One of these mobile groups was the so-called 'Ghulam Jam' militia, renowned for its ferocity. The unit, perhaps a 1,000-strong regiment, was founded by Amanullah, a teacher of pedagogy who had lost his whole family in a mujahidin attack. Based around Mazar-i-Sharif, it often operated in Baghlan.[9]

The role of the intelligence service increased significantly after the creation of a Ministry of State Security (WAD). Shortly before the Soviet withdrawal, the responsibility for managing most tribal units was transferred from the Ministry of Defence to WAD. Even before this, some small former-opposition groups had been assimilated into KhAD, as was the case of some resistance groups belonging to the far left organization SAMA, North of Kabul. Militias under KhAD/WAD control also operated with Soviet special units, while at a certain point some regional units active in the North were placed under KGB control, particularly following the death of their commanders in inter-militia confrontations or in clashes with the regular forces.[10]

---

[8] RA, 17 Jan. 1988; Ludwig, 'Einige Probleme', p. 109.

[9] *Bakhtar*, 28 Sept. 1989; Interview with Zahir Tanin, London, 16 June 1995; interview with Farid Mazdak, Berlin, 31 March 1996.

[10] Interview with Zahir Tanin, London, 16 June 1995; Interview with 'Sasha', Moscow, 28 May 1996; *Jane's Intelligence Review*, 1 Nov., 1990.

The militia manpower came mainly from the rural population. The main source for the Border Militia were the tribal *jirgahs* organized by the Ministry of Nationalities and Tribal affairs, which were 'duty-bound to "create" border militia'. Faiz Mohammed was the first to stipulate agreements with the tribes (see Part III, Ch. 11, Section 2), but the process continued after his death. At the end of 1982 the Achekzai and Nurzai tribal notables agreed, for example, to supply 10,000 young men to the Border Militia. The agreement of tribal notables was (formally at least) necessary, although in some cases the original nucleus of the militia unit consisted of a former mujahidin group, as in the case of Ismatullah Muslim in Kandahar province.[11]

Former mujahidin formed a more substantial presence in the regional forces. Sources close to the Resistance identified militia recruits as uprooted individuals or mercenaries and the groups which were striking deals with the government as clans defeated in intra-mujahidin rivalries or ethnic/religious minorities or gangs of pillagers and bandits.[12] These judgements may well be too harsh, but it appears that especially in the beginning militias recruited some elements from the lowest strata of society, often belonging to ethnic minorities or to weak clans. They were attracted by the relatively good pay and the prospect of having some power in their hands. According to S.B. Majrooh, an Afghan observer sympathetic to the opposition, while previously a tribesman had nothing better to do than collect wood in the mountains, now the government was offering him a rifle and a salary to join the militias. For the first time in his life he had some dignity. Originally, many mujahidin units were transformed into self-defence groups, included in the Revolution Defence Groups or directly recruited into the Interior Ministry forces (*sarandoy*). In 1984, 40,000 'counter-revolutionaries' surrendered to the government (i.e. 40,000 adult males living outside the government's reach willingly gave themselves up) and 13,000 of them entered some sort of militia.[13]

So by 1985 more than 200 village militias had been formed by former mujahidin, while 2,000 of them joined the *sarandoy*

---

[11] *Bakhtar*, 8 Sept. 1986; RA, 3 Dec. 1982.

[12] *Est et Ouest*, Nov. 1985, pp. 15, 16.

[13] *KZ*, 22 Feb. 1984; Ludwig, 'Einige Probleme', p. 104; RA, 17 Jan. 1988; *Asiaweek*, 19 June 1986.

in that year alone. In fact by the end of 1983, twenty-four of the twenty-eight Regional Battalions were made up of former mujahidin. Later the influx of former rebels seems to have been channelled to a larger extent into the Regional Forces. As early as February 1987 about 100 mujahidin commanders had signed contracts to fight in the *Gund-i Qaumi* and *Milishia-i Sahard*. In the first year of National Reconciliation 15,000 of them joined the Tribal Units, making up more than half of the 28,300 men recruited by the *Ghund-i Qawmi* in 1987. In mid-1987 in a province like Paktia former mujahidin were in charge of about seventy villages. By the end of 1989 and beginning of 1990, 50-60,000 former mujahidin were serving in these militias, – or 100,000 if those who joined other irregular armed formations are included.[14]

As can be seen from Table 53, government efforts were relatively successful, particularly from 1986 onward, whereas till that year growth had been steady, but still quite limited as compared to overall needs. For example, in mid-1986 in Farah province the regional forces covered fourteen villages, i.e. 2.5% of the total, thirty more being covered by the GDRs. One and a half years later the nationwide figure for villages 'protected' by the regional forces was 5-6%, while on the whole about 15-16% of the villages were covered by one or other militia of the Ministry of Defence. The *sarandoy* took care of another 19%.[15]

It remains to be assessed how reliable these formerly-confidential figures are. Significantly, Western estimates do not differ very much, as it was estimated that in 1981, 10,000 militiamen were fighting for the DRA and 20,000 in 1984. In 1990 most estimates were around 60-70,000, often including even some units that had been transferred to the army, like the 53rd Division.[16] Although

---

[14] M. Koloskov, *Fighters for the Faith? No, Hired Killers*, Novosti 1986, p. 95; Glavnoe operativnoe upravlenie general'nogo shtaba, *Karta khoda formirovaniya dobrovol'nykh polkov iz plemen ichtvertykh batal'onov iz byvshikh bandgrupp po sostoyanyu na 1983 g. (10.I.84)*; KNT, 6 March 1988; Najibullah, RA, 17 Jan. 1988; TASS, 11 Aug. 1987; Najibullah, RA, 19 Feb. 1987; *FEER*, 26 Oct. 1989; KNT, 13 Feb. 1990; Reuters, 24 Jan. 1990.

[15] *Bakhtar*, 27 June 1986; Najibullah, RA, 17 Jan. 1988.

[16] *Nouvelles d'Afghanistan*, no. 3 (Feb./March 1981); Franceschi, *Guerre en Afghanistan*, La Table Ronde, 1984, p. 92; Rubin, *The Fragmentation of Afghanistan*, p. 161.

government figures are to some extent an overstatement, due to well-known causes, militia manpower did grow dramatically.

One of the most prominent former mujahidin leaders to join the militias in the early years was Ismatullah Muslim in Kandahar province. As an important Achekzai leader, he claimed to lead 100,000 people, counting more realistically on the loyalty of half that number. With a past as an army officer, he had taken refuge in Pakistan in the Amin period and organized an armed movement there. In 1984, out of disagreement with the mujahidin parties over a delivery of weapons that he had stolen, he joined the government with several hundred men, taking up the task of guarding all the Achekzai settlements and 130 km. of the border with Pakistan. A variety of sources recognize his high degree of activism against the mujahidin. He himself claimed to have successfully carried out twenty ambushes against mujahidin and to have captured six caravans loaded with weapons in the second half of 1985. By 1988 General Ismatullah (though he styled himself 'Marshal') could field at least 4,000 men, with some sources estimating them at as many as 6-10,000, equipped with armoured vehicles and heavy guns. Even after the loss in 1988 of his HQ in Spin Boldak, on the border with Pakistan, he continued to fight alongside the Afghan Army around Kandahar, where he took part in a victorious counter-offensive in Tor Khowtal. Although he appears to have been a friend of President Karmal, he was keen to distance himself from the 'communist' government, while after 1987 he emerged as an admirer of President Najibullah. He is reported to have considered the possibility of crossing over to the mujahidin again, but he never put into practice such a project.[17] Ismatullah Muslim did inflict severe losses on his fellow mujahidin during the war, but remained a kind of self-styled warlord even more than the average militia leader, ultimately unreliable and unsuited for playing a more ambitious role within the 'pacification' policy. The other, smaller militia leaders who joined the government in the early years were not as unruly and autonomous, but their impact on the economy of the war was in most cases limited.

[17] TASS, 3 Feb. 1986; *The Times*, 26 Jan. 1989; J. Hill, 'Afghanistan in 1988: year of the Mujahidin', *Armed Forces Journal International*, March 1989; *Le Monde*, 5/6 Feb. 1989; A. Bonner, *Among the Afghans*, Duke University Press, 1987, p. 257.

16

THE RISE IN IMPORTANCE
OF THE MILITIAS

The early, limited impact of non-party militias on the war was
mirrored in the modest ambitions that the DRA leadership had
for them. In 1983 their personnel charts were fixed at 20-25,000
for the Self-Defence and Revolution Defence groups and 10-12,000
for the Regional Forces. In mid-1984 in a key province like
Kandahar, party and trade-union members still represented a substantial majority of the militiamen, with 4,700 of them, while
the NFF, which recruited militiamen mainly for the *Gund-i Qaumi*,
enlisted only 200. In fact the Regional Forces were utilized as
auxiliary troops, with a marginal role in the economy of the
conflict. Things evidently changed later on. Table 53 shows eloquently that their importance grew considerably over time and
it is unfortunate that no figures are available for 1990-1, when
their numbers grew further (see also Table 54 and Map 4 and,
for some regional detail, Maps 5 and 6). Not only did the relative
weight of other militias diminish, but a number of Revolution
Defence Groups were transformed into Regional Units, as for
example in Herat province in 1987, where the 509th Tribal Regiment was established out of former GDRs.[18]

At the outset, the militias were basically expected to deal with
the control of villages and the protection of the 'local organs of
power', and their extension was planned and desired as a means
of creating 'civilian and mass defence of the Revolution' 'everywhere'. Because of the weaknesses of the regular forces, their
military tasks increased constantly. They began to take over part
of the duties of the *sarandoy*, particularly at the local and village

18 *Aktual'nye problemy afganskoi revolyutsii*, p. 443; *Otchet o sostoyanii territorial'nykh
voisk v pr. Gerat, 8.11.87 g.*; *KNT*, 5 June 1984.

level. From 1364 (1985/6) onward they were entrusted with recruitment in the countryside, which in fact became one of their main tasks. On one occasion Najibullah praised one regional unit for its exemplary activity, which in 1987 consisted in taking part in seven joint operations, two convoy escorts, six clashes with the enemy (which led to the elimination of ten adversaries and to the capture of 'several' of them), the seizure of 109 weapons and the drafting of 677 people. Besides, particularly after the Soviet withdrawal, they were requested to go beyond local defence and to be active over the whole national territory. But their political role increased also. In fact they became the main tool of 'pacification', as the local organs of power and the NFF went into eclipse after 1987. The stress was no longer on attempting to convince notables and the population to join the regime, and then form militias or convince mujahidin group leaders to follow suit, but rather on directly bringing onto Kabul's side the armed groups, which in turn would guarantee control over the population. In this shift of emphasis one can discern an acknowledgement of the transformations caused by several years of war, in which the traditional notables had been supplanted by warlords throughout most of the country. At the autumn 1989 Plenum great stress was laid on the role of the former mujahidin commanders in 're-establish[ing] peace in the country'. On that occasion a special fund was created to supply them with goods and provide sanitary and educational services.[19]

How the decision to upgrade the role of the Regional Forces was taken is not clear. Certainly some Soviet observers were impressed by the fighting ability of some of the militias, which outmatched the regular forces. This is the case of Shir Agha, a mujahidin commander from Harakat-i Inqilab who went over to the government in 1981 and formed a militia. His group was quite large and more active than most other militias of the time. It numbered 500 men and covered a cluster of villages south-east of Herat, but was also able to carry out offensive operations and took part in joint operations with the army. Indeed, in 1983,

[19] Karmal, XV plenum, RA, 27 March 1985; Krivov, 'Vooruzhennye sily v politicheskoi zhizni Afganistana', p. 183; RA, 17 June 1986; Najibullah, RA, 17 Jan. 1988; TASS, 20 Sept. 1989; *Pravda*, 1 Nov. 1989.

during a clash carried out jointly by Shir Agha's unit and another such militia commanded by Mohammed Aref Barakzai, 'for the first time in the history of the struggle against the counter-revolution a strong and well trained enemy' was 'defeated not by regular troops but by detachments from home defence formations', to which so far only 'auxiliary functions' had been assigned. In the words of the Defence Minister, 'the conduct of the operation and its results make it possible ... to conclude that a new force has emerged in the country capable of independent combat actions against the counter-revolutionaries'. As a consequence a stronger interest began to be paid to organizing 'cooperation between irregular formations and supporting army subunits' and to exploit such potentialities in order to increase the armed forces' active manpower.[20]

Even sources favourable to the mujahidin noted that in some localities, like Chakhcharan, Maimana and Herat, the militias were more pugnacious than the regular army; militiamen in Maimana were reported by Western travellers to have a particularly strong ideological commitment and even sometimes to have undergone training in the USSR. In other militias a number of militiamen did 'tours of duty' with Soviet units. A high level of commitment is attributed to Firdaus Khan's militia in Nangrahar, whose leader was defined by a pro-government source as 'a serious person', in contrast with such unreliable commanders as Ismatullah and Sayyid Khan (see Chapter 18), even though he had himself defected from Hizb-i Islami in 1985.[21]

High salaries played a fundamental role in the rise of the regional and border militias. Table 55 is of interest in this regard. It should be borne in mind that in 1987 a regular soldier received 1,500 Afs. and that in 1990 the average salary for civilians was 4/5,000 Afs. Furthermore, bonuses were available to militiamen for the capture of deserters, etc. A large part of the money printed after 1986 went to the militias. In 1983, when the regional forces

---

[20] *KZ,* 27 Dec. 1983 and 6 Jan. 1984.

[21] O. Roy, 'La politique de pacification sur le terrain' in A. Brigot and O. Roy, *La guerre d'Afghanistan,* La Documentation Française, 1985, p. 69; Dorronsoro and Lobato, 'The Militia in Afghanistan', p. 100; RA, Jan. 1988; Khan, 'The Militias in Afghanistan', p. 59; interview with Juma Khan Sufi, London, 22 Oct. 1995; M. Pohly, *Krieg und Widerstand in Afghanistan,* Das Arabische Buch, 1992, p. 320.

were officially formed, 192 millions Afs. were spent on them, i.e. 0.39% of circulating currency and 0.44% of state expenditure. This compares favourably with 65 million spent on pro-government mullahs, but was still much less than the 4 billion spent in supporting peasants with seeds, fertilizer, etc. around the mid-1980s. Things had changed radically by 1990, when 24-25 billion Afs. were spent on the tribal units, i.e. 7.85% of circulating currency. The commander of the 53rd Division, Dostum, alone was reportedly given 40 millions Afs. each month to build up his personal influence. B. Rubin noted a very sharp increase in the supply of currency in the country after 1985 and calculated that, while circulating currency grew 17% each year between 1357 (1978/9) and 1365 (1986/7), in 1366, 1367, 1368 and 1369 (1990/1) the growth was respectively 58%, 35%, 46% and 40%. In 1990 it was reported that militia commanders received whole containers of money from the government.[22]

Some Uzbek militiamen openly stated that they had gone over to the government because economic assistance from the mujahidin parties was no longer arriving in their area and the government had offered to replace them as a supplier. They declared they would stay loyal to Kabul forever provided assistance continued to be given.[23]

Other advantages offered to militiamen included electricity and televisions in the villages. Commanders were also seduced by offers of military hardware, particularly after 1987. In the autumn of that year the typical arsenal of a Regional Unit, taking as an example a unit which deserted in Herat at that time, included a BM 21 multiple field rocket launcher, two 82 mm mortars, two 14.5 mm, eleven 12.7 mm and four 7.62 mm machine guns, 500 Kalashnikov, 350 carbines and 200 Enfields. It appears clear that heavy equipment was still in short supply. In Herat province many commanders protested against the failure to deliver heavy

---

[22] Rubin, *The Fragmentation of Afghanistan*, p. 161-4; Glavnoe operativnoe upravlenie general'nogo shtaba, *Karta khoda formirovaniya*, Starodubova, 'Moral'no-politicheskii potentsial', p. 62; interview with Juma Khan Sufi, London, 22 Oct. 1995; Anwar, *The Tragedy of Afghanistan*, p. 218; V. Butenas, 'Dorogoi aprel'skoi revolutsii', *Kommunist* (Vilnius), no. 9, 1986 p. 89.

[23] Reuters, 16 Dec., 1991.

weapons during 1987 and also lamented the limited quantity of ammunition delivered. The unprecedented wave of mujahidin groups going over to the government in the region in 1986 and 1987 may explain difficulties supplying them; it is also probable that the government, or part of it, did not really trust the newcomers and was reluctant to give them too much, as a Soviet journalist reported in 1989. Anyway in Baghlan province even a Soviet adviser lamented the lack of heavy weapons, communication devices and armoured transport in the tribal formations. He recommmended they should be supplied with such equipment and that special battalions should be created in each regiment with two heavy weapons' companies and some reconnaissance units. Similarly, in Herat province at the end of 1987 only 16% of the scheduled means of transport and 19% of the communications equipment were available to the Border Militia and the Regional Forces. Some units continued to experience supply shortages even later, like one tribal unit in Kandahar province, which in 1988 claimed to have fulfilled 75-80% of its obligations towards the government which in turn had fulfilled only 2-3% of its own. At the end of 1989 a 600-strong group in Faryab province, led by Sharafbek, went back into opposition after having waited several months without seeing any supplies from the government.[24]

From 1988 and particularly from 1989, however, heavy weapons and armoured vehicles, including armoured transports (BTR) and even tanks, were finally distributed in large quantities to trusted militias. Commander Doud in Herat province, for example, who was not even the most powerful commander in the area, had five tanks in his 1,000-strong militia in 1989. Over time, militia commanders grew more and more demanding. In 1990 they became angry when the government tried to equip their units with the 58,000 carbines left over for this purpose by the Soviets in Hairatan.

---

[24] Christina L'Homme and S. Thiollier, *Défis afghans*, no. 22 (Feb. 1990); A. Cordesman and A.H. Wagner, *The lessons of modern wars*, vol. III, Westview, 1990, p. 74, n. 59; *Otchet o komandirovke v pr. Gerat 8-10 noyabrya 1987 g.*; *Operativnaya obstanovka v territorial'nikh chastyakh (donesenie VKR 20 PD pr. Baghlan, 17.12.87 g.)*; *Otchet o sostoyanii territorial'nykh voisk v pr. Gerat, 8.11.87 g.*; V. Plastun, *Informatsiya*, 20.04.88; O. Zharov, 'Est' li pochva u pantyurkizma?', *Aziya i Afrika Segodniya*, 3 (1996), p. 31; Iunin S., 'V poiskakh geroya', *Podvig*, no. 34 (1989), p. 132.

In the end even Najibullah had to agree that it would be insulting to distribute such antiquated equipment to the militias.[25]

Moreover, ranks were generously distributed to former mujahidin commanders. The case of Djahangir, who commanded a tribal Regiment along the Jallalabad-Torkham road and was appointed general, rather than colonel as was appropriate, was just one of many.[26]

[25] Reuters, 10 Oct., 1989; Gareev, *Moya poslednyaya voina*, p. 269.

[26] Shebarshin, *Ruka Moskvy*, p. 195.

17

THE PLACE OF THE MILITIAS IN THE ECONOMY OF THE WAR

Activities of the militias

Several Soviet advisers seem to have been quite wary of the growing role of the militias, although their creation and development was in general favoured on the ground that the same strategy had brought victory in Central Asia in the 1920s. The assessment of the militias by these critics was very negative: they were not trustworthy, they could go over to the enemy, they did not fight very well. In short, in their eyes the growing emphasis on the development of the Regional Forces was to prioritize the quantitative aspect, increasing at the same time the risk of massive defections that might endanger the whole defensive system of the government. If we look at the balance of forces in Herat province in 1988, we can understand what the advisers were worried about: out of a total of 55,000 government troops there, more than 30,000 were from the militias. From this point of view the situation was even more worrying in 1990, when the 17th Infantry Division in Herat counted 3,400 regular troops and 14,000 militiamen, while the 21st in Shindand had the same number of militiamen and 1,645 regular troops. The fact that many militia commanders maintained contacts with the opposition parties, a fact of which Soviet intelligence was aware, made the prospect of full-scale rebellions all the more likely in their eyes.[27]

The difficulty of many advisers in accepting these developments continued till the end of the war. There is little record of a

[27] Interview with Farid Mazdak, Berlin, 31 March 1996; Lyakhovskii and Zabrodin, *Tainy afganskoi voiny*, p. 189; *Iz besed ruzh. sostava RA s Shevarnadze. VPO v RA avgust 1988 g.*; Gareev, *Moya poslednyaya voina*, p. 269.

213

similarly negative judgement on the part of the large majority of
Afghan officers. They seem rather to have been somewhat afraid
that the militias would be assigned resources at the expense of
the regular army. Hostility towards some militias was indeed
reported at times and it led to long delays in the payment of
salaries to the militiamen. In 1982, for example, GDRs in Kunar,
Nangrahar and Laghman provinces received no salary, while in
1981-1982 Border Militias in Kunar and Nangrahar received no
salary for fourteen months; long delays were reported even several
years later. This seems anyway to have been due more to factional
strains within the party than to hostility to militias as such.[28]

A well-known Soviet journalist summed up his opinion about
the militias when he wrote that the groups 'can take sides with
the government and hospitably open the gates of their villages
for us to enter but the following day they are likely to shut them
again and to shoot us in the back'.[29]

Is this a fair judgement or did the Soviet Army just find it
difficult to reconcile itself with war methods so different from its
own? Certainly the militias had an impact on the development
of the war. The number of operations carried out by the militias
became quite considerable in the second half of the mid-1980s.
In the first quarter of 1365 (1986/7) they carried out an average
of twenty-six operations each month, while in the first three
quarters of 1366 (1987/8) this rose to thirty-one each month,
twenty-four or twenty-five of them independently. In 1987 they
were credited with an average of twenty-two to twenty-three
successful ambushes each month, while 1,200 villages were
protected by them and 150 more had been 'freed' by them over
March–December 1987.[30]

At this time the role of the militias in active fighting was just
beginning to gain importance. This role actually increased very
sharply from 1989, particularly in Herat province, where most
of the fighting was actually carried out by the militias. After about

---

[28] *KP*, 29 June 1991; General Khalil, Interview, Moscow 21 May 1996; Interview
with Farid Mazdak, Berlin 31 March 1996; Najibullah, RA, 17 Jan. 1988;
Gankovskii, 'Polosa pushtunskikh plemen Afganistana', p. 115.

[29] A. Prokhanov, 'Afghanistan', *International Affairs*, Aug. 1988, p. 20.

[30] Najibullah, RA, 17 Jan. 1988; RA, 17 June 1986.

that time, any actual pressure on the mujahidin in the war of attrition was exerted by the militias. While in March 1984 internal party documents stated that the border tribes of Herat played a limited role in the conflict, Table 57 clearly shows the dramatic developments which took place from 1986 onwards. The figure for 1991 might leave one somewhat perplexed, but it is true that the fastest expansion was reported by pro-mujahidin sources from spring 1989 onwards.[31]

Initially, militia recruitment was most successful among some border tribes in Paktia and Nangrahar, notably Afridis, Waziris, Shinwaris, Hill Mohmands, and in Kabul provinces. Paktia in particular saw the formation of the first Tribal Division in 1987 (drawn from Najibullah's own tribe), apparently the first Tribal Unit to receive sizeable quantities of heavy weapons, including tanks.[32] Table 56 shows how Balkh and Badakhshan provinces followed, together with the border areas of Kandahar province, where Ismatullah Khan was active. Other sources confirm that Jowzyan, Northern Takhar and Faryab became also militia strongholds.

In the areas where their network was relatively thick, the militias managed to jeopardize the infiltration routes of the mujahidin, like in Sayd Karam district of Paktia province, where the militias controlled sixty villages and reportedly captured six convoys in 1987. Elsewhere they were able to check even the most expert mujahidin commanders, as when SAZA's (Sazman-i Inqilab-i Zamatkashan-i Afganestan, Revolutionary Organization of Afghan Workers, a left wing party allied to the PDPA) militia in Shar-i Bozorg (Badakhshan) repelled an attack by commander Massud.[33]

---

[31] 'Postanovlenie sekretariata TsK NDPA o rabote geratskogo provintsial'nogo komiteta partii po vypolnenyu reshenii XII plenuma TsK NDPA, 10 marta 1984 g.' in *NDPA (sbornik dokumentov)*, Tashkent, 'Uzbekistan', 1986, p. 157; C. Lobato, 'Civils et résistants dans la province d'Herat à l'automne 1989', *Afghanistan Info*, Nov. 1989.

[32] Isby, *War in a Distant Country*, pp. 90, 92; *Sel'skaya Zhizn'*, 25 Feb. 1988.

[33] TASS, 14 Feb. 1988; Dorronsoro, 'La politique de pacification en Afghanistan', pp. 459-64.

Loyalty of the militias

Not all the Regional Units were very active and in January 1988 Najibullah in fact complained that some of them had not taken part in any operation yet and did not even try to complete their personnel charts. Border militias were particularly disappointing and according to a Soviet scholar they did whatever they could to wriggle out of their duty to defend the border and to stop the passage of rebel convoys. Many Western travellers reported cases of militias which did not really fight any mujahidin or were taking bribes to let them through the roadblocks. Even Soviet sources complain about the fact that Paktia and Paktika tribes received weapons from the government but actually refused to fight against the mujahidin, although it should be noted that some of these militias were self-defence ones, which had only undertaken to keep their territory free from the opposition. They too broke the agreements signed with the government, allowing the mujahidin to move relatively freely. Instances of fraternization with.mujahidin groups were also reported.' The existence of the militias itself, however, 'brought a great deal of pressure on the people', as it 'forc[ed] them to take sides'. In other words, the expansion of the militia system may have gained the government few sincere friends and many 'spongers', but it did represent a form of increased 'collaborationism' on the part of the population, which certainly caused trouble for the mujahidin.[34]

One controversial issue is the loyalty of the militias to the government. A considerable number of militia groups did desert over the course of the war, but it does not seem that the desertion rate among them was higher than among regular army units, although this may not be true of the desertion of whole units after the early 1980s. The most critical phase in the process of joining the government seems to have been the initial one, particularly after the reception of the first substantial batch of supplies, as some groups were only trying to tap weapons and ammunition from Kabul. The most dramatic case took place in the early 1980s,

---

[34] Najibullah, RA, 17 Jan. 1988; *Aktual'nye problemy afganskoi revolyutsii, op. cit.*, p. 574; *Iz besed ruzh. sostava RA s Shevarnadze. VPO v RA avgust 1988 g.*; *CSM* 19 July 1982; *WP*, 17 Oct. 1983; Dominique Vergos, quoted in *CSM*, Dec. 22, 1986; J. B. Amstutz, *Afghanistan: the First Five Years of Soviet Occupation*, National Defense University, 1986, p. 291.

when Khair Mohammed's unit, after having been engaged in discussions with government representatives in Nangrahar province for two years, on the day of the reconciliation ceremony attacked the party's activists and killed seventy-seven of them before leaving for Pakistan. Otherwise, whatever the initial feeling among the mujahidin, the sort of patronage relationship established with the government proved relatively strong. Some of the Herati militiamen might even confide their ongoing support for the mujahidin to a Western traveller, as reported in 1989, but this did not compromise the operation of the militia system in the province until the end of the war. The relationship with the government was in most cases based not on friendship or on shared outlook, but on mutual interest. Many groups may have approached the government just as an expedient, but then became dependent on its patronage. Therefore, intimacy among militiamen and mujahidin was susceptible to harm the latter too, as is shown by Ismail Khan's warning to his men to avoid any excessive closeness with the militia leaders.[35]

Although reports of desertions of whole units well after their incorporation in the militia ranks abound, many of these events were actually determined by unbearable situations. Militia commander Ashar Khan in Herat province did desert in 1989 but, as sources close to the Resistance report, only because he was surrounded by the mujahidin; he and his men were expected to link back with the government as soon as possible. Some commanders traded with the mujahidin in weapons given by the government, but more out of greed than of loyalty to them.[36]

One significant case is that of Rasul Pahlawan, an important mujahidin commander in Faryab province. He joined the government in 1982 with a large number of men, in the long run decisively altering the balance of forces in the province, particularly in the Northern part of it. In September 1987 his 'desertion' was widely reported, but in fact he was only trying to extort more

---

[35] A.A. Kotenev, 'Natsional'no-etnicheskii faktor v vooruzhennoi bor'be s kontrrevolyutsei v DRA', diss., 1983, DSP, IV AN SSSR, p. 122; *The Independent*, 22 Sept. 1989; Dorronsoro, 'La politique de pacification en Afghanistan', pp. 459-64.

[36] Christina L'Homme and S. Thiollier in *Défis afghans*, no. 22 (Feb. 1990); Najibullah, RA. 17 Jan. 1988.

favourable terms for his militia. He took his regiment to the mountains and then entered negotiations with the command of the 18th Infantry Division, to which he had been previously assigned. In the end a new protocol was signed, where Pahlawan was given what he asked for, i.e. 'protection' of the Shiberghan-Maimana road. The protection of main roads was greatly desired by the militias, as it enabled them to raise much additional money through the 'taxation' of drivers and travellers. The existence of a link between the size of the militias and the extortion of tolls along the roads is confirmed by the fact that all the most important militia leaders were involved in it, including Dostum and Ismatullah Khan. Often militia commanders could choose relatively freely the areas of their activity, as in the case of the 507th Regiment in Andarab Valley.[37]

A Soviet observer noted in 1988 that the 3,000 village militias supported neither the government nor the mujahidin, but were only protecting their own way of life and their property. Large scale desertions did take place among them, but only after the withdrawal of Soviet and Regular Afghan units from their areas, within the framework of the 'strategic redeployment' executed after the Geneva agreements. More generally, desertions were relatively common during the winter, when the regular forces were often unable to support isolated militias.[38]

Cases in which mass desertions from the militia apparently really endangered a situation which was not already totally compromised are few, obviously excluding the events of 1992. They seem to be limited to three: Asmar in 1988 and Khost and Kwaja Ghur in 1991. Only the first of these seems to have been a form of treachery, although even in this case the military situation was bad and the regular troops were so quick to abandon the area that one might suspect the militias to have only run ahead of the events. Khost and Kwaja Ghur will be dealt with later, in the conclusion, suffice it to say here that their fall was connected

---

[37] Dorronsoro, 'La politique de pacification en Afghanistan', pp. 459-64; Lyakhovskii, *Tragediya i doblest' Afgana*, p. 410; *Asiaweek*, 29 June 1986, p. 41; telephone interview with Mark Urban, London, 19 May 1995; A. Borovik, *Afganistan. Echshe raz pro voinu*, Mezhdunarodnye Otnosheniya, 1990, p. 26.

[38] L. Shershnev in *Agitator*, no. 17 (11 Aug. 1988).

with the inability of the government to maintain the supply of goods.

This relative 'loyalty' to the government is particularly noteworthy when one considers that the mujahidin were trying their best to reduce the seduction exercised by the government's offers: A source from the refugees camps in Peshawar reports for example the seizure of some Zakhel tribe elders by the mujahidin in 1984, in order to convince the militiamen belonging to the tribe to desert. Even assassinations were common. In 1988-9 in particular the campaign to convince the militia leaders to go over to the mujahidin was very intensive. Ismael Khan, the mujahidin amir of Western Afghanistan, campaigned widely, holding discussions with the most important militia commanders in the area, but was only successful in 1990 in Baghdis province, where he managed to bring back onto his side part of the wave of commanders who had joined the government in the previous two years.[39]

Attempts to increase the reliability of the militias

A Soviet observer was already warning in early 1984 of the danger of creating 'a state within a state', a process which could have decisively influenced the final outcome of the Afghan crisis. In 1989, Soviet advisers recommended the government to take some measures to safeguard against the eventuality of a massive betrayal by the tribal troops. In particular it was advised not to increase the number of tribal units any further, and instead to increase recruitment to the regular units, even among the tribes. It was also recommended to create reserves of regular troops in the areas controlled by the militias.[40]

The government did not make much of these recommendations, as the number of tribal units continued to grow. On the other hand, to follow the Soviet recommendations would have meant re-starting the old vicious circle of pressganging and massive desertions. The government was, anyway, aware of the potential trouble that could have arisen due to the incipient supremacy of the

---

[39] *AIC MB*, 42, Sept. 1984; Lyakhovskii, *Tragediya i doblest' Afgana*, p. 411; *Afghan News*, 1 Sept. 1990, p. 2.

[40] *Aktual'nye problemy afganskoi revolyutsii*, p. 574; Gareev, *Moya poslednyaya voina*, p. 270.

tribal sector of the armed forces. In the first place, some Guard Brigades were deployed in the North, where militias formed the great majority of the armed forces and where no serious enemy threat was conceivable. Earlier, attempts had been made to make regional units look more like the regular ones, by increasing discipline. A bill envisaging the introduction of military uniforms for the tribal units was examined in 1987,[41] but apparently it was not approved, as such troops continued to wear no uniform.

The most significant efforts were aimed at really transforming regional units into regular ones. Seven units, numbering 2,650 men, underwent such a process in 1987, in most cases becoming *sarandoy* detachments. Several of the new regular army divisions formed since 1988 were mainly drawn from former regional troops. This is certainly the case of the 53rd, 55th, 80th, 93rd, 94th, 95th, and 96th Infantry Divisions, while it is not clear whether a division in Lashkargah was transferred to the regular forces or not. In 1990 General Olumi, head of the Supreme Defence Council, stated that the aim was slowly to transform the whole of the Regional Forces into regular units. In reality this proved easier said than done. In 1990 Najibullah faced a crisis when he tried to speed up the process, which in fact had been stagnating for a while, but he had to backtrack. Moreover, the transfer of troops and units to the regular forces was in itself no guarantee that a real change was in the making; certainly the 53rd Division was widely reported to have continued to behave in the usual way —it did not even adopt uniforms.[42]

Similarly, political work was expected to transform former 'bandits' into real 'soldiers of the Revolution'. Political workers in the tribal units were asked by Karmal to work with 'patience, courtesy and observing [tribal] traditions', in order to raise the 'political awareness of the personnel'. Najibullah pointed out the importance of political work in such units, otherwise the enemy would infiltrate them.[43]

Like the model battalion shown to a French journalist in March

[41] RA, 19 May 1987.

[42] Najibullah, RA, 17 Jan. 1988; *FEER*, 26 Oct. 1989; Inter Press Service, Feb. 26, 1990.

[43] *KZ*, 29 June 1983; Karmal, XV plenum, RA, 27 March 1985; Najibullah, RA, 17 Jan. 1988.

1985 in Kachkak village (Balkh province), every regional unit was supposed to be supplied with political officers. In some militias, like Dostum's, Pahlawan's, Jabar Kahraman's (a Khalqi active in Helmand province), some groups among the Shinwaris and the Mohmands (including Firdaus Khan Mohmand's), political work was actually carried out. At the same time great efforts were made to recruit party members among the rank and file. Unfortunately, reality did not always match the aims of the government. Table 58 shows the actual situation in Baghlan province in 1987, with regard to party membership. Given the fact that most members of the tribal units were former mujahidin, sluggish PDPA recruitment among them is not very surprising. Yet the regime stressed the need to increase the network of party and DYOA organizations, as well as the spread of political propaganda, possibly 'by making use of the epic traditions of the Pashtuns, Baluchis and Nuristanis'.[44]

Furthermore, many political officers were missing. Regiment 507 did not count a single one of them in its ranks. Table 58 also shows the lack of regular army officers. The same applies to the province of Herat in the same period, when only 27% of the regular officers and 25% of the political ones were present, as against 88% of the rank and file.[45]

There are more reasons to think that the armed forces did not pay too much attention to the development of a proper organization among the militias. Most army commands did not seem to care or at least no specific approach was developed to deal with tribal troops; the traditional ones were tried instead and they did not prove to be well suited. Often militias and regular army did not cooperate at all, as the army let village militias be attacked by mujahidin without intervening. To return to the situation in Baghlan province in 1987, Soviet Army sources reported that while Tribal Regiments 504 and 508 and battalions 4, 5 and 7 of the 24th regular Infantry Regiment fought well and cooperated with the regular units, the 507th Tribal Regiment and battalions 4 and 5 of the 10th regular Infantry Regiment were of very poor quality. Joint operations between regular units and militias were considered

[44] *L'Humanité*, 1 March 1985; interview with Zahir Tanin, London, 16 June 1995; Najibullah, RA, 27 May 1986.

[45] *Operativnaya obstanovka v territorial'nikh chastyakh (donesenie VKR 20 PD pr. Baghlan, 17.12.87 g.); Otchet o sostoyanii territorial'nykh voisk v pr. Gerat, 8.11.87 g..*

an important aim, particularly with regard to the border troops, which for this reason were given a certain degree of priority with regard to the assignment of available manpower. It seems, however, that only in Nangrahar province was a good degree of coordination achieved.[46]

However disappointing such efforts to improve the discipline and reliability of the tribal troops may have been, the strengthening of the militias still proved to be the only way by which the government could gather combat-worthy infantry. The most pugnacious division of the army after 1987 turned out to be the 53rd, originally a militia regiment. Its commander, Dostum, was not a former mujahid. Born in 1955 in a village near the future PDPA-stronghold of Shiberghan from a family of peasants, he later joined the PDPA and entered the army, as a paratrooper in 1973 and rose to command an armoured unit at the time of the April 1978 Revolution. In 1978, after the demise of Parcham, to which he belonged, he travelled to Pakistan in search of contacts, reportedly planning to start armed opposition to the Khalq regime. The heavily fundamentalist atmosphere of Peshawar discouraged Dostum, who was back in the ranks of the armed forces after the Soviet occupation. He first commanded a militia battalion near the gas fields in Shiberghan, later expanded to a regiment and then to a brigade. Having shown remarkable skills in forming disciplined and battle-worthy troops, in 1987 he was assigned the duty to form the 53rd Infantry Division and began to be active even outside his home area. At that time, what was by then known as the 'Jowzyani militia' was already renowned for its fighting discipline (which did not rule out looting at the end of the battle) and its ferocity. The core of the militia was made up of relatively politicized troops, but a growing number of former mujahidin were also accepted. In March 1990 he was in fact promoted to division commander and shortly later he joined the Watan CC, being present at its plenum in June 1991. It is hard to imagine a clearer assertion of the importance of his division, defined by an analyst as 'the only real mobile reserve' of the

[46] *Otchet o komandirovke v pr. Gerat 8-10 noyabrya 1987 g.*; Dorronsoro, 'La politique de pacification en Afghanistan', pp. 459-64; *Operativnaya obstanovka v territorial'nikh chastyakh (donesenie VKR 20 PD pr. Baghlan, 17.12.87 g.)*; Najibullah, RA, 10 July 1986; Cordesman, *The Lessons of Modern Wars*, p. 60; Najibullah, RA, 17 Jan. 1988.

regime. It appears that by the early 1990s the division actually expanded beyond the three standard brigades which should normally have composed it. More brigades seem to have been added and most sources estimated its strength at 20,000 (instead of the supposed divisional full-strength of 8,000), while one puts it at 45,000 in early 1992. It is probable anyway that such huge figures are overestimated, or at least that they include units from other militias and *sarandoy* deployed in the area, in virtue of the new structure of the army established in 1986-7 (see Part II, Ch. 5, Section 3).[47]

Another militarily effective militia appears to have been that of Jabar Khan, based in Lashkargah, Helmand province. In early 1992, after the beginning of troubles with Dostum, the government tried to transfer the latter's role of mobile force *par excellence* to Jabar, but events took over. Jabar's militia, which by then was a full division, showed remarkable solidity, as it was the only one in the Pashtun belt to remain active on its own for a couple of years after the fall of Najibullah.[48]

If Dostum's militia had a prominent military role, others showed a remarkable ability at stabilizing certain areas of the country. This is the case of the Ismaili militia centred in Baghlan province. Some 100-200,000 Ismaili are based in Badakhshan, Baghlan and Samangan provinces in North-east Afghanistan. A tribal regiment was formed in 1984 by a leading Ismaili notable, Sayyid Mansour, who argued the progressive character of the Ismaili social doctrine, as it allocated land to the toilers and was in favour of education for everybody, allowing mixed female-male classes till the 12th grade, while in Kabul they did not go beyond the 6th. Sayyid Mansour's son, Jaffar, who was actually in command of the militia, became governor of the province after the launch of the National Reconciliation. The 1,200-strong regiment was initially entrusted with the safety of 80 km. of road and was later expanded to a brigade, finally becoming the 80th Infantry Division in 1988, with the incorporation of other, mainly non-Ismaili, units. In

[47] A. Davis in *Jane's Intelligence Review*, March 1993; *Der Spiegel*, Nov. 1993; *Le Monde*, 29 May 1992; *AIC MB*, 92 (Nov. 1988), pp. 8-9; *Libération*, 26 May 1992; telephone interview with Mark Urban, London, 19 May 1995.

[48] Khan, 'The Militias in Afghanistan', p. 59.

1989 it numbered 13,000 men and 18,000 in 1992, again probably including other units which answered to its HQ. Its capacity to conduct operations far away from its home area was limited, although small contingents were dispatched here and there, like for example to Jallalabad in 1989. However, thanks to its ability to manage successfully the plentiful government funding (Baghlan being one of the most strategic provinces) and to keep good relationships with the Resistance forces, for example by allowing their supplies through, a large part of Samangan and most of Baghlan provinces were pacified. Support was gathered even among non-correligionists and economic help offered to those who did not attack government convoys along the main road. Even resistance sources confirm the marked decline in fighting in these areas in the two years after the beginning of the National Reconciliation. At Kayan, Mansour's personal residence, the government had built a hospital, a metal workshop, a repair garage and a veterinary centre. Under his control, Pul-i-Khumri in the late 1980s became the most 'normal' town in Afghanistan, with working services and a health system.[49]

In the end, militias played a fundamental role in the 'pacification' policy in the provinces of Herat, Farah and Baghdis in the West of the country, in Balkh, Jowzyan and Faryab in the North, and in Baghlan, Takhar and Badakhshan in the North-East. Their role was much more limited elsewhere, including in the whole of the Pashtun belt, where even strong militias like Ismatullah's and Jabar Khan's remained more or less isolated. Furthermore, the new regular divisions drawn from the militia manpower in certain cases gave the government some of the hard-fighting infantry it badly needed.

---

[49] Telephone interview with Mark Urban, London, 19 May 1995; Rubin, *The Fragmentation of Afghanistan*, p. 160; *NT*, 26 (1989); *FEER*, 13 July 1989; *La Repubblica*, 23 Dec. 1983; *Sunday Times Magazine*, 21 May 1989; *Le Monde*, 20 Sept. 1989; Keshtmand, personal interview, London, 10 Dec. 1993.

18

PERVERSE EFFECTS OF THE SPREAD
OF THE MILITIAS

The government's plans with regard to the extension of the role of the militias in the conduct of the war were fairly successful by the end of the 1980s – beginning of the 1990s and many of the obstacles met in the earlier phases had been overcome. This success, however, carried with it several collateral effects. The priority given to their quantitative expansion, for example, reduced the pool of recruitable manpower for the regular forces, which already had their share of problems in trying to increase their size. Many in fact enrolled in the militias just to avoid being recruited into the army. This was already a problem in 1984, when Defence Minister Rafi complained to a Soviet interlocutor that 8,000 young, recruitable men were avoiding the draft by serving in the Revolution Defence Groups. In 1987 a Soviet Army internal report accused five tribal units (three regiments and two battalions) of the 20th Infantry Division of being a sort of refuge for potential recruits for the army. The same units also refused to deliver to the army the 20% of recruits agreed upon. The problem was made worse by the fact that even city-dwellers sometimes entered militias to avoid the draft, like Ismailis from Kabul who joined Mansour's militia in Baghlan, without actually taking part in any fighting. Najibullah himself even accused some regional units of sheltering deserters and draft dodgers, while others did not do much anyway to implement the draft.[50]

[50] 'Sasha', interview, Moscow, 28 May 1996; *Zapis' besedy zamestitelya zaveduyushcgo Mezhdunarodnym otdelom TsK KPSS t. Ul'yanovskogo R.A. s chlenom Politbyuro TsK NDPA, zamestitelem Predsedatelya Soveta Ministrov DRA t. M. Rafi*, Kabul, 18 oktabrya 1984 goda, n.p., p. 3; *Operativnaya obstanovka v territorial'nikh chastyakh (donesenie VKR 20 PD pr. Baghlan, 17.12.87 g.)*; interview with Farid Mazdak, Berlin, 31 March 1996; Najibullah, RA, 17 Jan. 1988.

The government was successful in transforming militia membership into a popular job, thereby obtaining a recruitment boom.
This success, however, attracted, in the words of an Afghan officer
who opposed the militias, large numbers of peasants 'who did
not want to work the land' and did not fight very actively, if
they fought at all. In his drive to expand the militias, the governor
of Kandahar province arrived at the point of abandoning recruitment
for the army, offering instead an incentive of 20,000 Afs. for
those willing to join the militias. Najibullah himself not only
offered exemption from military service to the tribal youth who
agreed to form local self-defence units, but also declared his readiness
to release from military service those already recruited.[51] It should
be borne in mind, however, that the expansion of the militias
had more than a purely military aim – it was part of the policy
of 'pacification' itself, as it offered an honourable and convenient
way of giving up opposition to the regime.

By far the biggest problem was the irredeemable lack of discipline
of the regional units. Although the army was instructed to prevent
abuses by the militias, it was not really able to do so. Far from
expending their energy on 'forming party organizations, reactivating
schools', doing 'work useful to the population' and reopening
agricultural cooperatives, as Najibullah had hoped in January 1988,
after the Soviet withdrawal, militias produced a 'Wild West' atmosphere around the country, with dozens of wounds caused by
their feuds being treated each month in just one Kabul hospital.[52]

It has been widely reported that the government eschewed
lodging any complaint with the militias. While it is true that
even regular army units indulged in various sorts of abuse, particularly in the first years of the conflict, the militias went beyond
that: they robbed refugees returning from Iran and Pakistan and
on one occasion they sacked a hospital in Kandahar. They also
laid mines without any warning and apparently without even
noting them down on maps. In the town of Balkh militias were
reported to 'smoke hashish, demand goods at half price and prey
on people travelling after dusk'. Regular officers acknowledged

---

[51] General Khalil, Interview, Moscow, 21 May 1996; *AIC MB*, nos. 123-4
(Jan.-July 1991), p. 50; Najibullah, First National *jirgah* of Nomads, RA, 5 July
1987.

[52] Najibullah, RA, 17 Jan. 1988; AP, 15 Jan. 1990.

that militias were 'beyond control' and visitors were warned to leave the town by 4 p.m. Unsurprisingly, the population did not seem to like them too much.[53]

The growing arbitrariness of the violence carried out by the militias was clearly damaging to both the government's reputation, the improvement of which had demanded a lot of work, and to the 'pacification' policy itself, as the attraction of a peaceful life had been one of the main trump-cards in Kabul's hand. Economic life, already in a bad shape, was further jeopardized. Besides, militias were fighting each other, sometimes with considerable human losses. In autumn 1990, for example, clashes in Herat province, originating in the theft of some sheep, caused thirty deaths among two rival militias.[54]

In December 1989 the Supreme Army Command took measures to re-establish discipline in the militias, but they do not seem to have worked at all. Militia-related disorder spread to the capital Kabul itself, where many important militia leaders had established their residence. In September 1990 the government was forced to decree the expulsion of the militias from the city; 130 militiamen were arrested for having failed to comply.[55]

The situation in Baghlan province in 1987 was probably quite typical. The local clans kept trying to place their own men at the head of the tribal units and the regular forces commands were besieged by lobbying notables. As a result, the commanders of the Regional Units often pursued the clan's interest rather then the government's. Most of them did not apply the protocols signed with the government and when the government tried to bring some pressure to bear on them, they reacted by refusing to obey and sometimes arranging desertions from one or two posts, as a warning that a mass desertion could take place if they were not left to themselves. The command of the 20th Infantry Division, to which they were subordinated, tried to instil some discipline in them, but progress was achieved only in a few units. Some

[53] Asia Watch, *Afghanistan: The Forgotten War*, Human Rights Watch, p. 40; AP, 3 Oct. 1989.

[54] G. Dorronsoro, 'Kaboul 1992. L'usure', *Est et Ouest*, Jan. 1992; *The Economist*, 13 Oct. 1990.

[55] Starodubova, 'Moral'no-politicheskii potentsial', p. 63; AFP, 5 Sept. 1990.

others, like the 513th Regiment, even considered themselves only logistically dependent on the Division, otherwise doing whatever they wanted. Most units did not respect the minimum requirements of personnel participation in military activities, fixed at 25%. The regulations for the Regional Forces stated that at least 30% of the manpower of each unit had to be at the barracks or at their posts at any given time. It has been widely reported that the actual manpower of the Regional Units was well below official figures and it seems that the clause above was exploited by the tribal commanders to claim a fighting strength larger than their actual one: many supposed tribal soldiers were in fact peasants who stayed in their villages and did not differ from other static (and less well paid) militias. Najibullah himself admitted that confusion reigned on the subject, when he stated that some regional commanders did not even know the numerical strength of their own units. At the XIX Plenum he had denounced the presence of false names in the membership lists of the Soldiers of the Revolution.[56]

On the other hand, if some commanders were pocketing money and making off with weapons rather than expanding their force, others were really doing their best to increase their manpower. In some militias boys as young as twelve were recruited for active fighting, and they could serve in other roles once they were eight.[57]

A perfect example of the conduct of the new, powerful militia commanders is given by Sayyid Ahmad, who went over to the government in 1987 with the fifty-seven villages he controlled and formed a Tribal Regiment in Guzara district (Herat), later expanded to a division. As a major and wealthy landlord he had been one of the promoters of the March 1979 rebellion in Herat. He joined the ranks of the mujahidin immediately thereafter and became regional commander of Jamiat in Guzara district. As a general in the tribal forces, he controlled a territory with a population

---

[56] *Operativnaya obstanovka v territorial'nikh chastyakh (donesenie VKR 20 PD pr. Baghlan, 17.12.87 g.); Ukaz prezidiuma revolyutsionnogo soveta DRA, 30 dekabrya 1984 g.*, p. 411; Najibullah, RA, 17 Jan. 1988; V. Plastun, 'NDPA: voprosy edinstva i soyuznikov na sovremennom etape revolyutsii', *Spetsial'nyi Byulleten' IV AN SSSR* no. 6 (1987), p. 122.

[57] Reuters, Oct. 10, 1989.

of 50,000. He made wide use of and enjoyed the symbols of power, with his four wives, his hashish-smoking bodyguards, his membership of Parliament, his guest house in Kabul and his Mercedes Benz car. He was also allowed by the government to run business activities, which included the ownership of the only cement factory in the province. The 1,000 men with whom he joined the government became at least 3,000 two years later. His force was equipped with tanks, BTR (including the most recent BTR 80), field rocket launchers and mortars. By means of checkpoints along the main provincial road he also extracted 'taxes' from lorry drivers in exchange for their safe passage.[58]

At the time he crossed over to the government he declared to a Soviet interviewer that 'only dialogue can bring us to peace. This truth is simple, but it must be understood even by those who still wage war and by those who equip them with weapons and money. It is impossible to win this war. It is necessary to search for compromises at the negotiating table.' The version given by pro-Resistance sources was quite different: Sayyid Ahmad, whose area of influence was close to the Herat airport and was exposed to violent reprisal bombings, had no choice but to strike a truce with the government, while at the same time continuing to grant freedom of movement to the mujahidin within his territory. If the first interpretation was typical Soviet rhetoric, the second was wrong too. A couple of years later, once his power was consolidated, Ahmad openly stated that he had switched sides because of the good deal offered by the government. 'I don't go with anyone forever, I only go with the one who works for my men. When that stops, I switch sides,' were his words. 'In my territory, I am the boss,' he added.[59]

In fact Ahmad really enjoyed substantial powers in his region. Disputes were regulated by himself or by his second in command. Criminals were brought to the *qazi* (Islamic judge) and, when condemned, delivered to government prisons. A military attorney followed the trials in the militia courts, but in fact the government accepted all the verdicts without complaint. Only prisoners charged

---

[58] A. Laurinchikas, 'Zelenie kraski zhizni', *Nash Sovremennik*, 11 (1987), p.153; Shebarshin, *Ruka Moskvy*, p. 200.

[59] *NT*, no. 30 – 1987, p. 13; R. Sikorsky, *Dust of the Saints*, Chatto and Windus, 1989, p. 150-1; AP, Jan. 15, 1990.

with political crimes were tried by the National Security Court. These conditions were not a special favour to Ahmad, as they were explicitly provided for in the 1989 Law on Local Autonomy (see Ch. 13, Section 3), although he might have been granted them some time in advance. As was claimed in some quarters at that time, it does not appear much short of a feudal relationship. In fact it has been alleged that the government encouraged the 'retribalization' of the local groups, i.e. the rediscovery of tribal/ethnic links which had faded away or had never been very important, like in the case of Ahmad, in order to facilitate their manipulation.[60]

Furthermore, Ahmad did his best to avoid political work being carried out among his units. He defended his only partial application of the protocols by pointing to the parallel non-compliance of the government; in particular he demanded that his troops be completely equipped with Kalashnikovs as stipulated. Therefore his relationship with regular troops was tense. On one occasion Ahmad was menaced with a pistol by a regular officer who wanted his bodyguards to deposit their weapons before entering Herat, as was requested by regulations. Ahmad gave up, but some time afterwards the officer was assassinated.[61]

Notwithstanding the contacts he maintained with Ismail Khan till at least 1988, Ahmad undoubtedly fought the mujahidin intensively in the years following his realignment. When finally Ismail asked him to make his final choice, he chose the government.[62] In the end, he was assassinated in 1990, either by someone from his former fellow mujahidin or by another rival militia commander.

Ismatullah Muslim enjoyed a similar authority over his territory. He too was quite unruly, not least because of his attraction to alcohol and drugs. In November 1987, while entering the *Loya Jirgah*, to which he was a delegate, his bodyguards took part in a shoot-out with the security forces, as the latter had not wanted to let him in armed. Fourteen people were killed, while more

---

[60] Asia Watch, *Afghanistan: The forgotten war*, p. 41; Dorronsoro, 'La politique de pacification en Afghanistan', pp. 459-64.

[61] *Otchet o sostoyanii territorial'nykh voisk v pr. Gerat, 8.11.87 g.; Otchet o komandirovke v pr. Gerat 8-10 noyabrya 1987 g.*

[62] Lyakhovskii, *Tragediya i doblest' Afgana*, pp. 412-14.

lost their lives when a new clash took place at his house in Kabul, as he was being arrested. One year later he was back in Kandahar.[63]

Clearly the idea of exercising relatively strict monitoring, if not control, over the tribal units was not realistic, given the vastness of the territory and the persistent weakness and ineffectiveness of the regular forces.[64] This was one important factor working in favour of the establishment of a sort of feudal relationship between the central government and the militia leaders. If the scarcity of cadre and political officers was added, any effort at reducing their independence was clearly bound to meet huge difficulties. Finally, it would seem that regular officers included in the militia ranks ended up being absorbed by them, rather than shaping them according to government wishes.

[63] *Asiaweek*, 29 June 1986, p. 41; Reuter, 30 March, 1989; V. Korgun, 'Natsional'noe primirenie i vnutripoliticheskaya situatsiya v 1988 g.', *Spetsial'nyi Byulleten' AN SSSR – IV*, no. 2 (1990), p. 56-7.

[64] *Operativnaya obstanovka v territorial'nikh chastyakh (donesenie VKR 20 PD pr. Baghlan, 17.12.87 g.).*

19

CONCLUSION

THE FALL OF NAJIBULLAH

The chronology of events which brought about the fall of Najibullah in the first four months of 1992, characterized by the alliance between some militia commanders and mujahidin groups, is fairly well known. The same cannot be said for the background to those events and the atmosphere in which they developed. By 1989-90 government policies were quite successful in guaranteeing at least the medium-term survival of the regime. In early 1991, however, signs of a crisis began to come into view. Strains within the party were exacerbated by its declining capacity to provide its members with jobs and career opportunities. The PDPA/Watan was only able to fund 55% of its financial needs, the rest had to come from the government and from the USSR; once government subsidies to the PDPA ceased in 1988, money did keep coming secretly from Moscow. By this time the PDPA had already sold its Social Sciences Institute to the state, which turned it into a school for officials. Problems got more serious in 1990, and by September about one hundred party cadres had either been 'released from services under the flag' or had lost their posts 'due to the new party structure'. In the late summer, it was decided that the practice of overmanning could no longer be afforded and a 40% reduction in staffing was decided by the Central Council of Watan, admittedly with the proviso that 'all those who are jobless will be assigned to new posts'. The tendency of the party to become 'a state apparatus or to be merged into it' was now sharply criticized by Najibullah, but the real reasons behind the changes were financial ones. After the coup attempt in Moscow in August 1991, the last external financial sources were cut and Watan had to dismiss full-time party functionaries on a larger scale; the party daily became a weekly.[1]

Another factor in the crisis was the spread of corruption. Al-

---

[1] TsK KPSS, 'Ob okazanii material'noi pomoshi Narodno-Demokraticheskoi partii Afganistana', 9 Jan. 1987, in *Soujetische Geheimdokumente* p. 455; Korgun,

though it had existed before, enough resources trickled down to feed the social base of the regime. But the degree of corruption had increased since the Soviet withdrawal. As early as 1988 *Pravda* reported that in the Kabul region one third of all goods supplied by the USSR had been stolen. Another Soviet source estimated that after the withdrawal only 10–15% of Soviet aid actually reached the population, the rest being absorbed by the bureaucracy.[2]

In reality, corruption was only a side effect of the growing scarcity of resources that the government could count on from 1990. During the occupation, the supply of wheat from the Soviet Union increased constantly, from 74,000 tons in 1360 (1981/2) to 160,000 in 1983 to 200,000 in 1984, stabilizing at around 250,000. Efforts by the government to increase its purchases of wheat on the domestic market were successful when compared to the very modest achievements of the 1983-6 period (when no more than 40,000 tons were collected each year) as 140,000 tons were purchased in 1988 and 150,000 in 1989, but this still represented only a mere 3.5 – 4% of the wheat production for 1977/8 and variously 5 or 10% of the production for 1986. A very severe crisis was experienced in 1989, but after some difficulties, a Soviet airlift managed to ease the situation, while after this it became possible to buy food from Pakistan. But a new crisis exploded in 1991, as the Soviet Union could not meet its commitment to supply 230,000 tons of food; by early October only half that figure had been delivered. The situation was further complicated by the particularly high deficit in wheat production recorded that year (amounting to 450,000 tons) as famine had hit the North and West of the country and the mujahidin were hindering road traffic with the South. During the summer, prices, which had already been going up for one year, began to soar, practically doubling. In August Prime Minister Khaleqyar urgently requested the delivery of 200,000 tons of wheat from Moscow and 50,000 more from India. The shortage was reflected in the distribution

---

'Natsional'noe primirenie i vnutripoliticheskaya situatsiya v 1988 g.', p. 59; *Bakhtar*, 20 Sept. 1990; *Pravda*, 29 Dec. 1980; *AFP*, 20 Oct. 1991 and 26 Nov. 1991.

[2] V. Korgun, 'Est' li vikhod iz tupika?', *Aziya i Afrika Segodnia*, no. 6 (1992); V. Korgun, 'Afganistan posle vyvoda sovetskikh voisk', *Vostok i Sovremennost'* no. 1 (1990), pp. 12-13; *Pravda* 26 Sept. 1988.

of coupons: from April petty officials and clerks lost their entit-
lement, while even families still entitled to the coupons (mainly
those of soldiers) received them after lengthening delays. These
reached several months by late 1991 and caused great dissatisfaction
among the population. The distribution of large quantities of wheat
from abroad in the form of emergency aid did begin at the end
of the year, but the climate of scarcity had already negatively
influenced the credibility of the regime.[3]

Furthermore by 1988, 75% of state revenue came from establishments and projects built with Soviet assistance that saw their
activity decline after the withdrawal of Soviet technicians, particularly from mid-1990. In June 1991 Najibullah admitted that
GDP had declined considerably over the previous year. Coupled
with the increasingly scarce supply of commodities and tools, this
trend worsened markedly from mid-1991. At that point, the
government could only rely on customs and indirect taxes, which
made up 30% of the budget, and what remained of Soviet financial
help in order to pay salaries and wages. In 1991 such help was
expected to amount to 100 million rubles plus 20 million more
distributed through the UN program, while credits were to be
granted for a further 150 million rubles.[4] After the final cut-off
in late summer 1991, the only way left to make up the difference
was to print money.

An even more critical aspect of the situation was the utterly
insufficient supply of fuel; in 1991 the government received only
10% of the fuel that the USSR had agreed to supply. This obviously
had a negative effect on the performance of the armed forces
and, despite the arrival of considerable quantities of fuel from
abroad between the end of 1991 and the beginning of 1992, the

---

[3] Strmecki, 'Power Assessment', p. 376; Rubin, *The Fragmentation of Afghanistan*,
pp. 139, 170; *FEER*, 26 Oct. 1989; *AFP*, 3 Oct. 1991; *Izvestia*, 23 Dec. 1991;
O'Ballance, *Wars in Afghanistan*, p. 225; C. Lobato, interview, *Nouvelles d'-
Afghanistan*, no. 56 (1992), p. II; RA, 27 Jan. 1992; Najibullah, RA, 6 Feb.
1988 and 5 Dec. 1991; Shah M. Tarzi, 'Afghanistan in 1991', *Asian Survey*,
Feb. 1992, p. 196; A.Q. Samin, 'War impacts on Afghan agriculture', WUFA,
April-June 1989, p. 23.

[4] Najib, RA, 6 Feb. 1988 and 11 June 1991; Harrison in *LMD*, Jan. 1991;
KP, 29 June 1991; TASS, 11-12 June 1991.

Air Force was grounded in January 1992 because of lack of fuel, while in the western part of the country the army depended on commercial purchases of fuel from Iran. Although Pakistani and Western observers in Kabul believed that the regime still held abundant reserves of military supplies, Russian sources estimated that they amounted to only 5-6 months of hard fighting.[5]

Financial difficulties and food shortages were necessarily reflected on the battlefield, and 1991 was characterized by a string of defeats for government forces. The most widely-publicized setback was the fall of Khost in April 1991, where the whole garrison surrendered or deserted. The reasons behind this collapse are not clear, as many have been given; bribes paid to the militias defending some key positions; the role of former Defence Minister Tanai in negotiations which guaranteed members of the garrisons their survival; an unprecedented degree of military preparations among the mujahidin. It does appear however, that the progressive exhaustion of ammunition supplies played a role.[6]

The other main defeats were in the North East, particularly in Takhar province, where in mid-1991 the 55th Division was wiped out. Although this event has sometimes been presented as an example of the great military prowess of Jamiat's leader Massud, in reality the collapse was due to the fact that the local SAZA-organized militias had not been paid since early 1991. Later on they no longer even received military supplies from the centre. The commander of the Division, Abdul Samad, left for Kabul shortly before the collapse in order to protest against what he defined as 'insufficient support from the government'. So it is not surprising that SAZA forces deserted *en masse* to the mujahidin.[7] In June 1991 the government controlled only one third of that very border with the USSR itself. Even in 1990 the number of desertions was higher than in late 1989, but it peaked only in the second half of 1991 (see Table 2, part II), with as much as

---

[5] Rubin, *The Fragmentation of Afghanistan*, p. 171; *KZ*, 24 Sept. 1991; *KZ*, 31 Jan. 1992; Najib, RA, 5 Dec. 1991.

[6] Dorronsoro, 'Kaboul 1992, l'usure'; C. Sigrist, 'Die Mujahidin am Scheidenweg' in *Tritt Afghanistan aus dem Schatten*, IAF, 1991, p. 17; O'Ballance, *op. cit.*, p. 222.

[7] C. Lobato, interview, *Nouvelles d'Afghanistan*, no. 56 (1992), p. II; Reuters, 30 July 1991 and 14 July 1991.

a 60% increase over the previous year. Soviet sources reported that the Air Force, the Jallalabad, Gardez and Salang garrisons and the troops busy ensuring the control of the road network were completely exhausted.[8]

Furthermore, problems were arising with the militias, even when they did not desert *en masse* as in Khost or in Northern Takhar. As the government had run out of money to pay them 'appropriate' salaries, they switched to drug smuggling, abductions and the like, to an unprecedented degree. One Soviet scholar commented in 1988 that the National Reconciliation policy was weak, because by becoming mujahidin the former peasants improved their status and were consequently not at all eager to go back to work the land.[9] It could be added that this was even more the case for the younger generations, who had grown up with the war. In fact, the government did manage to turn this situation to its favour, by hiring them to fight in its ranks. Unfortunately, this fostered the creation of warlords all over the country, a process which had already been encouraged by the weak links between the exiled parties and their commanders in the interior and the plentiful and unconditional supply of military hardware from abroad to the mujahidin. Such a process turned out to be a very strong disincentive to the re-establishment of anything resembling a 'normal' economy.

Such a complicated situation favoured the exacerbation of rivalries between the various components of the regime. 'Reciprocal betrayal' among party officials and army officers was widespread. The ideological crisis of the party did not make things better. Diplomats reported in 1990 that many party members were reluctant to exchange their PDPA cards for membership of Watan. The adoption of a political platform based on 'nationalism' could not but encounter serious trouble in such a multiethnic country, as demonstrated by the ethnic conflicts which marked the end of the regime in 1992. Moreover, the failure to transform the PDPA into Watan was openly admitted by Najibullah in early 1991,

---

[8] Starodubova, 'Moral'no-politicheskii potentsial' p. 62; *Trud*, 14 June 1991; M. Gareyev, 'The Afghan problem : Three years without Soviet troops', *International Affairs*, March 1992, p. 21.

[9] *LAT*, 13 September 1991; V.N. Plastun, *Situatsiya v Afganistane*, lecture given in Moscow, 1988, p. 36.

when he stated that 'the work to complete the basis of ideological and political activity [...] has not been carried out as it should have been. [...] Some party members live in a limbo between the ideas of yesterday and those of today; in some way we got rid of ours [*sic*] previous ideas and we got stuck with generic slogans about the future. [The educational system and the press] did not succeed in instaurating new ideological basis'. In June 1991 Najibullah was even more explicit, criticizing the inactivity of the party and its incapacity to establish a new policy. The ideological vacuum, coupled with the financial and material crisis, explains why some factions of the party were so busy in late 1991 trying to strike separate deals with the mujahidin.[10]

The ultimate limitation of Najibullah's strategy lay in its external dependence. In the end, the pro-Soviet regime in Kabul was not defeated on the field, rather it disintegrated when it became clear that it was running out of resources. It is difficult to imagine how the communist regime in Afghanistan could have survived the Soviet Union for much longer that it actually did, whatever it might have done. On the other hand, it would not have been easy in 1989 for anybody to foresee such an abrupt collapse of the Soviet Union two years later. At that time the regime could have expected more than a fair chance of survival in the long term, provided even a moderate degree of external support could be maintained and if it could manage to strengthen the centre in order to offset the growing devolution of local power to the militias. How this could have been achieved is difficult to say, given the difficulty of reconciling patronage in the countryside with the strengthening of whatever genuine political basis the regime had in the main towns, an aim which was also greatly hampered by the decline of the Soviet ideological model. Playing the card of 'Afghan nationalism', a move possibly inspired by the Ba'athist model, did not prove to be the right answer, in part because of the lack of credible external enemies. Had the regime been able to find a solution to this dilemma, it might also have guaranteed itself some degree of economic self-sufficiency by keeping the gas fields in Northern Afghanistan in activity, but in ten

[10] Lyakhovskii and Zabrodin, *Tainy afganskoi voiny*, p. 184; RA, 11 June 1991; Dr. S. Hamidullah Rogh, member of CC – Watan, quoted in *Link*, 27 Sept. 1992; RA, 11 Jan. 1991; AFP, 14 Sept. 1990.

years of occupation only scant efforts appear to have been made to train local technicians to do this.

To some extent, it is possible to say that Najibullah's regime was strangled by its own 'flexible strategy', whose main instrument (the militias) ran out of control when the availability of the means needed to manage them began to dwindle. The other core policy of Najibullah – the establishment of a strong 'presidential' regime – also facilitated the development of the crisis; Najibullah was caught in a difficult transition, at a time when his control over the state was still relatively shaky and the many enemies he had made within the PDPA/Watan were not yet completely marginalized. There are, however, lessons to be learnt. It would in fact be wrong to overstate the limits of these policies. For it is clear today that the processes set off by the Saur Revolution, while they could not be stopped, had to be re-directed if any way out of the regime's permanent state of crisis was to be found. When this was actually put into practice after 1986, however, it in turn served to re-intensify the tensions within the PDPA. Having already been critically damaged by factional infighting during the first phase of the Revolution, the party now began to crack. The reasons for this were in part ideological, but one key factor was the difficulty experienced by a factionalized party in handling a divide-and-rule policy among the local communities. Inevitably, competition developed among the factional leaders to secure informal affiliations and 'connections' at the local level.

Najibullah's move towards a regime more decisively based on his personality, whatever the actual motivation, was clearly also an attempt to address such a contradictory situation. Could he have been ultimately successful? Many commentators point out the weakness of his legitimacy. However, the way one attains and develops legitimacy is still a matter of debate. Judging from the historical record, it could be argued that, if he had managed to strengthen his hold and resist for some time, a certain degree of legitimation would have followed. Power often legitimizes itself by its own durability. Najibullah did understand that politics in Afghanistan is not made with the bolshevik-style 'proletarian masses', nor with Western-style 'citizens', but with notables and warlords, and he had the skills to put into practice a policy consistent with this view. What Najibullah was actually building up in

Afghanistan was a sort of feudal state,[11] where he would have played the role of 'king' and the militia warlords would have been his vassals. From Najibullah's point of view this had the merit of making him indispensable, as such a feudal state could only rest on the 'king's' personal capabilities and relationships. But it is also possible to argue in favour of such a project as the most (or only?) realistic choice to guarantee some future to anything worth the name of 'Afghan state'. The policies worked out by the late 1980s were achieving some success in cornering the mujahidin. Although it is not clear who actually lobbied in favour of the utilization on an ever larger scale of semi-regular militias, clearly these proved to be a relatively well-suited means of 'indirect intervention' from the Soviet point of view, as they could at least guarantee some minimal strategic and security requirements at a low cost. It became a sort of indirect 'neutralization' of Afghanistan, by its transformation into an endless battlefield. In fact, many in Russia regretted having abandoned Najibullah when the Tajik crisis exploded and attempts were made to establish strong links with the leading former militia 'general' in Northern Afghanistan, Dostum.

Militias were not as successful from the Afghan government point of view, as it had to pay the price of growing anarchy within the country, due to its inability to fine tune the policy once it developed beyond its early stages. The consolidation of Najibullah's feudal state would surely have been a long and troublesome process. Still, in itself the project was not necessarily doomed to fail. After all, hiring enemies to fight on one's own behalf is a strategy which will hardly surprise scholars of European history, and the depredation of the militias should sound familiar too. The failure of these policies, therefore, in absence of the fall of the Soviet Union, should not be taken at all for granted. However, because of their very nature, not only did the regime become utterly vulnerable to unfavourable developments in the Soviet Union, but it also helped create the conditions for the disintegration of the Afghan state when those resources which made such policies possible, were no longer available.

---

[11] The term 'feudal' suffers from a negative bias in today's literature, but it is used here in its technical meaning.

20

THE AFTERMATH: AFGHANISTAN'S DISINTEGRATION

'Warlord' and 'warlordism' are terms which are enjoying a new period of popularity. They appear to suit a whole range of situations in many parts of the globe, where a state collapses and no political force is either willing or able to rebuild it. A good definition of warlordism stresses the 'decay of nationalism into regionalism and sectarianism', the links between such provincial power centres and foreign interests, the 'disintegration of the military hierarchy and the rise of lower-ranked officer strata', and the 'burden imposed on civil society by the extortion and violence occasioned by warlordism and by the obstacles it places in the way of political solutions to problems'.[1] The 'perfect' warlord is a military leader devoid of any political ideology or affiliation, who has stolen or picked up the 'right' to rule over part of the country, although in real life a weak or remote commitment to a party or ideology is no obstacle to applying such a label. Warlords anyway generally have some sort of broad political project; for no other reason, this is because they are forced by the competitive environment where they operate to consider their own position relative to matters such as the reconstruction of the state (which model of state?), their alignment to the interests of regional and international powers (i.e. whether one is offering one's own services in the fight against communism or islamism, to support ethnic separatism abroad, etc.) and of the 'international community' (e.g. what to do regarding the opium trade or weapons smuggling).

Such definition clearly suits the Afghan case, but how modern warlordism developed in Afghanistan remains to be assessed. Was

[1] J.A.G. Roberts, 'Warlordism in China', *Review of African Political Economy*, n. 45-6 (1989), p. 26.

the Afghan state set to collapse anyway, 'or did specific policies put into practice between the late 1970s and the early '90s determine this outcome? Are warlords a 'natural' feature of Afghan society?

Other long-term factors, apart from the weakness of the communist regime which has been dealt with in detail in this volume, played an important role in the crisis of the Afghan state; first and foremost among these was the inability of the opposition parties to fill the vacuum. The weakness of their party structures, the limited number of trained and ideologised militants and the absence of an overall strategy, coupled with difficult communications and the reluctance of the local population to accept any form of organization, largely contributed to the creation of regional, almost indipendent leaderships among the mujahidin. The inefficiency of the so-called 'traditionalist' parties is notorious, but even the two best structured parties, Jamiat-i Islami and Hizb-i Islami, experienced great difficulties. The former, which by the mid-1980s had emerged as the largest opposition party, suffered from frictions between main commanders and smaller ones, who resented the centralization of the decision process, and (after 1992) between its two main field commanders, Ismail Khan in the West and Massoud in the East. At the beginning of the resistance aganist the communists, the party only had a few hundred activists. Although they multiplied by ten or fifteen times over the following ten to twelve years, they were never enough to guarantee a real party control over most of the territory. Hizb-i Islami counted just a few hundred more at the beginning of the war and, although it grew faster during the first few years, it soon stalled. Overall, by the late 1980s the Afghan Islamist parties counted on an estimated 15,000 trained cadres,[2] thinly spread over a mass of hundreds of thousands of armed mujahidin. After all, even the Afghan Islamist movement was a product of the Afghan urban society like the Communists, and its success in finding roots in the countryside only came at the price of striking alliances with local notables and clergymen. Many thousands of young Afghans of rural origin were 'educated' in the religious schools (*madrasa*) of the North West Frontier Province, supposedly under the strict supervision of the Islamist parties. In reality they were transformed instead into more traditionalist-oriented fundamentalists. They did not

---

[2] This figure is given by S. Harrison.

develop equally good skills in organizing a 'modern' guerrilla movement, but in the end these young fundamentalists found it easier to root themselves in the Afghan countryside than the Islamists with their urban background, who continued to make up the thin upper crust of these parties. As the advent of the Taliban has shown, notwithstanding their military ineptitude, they could easily sweep away the Islamists from the Pashtun belt, thanks to their influence over the rank and file of the Islamist parties themselves.

By the second half of the 1980s there were at least 6,000 mujahidin commanders in Afghanistan, about a third without affiliation to any political party and most of the others with only loose affiliations. They controlled areas ranging from a single village to a whole province or more.

A controversial point in the crisis of the Afghan state is the ethnic issue. Some factions of the anti-communist opposition, identified with the monarchy and the Pashtun rule over the country, claimed that ethnic turmoil in Afghanistan was caused by the ethnic policies of the revolutionary regime. Some other factions, notably Jamiat (a mainly Tajik party) and most of all Hizb-i Wahdat (the party of the Hazara), would not subscribe to this argument, since they proved to be among the beneficiaries of the ethnic reshaping of the country. In the early 1980s, certainly, the PDPA was eager to carry out Soviet-style ethnic policies, imagining that this would earn it the support of the minorities. This approach was championed in particular by some leftist factions which had generally come out of the PDPA in the 1970s and aimed at establishing a federal republic and enjoyed the support of some Soviet advisers. There was no unanimity, however, and the Pashtun component of the communist regime fiercely opposed the most radical aspects of these ethnic projects. Despite much talk, the outcome was eventually limited. To some extent government policies succeeded in awakening the ethnic consciousness of the Uzbek and Hazara minorities, although in the latter case the early repression (1978-9) against the local opposition counted more than the subsequent 'positive' policies. This was mainly achieved through the establishment of schools and radio broadcasts in the languages of the minorities and, in the case of the Uzbeks, also thanks to the efforts of a sizeable number of advisers from the Uzbek SSR. The whole process, however, remained limited mainly to the thinly-spread ethnic intelligentsia and the middle class, particularly those with education. There are few signs that the majority of the members of the minorities shared anything close to a strong sense of ethnic consciousness. The only possible exception might have been the Hazara, but their commitment to political autonomy was never really tested, as they were left alone by the government in the strategically unimportant central area of the country.

Whatever increase in ethnic consciousness may have taken place in Afghanistan in the 1980s and early '90s, it was probably more the effect than the cause of the crisis of the Afghan state, since the élites of the minorities stepped in to fill a vacuum, sometimes at the invitation of the central state, sometimes in open opposition to it. However, by the early 1990s the dynamic of the minorities had developed its own logic. At least two of the main protagonists of the Afghan conflict, Massoud and Dostum, played the ethnic card to some extent, the latter much more heavily. The immediate cause of Dostum's mutiny against President Najibullah was obviously the ethnic strife within the upper echelons of the army, as he reacted to an attempt to check his rising power in Northern Afghanistan. Once the communist regime had collapsed, Dostum clearly favoured the emergence within his own army of an officer corps with an unprecedentedly large and powerful Uzbek component at the expense of other ethnic groups, although his army remained a mixed one, including also Pashtuns. At times he also openly toyed with the idea of presenting himself as the paladin of the Afghan Uzbeks, but never really adopted this policy. Massoud and Jamiat were more careful, as they aspired to be the dominant party in the whole of Afghanistan. Although there were also a sizeable number of Pashtuns in Jamiat ranks, its overwhelming support among Tajiks, particularly in the countryside, was clearly due to their identification of it as 'their' party. At the same time, even other ethnic groups and in particular Pashtuns began gradually to identify Jamiat as a Tajik party, a circumstance that clearly hampered its efforts to expand its influence beyond its traditional strongholds.

However, the main factor behind the crisis of the Afghan state was the power accumulated by the most powerful militia commanders, resembling that of a feudal lord. The opium trade, the extortion of taxes on the highways, the looting of the civilian population and the money coming directly from the government joined together to transform many militia groups into the main economic power in their areas of activity. Even the local judiciary was strongly influenced by them, as it was stipulated that the government could only send observers to the local courts, whose *qazis* (judges) generally had obligations to the local militia commander.

The 'pacification' policy of the government met a degree of success exactly because it matched what the opposition parties had been offering after 1980. Indeed, by late 1989 the mujahidin parties began to find themselves at a disadvantage in this competition. Dealing with armed groups operating inside Afghanistan was more difficult for the mujahidin than for the government, both because of the country's difficult geography (the main roads were in the hands of Kabul) and because of their weak organization and logistics. This was particularly true of the areas of the country further away from the border with Pakistan, like the North. In any case, even when commanders were not particularly eager to go over to the government side, the increasing multiplicity of sources of support was to weaken the allegiance of local commanders to the opposition parties, as they could always threaten to switch to Kabul if unsatisfied and could more easily resist pressure to join difficult or unrewarding military operations against the Afghan army.

Some parties, notably Hizb-i Islami and Jamiat-i Islami, did implement plans to create regular 'regiments' out of their semi-regular units. Formally, several score of such regiments were formed before the fall of Najibullah in April 1992, but in practice most of them differed only in name from the old formations. In sum, by 1992 actual regular mujahidin forces did not exceed 12-13,000 men, mostly belonging to Jamiat. Even these, though definitely better trained and organized than the mass of the mujahidin, were not subjected to unconditional military discipline. Their operation still depended on personal relationships between commanders and their subordinate 'officers'. The mujahidin found it difficult even to maintain the army units which fell into their hands when the regime crumbled – in this only Jamiat was at least partly successful.

Before 1992 the mujahidin's command and supply system could still do its job, though with increasingly evident shortcomings, but things changed when the mujahidin, in coalition with the rebellious militia leaders, came to power in Kabul. What had been at least acceptable in opposition was not adequate to prevent the country from sliding into anarchy. The situation was made even worse by the fact that, with large quantities of weapons and ammunition falling into the hands of regional commanders, the leverage of the mujahidin parties over them was virtually cancelled. The situation was made worse by the cut of most outside help to the parties. The only residual link was ideological in nature, but most of the mujahidin commanders, particularly in the southern Pashtun belt, had no real allegiance to parties. Even when party links had some substance, it proved difficult to control commanders in remote areas only on this basis.

The interference of foreign powers in the internal affairs of Afghanistan hardly needs to be introduced either, although its increasingly manipulative character after the Soviet withdrawal should be stressed. While up to 1991 'only' four countries were involved – the United States, Saudi Arabia and Pakistan with the mujahidin, and the Soviet Union with the government – siding permanently with the same faction throughout the war, since 1992 external powers have switched from one faction to the other with extreme opportunism. Russia at times supported Jamiat at certain periods, and Dostum at others. Saudi Arabia first supported Jamiat (thanks to the good offices of Ittehad, a small 'Wahabi' party aligned to Rabbani), then the Taliban. Pakistan first sustained Hizb-i Islami, and then the Taliban, with a transitory phase when, owing to rivalries between different services, it supported both of them. Iran helped first Hizb-i Wahdat, then Jamiat and (possibly) Wahdat, and finally Dostum. Only India and Uzbekistan stuck all the time to Jamiat and Dostum respectively.

However, some aspects of foreign intervention are less well known. The general scale appears quite clear, at least in gross terms, but some very relevant details remain obscure, like the actual quantity of small weapons introduced into Afghanistan. According to one source, 3 million Kalashnikovs were available to the Pakistani intelligence for delivery to some Afghan faction in 1993.[3] Many others had obviously been shipped in 1980-92 –how many is difficult to guess. It has been estimated that by the early 1990s 2 million weapons were circulating inside Af-

---

[3] Amnesty International, *Afghanistan: The world's responsibility*, 1995.

ghanistan, including thousands of heavy ones. The choice of the CIA and of the Pakistanis – soon emulated by the Afghan government and by the Soviet Union – to distribute weapons to supposedly cooperative Afghans with largesse was largely a matter of Cold War politics, but not entirely so. Because of the disintegration of state control in the countryside, and the resistance parties' inability to replace it effectively what might be called a state of nature became dominant there. The ability to offer protection (against the government or the opposition, against rival clans, against bandits) became the driving factor in local politics. Armed groups sprang up everywhere, and at least in the south, south-east and south-west of the country practically every village got at least one. Weapons were in heavy demand, but isolated villages could get a sufficient supply without linking up to some external power, which could be a mujahidin party, the state itself or some middleman who in turn enjoyed privileged access to one of these sources. A better guarantee of protection could often be obtained by joining a larger conglomeration of villages, headed either by a renowned and powerful mujahidin leader or by a government militia leader or some independent 'warlord'. In other words, the availability of guns and ammunition was one of the main factor behind the expansion of political influence in the Afghan countryside. Even if most of the weapons supplied to the mujahidin never fired a single shot against Soviet or Afghan government troops, they played an important role in the politics of the conflict as the 'currency' needed to buy the allegance of the villages to the cause of the mujahidin parties, which would easy the passage of supply caravans to the interior.

However, this relative success was clearly not without important side effects. The government, at first wary of supplying weapons to people it could not really trust, changed its mind once it became clear that no other solution was available to achieve a breakthrough in the countryside. Furthermore, it also became apparent that the militant opposition already had as many weapons as it could use and probably more. After 1986 the government began to grab back some influence in the countryside, using the same tools of the mujahidin.

Another side-effect was on the structural development of the mujahidin parties, as they had now little incentive to improve their organization and recruit people on a properly political basis.

Furthermore, once the policy of massive distribution of weapons to the opposition parties had been chosen, it became difficult to change – particularly after it had been into effect for some years – because the mujahidin had become 'addicted' to it. When the pro-Soviet government adopted a similar approach, this had a multiplier effect and actually raised the stakes, since from 1987 it began to deliver armoured vehicles, including tanks and heavy artillery, to some militias. Soon militia commanders could afford to refuse to accept weapons they considered unworthy of their status, like carbines rather than Kalashnikovs. When a number of militia units were integrated into the regular army, their equipment was correspondingly further upgraded. Although all such units were classified as 'infantry divisions', they received quite large quantities of tanks and other given armoured vehicles, given the plentiful armour the Soviet Union made available to the Afghan government in 1988-90. Because of the country's geography, armour rarely proved really decisive in the Afghan context, but it was an asset, particularly in controlling the main highways, which in turn was decisive to the survival of some sort of national government.

Could the process which at brought about the collapse of the Afghan state have been stopped at some stage? It might be argued that because in 1980 the strategic initiative in Afghanistan actually lay with the Americans and it was up to them to decide how to arm the mujahidin, how much to give them and how to distribute this help, they could have taken a longer-term view. It appears that some debate actually took place with the Pakistanis whose long-term aim was to gain (indirect) control of Afghanistan once it was freed of Soviet presence. Thus Pakistan tried favouring the one party which seemed able to deliver a unified and friendly Afghanistan at the end of the war, i.e. Hizb-i Islami. Its interests would have been best suited by a largely dominant Hizb, with the other parties allowed to survive though not to (prosper) in order to maintain some leverage on the Hizb. The Americans, on the other hand, appear to have been mainly interested in maximising damage to the Soviets in the short and medium term. To favour a radical and centralized party like Hizb would have allowed the quantity of weapons shipped inside Afghanistan to be drastically contained, but it would also have meant alienating a significant part of the population and therefore weakening the resistance, at least in the short term and politically if not militarily. So they favoured a 'fairer' distribution of resources among the mujahidin parties, an approach that would maximise the extension of the resistance effort, again in the short term at least. In the end, the solution adopted was much closer to the American approach, although Hizb-i Islami was specially favoured in the distribution of resoureces. It can be argued that this choice prepared the ground for the future disintegration of Afghanistan. To be fair, the United States tried to bring together the mujahidin parties based in Pakistan in a single alliance and eventually succeeded (after years of failed attempts), but only from the formal point of view, as the various parties continued to pursue their own separate and indeed opposite agendas, not to speak of any coordination on the field.

However, it is doubtful whether the Pakistani approach could have worked. Hizbi-i Islami was really far too radical for the Afghan enviroment, and rapidly alienated many groups which had established links with it in the very early phase of the Soviet occupation. It is difficult to speculate what would·have happened if groups hostile to Hizb had not been given the chance to join other opposition groups – i.e. how many would actually go over to the government, particularly among the ethnic minorities – but it appears that the pacification policy of the government would have been made easier. Furthermore, Hizb's performance was impressive only when compared to most of the other, extremely disorganized opposition parties. Although (alone among the opposition) it did have something resembling a general strategy, its capacity to carry it out on the ground was limited. It was aware of the need to concentrate forces along the highways and other strategic points and tried rather seriously to achieve this with its mobile forces, but these were not available in quantities large enough to have a real strategic impact, and it is not sure whether it would have been possible to expand them in any case. The Pakistani intelligence (ISI) did not even consider switching its support to Jamiat, the other more likely candidate for such a role, because of ethnic prejudice (Hizb being mainly Pashtun, like many in the high echelons of the Pakistani armed forces) and because of the influence exerted over ISI by the Pakistani radical Islamists, who strongly sympathized with Hizb.

Another chance to avoid the collapse of the Afghan state could have come through a dramatic turnaround in US policy in 1989 (after the Soviet withdrawal), when American policy-makers could have decided to withold (or dramatically reduce) their help to the mujahidin. This would have enormously increased the chances of survival of the Najibullah regime in the medium and long term. This could have allowed the survival of some sort of political centre in Afghanistan, avoiding the almost total disintegration of the state which took place in 1992. President Najibullah did actually try to make a similar choice more attractive to Americans, with a campaign aimed at 'de-marxistizing' the regime and allowing more freedom to the urban-based middle class, including the legalization or semi-legalization of certain small 'opposition' parties (some actually were just bogus, creatures of the Afghan security services). Such alternative US policy, however, was extremely unlikely. Overall considerations of foreign policy (mainly having to do with the American desire to inflict a blow to the Soviet Union) prevented this.

Probably the most concrete chance of preventing a total disintegration of the Afghan state (taking into account international constraints) was rather in 1992, as the mujahidin took control of Kabul, with the help of some militia wardlords, led by Dostum. It would not have been impossible at that time for the Americans to exert some leverage on the strongest muhahidin party, Jamiat-i Islami, to push it towards a more accommodating attitude towards other parties and most of all towards the militia leaders. After all, Jamiat had been seeking the friendship of the United States since 1986, abandoning its earlier 'anti-imperialism'. At that point anti-American rethoric, which had been almost as strong as Hizb-i Islami's, disappeared for Jamiat's publications. The party already enjoyed a favourable press in certain countries, such as France, and set out to conquer US public opinion. Whatever the success of this campaign, US policy changed litle, probably as policy-makers wanted to avoid contrasts with Pakistan, while their fundamental aim (defeating a communist regime) had already been achieved. However, even if the United States had switched to Jamiat and pressed it to become more conciliatory, the outcome would still have been a definitely weak state. It is extremely doubtful whether foreign 'benefactors' would have been ready to supply the (considerable) resources needed to strengthen it and make it viable. Moreover, some troubles would have been met with anyway:

Hizb-i Islami, for example, would not easily have accepted the supremacy of Jamiat, however mild, especially with US sponsorship. However, the situation would probably not have been as bad as what actually followed.

With the mujahidin unable to rebuild the state after its collapse in 1992, a situation seemed to develop in which most of the southern Pashtun belt was in complete anarchy or ruled by local, non-political *jirgahs*, and a few warlords ruled most of the rest of Afghanistan. However, the warlords' power proved not to be very stable. The country's impoverished condition and the often predatory character of their rule made it difficult for them to sustain their mini-states. As their legitimacy was based mainly or exclusively on military skills, their troops would fight only for money or for the prospect of loot. Because of the international environment, there was pressure for the collapsed condition of the state to be only temporary or transitional, and the warlords had to compete fiercely among themselves to have any chance of being part of the final settlement. Given such premises, the situation could only evolve in one of two opposite directions.

Either the warlords could have succeeded in establishing a 'feudal state', i.e. having their status as autonomous local rulers acknowledged as legitimate by a (possibly internationally recognized) government based in Kabul, which would have been too weak to undermine their power. This would have been, to some extent, a return to the situation that was developing in Afghanistan during the last years of the Najibullah regime. The other possibility was the appearance of a reaction against the warlords from some quarter, probably outside their areas of influence, e.g. from the southern Pashtun belt, where it could also have exploited ethnic resentment against the dominance of the ethnic minorities in Kabul. This is what actually happened with the Taliban.

A

STATISTICAL TABLES

1. AGE GROUPS IN THE P.D.P.A., END 1983 (%)

Up to 20 years	12.4
21-30	51.4
31-40	27.1
40-60	9.0
60+	0.1

Source: Ludwig, 'Einige Probleme', tables 4 and 5 (appendixes).

2. PERCENTAGE OF P.D.P.A. AND D.Y.O.A. MEMBERS IN THE ARMED FORCES

	PDPA	DYOA
1983		32
1984	60	
1985	62	40
1986	64	almost 50
1988		36
1989	65.4	

Sources: Krivov, 'Vooruzhennye sily v politicheskoi zhizni Afganistana', p. 188; V. Basov, 'Postup' afganskoi revolyutsii', *Agitator* no. 7, 1985, p. 46; *Komsomolskaya Pravda*, 14 Sept. 1986; RA, 15 Aug. 1988; Najibullah, RA, 31 Dec. 1989; Karmal, RA, 4 March 1984; Basov and Poliakov, 'Afganistan: trudnye sud'by revolyutsii', p. 45; Najibullah, RA, 21 Oct. 1986; Ludwig, 'Einige Probleme', p. 124.

3. SOCIAL COMPOSITION OF DELEGATES AT THE II NATIONAL CONFERENCE OF P.D.P.A., 1987 (%)

Armed forces	52.2
Workers, peasants, artisans	15.5
Intelligentsia	3.9
Party cadres	20.9
State and social organizations employees	7.5

Source: Umarov, 'Stanovlenie i tendentsii razvitiya politiki', p. 89.

4. LITERACY COURSES: NUMBERS OF PARTICIPANTS AND TEACHERS, 1980-6

	Participants	*Teachers*
1980	347,714	17,540
1981	550,000	13,750
1982	632,500	15,812
1983	306,628	14,686
1984	376,106	12,485
1985	317,071	12,491
1986	325,300	12,731

Source: E.P. Belozershev, *Narodnoe obrazovanie v respublike Afganistan*, Moscow Pedagogika, 1988, p. 49.

5. D.Y.O.A. MEMBERSHIP

March 1978	10,000
July 1980	20,000
Beginning 1981	50,000
End 1982	90,000
Beginning 1983	100,000
End 1983	125,000
Nov. 1984	128,500
1984	157,960
Beginning 1985	130,000
	150,000
Sept. 86	200,000

Sources: 'Postanovlenie politburo TsK NDPA o deyatel'nosti TsK DOMA po dal'neishemy uluchsheniyu organizatsionnoi, politicheskoi i vostitatel'noi raboty sredi molodezhi v svete reshenii..., 17 noyabrya 1984 g.' in *NDPA (sbornik dokumentov)*, Tashkent: 'Uzbekistan', 1986, p. 313; *KP*, 14 Sept. 1986; N.I Marchuk, *Neob''yavlennaya voina v Afganistane*, Luch, 1993, p. 26; G.M. Mohsenzada, 'Die Rolle der afghanische Jugend im Kampf für die revolutionäre Umgestaltung Afghanistans', diss., Humboldt Universität, Berlin, 1985, p. 103; *KP*, 14 Sept. 1986; P. Bonovsky, *Washington's Secret War against Afghanistan*, International Pub., New York, 1985, p. 115.

6. P.D.P.A. MEMBERSHIP

	Full	Candidate	Total
End 1978			18,000
End 1979			22,068
Aug. 1980			41,000
End 1980	27,695	22,904	50,599
March 1982	35,874	31,003	66,876
March 1983	48,899	40,772	89,671
March 1984	65,415	46,166	111,581
Dec. 1984			122,000
March 1985	84,689	48,389	133,628
March 1986	104,449	50,404	154,853
March 1987	125,165	51,534	176,699
March 1988			205,000
June 1990			173,600
1991			155,000

Sources: News Bullettin, 20 July 1990; Ya.A. Plyais, 'Voznikovenie i nikotorye aspekty teoriticheskoi i organizatsionnoi deyatel'nosti NDPA', diss. Moscow, 1992, pp. 341-2; *Organisational structure and composition of the PDPA,* Kabul, n.d.; Ludwig, 'Einige Probleme', p. 138; AFP 9 Nov. 1991.

7. ASSASSINATIONS OF TEACHERS, STUDENTS, OFFICIALS, CLERKS BY MUJAHIDIN IN SOME AFGHAN PROVINCES, JANUARY 1980-JULY 1982

	Teachers	Students	Officials	Clerks
Jowzyan	31	8	30	39
Parwan	33		6	2
Paktia	8		1	
Takhar	32	7	1	
Nimroz	3		1	
Badakhshan	39		1	

Source: D.R. Goyal, *Afghanistan behind the Smoke Screen,* New Delhi, Ajanta 1984, p. 143.

8. RECRUITMENT TO THE P.D.P.A.

(*I = first half of the year; 1, 2, 3... = January, February, March...*)

I 1360 (1981/2)	10,000
1361	31,000
1362	32,000
1363	34,000
I 1364	18,500
1364	45,000
1365	39,000
I 1366	17,213
1-10 1366	40,000
1987 – 6-1990	114,853
11 1987 – 6 1990	75,000
7-12 1990	10,000
Total c.	350,000

Sources: Babrak's Karmal Speech to the Seventh Plenum of the PDPA, CC, p. 2; Basov and Poliakov, *Afganistan: trudnye sud'by revolyutsii*; RA, 20 Oct. 1987, 27 June 1990; *Babrak Karmal's Speeches at 15th Plenum of the PDPA, CC March 1985*, p. 7; *Pravda*, 28 Dec. 1990.

9. EDUCATIONAL LEVELS OF P.D.P.A. MEMBERS (%)

	1360	*1362*	*1363*	*1364*	*1365*
Ph.D.	0.2	0.2	0.1	0.1	0.1
Master's	0.8	0.8	0.9	1.2	1.3
Higher ed. (HE)	16.2	10.1	10.4	10.2	9.4
HE not comp.	6.8	5.9	5.7	5.3	5.5
Middle education (ME = 12th class)	32.7	30.4	29.5	29.6	27.3
ME not comp.	19.2	17.4	17	17.1	17
Primary ed. (PE)	9.2	11.8	12.5	12	11.5
Partial PE	3	4.2	5.3	5.1	6
Literacy courses				1.3	5.2
Illiterate	11.9	19.2	18.6	18.1	16.7

Source: Plyais, 'Voznikovenie i nikotorye aspekty', pp. 341-2.

10. MEMBERSHIP OF VARIOUS PROVINCIAL PARTY ORGANIZATIONS

	1980	1981	1982	1983	1984	1985	1986	1987	1988
Jowzyan	963			2,700			1,500		
Balkh		1,277	1,500				3,000		
Samangan	364					1,000			
Kunduz	386	973				3,000		3,252	
Faryab		263	1,300					1,500	4,000
Takhar		124	517					2,000	2,600
Herat p.	1,000	985				2,900			
Herat c.		500							
Parwan	564					1,560			
Ghor							500		
Baghdis						500			
Bamyan						285			
Helmand	845					1,500			
Kapisa							728		
Kunar							4,000		
Paktia	2,300		555				1,300		1,427
Laghman						977			1,500
Uruzgan						600			
Nimroz	47					412			
Logar						500			
Nangrahar	616					5,190			
Jallalabad (not off)									12,000
Nangrah.	1,109 (b)								
Badakhsh.	292					4,000	4,500		5,953
Kandahar						1,000		4,500	
South	17 (b)								
Paktika	50 (b)		236						
Farah		253					1,200		2,000
Ghazni	152 (b)					1,600			1,700
Zabul							300		
Wardak							1,000		
Baghlan	576						3,000		
Kabul c.	9,058								
Kabul p.	993								
Zabul			63 (b)						

b = beginning of the year. In many cases female members, who always made up less than 10% of membership, are not included.

Sources: KNT; Bakhtar, RA; I. Shedrov, Afghanistan. Molodost' Revolyutsii, Molodaya Gvardiya, 1982, pp. 96, 112; ND, 8/9 Aug. 1981; KZ, 28 May 1988; Tanjug, 23 June 1988; F. Halliday, 'Report on a visit to Afghanistan 20-27.10.1980', unpubl. typescript, p. 14; Aktual'nye problemy afganskoi revolyutsii, p. 598; Izvestia, 1 March 1983; List of reports about all the provinces except Kabul; Voenno-politicheskaya obstanovka v pr. Nimruz na konets febralya 1988g; Voenno-politicheskaya obstanovka v provintsii Kandagar, af. variant, febr. 1988 g.; Voenno-politicheskaya obstanovka v provintsii Kunar po sostoyanie na 1 Maya 1985; Provintsiya Baghlan; D.V. Ol'shanskii, Natsional'noe primerenie, ION pri TsK KPSS, Moscow, 1988; Yu. Gankovskii, 'Polosa pushtunskikh plemen Afganistana'; Provintsiya Paktika, 1360-1; Provintsiya Paktia, 1360.

11. MEMBERSHIP OF VARIOUS D.Y.O.A. PROVINCIAL ORGANIZATIONS

	1978	1979	1980	1983	1984	1985	1986	1987	1988
Herat					3,000				
Balkh					1,000		7,180		
							5,700		
Faryab								4,000	
Ghazni							2,000		
Jowzyan					5,200	6,000			
Kabul	1,800 (Mar.)	4,500						74,000	
	4,000 (June)								
Kandahar					3,000				
Kunar					1,700	2,200			
Kunduz					1,800				
Laghman									1,827
Nangrahar			5,000			6,542			
Paktia							1,120		
Parwan							2,000		
Samangan							1,800	2,283	

Sources: V.I. Yurtaev, 'Demokraticheskaya organizatsiya molodezhi Afganistana' in *Aprel'skaya Revolyutsiya 1978 g. v Afganistane, referatnyi sbornik,* INION/IV, Moscow, 1982, pp. 211, 212; I. Shedrov, *Afganistan: molodost' revolyutsii,* Molodaya Gvardiya, 1982, p. 40; *KNT;* RA.

12(a). ETHNIC COMPOSITION OF PDPA (%)

	1360 (1981/2)	1362 (1983/4)	1363 (1984/5)	1364 (1985/6)	1365 (1986/7)	1368 (1987/8)
Pashtuns	47.6	42.7	40.3	38.8	39.2	37.7
Tajiks	41.9	44.6	45.6	47.0	46.0	47.1
Uzbeks	5.1	6.9	7.3	7.6	7.5	8.1
Hazaras	2.8	3.1	3.5	3.8	4.1	4.0
Turkmens	0.8	1.1	1.4	1.4	1.4	–

Sources: N. Kaviani in *25 let PDPA,* Moscow, It. ON pri TsK KPSS, 1990, p. 69; Plyais, 'Voznikovenie i nikotorye aspekty', pp. 341-2; *KNT;* 31 Dec. 1989.

12(*b*). ETHNIC COMPOSITION OF P.D.P.A. (%)

	Oct. 1980	Nov. 1982	May 1983	Jan. 1986
Pashtun	56	53	48	43
Tajiks	35	40	42	44
Others	9	7	10	13
– Uzbeks	–	–	–	7
– Hazaras	1	–	–	3
– Turkmens	–	–	–	1

Sources: Aktual'nye problemy afganskoi revolyutsii, p. 595; Yu. V. Bosin, 'Natsional'nye problemy sovremennogo Afganistana', diss., IV AN, Moscow, 1992, p. 137.

13. P.D.P.A. PRIMARY ORGANIZATIONS

	Total	Villages covered
1982	1,656	
1362 (1983/4)	3,029	,277
1363 (1984/5)	3,931	556
1364 (1985/6)	4,669	605
1985		673
1986		750
1365 (1986/7)	5,703	1,074
1987	6,160	1,160

Sources: Plyais, 'Voznikovenie i nikotorye aspekty', pp. 341-2.

14. AGITPROP ACTIVITIES

Recipients per month

	Goods	Medical aid	Carried out by
June 1981–May 88	11,904	4,761	Sov. army
1982	2,926	1,974	Afg. army
1987	11,250	10,700	Sov. army
1366 (1987/8)		5,000	Sarandoy

Sources: Aktual'nye problemy afganskoi revolyutsii, p. 441; Lyakhovskii, 'Na afganskoi vizhzhennoi zemle', p. 60; Yu. Krasikov, 'Internatsional'naya missiya sovetskogo voina', *Voennyi Vestnik*, no. 10 (1988), p. 5; RA, 19 May 1987; *KP*, 2 July 1988.

15. SOCIAL COMPOSITION OF P.D.P.A. RECRUITS (%)[*]

	Workers, peasants and craftsmen	Peasants	Workers
1360 (1981/2)	38		
1362 (1983/4)	43.5		
1363 (1984/5)	45		
1365 (1986/7)		27.8	18
1985-7	45		

Source: Politburo Session, RA, 6 July 1985; Najibullah, RA, 14 June 1987, CC Plenum.
[*] For comparative purposes, consider that craftsmen averaged around 2%.

16. SOCIAL COMPOSITION OF P.D.P.A. (%)

	1978	1360	1361	1362	1363	1364	1365
Workers		11.2	11.2	12.7	13.7	14.1	14.1
	5.0						
Peasants		16.7	17.1	17.2	18.3	17.9	18.5
Craftsmen		0.7	1.0	1.0	1.2	1.6	2.1
Intellectuals		60.7	62.0	58.9	57.0	55.8	54.4
Small landowners		0.3	0.2	0.1	0.1	0.1	–
Students		9.7	8.2	9.6	9.0	9.5	8.9

Sources: Plyais, 'Voznikovenie i nikotorye aspekty' pp. 341-2; *Organisational structure and composition of the PDPA,* Kabul, n.d.

17. VARIATIONS IN THE SIZE OF G.D.R.S. IN SEVERAL PROVINCES

	1981	1982	1983	1984	1985	1986	1987	1988
Badakhshan					1,400			3,240
Baghlan				17,000				
Balkh						1,380	1,500	
Farah								800
Ghazni								600
Herat			4,500			3,800		3,500
Helmand					900		800	
Jowzyan				1,553		1,600		
Kabul				10,400				
Kandahar				200	370		960	
Kunar					993/700			
Laghman				292				
Nangrahar								6,000
Paktia	200					2,000		2,100
Samangan			600			830	700	
Sar-i-Pul						534		

Sources: KNT; RA; *Haqiqat-i Inqilab-i Saur,* 9 Oct. 1986.

18. MILITARY OPERATIONS CARRIED OUT BY AFGHAN ARMED FORCES, INDEPENDENTLY OR JOINTLY WITH 40TH ARMY

	Total		Army		
	Large	Small	Large	Small	Sarandoy
1979				400	
1360 (1981/2)					
Joint					900
Independent					800
Jan.–May 1984					
Joint			51		
Independent			34		
Jan.–May 1987					
Joint			17		
Independent			14		
1366 (1987/8)					
Independent			26		
April–Aug. 1988					
Independent	35	1,865			

Sources: RA, 24 March 1982; *Iz besed ruzh. sostava RA s Shevarnadze. VPO v RA avgust 1988 g.*; V.A. Merimskii, 'Voina v Afganistane: zapiski uchastika', *Novaya i Noveyashaya Istoriya*, no. 3 (1995), p. 112; Lyakhovskii, *Tragediya i doblest' Afgana*, pp. 284, 339.

19. DESERTIONS AND M.I.A.s IN THE AFGHAN ARMED FORCES[*]

	Desertions	%	MIAs
1980	25,432		721
1981	30,680	21.9	8,644
1982	30,945	15.8	1,918
1983	42,544	19.7	401
− Border Guards Jan.-Jul. 1983	4,000		
1984	35,058	13.2	1,870
− Army (1363)	25,600	18.2	
Sarandoy	6,400	8	
1985	28,550	10.4	2,853
− Sarandoy	4,000	4.4	
1986	32,433		2,905
1987	29,048	10.3	2,773
− Sarandoy	1,000		
1988	30,941	9.9	5,917
− Army	25,422	19.3	
− Sarandoy Apr.-Aug. 1988	2,600		
Jan.-Nov. 1989	38,600		5,600
− Army	27,800		
1990	3,000 per month		
Jan.-Jun. 1991	30,000		
Oct.-Nov. 1991	9,000		

[*] Details for each service are given when available. Percentages represent desertions over total manpower. Most MIAs were deserters too.

Sources: Starodubova, 'Moral'no-politicheskii', pp. 57, 58; Gankovskii, 'Vooruzhennye sily respubliki Afganistan', Gareev, *Moya poslednyaya voina*, pp. 103, 204; Merimskii, 'Voina v Afganistane', p. 112; Lyakhovskii, *Tragediya i doblest' Afgana*, p. 592, appendix 14; Lyakhovskii and Zabrodin, *Tainy afganskoi voiny*, p. 184; Marchuk, *Neob"yavlennaya voina v Afganistane*, p. 109; *Iz besed ruzh. sostava RA s Shevarnadze. VPO v RA avgust 1988 g.*

20. RECRUITMENT IN NORTHERN AND NORTH-EASTERN PROVINCES, *MIZAN* AND *AKRAB* 1366 (23 SEPT.-21 NOV. 1987).

	Sarandoy		WAD		Army	
	Planned (1)	Recruited (%) (2)	(1)	(2)	(1)	(2)
Baghlan	1,120	16	640	19	734	5
Kunduz	1,120	52	700	78		
Takhar	1,180	30	740	34		
Badakhshan	1,120	17	680	28		
Balkh	1,140	22	860	36	506	99
Samangan	720	33	440	23		
Jowzyan	1,340	35	800	27		
Faryab	1,100	45	700	43		

Source: *Rezul'taty prizyva 2 mesyatsev (mizan-akrab) 1366 g. v provintsiyakh Severa i Severo-Vostoka.*

21. LEVELS OF DESERTIONS AMONG OFFICERS OF THE AFGHAN ARMED FORCES.[*]

1363 (1984/5)	628 out of 25,660	2.4%
1364 (1985/6)	850 out of 28,000	3.0
Apr.-Dec. 1986	605 out of 18,936	3.1
1989	3,000 out of 24,215	12.3
Oct.-Nov. 1991	300 out of 9,000	3.3

[*] Percentages represent the proportion over the total number of desertions.

Sources: Starodubova, 'Moral'no-politicheskii potentsial', p. 58; Marchuk, *Neob"yavlennaya voina v Afganistane*, p. 109; Gareev, *Moya poslednyaya voina*, p. 103; Lyakhovskii, *Tragediya i doblest' Afgana*, p. 592.

22. MEMBERS OF P.D.P.A. AND D.Y.O.A. ORGANIZATIONS IN THE ARMED FORCES[*]

	Army		WAD	Sarandoy		Total	
	PDPA	DYOA	PDPA	PDPA	DYOA	PDPA	DYOA
April 78*	970/1,100						
(Plus Qader's group: 600/800)							
Sept. 78	4,000	8,000					
March 79	5,200						
Nov. 79	9,000						
End 79	10,176						
Spring 80	12,450						
End 1980	15,153						
1981	32,000			3,000			
1981/2	20,425		4,246	7,035	9,000	31,706	
1982/3	26,515		6,072	18,515		51,102	
1983/4	31,074		9,819	23,154		64,047	
1984/5	36,157		13,460	30,744		80,361	
1985						40,000	
1986	42,363						
1985/6	40,598		16,727	33,884		91209	
1986/7	43,802		22,893	37,460		104,155	
Beg. 1987							76,500
1988	48,684			44,000		25,000	
	47,000		28,500	31,400		106,900	

[*] Figures for 1978 also show the size of A. Qader's pro-Soviet organization, which later joined the PDPA.

Sources: RA 24 March 1982; Starodubova, 'Moral'no-politicheskii potentsial', pp. 78, 170; Ludwig, 'Einige Probleme', pp. 74, 108, 124; Umarov, B. Kh., 'Stanovlenie i tendentsii razvitiya politiki natsional'nogo primireniya v Afganistane', Tashkent, diss., 1990, p. 116; Gankovskii, 'Vooruzhennye sily respubliki Afganistan', p 9; Marchuk, *Neob"yavlennaya voina v Afganistane*, p. 20, 27; Lyakhovskii, *Tragediya i doblest' afgana*, appendix 14; Bradsher, *Afghanistan and the Soviet Union, III unpublished edition*, ch. 3 p. 19; *Iz besed ruzh. sostava RA s Shevarnadze. VPO v RA avgust 1988 g.*; Ya.A. Plyais, 'Voznikovenie i nikotorye aspekty teoriticheskoi i organizatsionnoi deyatel'nosti NDPA', Moscow, 1992, diss. p. 343; Z. Gol', 'Revolyutsionnaya Armiya v natsional'no-demokraticheskoi revolyutsii (na primere Afganistana)', diss. Moscow 1988, p. 86.

23. MEMBERS OF THE ARMED FORCES WHO WERE MEMBERS OF THE PARTY (%)

	1979	1980	1981	1982	1983	1987	1988	1989	1990
Armed forces				45	43	60[*]		60[*]	
Officers	33		58	75[*]			83[*]		70-80[*]
NCOs			17			47			
Soldiers			5			11			
Sarandoy		5		12 (PDPA)			46 (PDPA)		
				16 (DYOA)			20 (DYOA)		

[*] *Including members of DYOA.*

Sources: Plyais, *Voznikovenie i nikotorye*, p. 343; TASS, 5 July 1988, *op. cit.* in A. Arnold, 'The ephemeral elite', in *The politics of social transformation in Afghanistan, Iran and Pakistan*, Syracuse University Press, 1994, p. 51; Lyakhovskii and Zabrodin, *Tainy afganskoi voiny*, p. 99; *Izvestia*, 27 May 1983; RA, 26 Oct. 1982; Najibullah, RA, 26 April 1988; Merimskii, 'Voina v Afganistane: zapiski uchastika', p. 79; Yu. Gankovskii, interviewed by V.K. Turadzhev, 'Nasha bol' –Afganistan', *Aziya i Afrika Segodnia*, no. 6, 1989, p. 5; S.A. Keshtmand, 'Uregulirovanie afganskoi problemy', *Partinaia Zhizn'*, no. 2, 1990, p. 76; RA, 24 March 82; Starodubova, 'Moral'no-politicheskii potentsial', p. 78; KP, 2 July 1988.

24. PARTY PRIMARY ORGANIZATIONS IN THE ARMED FORCES

	Army	WAD	Sarandoy	Total
Sept. 1978	176			
1981/2	503	63	240	806
1982/3	554	94	350	998
1983/4	716	164	440	1,320
1984/5	814	278	516	1,608
1985/6	920	376	551	1,847
1986/7	1,041	467	566	2,074

Sources: Plyais, *Voznikovenie i nikotorye*, p. 343; *Aktual'nye problemy afganskoi revolyutsii*, 1984, p. 417

25. FULFILMENT OF RECRUITMENT PLANS, NATIONWIDE AND AT THE PROVINCIAL LEVEL (%)

Provinces, zones and cities		Nationwide
		Jan.-April 1980 1.4
		1980, 1981 40
		1983 60
March-Sept. 1984		*March-Sept. 1984*
Kandahar	39	82
1363 (1984/85)		*1984, 1985, 1986*
Kandahar	33	59-69
Beginning 1987		*First half 1987*
Kabul city	92	58
Mizan and Akrab 1366		
(23 Sept.-21 Nov. 1987)		
Baghlan	11.4	
Kunduz	58.8	
Takhar	33.4	
Badakhshan	24.5	
Balkh	43.3	
Samangan	31.1	
Jowzyan	31.5	
Faryab	44.1	
Jan.-Jun. 1987		
Baghlan	46	
Laghman	30	
Baghdis	29	
Kunar	13	
Kapisa	9	
Bamyan	5	
June-Nov. 1987		
20th Infantry Div.	90	
(North-east)		
1988		*1988*
All provinces except		42
Kabul City		20
		1989
		73

Sources: Starodubova, 'Moral'no-politicheskii potentsial', p. 74; 'Postanovlenie politburo TsK NDPA o rabote kandagarskogo provintsial'nogo komiteta partii po ukrepleniyu partiinogo edinstva i distsipliny v svete trebovanii XIV plenuma TsK NDPA, 10 otkyabrya 1984 g.' in *NDPA (sbornik dokumentov)*, Tashkent, 'Uzbekistan', 1986, p. 163; *Otchet p-ka yu...tsiy Dud..na V.I. o prodenyannoi rabote za period prebyvaniya v komandirovke s X-83 po VIII-85g., g. Kandagar 1985g.; Rezul'taty prizyva 2 mesyatsev (mizan-akrab) 1366 g. v provintsiyakh Severa i Severo-Vostoka; Otchet o komandirovke v pr. Baghlan, 15-18 dekabrya 1987 g.*; Najibullah, RA, 14 June 1987, CC Plenum; Lyakhovskii, *Tragediya i doblest' Afgana*, p. 407; Lyakhovskii and Zabrodin, *Tainy afganskoi voiny*, p. 187; Gankovskii,

'Vooruzhennye sily respubliki Afganistan'; Gareev, *Moya poslednyaya voina*, p. 203; *Aktual'nye problemy afganskoi revolyutsii*, p. 436; *Zapis' besedy zamestitelya zaveduyushego Mezhdunarodnym otdelom TsK KPSS t. Ul'yanovskogo*, p. 3; Merimskii, 'Voina v Afganistane: zapiski uchastika', p. 112.

26. POLITICAL WORKERS IN THE AFGHAN ARMED FORCES

	Total	Army	Sarandoy	KhAD/WAD
1982				600
1986	7,000	4,273	2,556	
1987	8,600			
1989	10,000			

Sources: S. Krivov, *op. cit.*, p. 188; RA, 24 March 82; D.V. Ol'shanskii, *Natsional'noe primerenie*, ION pri TsK KPSS, Moscow, 1988, p. 63; Starodubova, 'Moral'no-politicheskii potentsial', p. 155.

27. STRENGTH OF THE AFGHAN ARMED FORCES, WITH DETAIL OF THE DIFFERENT BRANCHES

(e = end of the year. Figures expressed in thousands)

	Tot. 1+2+ 3+4	Min. of Defence	(1) Regular Army	Border Guards	(2) Sar- andoy	(3) KhAD/ WAD	(4) Special Guard
1978	126	98	90	–	28	–	–
1979e	70		50	–	8		–
	87	60		–	20	7	–
1980	100e	45		–	13.4	5.1	–
					29.6		
1981	137	97		8	32.1	6.5	–
1982	180	115			54.3	9.8	–
		100					
1983	200	121			74.8	17.3	–
March:		140					
1984	240	139	98		79.5	20.2	–
		150					
1985	260	146			90.2	26.7	–
1986	300				91.7	58.8	–
1987	310	160		30	98.7	64.3	–
1988	310	132	90		96.7	68.6	11.5
	340	157			105	80 (3+4)	
	370	148					
					117		
1989	329	165			97	57	
		150			155		12-15
1990	400	220			93	90 (3+4)	
1991	160				100	40	

Sources: Plyais, *Voznikovenie i nikotorye aspekty*, p. 343; 'Zacedanie Politbyuro TsK KPSS 10 marta 1983 goda' in *Soujetische Geheimdokumente* p. 408; Umarov 'Stanovlenie i tendentsii', p. 116; Gankovskii, 'Vooruzhennye sily respubliki Afganistan', V. Korgun, 'Natsional'noe primirenie i vnutripoliticheskaya situatsiya v 1988 g.', *Spetsial'nyi Byulleten' AN SSSR – IV*, no. 2 (1990), p. 61; Yu. Gankosvkii, 'Afghanistan: from intervention to National Reconciliation', *The Iranian Journal of International Affairs*, vol. IV, no. 1 (spring 1992), p. 135; S. Krivov, *op. cit.*, pp. 180–1; Starodubova, 'Moral'no-politicheskii potentsial', pp. 56, 60; Gareev, *Moya poslednyaya voina*, p. 192; Lyakhovskii and Zabrodin, *Tainy afganskoi voiny*, pp. 82, 99; Sarin and Dvoretsky, *The Afghan Syndrome*, Presidio Press, 1993, p. 77; AFP 13, 19 Feb. 1988; *Aktual'nye problemy afganskoi revolyutsii*, p. 441; Basov and Poliakov, *Afganistan: trudnye sud'by revolyutsii*, p. 32–3; Najibullah, *Aziia i Afrika Segodnia*, SWB 28 May 1987; Lyakhovskii, *Tragediya i doblest' Afgana*, Appendix 14; Ludwig, *Einige Probleme*, p. 107; Bonovsky, *Washington's secret war against Afghanistan*, p.110.

28. DEGREE OF COMPLETION OF THE PERSONNEL CHARTS OF THE ARMED FORCES (%)

	1980	1983	1984	1986	1987	1988
TOTAL	65	67		61	51^e 74^m 62.4^b	53
Army		62	70	66	54^b 61.6^e	
Sarandoy	60		85		60	
WAD					70.5	

^{b} = beginning of year
^{m} = mid-year
^{e} = end of year

Sources: see Table 35.

29. PERSONNEL CHARTS OF THE ARMED FORCES
(*A further extension was probably planned after 1988.*
Figures are expressed in thousands.)

	1990	1988	1986	1984	1982	1981	1979
Min. of Def.		240	200	150	115	100	
Army			160	140		80	
Border guards						25	
Air Force						10	
WAD		100					
Combat units		20					
Guards	40	16					
Sarandoy		160	115		100	90	50
Total		500					

Sources: Gankovskii, 'Vooruzhennye sily respubliki Afganistan'; *Aktual'nye problemy afganskoi revolyutsii*, p. 443; Ludwig, 'Einige Probleme', p. 107; Lyakhovski and Zabrodin, *Tainy afganskoi voiny*, p. 187; *Vjesnik*, Zagabria, 28 Dec. 1982; Lyakhovskii, *Tragediya i doblest' Afgana*, p. 455; Rubin, *The Fragmentation of Afghanistan*, p. 157; Gromov, *Ogranichennyi kontingent*, p. 237.

30. GOVERNMENT FORCES IN SEVERAL PROVINCES

	Total	Army	Sarandoy	WAD/ KhAD	Militias
1985					
Ghazni	7,800	5,000	2,500	300	
1366 (1987/8)					
Bamyan	700	1 batt.	1 batt.	1 batt.	
Laghman	2,940		1,150	1,500 (incl. GDRs)	290
Jowzyan	19,124		7,474	1,737	9,913
Baghlan	19,042	7,280	4,232	968	6,562
Samangan	5,370		1,653	1,137	2,580
Balkh	19,614	5,596	4,748	2,986	5,922
			Border Tr. 362		
Badakhshan	10,914	1 Regt.	4,204	1,596	4,475
			Border Tr. 639		
Faryab	10,528	1 Regt.	3,109	1,793	
			Border Tr. 230		
Takhar	6,126	1 Regt.	2,569	1,321	2,176
			Border Tr. 60		
Kunduz	7,875		2,958	1,899	2,567
			Border Tr. 451		

Sources: List of reports on all the provinces àxcept Kabul; Informatsiya o regulamykh silakh VS i grazhdannskikh vooruzhennykh formirovaniyakh, 1987; Obstanovka v provintsii Laghman, 6.02.88 g.; Lyakhovskii, Tragediya i doblest' Afgana, p. 405; M. Olimov, 'Iz zapisok perevodchika', Vostok, no. 3 (1991), p. 60.

31. ACTIVE DIVISIONS AND BRIGADES IN 1980 AND NEW ONES ACTIVATED IN SUBSEQUENT YEARS[*]

1980

7th Inf. Div. Moqor
8th Inf. Div. Kabul
11th Inf. Div. Jallalabad, resumed active operations only in 1982
12th Inf. Div. Gardez
14th Inf. Div. Ghazni
15th Inf. Div. Kandahar
17th Inf. Div. Herat
18th Inf. Div. Mazar
20th Inf. Div. Baghlan
25th Inf. Div. Khost
4th Armd. Brig. Kabul
15th Armd. Brig. Kabul
7th Armd. Brig. Kandahar
21st Mech. Brig. Shindand, transformed into division in 1987
Guards Brig. Kabul, merged with Special Guards in 1988
88th Artillery Brig. Kabul
37th Commando Brig. Kabul
38th Commando Brig. Kabul

1980-5

3th Border Brig. Kandahar
8th Border Brig. Paktia
6th Border Brig. Paktika
9th Border Brig. Kabul, Paktika
10th Border Brig. Kunar
7th Border Brig. Farah
1st Border Brig. Jallalabad
2nd Border Brig. Khost
4th Border Brig. Nimroz
5th Border Brig. Herat
11th Border Brig. Helmand

1981?

9th Inf. Div., reformed after disbandment 1979-1980

1984

2nd Inf. Div. Jabal ul Saraj

1986-

24th Sarandoy Brig. Badakhshan
?7th Sarandoy Brig. Jallalabad
8th Sarandoy Brig. Pul-i-Alam
? Sarandoy Brig. Gardez
? Sarandoy Brig. Charikar

7th Sarandoy Brig. Kandahar
? Sarandoy Brig. or regiment Parwan
? Sarandoy Brig. or regiment Baghlan
4th Sarandoy Brig. Herat
15th Sarandoy Brig. Kapisa
(One brigade was formed for most provinces)

1987

21st Inf. Div. Shindand

1988-9

40th Inf. Div. Parwan
53th Inf. Div. Shiberghan
54th Inf. Div. Kunduz
60th Inf. Div. Sarobi
80th Inf. Div. Pul-i-Khumri
3rd Inf. Div. Sarandoy Kabul
5th Inf. Div. Sarandoy Kabul
4th Inf. Div. WAD Kabul
10th Inf. Div. WAD Kabul

1988-90

1st Guards Div. Kabul
16th Guards armd Div. Kabul
55th Guards Brig. Kabul
? Guards Brig. Kabul
70th Guards Brig. Heiratan
72nd Guards Brig. Mazar
76th Guards Brig. Mazar
73rd Guards Brig. Shiberghan

1989-90

55th Inf. Div. Takhar
93th Inf. Div. Girishk
95th Inf. Div. Hazara Kabul
96th Inf. Div. Hazara Kabul

1990-1

94th Inf. Div. Hazara Kabul
? Inf. Div. Lashkargah

* The list may be incomplete for the last few years

Sources: Gankovskii, 'Vooruzhennye sily respubliki Afganistan', p. 12; Gareev, *Moya pos-lednyaya voina*, p. 230; Lyakhovskii, *Tragediya i doblest' Afgana*, pp. 337, 579, 589; Lyakhovskii and Zabrodin, *Tainy afganskoi voiny*, p. 165; Davis, *Jane's Intelligence Review*, March 1993; *List of reports on the situation in all the provinces except Kabul;* Cordesman, *The Lessons of Modern Wars*, p. 44.

32. BORDER-SEALING ACTIVITIES BY AFGHAN GOVERNMENT AND SOVIET FORCES

	Ambushes prepared daily		Caravans intercepted monthly	
	Soviet	Afghan	Soviet	Afghan
May-Sept. 1983	18-19		52-53	
Jan.-Oct. 1984		16		
May-Sept. 1984	13-14		36-37	
Winter 1984		16-17		85
1987				
1366		12-13	30	
July-Dec. 1988				69-70

Sources: Lyakhovskii, *Tragediya i doblest' Afgana*, pp. 288-9, 341, 355-6; A.V. Tchikichev, *Spetnaz en Afghanistan*, CEREDAF, 1994, p. 29; Gromov, *Ogranichennyi kontingent*, p. 323; Ludwig, 'Einige Probleme', p. 104; *KZ*, 11 March 1988 and 14 Aug. 1988.

33. LOSSES OF THE AFGHAN AIR FORCE

	1980	1981	1982	1983	1984	1985	1986	1987	1988	1989
Planes	2	2	7	6	9	28	12	21	24	
Helicopters	2	4	8	15	15	22	17	33	44	
Total	4	6	15	21	24	50	29	54	68	102

Sources: Lyakhovskii *Tragediya i doblast' afgana*, appendix 14; Gareev, *Mova poslednyaya voina*, p. 208.

34. CASUALTIES, KABUL REGIME FORCES

	Killed	Wounded	Missing/captured
1980	9,051	10,087	3,187
1981	3,303	8,323	2,341
1982	2,885	7,819	500
1983	3,408	9,242	1,327
1984	3,353	9,011	432
1985	3,690	8,898	556
1986	5,772	11,876	1,162
1987	6,229	12,786	986
1988	10,127	16,529	3,809
1989	11,133	22,018	2,945
1990	7,977		
Jan.-May 1991	1,628		
Totals	68,556	116,589	17,245

Source: K. Matinuddin, *Power Struggle in the Hindu Kush, Afghanistan 1978-1991*, Wajidalis, Lahore, p. 167.

35. MONTHLY LOSSES OF AFGHAN ARMED FORCES
(KILLED AND WOUNDED)

	Army	Sarandoy
1980	135	
1981	560	
1982	209	
1983	207	
1984	222	
1985	201	
1986	235	
Jan.-Jun. 1987	291	
1987	207	133
Mar.-Aug. 1988	218	
Apr.-Aug. 1988		580
1988	236	
Mar.-Jun. 1989	1,866	
Jan.-Nov. 1989	1,900	

Sources: Lyakhovskii, *Tragediya i doblest' Afgana*, p. 339 and Appendix 14; *Iz besed ruzh. sostava RA s Shevamadze, VPO v RA avgust 1988 g.;* 27 June 1989; Gareev, *Moya poslednyaya voina*, p. 204.

36. LOSSES OF EQUIPMENT IN AFGHAN ARMED FORCES

	1980	1981	1982	1983	1984	1985	1986	1987	1988
Tanks	21	23	21	37	32	32	25	27	144
Armoured vehicles	52	49	45	141	77	89	51	57	243
Guns and mortars	65	40	62	90	29	35	47	33	349

Source: Lyakhovskii, *Tragediya i doblest' Afgana*, appendix 14.

37. EQUIPMENT OF THE AFGHAN ARMED FORCES

	1978	1988	1990
Tanks	650	843	1,568
BMP	87		828
BTR	780		
Artillery	1,919		4,880
Planes	150		126 (combat)
Helicopters	25		14 (combat)

Sources: Gai and Snegirev, *Vtorzhenie*, p. 72; Gareev, *Moya poslednyaya voina*, p. 192.

38. DEGREE OF COMPLETION OF THE PERSONNEL CHARTS OF THE ARMED FORCES (%)

	1979	1980	1983	1984	1986	1987	1988	1989	1991
Armed forces			65	67		61	51f	53	
						74^m			
						62.4^b			
Army			62	70	66	54^b			
						61.6^c			
Officers			96		75	70			
Combat Units						25	22-32		
Infantry									7-10
Services							50-60		
Infantry			45-50						
Tanks						56	40^*		
Artillery							28		
Specialists						50			
Air Force						81	64		
Border Guard	30		50			60			
Political cadres		19							
Sarandoy		60		85		60			
Operative units		72.5^b							
Officers		45							
NCOs		39							
Soldiers		40.7							
WAD						70.5			

^{b} = beginning of year
^{m} = mid-year
^{c} = end of year

Sources: Lyakhovskii, *Tragediya i doblest' Afgana*, pp. 189, 375, 592; *Aktual'nye problemy afganskoi revolyutsii*, pp. 402, 436; T. Gaidar, *Pod afganskim nebom*, Sovetskaya Rossiya, ʼ1981, p. 52; *Iz besed ruzh. sostava RA s Shevarnadze. VPO v RA avgust 1988 g.*; Gareev, *Moya poslednyaya voina*, pp. 203, 204; Merimskii, 'Voina v Afganistane: zapiski uchastika', p. 112; Umarov, 'Stanovlenie i tendentsii', p. 117; Gankovskii, 'Vooruzhennye sily respubliki Afganistan', pp. 14-15; Lyakhovskii and V.M. Zabrodin, *Tainy afganskoi voiny*, pp. 165-6, 187; A. Lyakhovskii and V. Zabrodin, 'Tainy afganskoi voiny', *Armiya* 9, 1992, pp. 64-5; Ludwig, 'Einige Probleme', p. 107.

39. MILITARY HELP FROM U.S.S.R. TO AFGHANISTAN
(WEAPONS SYSTEMS)

	Up to 1989	1989	Left over by 40th Army	1990
Tank	767	305 ⎱		380
BMP	491	283 ⎰ 990		211
BTR	1,338	705 ⎰		651
Field rocket-launchers	116	16	43	50
Guns and mortars	1,212		224	114
RPG	3,804		1,706	820
Flamethrowers	5,680		14,443	1,000
Light weapons	119,000	40,000	231	95,400
AA guns	700			680
Planes	76	59		66
Helicopter	36	12		37

Sources: Gareev, *Moya poslednyaya voina,* pp. 85, 310, 311; TsK KPSS, 'O doplonitel'noi postavke spetsimushestva Respublike Afganistan, 1989' in *Sowjetische Geheimdokumente,* pp. 606, 608.

40. MILITARY HELP FROM U.S.S.R. TO AFGHANISTAN
(MILLIONS OF RUBLES)

1980	1981	1982	1983	1984	1985	1986	1987	1988	1989	1990
267.6	231.5	277.9	221.4	366.3	516.3	579.1	1,063.4	1,629.0	3,972.0	2,200.0

Source: Lyakhovskii, *Tragediya i doblest' afgana,* Appendix 14.

41. MUJAHIDIN EQUIPMENT

	1989	Summer 1990	Mid-1991	Oct. 1991
Anti-tank missiles				
	30 (launchers)	1,400		
Anti-tank rocket launchers	10,200	11,400		1,1550
Guns	100	550 ⎫		1,900
Guns and mortars		⎬ 4,000		
Mortars	3,000	3,500 ⎭		3,860
Recoiless guns	1,550	2,000		
Field				
Rocket launchers	1,000	1,200		1,675
Heavy machines and anti-aircraft guns	800	4,600		4,300
Anti-aircraft missiles	700	402		
Tanks		92	150	202
Armoured vehicles		1,100	250	280

Sources: Gareev, *Moya poslednyaya voina,* p. 186; Lyakhovskii, *Tragediya i doblest' Afgana,* p. 580; Lyakhovskii, 'Na afganskoi vizhzhennoi zemle', p. 58; Gromov, *Ogranichennyi kontingent,* p. 322.

42. LIGHT WEAPONS SEIZED FROM THE MUJAHIDIN, PER MONTH

1360 (Sarandoy)	333
1361 (Army)	750
May – Sept. 1983 (Red Army)	866
May – Sept. 1984 (Red Army)	811
Winter 1984/5 (Red Army)	581
1985 (Afghan armed forces)	541
Jan. – 15 June 1987 (Red Army)	392
March – June 1987 (Afghan armed forces)	385

Sources: RA, 24 March 1982 and 16 April 1983; Lyakhovskii, *Tragediya i doblest' Afgana,* pp. 285, 288-9, 339; I.G. Maidan, *Problemy sotsial'noi bazy Aprelskoi Revolyutsii i politiki natsional'nogo primirenie v Afganistane,* Kiev, 1988, p. 35.

43. ETHNIC COMPOSITION OF THE AFGHAN ARMED FORCES (%)

	Pashtun	Tajiks	Uzbeks	Others
		ARMY		
1978				
Officers				
Senior	70	20		10
Junior	45	35		10
Troops	60	30		10
1985				
Total	50			
1987/8				
Senior and political officers	55	35	2.2	
1989				
Troops	almost 50	35–40		
		SARANDOY		
1987				
Officers and NCOs	46.9	41	5.7	
1990				
Total	90	*(might apply only to mobile units)*		

Sources: V. Korgun, *Intelligentsia v politicheskoi zhizhne Afganistana*, Nauka, 1983, p. 12; Gankovskii, 'Vooruzhennye sily respubliki Afganistan', *Mainstream*, 12 Jan. 1985; Lyakhovskii and Zabrodin, *Tainy afganskoi voiny*, p. 99; S. Krivov, *op. cit.*, p. 184; Starodubova, 'Moral'no-politicheskii potentsial', p. 105; Yu. V. Bosin, 'Natsional'nye problemy sovremennogo Afganistana', diss., IV AN, Moscow, 1992, p. 138.

44. TOTAL STRENGTH OF THE N.F.F. BY REGION (*x* 100)[*]

	1982	1983	1984	1985	1986	1987	1988	1989
NORTHERN PROVINCES								
Badakhshan		160						
Takhar			96		157	226		
Kunduz			162	247		327		
Baghlan		60		76	268			
Samangan					90	112		120
Balkh			300	354	410	390		
Jowzyan			240		370			
Faryab			99			250		
Baghdis		20	41		125	130	75	
Kapisa					76			
Parwan		103.5	115					
OTHER PROVINCES								
Kabul prov.		120				200		230
Logar				12				
Wardak							16	
Bamyan	10.5	70						
Ghor						29		
Herat		170	179	304	355			
Nimroz					26			
Farah			13.5		115			
Helmand		95	140		190			
Ghazni					190	150		
Kandahar		6	70		132	164		
Kunar					90	105		
Laghman		8		55	84		40.5	51
Nangrahar			250		90			
Paktia				66	100	110		

[*] Data incomplete.

Sources: See Table 45.

45. INDIVIDUAL MEMBERSHIP IN THE N.F.F. BY REGION*

	1984	1985	1986	1987	1988	1989
NORTHERN PROVINCES						
Balkh			6,437	15,000	14,993	13,100
Kunduz	1,293	6,500		7,400		
Takhar		4,322				
Samangan					3,500	
Faryab					6,000	
Parwan					3,000	
OTHER PROVINCES						
Farah	450					
Ghazni			5,630			
Kandahar	1,840		4,000	5,413	5,688	
Laghman					4,048	5,100
Paktia	1,176		5,400			
Kunar						
Narang district			700			

* Data incomplete.

Sources: KNT; RA; *Haqiqat-i Inqilab-i Saur,* 2 April 1987.

46. MONTHLY AVERAGES OF CLASHES BETWEEN MUJAHIDIN AND GOVERNMENT/SOVIET FORCES

1983	200
Jan. – May 1986	362 (42 against Soviets)
Jan. – May 1987	796 (126 against Soviets)

Sources: Lyakhovskii, *Tragediya i doblest' Afgana,* pp. 329, 355-6; Leonov, *Likholet'e,* p. 269.

47. MUJAHIDIN ACTIVITIES: NUMBER OF ARMED MEN

	Active	Active + inactive	All armed groups hostile to government
1981	30,000		
1983	40,000		
1985	50,000	105,000	
1986	80,000	125,000	
1987	60,000	130,000	
1988	75,000	140,000	274,000
1988-9	85,000	170-190,000	
1989	55,000		
1990	55,000	190,000	
1991	55,000	180,000	212,000

Sources: Pravda, 26 Sept. 1988; Lyakhovskii, *Tragediya i doblest' Afgana*, pp. 204, 290, 312, 318, 328, 418, 455, 575, 581-2; Gareev, *Moya poslednyaya voina*, pp. 185-6; *NT*, 11 (1989); *Izvestiya*, 7 Aug. 1989; *Vyvody po obstanovke, gruppirovki i kharakteru deistvii myatezhnikov na territorii RA na 1.06.88 goda; Internal document of 40th Army, title unreadable; Spravka o politiko-voennoi obstanovke, gruppirovkakh, kharaktere deistvii, planakh i namereniyakh kontrrevolyutsii v respublike Afganistan na 6.12.87 g.; Pravda*, 18 March 1989; Lyakhovskii, 'Na afganskoi vizhzhennoi zemle', p. 58; *Vostok*, 5, 1992; Gromov, *Ogranichennyi kontingent*, pp. 231, 322; *L'Unità*, 22 Jan. 1987.

48. MILITARY POTENTIAL OF AFGHAN TRIBES AND ETHNIC GROUPS, 1983

	Population	*Armed men*
PASHTUN TRIBES		
Durrani		
Popolzai	100–150,000	10–18,000
Barakzan	200–250,000	20–30,000
Nurzai	150–200,000	15–20,000
Other Durrani tribes	500,000	30–35,000
Ghilzai		
Suleimankhel	250–300,000	30,000
Khattaki	40–60,000	10,000
Other Ghilzai tribes	900–1,050,000	50,000
SMALLER TRIBES		
Kakar[1]	250–300,000	25,000
Wazir	200,000	20,000
Afridi[2]	250,000	40,000
Mohmand[3]	100–130,000	40,000
Yusufzai[4]	700,000	80,000
Shinwari		15,000
Total Pashtuns		515–543,000
OTHER ETHNIC GROUPS		
Tajiks		60,000
Hazara		60,000
Uzbeks		40,000
Turkmens		15–20,000
Total non-Pashtuns		180–200,000

[1] Both in Afghanistan and Pakistan – the tribe migrates yearly across the border
[2] Mostly in Pakistan
[3] Mostly in Pakistan
[4] All in Pakistan

Source: A.A. Kotenev, 'Natsional'no-etnicheskii faktor v vooruzhennoi bor'be s kontrrevolyutsei v DRA', diss., 1983, IV AN SSSR, pp. 118–21.

49. MEMBERS OF NON-GOVERNMENT ARMED GROUPS INVOLVED IN 'PACIFICATION' PROCESS FROM 1980

	Over to government		Ceasefires		Holding discussions with govt.
	Armed	*Total*	*Armed*	*Total*	
Dec. 1983		21,000		30,000?	56,000
1984				100,000	50,000
1986	12,000	42,000			6,000
1987	27,000	82,000		114,000	6,913
1988	32,000	60,000		120,000	11,533
1989	57,000	125,000			7/45,000
1990	91,000	217,000	92,316	296,000	
1991	96,000	239,000	146,239	358,800	

Sources: see Graph 4.

50. PERCENTAGE OF TERRITORY CONTROLLED BY THE KABUL GOVERNMENT

	Controlled by government	(1) By Mujahidin	(2) Neutral or contested
Sept 1980[a]	20	20	60
Spring 1981[b]	25	10	65
1982[c]	18	82	
1983[d]	25		
1985[e]	20	80	
1985[f]	35		
1986[g]	30	70	
1986[h]	23		
1987[i]	15	85	
1987[j]	20		
1987[k]	35		
1988[l]	20		
1989[m]	18		
1991[n]	15	85 (1+2)	
1991[o]	30	40	30
Mid-1991[p]	10–11		

[a] Sh. Khanif, 'Afganskii dnevnik', *Pamir*, no. 12 (1989), p. 122
[b] PAP, cited by *Le Monde*, 29 May 1981
[c] Afghanistan Information and Documentation Centre, Peshawar, Jan. 1983
[d] M. Urban, *War in Afghanistan*, p. 214.
[e] *Afghan realities*, no. 72 (2 Jan. 1987), p. 6.
[f] Najibullah's interview with an Indian journalist, cited in C. Karp, *Afghanistan: six years of Soviet occupation*, US Dept. of State, Special Report, no. 135 (1985), p. 9.
[g] E
[h] V.G. Safronov, 'Kak eto bylo', *Voenno-istoricheskii Zhurnal* , no. 5 (1990), p. 69
[i] Gromov, *Ogranichennyi kontingent*, p. 260.
[j] Gankovskii, 'Vooruzhennye sily respubliki Afganistan', p. 14.
[k] Urban, *War in Afghanistan*, p. 214.
[l] *Le Monde*, 12 May 1988
[m] Gromov, *Ogranichennyi kontingent*, p. 322.
[n] KP, 29 June 1991.
[o] Y. Gankovsky, 'Afghanistan: from intervention to National Reconciliation', *The Iranian Journal of International Affairs*, vol. IV, no. 1 (spring 1992), p. 136.
[p] Lyakhovskii, *Tragediya i doblest' Afgana*, p. 575.

* *Western or mujahidin sources.*

51. CONTROL EXERCIZED BY GOVERNMENT AND MUJAHIDIN OVER DISTRICTS/SUBDISTRICTS

	Dec. 1980	Nayar 1981	End 1982	May 1983	June 1983	May 1988	March 1989
	a	b	c	d	e	f	g
Controlled by government		48	32	35	50	39	61
Controlled by Resistance	74	90	130	127	80	160	108
Contested, of which		48	99	124	156	91	118
– pro-govt							(44)
– pro Mujahidin							(47)

a Lyakhovskii, *Tragediya i doblest' Afgana*, p. 179.

b K. Nayar, *Report on Afghanistan*, 1981.

c Afghan Documentation Centre, in *Dawn*, 5 Jan. 1983; here 'controlled by government' indicates '50–100% control' and 'controlled by Resistance' 90–100% control.

d *Asia and Africa Today*, June 1989, p. 21.

e S. Sokolov, quoted, in Lyakhovskii, *Tragediya i doblest' Afgana*, p. 260.

f Lyakhovskii and Zabrodin, *Tainy afganskoi voiny*, p. 139; Gromov, *Ogranichennyi kontingent*, p. 322.

g *NT*, 11, 1989.

52. TERRITORY/VILLAGES * UNDER GOVERNMENT CONTROL IN VARIOUS PROVINCES (%)

	1981	1982	1984	1985	1986	1987	1988	1989	1990
Kabul					86*				
Farah						40	50+*		
Nimroz				17.6*			50+ 24.6*		
Balkh				19.8*		70.2*	50+*		
Balkh d.								50*	
Jowzyan							50+*		
Poktia	10.5	40		42*					
Khost major d.				11.3*					
Laghman		25					30*		
Nangrahar		33					69*		
Logar		15*							
Takhar							40*		40
Kunduz					75.9*	67*	73.6*		
Kandahar				63*		5.9*	40*		
Maiwand d.						25			
Zabul				14.1*		4.4*			
Uruzgan				0.5*		0.5*			
Helmand				13.1*		24			
Ghazni				14*					
Baghlan				14.1*		48.6*	50+		
Pul-i Khumri d.				47.1*					
Andarab d.				46.8*					
Other districts				0					
Paktika		8.5*							
Badakhshan			35.5*				43.5*		
Samangan							48.5*		
Faryab							49.1*		
Qaysar d.								27*	
Jowzyan							48*		
Kunar				24*					

Bamyan, Kapisa: government control very weak at any time.

Sources: News Bulletin, 23 July 1990; *FEER*, 6 Aug. 1987; *Haqiqat-i Inqilab Saur*, 5 Oct. 1987; *Pravda*, 20 Jan. 1988; *Izvestia*, 16 Jan. 1988; Muzaffar Olimov, 'Iz zapisok perevodchika', *Vostok*, no. 3 (1991) pp. 59, 60; Sarin and Dvoretsky, *op. cit.*, p. 78; *KNT*, 5 Nov. 1986; *Aziya i Afrika Segodnia*, no. 8 (1987), p. 40; *SR*, 2 Dec. 1987; *KP*, 3 Nov. 1987; *Pravda*, 28 Jan. 1985; *L'Humanité*, 1 March 1985; *Obstanovka v provintsii Laghman, 6.02.88 g.; Voenno-politicheskaya obstanovka v zone otvetstvennosti 11 pd za poslednii kvartal 1366g.; Voenno-politicheskaya obstanovka v pr. Nimruz na konets febralya 1988g.; Otchet p-ka yu...tsiy Dud..na V.I. o prodenyannoi rabote za period prebyvaniya v komandirovke s X-83 po VIII-85g., Kandagar 1985g.*; A. Podlesnyi, 'Politika Natsional'nogo Primireniya i osobennosti ee provedeniya v yuzhnykh raionakh Afganistana', *Spetsial'nyi Byulleten' IV AN SSSR* no. 2 (1990), pp. 158-9; 'Postanovlenie sekretariata Tsk NDPA o rabote badakhshanskogo provintsial'nogo partiinogo komiteta po vypolneniyu postanovleniya politburo Tsk NDPA ot 17.9.1361, 30 dekabrya 1984 g.' in *NDPA* (*Sbornik dokumentov*), Tashkent, 'Uzbekistan', 1986, p. 259; Yu. Gankovskii, 'Polosa pushtunskikh plemen Afganistana', *Spetsial'nyi Byulleten'" AN SSSR IV* no. 6 (1987), p. 110; *List of report about all the provinces except Kabul; Voenno-politicheskaya obstanovka v pr. Nimruz na konets febralya 1988g.; South* Feb. 1989 p. 14; *Provintsiya Paktika*, 1360-1; *Provintsiya Paktia* 1360.

53. MILITIA MANPOWER

	Total	Tribal (1+2)	Regional (1)	Frontier (2)	GDR	Self-defence
1980						8,000
1981				3,000		
1982					8,000	
1983		16,000	10,000	6,000	18,000	12.000
1983 (end)			11,892			14,000f
1984		20,000				
1985		25,000				
1986	90,000	40,000	17,000	21,700		
1987	130,000	52,000	36,000	16,000	33,000	42,000
1988	150,000	62,000	42,000	20,000	35,000	
	160,000					
1989	170,000					

Sources: Glavnoe operativnoe upravlenie general'nogo shtaba, *Karta khoda formirovaniya dobrovol'nykh polkov iz plemen ichtvertykh batal'onov iz byvshikh bandgrupp po sostoyanyu na 1983 g. (10.1.84);* Bakhtar, 8 Feb. 1988, 27 March 1988; *KNT,* 25 April 1984, 10 Oct. 1983, 25 May 1983, 28 March 1988; *News Bulletin,* 7 Oct. 1985; Najibullah, *RA,* 17 Jan. 1988; Ludwig, 'Einige Probleme', p. 110; *Informatsionnyi byulleten' po materialam XX plenuma TsK NDPA,* Kabul, 1986, p. 1; V. Basov, 'Postup' afganskoi revolyutsii', *Agitator,* no. 7 (1985), p. 46; Lyakhovskii and Zabrodin, *Tainy afganskoi voiny,* p. 99; Krivov, 'Vooruzhennye sily v politicheskoi zhizni Afganistana', pp. 180–1; Starodubova, 'Moral'no-politicheskii potentsial' p. 56; *ND,* 17 April 1981; *Guardian,* 2 May 1989, 20 April 1988; *Radyansika Ukrayina,* 15 Dec. 1983.

54. ACTIVE REGIONAL UNITS

	1983	1984	1986	1987	1991
Battalions	28	36	27	57[*]	
Regiments	7	9	13	21[*]	
Divisions				1	4-5[†]

Sources: Najibullah, *RA* 17 Jan. 1988; *KNT,* 18 June 1986; Glavnoe operativnoe upravlenie general'nogo shtaba, *Karta khoda formirovaniya dobrovol'nykh polkov iz plemen ichtvertykh batal'onov iz byvshikh bandgrupp po sostoyanyu na 1983 g. (10.1.84).*

[*] Figure may be overestimated as some battalions had been transformed into regiments and some regiments included in newly formed divisions over the previous year.
[†] Plus 7 more, probably with mixed personnel, transferred to the regular forces.

55. SALARIES IN THE BORDER MILITIA AND REGIONAL FORCES (*in Afghanis*)

	Border militia		Regional forces		
	1982	*1984*	*1987*	*1989*	*1990*
Militiaman	2,500*	2,000	3,000	4-10,000	15-20,000
Platoon commander	3,500*	3,000			
Company commander	4,500*	3,500	4,500-6,500		
Battalion commander	5,500*	4,000 ⎫ above regular			
Regimental commander		6,000 ⎭ army salary			

* + 600 Afs ration allowance.

Sources: A.H. Khan, 'The Militias in Afghanistan', *Central Asia*, no. 31 (winter 1992), pp. 63, 69, 71; 'Ukaz prezidiuma revolyutsionnogo soveta DRA, 30 dekabrya 1984 g., O Prinyatii Polozheniya o territorial'nykh voiskakh Vooruzhennikh Sil Demokraticheskoi Respubliki Afganistan' in *NDPA (sbornik dokumentov)*, Tashkent, 'Uzbekistant', 1986, pp. 413-14; RA, 19 May 1987; Najibullah, RA, 28 June 1987, Christina L'Homme, S. Thiollier in *Défis Afghans*, no. 22 (Feb. 1990); AFP, 22 Nov. 1989.

56. MILITIA STRENGTH IN VARIOUS PROVINCES, DISTRICTS AND ZONES

	1980	1982	1983	1984	1985	1986	1987	1988	1990
Kabul					12,300				
Paghman						2,000			
North-Eastern zone							5,743*		
Baghdis									
Bala Murghab			100						
Faryab									
Shirin Tagab					1,000*				
Qaysar								3,000*	
Daulatabad					6,000				
Takhar								1,400*	
Sar-i-Pul							1,100*		
Kandahar				4,900					
Spin Boldak			1,000						
Nangrahar									
Shinwar					1,100†* / 300*	5,500			
Kisharak			100						
Nangrahar, Kunar			3,500†						
Kunar					300†* / 450 / 2,600	1,400†			
Chauki dist.				44†					
Sarkanai				91†					
Balkh									
Laghman				881*			14,000	1,000*	
Nuristan dist.				165*				290*	
Jowzyan					1,900				
Badakhshan							1,467* / 4,811		
Ghazni	1,000	1,000*							
Bahyak	400								
Andar dist.						2,000			
Paktia									
Khost									
Jaji			600*						1,300*

* Tribal units only
† Border militia only

Sources: Otchet o sostoyanii territorial'nykh voisk v pr, Gerat, 9.11.87 g.; Haqiqat-i Inqilab-i Saur, 23 Sept. 1985; *Obstanovka v provintsii Laghman, 6.02.88 g.; Otchet o komandirovke v pr. Baghlan, 15-18 dekabrya 1987 g.;* Gareev, *Moya poslednyaya voina,* p. 269; *Otchet o komandirovke v pr. Gerat 8-10 noyabrya 1987 g.; Voenno-politicheskaya obstanovka v zone otvetstvennosti 11 pd za poslednii kvartal 1366g.; Izvestia,* 11 Aug. 1983; *KP,* 30 March 1989; *KNT,* 26 March 1985, 15 Nov. 1986, 28 Jan. 1988, 6 June 1984, 6 June 1984, 10 July 1988, 5 March 1985, 17 March 1985; *Der Spiegel,* 20, 1986, p. 162; *RA,* 4 Sept. 1980, 10 Nov. 1984, 11 Jan. 1984; *Bakhtar,* 4 Sept. 1986, 27 Nov. 1987, 24 Sept. 1987; *TASS,* 22 March 1988; *NT,* 3 – 1990; *Iz besed ruzh. sostava RA s Shevarnadze. VPO v RA avgust 1988 g.; KNT,* 25 May 1983; *KNT,* 27 June 1991; Yu. Gankovskii, 'Polosa pushtunskikh plemen Afganistana', *Spetsial'nyi Byulleten' AN SSSR IV* no. 6 (1987), p. 115 n. 13.

57. MILITIA STRENGTH IN HERAT PROVINCE

	1983	1984	1985	1986	1987	1988	1989	1991
Border	1,000	800	3,000	4,400				
			3,600					
Tribal				5,030	20,000			
Border and tribal						31,000	35,000	
All militias				13,862				70,000

Sources: see Table 56.

58. OFFICER STAFF AND P.D.P.A. AND D.Y.O.A. MEMBERSHIP AMONG REGIONAL UNITS, NORTH-EAST ZONE, 1987

	Cadre officers	Tribal officers	Cadre NCOs	Tribal NCOs	Soldiers
Tribal regiments:					
504 Reg.	33	48		19	1,016
PDPA		39+4*		4+0*	16+8
DYOA					237
507 Reg.	32	49	5	7	1,193
PDPA		13+8*		2+5*	9+11
DYOA					214
518 Reg.	16	27	5	8	704
PDPA		20+0*		6+0*	52+17
DYOA					50
513 Reg.	36	63	8	16	1,543
PDPA		25+1*		1+0*	18+0
DYOA					150
10 Reg. Regular Army, tribal battalions					
4 batt. 10 Reg.	16	21		16	348
5 batt. 10 Reg.	5	21		6	452
24 Reg. Regular Army, tribal battalions and companies					
4 batt. 24 Reg.	7	18			376
5 batt. 24 Reg.	14	18			376
6 batt. 24 Reg.		14*			132
7 batt. 24 Reg.	16	9			247
8 batt. 24 Reg.	4	15			204
4 co. 24 Reg.	1	4			5
75 Reg. Regular Army, tribal battalions					
4 batt. 75 Reg.	6	11		7	208
5 batt. 75 Reg.	2	14			130

* Cadre plus tribal.

Source: Operativnaya obstanovka v territorial'nikh chastyakh (donesenie VKR 20 PD pr. Baghlan, 17.12.87 g.). The source does not distinguish between cadre and tribal offer and NCO party members.

B

MAPS

Note. For comparative purposes, all maps include the province of Sar-i-Pol, which did not exist till 1987. Squares represent town and cities.

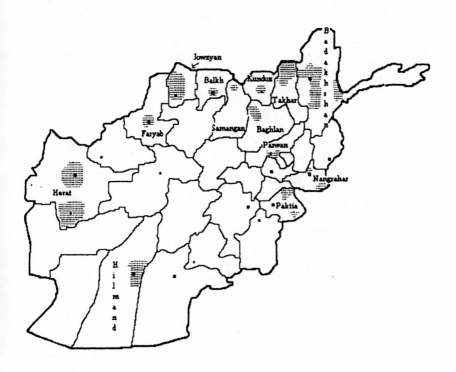

1. Main Areas of PDPA recruitment among peasants, 1980-9.
Sources: KNT, RA, *Bakhtar.*

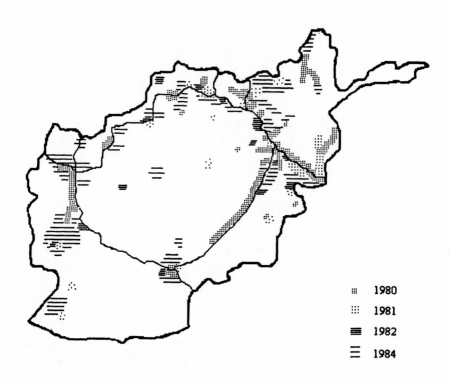

::: 1980
::: 1981
≡ 1982
≡ 1984

2. Expansion of the area of operations, 1980-4
(main highways also represented)

Sources: Les Nouvelles d'Afghanistan, no. 23, 1985, p. 12; Comitato italiano di soldiarità
con la Resistenza Afghana, *La Resistenza Afghana*, Roma, Città del Sole, 1982,
pp. 307-9.

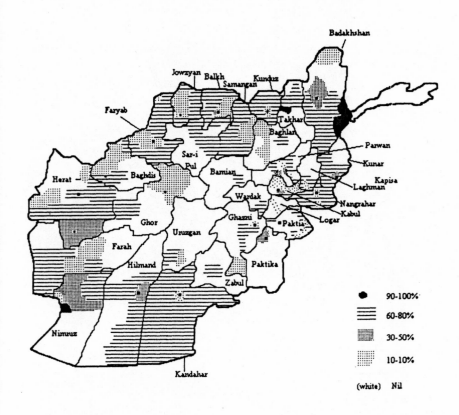

3. Degrees of government control over different areas of the country, according to mujahidin sources

Source: as for Table 50, C.

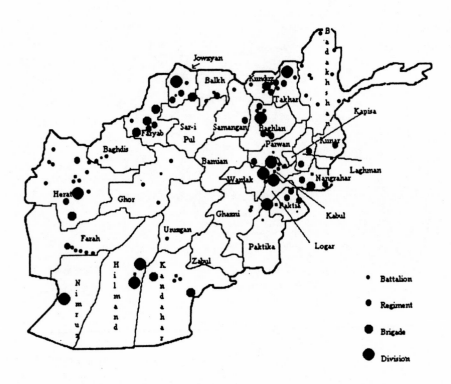

4. Creation of Regional Forces units, 1982-91.   Incomplete; represents available data.

Sources: Voenno-politicheskaya obstanovka v pr. Gil'mend (Uezdy Kadzhani, Sangin i Musa Kala) na konets febralya 1988g.; Bakhtar, 5 Dec. 1988; Izvestia, 15 July 1983; Voenno-politicheskaya obstanovka v zone otvetstvennosti 11 pd za posle dnii kvartal 1366g.; O. Kviatkovskii, 'Komandirovka na voiny', *Prostor,* 2/1988, p. 189; *KNT,* 29 March 1988; *Haqiqat-i Inqilab-i Saur,* 23 September 1985; *KNT,* 26 March 1985; *Link,* 30 Dec. 1990; *Otchet o sostoyanii territorial'nykh voisk v pr. Gerat,* 8.11.87 g.; L.V. Shebarshin, *Ruka Moskvy,* p. 200.

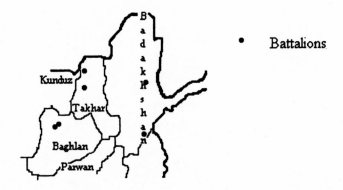

• Battalions

5. Regional units active in North-eastern Provinces, Dec. 1983. Information incomplete.

Source: Gllvnoe operativnoe upravlenie general'nogo shtaba, Karta khoda formirovaniya dobrovol'nykh polkov iz plemen ichtvertykh batal'onov iz byvshikh bandgrupp po sostoyanyu na 1983 g. (10.I.84).

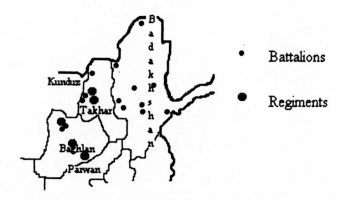

• Battalions

● Regiments

6. Regional units active in North-eastern Provinces, Dec. 1987/early 1988. Information almost complete – some independent units not included.

Source: Operativnaya obstanovka v territorial'nikh chastyakh (donesenie VKR 20 PD pr. Baghlan, 17.12.87 g.); T. Ruttig, Gesprach mit Zuhhurullah Zuhhuni (SAZA), May 1988, p. 4.

C

GRAPHS

Note. Quantitative values are given by the area included between the x-axis and the curve.

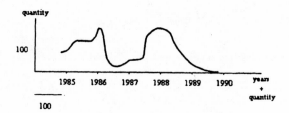

1. Growth in the membership of agricultural cooperatives

Sources: KNT, RA.

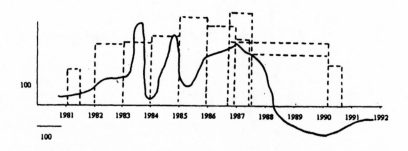

2. Membership growth of PDPA (represented from the area between the x axis and the curve) and variations in the number of new members (the area of the columns). After 1988 membership declined. The figures are official ones, apart from those for 1992, which are unofficial (*International Defense Review*, 4/1992).

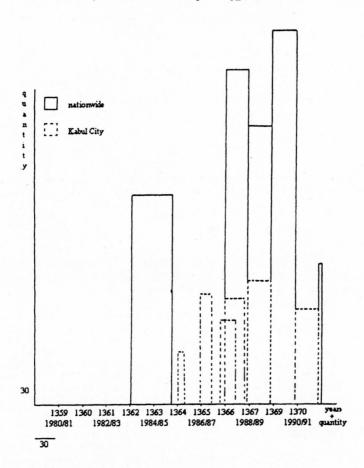

q
u
a
n
t
i
t
y

☐ nationwide

[___] Kabul City

30

| 1359 | 1360 | 1361 | 1362 | 1363 | 1364 | 1365 | 1366 | 1367 | 1369 | 1370 | years |
| 1980/81 | | 1982/83 | | 1984/85 | | 1986/87 | | 1988/89 | | 1990/91 | + quantity |

30

3. Recruitment to the Afghan armed forces

Sources: Umarov, 'Stanovlenie i tendentsii razvitiya politiki', p. 117; Gankovskii, 'Vooruz-hennye sily respubliki Afganistan'; Starodubova, 'Moral'no-politicheskii potentsial', p. 74; Gareev, *Moya poslednyaya voina*, p. 203; *Zapis' besedy zamestitelya zaveduyushego Mezhdunarod-nym otdelom TsK KPSS t. Ul'yanovskogo R.A. s...*, op. cit., p. 3; Najibullah, RA, 17 Jan. 1988; Merimskii, 'Voina v Afganistane zapiski uchastika', p. 112.

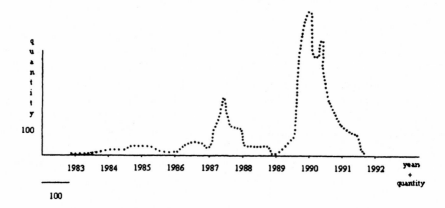

q
u
a
n
t
i
t
y

100

1983   1984   1985   1986   1987   1988   1989   1990   1991   1992   years
                                                                        +
                                                                     quantity

100

4. Pace of the 'pacification' process: number of mujahidin surrendering to the government, 1980-92. The quantity is given by the area included between the X axis and the curves (armed mujahidin).

Sources: NT, 13–1983, 17–1987, 43–1986; FEER, 28 April 1988; Ludwig, 'Einige Probleme', p. 104; Bonovsky, *op. cit.,* p. 258; IISS, *Strategic Survey 1985/1986; Bakhtar,* 26 Sept. 1986, 16 Oct. 1987, 20 Oct. 1987, 2 Dec. 1987, 27 Dec. 1987, 2 Jan. 1988, 18 Nov. 1988, 4 Oct. 1990, 13 June 1991, 16 Feb. 1991, 12 Sept. 1991, 16 Feb. 1991, 26 Sept. 1986, *KNT,* 29 Oct. 1986, 1 Jan. 1987, 3 Jan. 1987, 3 March 1987, 8 March 1987, 18 April 1987, 17 May 1987, 27 May 1987, 18 June 1987, 6 Oct. 1987, 16 Jan. 1988, 3 Feb. 1988, 20 Sept. 1988, 23 Oct. 1988, 18 Dec. 1988, 15 Nov. 1989, 14 Feb. 1990, 18 Jan. 1992, 16 Jan. 1988; *L'Humanité,* 24 May 1988; *Informatsionnvi Bulletten' po materialam XX Plenuma TsK NDPA,* Kabul, 1986; TASS, 6 Feb. 1987; AFP, 7 Feb. 1987 and 13 Feb. 1987; *Pravda,* 26 Feb. 1987; Kyodo, 28 Feb. 1987; RA, 8 March 1987, 17 Jan. 1988, 14 May 1988, 2 May 1989, 27 Nov. 1989, 25 Feb. 1990, 2 Oct. 1990, 29 May 1989, 27 Nov. 1989, 25 Feb. 1990; Najibullah, RA, 27 Dec. 1989; Najibullah, RA, 28 May 1990; RM, 9 April 1987; *NYT,* 28 April 1987, 6 May 1987, Lyakhovski, *Tragedia...,* pp. 330, 418-19; *Literaturnaya Gazeta,* 16 Sept. 1987; *O kolichestve... op. cit.,* *Vyvody po obstanovke...,* op. cit., *Chronique des événements,* Ceredaf, 1988 p. 5; CTK, 3 Jan. 1988; ND, 19-20 March 1988; Reuters 4 July 1988; SR, 4 April 1989; *La Repubblica,* 9 May 1989; TASS, 9 July 1989; Reuters 4 July 1989; *Le Monde,* 20 Sept. 1989; *Pravda,* 13 Dec. 1989; TASS, 29 Dec. 1989; Reuters 11 May 1989; *Süddeutsche Zeitung ,* 27 July 1990; Reuters, 14 Jan. 1991; FEER, 17 Oct. 1991; TASS, 9 March 1983; Lyakhovskii and Zabordin, *op. cit.,* 185; AFP, 3 Aug. 1989; Reuters 14 Jan. 1991; TASS, 15 Feb. 1992; Kotenev, *op. cit.;* *O kolichestve band myatezhnikov, pereshedshikh na storonu gosudarstva i vyshedshikh na peregovory (na 20 noyabrya 1987 goda); Vyvody po obstanovke, gruppirovki i karaktery deistvii myatezhnikov na territorii RA (na 1.06.88 goda);* D. Hiro, *Between Marx and Muhammed,* HarperCollins, 1994, p. 255.

BIBLIOGRAPHY

Note Short articles in newspapers and journals, and radio broadcast transcripts are not included.

Oral sources

Anifi, J., BBC Monitoring, born in Faryab province; telephone communication, 13 December 1993.

Januf, Mohammed, adviser of Komsomol in Afghanistan, Kunduz province, 1983-4; personal communication, London, 23 February 1995.

Keshtmand, S.A., high-ranking member of PDPA, Prime Minister; personal communication, London 10 December 1993.

Khalil, General, Vice-Minister of Defence, military governor of Western zone; personal communication, Moscow, 21 May 1996.

Khan, Sufi Juma, from Baluchistan, Pakistan, founder of the Communist Party of Pakistan, in exile in Kabul 1980-92; personal communication, London, 22 October 1995.

Mazdak, Farid, high-ranking member of PDPA, general secretary of DYOA, member of Politburo; personal communication, Berlin, 31 March 1996.

'Sasha', Soviet adviser in Afghanistan, Ministry of Defence, Dept. of Regional Units; telephone communication, Moscow, 28 May 1996.

Tanin, Zahir, member of CC – PDPA, journalist; personal communications, London, 8 March 1994 and 16 June 1995.

Urban, Mark, journalist, author of book on Afghanistan; telephone interview, London, 19 May 1995.

DOCUMENTS AND OTHER UNPUBLISHED SOURCES

Unpublished documents

Glavnoe operativnoe upravlenie general'nogo shtaba, 'Karta khoda formirovaniya dobrovol'ykh polkov iz plemen ichtvertykh batal'onov iz byvshikh bandgrupp po sostoyanyu na 1983 g. (10.1.84)', Red Army map.

Hakim, 'Nedostatki (negativnye yavleniya) v rabote voenno-politicheskogo uchilisha, 10.10.87g.', report to unspecified Red Army official.

'Informatsiya o regularnykh silakh VS i grazhdanskikh vooruzhennykh formirovaniyakh', Red Army intelligence report, 1987.

Internal document of 40th Army, title illegible.

'Iz besed ruzh. sostava RA s Shevarnadze. VPO v RA avgust 1988 g.', transcript from a Red Army adviser.

'Iz donesenii o rabote agitgrupp s naseleniem za 19.01', Red Army report.

Kasperavichius, 'Nachal'niku politotdela-zamestitelyu glavnogo voennogo sovetnika v DRA po politicheskoi chasti, General-Leitenantu Aunapu E.M.', October 1986, Red Army report.

List of reports about all the provinces except Kabul, n.d., Red Army intelligence report.

'O khode realizatsii politiki natsional'nogo primireniya 26.04.88', Red Army periodical report.

'O kolichestve band myatezhnikov, pereshedshikh na storonu gosudarstva i vyshedshikh na peregovory (na 20 noyabrya 1987 goda)', Red Army report.

'Obstanovka v provintsii Laghman, 6.02.88. g.', Red Army intelligence report.

'Operativnaya obstanovka v territorial'nikh chastyakh (donesenie VKR 20 PD pr. Baghlan, 17.12.87 g.', Red Army report:

'Otchet o komandirovke v pr. Baghlan, 15-18 dekabrya 1987 g.', Red Army report.

'Otchet o sostoyanii territorial'nykh voisk v pr. Gerat, 8.11.87 g.', Red Army report.

'Otchet p-ka yu...tsiy Dud..na V.I. o prodenyannoi rabote za period prebyvaniya v komandirovke s X-83 po VIII-85g., g. Kandagar 1985g.', Red Army report, title partially unreadable.

'Provintsiya Baghlan', Red Army report, undated.

'Provintsiya Paktia', Red Army report, 1360 (1981/2).

'Provintsiya Paktika', Red Army report, 1360-1.

'Rezul'taty prizyva 2 mesyatsev (mizan-akrab) 1366 g. v provintsiyakh Severa i Severo-Vostoka', Red Army report.

Ruttig T., 'Gesprach mit Zuhhurullah Zuhhuni (SAZA)', May 1988, Report to the DDR Embassy in Kabul.

'Spravka o politiko-voennoi obstanovke, gruppirovkakh, kharaktere deistvii, planakh i namereniyakh kontrrevolyutsii v respublike Afganistan na 6.12.87 g.', Red Army report.

'Svedeniya o sostave "Yader" dlya formirovaniya i ukrepleniya vlasti v zone "Severo-Vostok" po sostoyanyu na ..... 1980 goda', Red Army report.

'Voenno-politicheskaya obstanovka v pr. Gil'mend (Uezdy Kadzhani, Sangin i Musa-Kala) na konets febralya 1988g.', Red Army report.

'Voenno-politicheskaya obstanovka v provintsii Kandagar, af. variant,. febr. 1988 g.', Red Army report.
'Voenno-politicheskaya obstanovka v provintsii Kunar po sostoyanie na 1 Maya 1985', Red Army report.
'Voenno-politicheskaya obstanovka v pr. Nimruz na konets febralya 1988g.', Red Army report.
'Voenno-politicheskaya obstanovka v zone otvetstvennosti 11 pd za poslednii kvartal 1366g.', Red Army report.
'Vyvody po obstanovke, gruppirovk i kharakteru deistvii myatezhnikov na territorii RA na 1.06.88 goda', Red Army report.
'Zapis' besedy zamestitelya zaveduyushego Mezhdunarodnym otdelom TsK KPSS t. Ul'yanovskogo R.A. s chlenom Politbyuro TsK NDPA, zamestitelem Predsedatelya Soveta Ministrov DRA t. M. Rafi, Kabul, 18 oktabrya 1984 goda', transcript.

Published Documents

20th anniversary of the People's Democratic Party of Afghanistan. Materials of the Jubilee Meeting of the PDPA CC, the DRA RC and the Council of Ministers January 10 1985.
Documents and Records of the National Conference of the People's Democratic Party of Afghanistan, Kabul, March 14-15, 1982.
Informatsionnyi byulleten' po materialam XX plenuma TsK NDPA, Kabul, DSP, 1986.
A Summary of the Babrak Karmal's Report on the Party Tasks Concerning the Intensification of Political Work among the Masses to the Ninth plenum of the PDPA, CC, Kabul, n.d.
Speech of B. Karmal, Kabul, 1365 (1986/7).
Speech given on the 25th Anniversary of the Foundation of the Party, end 1989, 'Party unity an earnest need for its might', Kabul, State Printing House, 1990.
Babrak Karmal's speech to the 7th Plenum of the PDPA, CC, n.d. (1981); at the 13th Plenum, March 1984; at the 15th Plenum, March 1985; at the 17th Plenum, 1986.
Babrak Karmal's Theses, Declaration of DRA RC, Kabul November 1985.
Najibullah M., *Comrade Najib's Speech at the Plenum of PDPA, CC Jauza 1366* (June 1987).
———, *Taking the Path of National Reconciliation*, Government Commitee of Press and Publication, Kabul, 1988.
National Conference of PDPA on National Reconciliation (oct. 18-20, 1987). Documents, Kabul, Afghanistan Today, 1987.
Organisational Structure and Composition of the PDPA, Kabul, n.d.
'Polozhenie o poryadke vedeniya peregovorov s predstavitelyami vooruz-

hennikh otryadov plemen i kontrrevolyutsionnykh band po skloneniyu ikh k perekhodu na storonu gosudarstvennoi vlasti, 30 dekabrya 1984 g.' in *NDPA (sbornik dokumentov)*, Tashkent, 'Uzbekistan', 1986.

'Postanovlenie politburo TsK NDPA o dal'neishem povishenii roli NOF DRA v dele splocheniya patrioticheskikh sil strany, 26 sentyabrya 1984 g.' in *NDPA (sbornik dokumentov)*, Tashkent, 'Uzbekistan', 1986.

'Postanovlenie politburo TsK NDPA o deyatel'nosti TsK DOMA po dal'neishemu uluchsheniyu organizatsionnoi, politicheskoi i vostitatel'noi raboty sredi molodezhi v svete reshenii..., 17 noyabrya 1984 g.' in *NDPA (sbornik dokumentov)*, Tashkent, 'Uzbekistan', 1986.

'Postanovlenie sekretariata TsK NDPA o rabote badakhshanskogo provintsial'nogo partiinogo komiteta po vypolneniyu postanovleniya politburo TsK NDPA ot 17.9.1361, 30 dekabrya 1984 g.' in *NDPA (sbornik dokumentov)*, Tashkent, 'Uzbekistan', 1986.

'Postanovlenie sekretariata TsK NDPA o rabote geratskogo provintsial'nogo komiteta partii po vypolnnyu reshenii XII plenuma TsK NDPA, 10 marta 1984 g.' in *NDPA (sbornik dokumentov)*, Tashkent, 'Uzbekistan', 1986.

'Postanovlenie politburo TsK NDPA o rabote kandagarskogo provintsial'nogo komiteta partii po ukrepleniyu partiinogo edinstva i distsipliny v svete trebovanii XIV plenuma TsK NDPA, 10 otkyabrya 1984 g.' in *NDPA (sbornik dokumentov)*, Tashkent, 'Uzbekistan', 1986.

'Postanovlenie sekretariata TsK NDPA o rabote tsentral'nogo soveta DOZhA po uluchsheniyu deyatel'nosti zhenskikh organizatsii v svete trebovanii..., 7 iyuliya 1984 g.' in *NDPA (sbornik dokumentov)*, Tashkent, 'Uzbekistan', 1986.

'Sekretnye dokumenty iz osobykh papok: Afghanistan', *Voprosy Istoriy*, no. 3 (1993).

TsK KPSS, 'K sobytiyam v Afganistane, 27-28 dekabrya 1979 g.' in *Soujetische Geheimdokumente zum Afghanistankrieg (1978-1991)*, VDF Zurich, 1995.

TsK KPSS, 'O dopolnitel'noi postavke spetsimushestva Respublike Afganistan, 1989' in *Soujetische Geheimdokumente zum Afghanistankrieg (1978-1991)*, VDF Zurich, 1995.

TsK KPSS, 'O meropriyatiyakh v svyazi s predstoyashim vyvodom sovetskikh voisk iz Afganistana', 23 January 1989 in *Soujetische Geheimdokumente zum Afghanistankrieg (1978-1991)*, VDF Zurich, 1995.

TsK KPSS, 'O rabochem vizite Ministra oborony SSSR v Respubliku Afganistan', in *Soujetische Geheimdokumente zum Afghanistankrieg (1978-1991)*, VDF Zurich, 1995.

TsK KPSS, 'Ob okazanii material'noi pomoshi Narodno-Demokraticheskoi partii Afganistana', 9 January 1987 in *Soujetische Geheimdokumente zum Afghanistankrieg (1978-1991)*, VDF Zurich, 1995.

TsK KPSS, 'Po voprosu rassmotreniya pros'b Prezidenta Respubliki

Afganistan', 5 October 1989 in *Sowjetische Geheimdokumente zum Af-ghanistankrieg (1978-1991)*, VDF Zurich, 1995.

'Ukaz prezidiuma revolyutsionnogo soveta DRA, 30 dekabrya 1984 g., O Prinnyatii Polozheniya o territorial'nykh voiskakh Vooruzhennikh Sil Demokraticheskoi Respubliki Afganistan' in NDPA (sbornik dokumentov), Tashkent, 'Uzbekistan', 1986.

'Vypiska iz protokola N. 149 zacedaniya Politbyuro TSK KPSS ot 12 apreliya 1979 goda' in Sowjetische Geheimdokumente zum Afghanis-tankrieg (1978-1991), VDF Zurich, 1995.

'Zasedanie Politbyuro TsK KPSS 10 marta 1983 goda' in Sowjetische Geheimdokumente zum Afghanistankrieg (1978-1991), VDF Zurich, 1995.

Dissertations

Bart, A.I., 'Partiino-politicheskaya rabota v voiskakh v usloviakh boevykh deistvii v Afganistane, 1979-1989 gg.', Alma Ata, 1990.

Bosin, Yu. V., 'Natsional'nye problemy sovremennogo Afganistana', IV AN SSSR, Moscow, 1992.

Dardmal, Rahim Jan, 'Die Herausbildung der sozialistichen Produk-tionsverhaltnisse in der Landwirtschaft Afghanistans', Martin-Luther-Universität, Halle-Wittenberg, 1985.

Gol', Z., 'Revolyutsionnaya Armiya v natsional'no-demokraticheskoi revolyutsii (na primere Afganistana)', Krasnoznamennaya Akademiya im. V.I. Lenina, Moscow 1988.

Gora, L., 'Analyse des sozialökonomischen und politischen Entwick-lungsstandes der Gesellschaft Afghanistans für den Zeitraum von 1973 bis 1978 und der hauptsachlichsten Veränderungen nach der April-revolution von 1978', Diplomarbeit, Humboldt Universität, Berlin, 1983.

Harpviken, K.B., 'Political Mobilisation among the Hazara of Afghanistan: 1978-1992', Dept. of Sociology, University of Oslo, 1995.

Katkov, I.E., 'Tsentral'naya vlast' Afganistana i pushtunskie plemena', DSP, Moscow, IV AN SSSR, 1987.

Kotenev, A.A., 'Natsional'no-etnicheskii faktor v vooruzhennoi bor'be s kontrrevolyutsei v DRA', 1983, DSP, IV AN SSSR.

Ludwig, J., 'Einige Probleme der Strategie und Politik der Demokratis-chen Volkspartei Afghanistans (DVPA) in der nationaldemokratischen Revolution in Afghanistan (1978 bis 1985)', Akademie fur Gesellschaftwissenschaften beim ZK der SED, Partei-internes Material, 1986.

Mahbub, C., 'Moralische Aspekte im Islam und deren gegenwärtige ideologische Bedeutung in den Auffassung fortschrittlicher Geistlicher der DRA', Humboldt-Universität, Berlin, 1986.

Mohsenzada, G.M., 'Die Rolle der afghanische Jugend im Kampf für die revolutionäre Umgestaltung Afghanistans', Humboldt-Universität, Berlin, 1985.

Nuristani, A.N., 'Zu Rolle, der Agrarfrage im revolutionäre Prozess Afghanistans', Hochschule fur Ökonomie, Berlin-Est, 1987.

Plyais, Ya.A., 'Voznikovenie i nikotorye aspekty teoriticheskoi i organizatsionnoi deyatel'nosti NDPA', Mos. Kommercheskii Un., Moscow, 1992.

Shaniyazova, S.K., 'Znachenie Aprel'skoi Revolyutsii 1978 g. v razvitii kultury narodov Afganistana 1978-1988 gg', Un. V.I. Lenin, Tashkent, 1989.

Starodubova, O.V., 'Moral'no-politicheskii potentsial vooruzhennikh sil Afganistana: problemy i trudnosti formirovaniya (1978-1990)', IV AN Uzbeskoi SSR, Tashkent, 1991.

Strmecki, J.M., 'Power Assessment: Measuring Soviet Power in Afghanistan', Georgetown University, Washington, DC, 1994.

Tavus, M., 'Filosofsko-sotsiologicheskii analiz roli religii i religiozniykh deyatelei Afganistana v relizatsii politiki natsional'nogo primireniya', Krasnoznamennaya Akademiya im. V.I. Lenina, Moscow, 1991.

Umarov. B. Kh., 'Stanovlenie i tendentsii razvitiya politiki natsional'nogo primireniya v Afganistane', IV AN Uzbeskoi SSR, Tashkent, 1990.

Other unpublished sources

Bradsher, H.S.A., 'Afghanistan and the USSR', 3rd unpublished version (1993) of book printed by Duke University Press, Durham, NC.

Ege, E., 'Confidence in Kabul: A political solution for Afghanistan', typescript, undated (1983).

Halliday, F., 'Political change and regime survival in Afghanistan, '1978-1992', ESRC End of Award Report, 1995.

——, 'Report on a visit to Afghanistan 20-27.10.1980', typescript.

Plastun, V.N., 'Situatsiya v Afganistane', lecture given in Moscow in 1988.

——, 'Voenno-politicheskaya obstanovka v DRA i polozhenie v NDPA', 23 July 1986, typescript.

SECONDARY SOURCES

Books

25 let PDPA, It. ON pri TsK KPSS, Moscow, 1990.

Adamec L.A., *A Biographical Dictionary of Afghanistan*, Akademische Druck – und Verlagsanstalt, Graz, 1987.

Afghanistan 1989-1995, Beiheft zur *Allgemeinen Schweizerischen Militär-zeitschrift* (ASMZ) 5/1996.

Aktual'nye problemy afganskoi revolyutsii, Nauka, Moscow, 1984.

Amin T., *Ethno-national Movements of Pakistan*, Institute of Policy Studies, Peshawar, 1988.

Anwar R., *The Tragedy of Afghanistan*, Verso, London, 1988.

Arney G., *Afghanistan. The Definitive Account of a Country at Crossroads*, Mandarin Books, London, 1990.

Arnold A., *Afghanistan's Two Party Communism*, Hoover Institution Press, Stanford, CA, 1983.

Asia Watch, *Afghanistan: the Forgotten War*, Human Rights Watch, New York, 1991.

Basov V.V./Poliakov G.A., *Afganistan: trudnye sud'by revolyutsii*, Znanie, Moscow, 1988.

Bazgar S., *La résistance au coeur*, Denoël, Paris, 1987.

Belozershev E.P., *Narodnoe obrazovanie v respublike Afganistan*, Pedagogika, Moscow, 1988.

Bensi G., *Allah contro Gorbaciov*, Reverdito Editore, Trento, 1988.

Bonner A., *Among the Afghans*, Duke University Press, Durham, NC, 1987.

Bonovsky P., *Washington's Secret War Against Afghanistan*, International Publishers, New York, 1985.

Borovik A., *La guerra nascosta*, Leonardo, Milano, 1990.

——, *Afganistan: echshe raz pro voinu*, Mezhdunarodnye Otnosheniya, 1990.

Bronner W., *Afghanistan, Revolution und Kontrrevolution*, Marxismus Aktuell, Verlag Marxistische Blätter, Frankfurt am Main, 1980.

Buchhorn M., *40 Tage in Kabul*, Beltz Verlag, Weinheim, 1982.

CEREDAF, *Chronique des évènements 1984-1985*, Paris, 1986.

Comitato italiano di solidarità con la Resistenza Afghana, *La Resistenza Afghana. Incontro internazionale a sostegno del popolo 'afghano aggredito dall'URSS, Firenze 26-28 marzo 1982*, Roma, Città del Sole, 1982.

Cordesman A.H./Wagner A.R. , *The Lessons of Modern Wars*, vol. III, Westview, Boulder, Co, 1990.

Danziger N., *Danziger's Adventures*, London, HarperCollins, 1992.

Davydov A.D., *Afghanistan: voiny moglo ne byt'*, Nauka, Moscow, 1993.

De Beaurecueil S., *Chronique d'un témoin privilégié*, vol. II, CEREDAF, Paris, 1993.

Franceschi P., *Guerre en Afghanistan*, La Table Ronde, Paris, 1984.

Fullerton J., *The Soviet Occupation of Afghanistan*, Far Eastern Economic Review, Hong Kong, 1983.

Gai D./Snegirev V., *Vtorzhenie*, IKPA, Moscow, 1991.

Gaidar T., *Pod afganskim nebom*, Sovetskaya Rossiya, Moscow, 1981.

Gareev M.A., *Moya poslednyaya voina*, Nisan, Moscow, 1996.

Goodwin J., *Caught in the Crossfire*, Dutton, New York, 1987.

Goyal D.R., *Afghanistan behind the Smoke Screen*, Ajanta, New Dehli, 1984.

Gromov B., *Ogranichennyi kontingent*, Progress, Moscow, 1994.

Harrison S./Cordovez D., *Out of Afghanistan*, Oxford University Press, 1995.

Hassan Kakar M., *Afghanistan: The Soviet Invasion and the Afghan Response*, University of California Press, Berkeley, 1995.

Heinamaa A./Leppanen M./Yurchenko Y., *The Soldiers' Story*, University of California Press, Berkeley, 1994.

Hiro D., *Between Marx and Muhammed*, London, HarperCollins, 1994.

Hoppe F., *Kabul '84*, Solidaritatskomitee der DDR, Berlin, 1984.

Hyman A., *Afghanistan under Soviet Domination*, Macmillan, Basingstoke, 1984.

Isby D., *War in a Distant Country*, Arms and Armour Press, London, 1989.

Jamir S., *Zum Problem des Analphabetismus in Afghanistan*, LIT Verlag, Hamburg, 1990.

Kaul R., *Democratic Afghanistan – forever*, Pulse Publisher, New Dehli, 1987.

Koloskov M., *Fighters for the Faith? No, Hired Killers!*, Novosti Press Agency Publishing House, Moscow, 1986.

V. Korgun, *Intelligentsia v politicheskoi zhizhne Afganistana*, Nauka, Moscow, 1983.

Krishna Iyer V.R./Vinod Sethi, *The New Afghan Dawn*, Indo-Afghan Friendship Society, New Dehli, 1988.

Lamb C., *Waiting for Allah*, Penguin, London, 1992.

Leonov N.S., *Likholet'e*, Mezhdunarodnye Otnosheniya, Moscow, 1994.

Lyakhovskii A., *Tragediya i doblest' Afgana*, Iskona, Moscow, 1995.

――――/ZabrodinV., *Tainy afganskoi vojny*, Planeta, Moscow, 1991.

Maidan I.G., *Problemy sotsial'noi bazy Aprelskoi Revolyutsii i politiki natsional'nogo primirenie v Afganistane*, AN UkSSR, Kiev, 1988.

Male B., *Revolutionary Afghanistan*, Croom Helm, 1982.

Malik H., *Soviet-Pakistan Relations and post-Soviet Dynamics 1947-1992*, Macmillan, Basingstoke, 1994.

Malinkovich V., *Afganistan v ogne*, Suchasnist', 1985.

Marchuk N.I., *Neob"yavlennaya voina v Afganistane*, Luch, Moscow, 1993.

Martyred for the Cause of Truth: The true Moslems Murdered by the Mujahidin, Kabul Government Press, n.d. (c. 1983).

Matinuddin K., *Power Struggle in the Hindu Kush: Afghanistan 1978-1991*, Wajidalis, Lahore, 1991.

Mezhdunarodnyi Ezhegodnik – Politika i Ekonomika 1981.

Mezhdunarodnyi Ezhegodnik – Politika i Ekonomika 1982.

Mezhdunarodnyi Ezhegodnik – Politika i Ekonomika 1984.

Mezhdunarodnyi Ezhegodnik – Politika i Ekonomika 1987.

Mo E./Pellizzari V., *Kabul Kabul*, Vallecchi, Firenze, 1989.

Moghadam V., *Modernizing Women*, Lynne Rienner, Boulder Co, 1993.

Mokrusov G., *120 dnei v Kabule*, Pravda, Moscow, 1981.

Musaelian G./Sukhoparov A., *Ekho razbuzhannykh gor?*, Moskovskii Rabochi, Moscow, 1988.

National Reconciliation in Practice, Afghanistan Today Publishers, Kabul, 1987.

Nayar K., *Report on Afghanistan*, Allied Publishers, New Delhi, 1981.

Nikolayev L., *Afghanistan between the Past and the Future*, Progress, Moscow, 1986.

O'Ballance E., *Wars in Afghanistan*, Brassey's, London, 1993.

Ol'shanskii D.V., *Natsional'noe primerenie*, ION pri TsK KPSS, Moscow, 1988.

Palmer L., *Adventures in Afghanistan*, Octagon Press, London, 1990.

Pashkevich M.M., *Afganistan: voina glazami kombata*, Voennoe Izd., Moscow, 1991.

Pedersen G., *Afghan Nomads in Transition*, London, Thames and Hudson, 1994.

Pohly M., *Krieg und Widerstand in Afghanistan*, Das Arabische Buch, Berlin, 1992.

Roy O., *Islam and Resistance in Afghanistan*, Cambridge University Press, 1990.

Rubin B.R., *The Fragmentation of Afghanistan*, Yale University Press, New Haven, CT, 1995.

Sadat A., *Afghanistan: Land of Jirgahs*, Kabul, 1986.

Sarin O./Dvoretsky L., *The Afghan Syndrome: The Soviet Union's Vietnam*, Presidio Press, Novato, 1993.

Schultheiss R., *Night Letters: Inside Wartime Afghanistan*, Orion Books, New York, 1992.

Schweizer P., *Victory. The Reagan Administration's Secret Strategy that Hastened the Collapse of the Soviet Union*, Atlantic Monthly Press, New York, 1995.

Sen Gupta B., *Afghanistan: Politics, Economics and Society*, Pinter, London, 1986.

Shahrani M.N./Canfield R., *Revolutions and Rebellions in Afghanistan*, Institute of International Studies, Berkeley, 1984.

Shedrov I., *Afghanistan. Molodost' Revolyutsii*, Molodaya Gvardia, Moscow, 1982.

Shebarshin L.V., *Ruka Moskvy*, Tsentr-100, Moscow, 1992.

Sikorsky R., *Dust of the Saints*, Chatto and Windus, London, 1989.

Spolnikov V., *Afganistan: islamskaya oppositsiya*, Nauka, Moscow, 1990.

Stahel A.A./Bucherer P., *Afghanistan 1986/87*, Schweizerisches Afghanistan-Archiv, Liestal, 1987.

Strategic Survey 1985/1986, IISS, London.

Strategic Survey 1989/1990, IISS, London.

Svetikov V.N., *Zharkii mesiats saratan*, DOSAAF, Moscow, 1988.

Tchikichev A.V., *Spetnaz en Afghanistan*, CEREDAF, Paris, 1994.

Trask R., *Grasping the Nettle of Peace*, Morning Star, London, 1987.

Tschernajew A., *Die letzen Jahre einer Weltmacht*, Deutsche Verlags-Anstalt, Stuttgart, 1993.

Urban M., *War in Afghanistan*, Macmillan, Basingstoke, 1990 (2nd edn).

Vassiliev A., *Russian Policy in the Middle East: from Messianism to Pragmatism*, Ithaca Press, Reading, 1993.

Vercellin G., *Afghanistan 1973-1978*, Università di Venezia, 1979.

Voina v Afganistane, Voenizdat, Moscow, 1991.

Zhtnukhin A.P./Lykoshin S.A., *Zvezda nad gorodam Kabbulom*, Molodaya Gvardiya, Moscow, 1990.

Articles

Afanas'ev A., 'Afganistan: pochemu eto proizoshlo', *Kommunist Vooruzhennikh Sil*, no. 12 (1991).

Ahmed F., 'The Khalq failed to comprehend the contradictions of the rural sector', *Merip Reports*, July/Aug. 1980.

Aristova L.B./Bosin Yu./V./Makhkamov M./Khashibekov Kh., 'Mnogonatsional'nyi Afganistan' in *Zapadnaya Aziya*, Nauka, 1993.

Arnold A. and R., 'Afghanistan' in 1985., 1987, 1988 and 1989 editions of the *Yearbook on World Communist Affairs*, Hoover Institution, Stanford, CA.

Arnold A., 'The ephemeral elite' in *The politics of social transformation in Afghanistan, Iran and Pakistan*, Syracuse University Press, 1994.

Atoev K., 'Religioznaya situatsiya v sovremennom Afghanistane' in *Voprosy teorii i pratiki nauchnogo ateizma*, Moscow, 1988.

Babakhodzhaev M.A., 'NDPA – krupneischaya i samaya vliyatelnaya sila afganskogo obschestva' in *Respublika Afganistan*, Akademiya Nauk Uzbeskoi SSR, Tashkent, 1990.

Baryalai M., 'Indispensable for the victory over counterrevolution', *World Marxist Review*, 6 (1985).

Baryalay M., 'National Traditions serve the revolution', *World Marxist Review*, 4 (1986).

Basov V., 'Postup' afganskoi revolyutsii', *Agitator*, no. 7 (1985).

Bhattacharya S.P., 'Soviet nationality policy in Afghanistan', *Asian Affairs*, June 1984.

Butenas V., 'Dorogoi Aprel'skoi Revolyutsii', *Kommunist* (Vilnius), no. 9 (1986).

Centlivres-Demont M., 'Afghan women in peace, war, and exile' in *The politics of social transformation in Afghanistan, Iran and Pakistan*, Syracuse University Press, 1994.

Coldren L., 'Afghanistan in 1984', *Asian Survey,*, Feb. 1985.

———, 'Afghanistan in 1985', *Asian Survey*, Feb. 1986.

Cymkin T.M., 'Aftermath of the Saur coup: insurgency and counter-insurgency in Afghanistan', *Fletcher Forum*, summer 1982.

Davidov A., 'Osnovnye aspekty sotsial'nykh konfliktov v derevne Afganistana', *Spetsial'nyi byulleten' AN SSSR – IV*, no. 2 (1987).

Davydov A.D., 'Osnovnye izmeneniya v kontsentsii agrarnoi reformy do i posle Aprel'skoi Revolyutsii v Afganistane', in *Aprel'skaya Revolyutsiya 1978g.*, Referatnyi sbornik, AN SSSR i INION, 1982

Dorronsoro G., 'Kaboul 1992, l'usure', *Est et Ouest*, Jan. 1992.

———, 'La politique de pacification en Afghanistan' in G. Chaliand (ed.), *Stratégies de la guerrilla*, Payot, 1994.

Dorronsoro G./Lobato C., 'L'Afghanistan un an après le retrait soviétique', *Est et Ouest*, Jan. 1990.

———, 'The Militia in Afghanistan', *Central Asian Survey*, 4 (1989).

Dupree L., 'Red Flag over the Hindukush', *Afghanistan Studies Journal*, vol. 1, no. 2.

Galster S. R./Hippler J., 'Report from Afghanistan', *Middle East Report*, May-June 1989.

Gankovskii Yu., 'Afghanistan: from intervention to National reconciliation', *The Iranian Journal of International Affairs*, vol. IV, no. 1 (spring 1992).

———, interviewed by V.K. Turadzhev, 'Nasha bol' – Afganistan', *Aziya i Afrika Segodnia*, no. 6 (1989).

———, 'O putiakh prekrasheniya grazhdanskoi voiny v Afganistane', *Vostok i Sovremennost'*, no. 3 (1993).

———, 'Polosa pushtunskikh plemen Afganistana', *Spetsial'nyi Byulleten' AN SSSR IV*, no. 6 (1987).

———, 'Vooruzhennye sily respubliki Afganistan', *Vostok i Sovremennost'*, no. 2 (1989).

Gankovsky Yu. V., 'The dynamics of Russian-Afghan relations' in M. Mesbahi (ed.), *Russia and the Third World in the post-Soviet era*, University Press of Florida, 1994.

Gareyev M., 'The Afghan problem : three years without Soviet troops', *International Affairs*, March 1992.

Ghani A., 'Gulab: an afghan schoolteacher' in E.Burke III (ed.), *Struggle and survival in the Modern Middle East*, I.B. Tauris, London, 1993.

Gibbs D., 'The peasant as a counter-revolutionary', *Studies in Comparative International Development*, vol. XXI, no. 1 (1986).

Giustozzi A., 'La resistenza afghana. Rivolta tradizionalista e movimenti politici moderni', *Rivista di Storia Contemporanea*, no. 1 (1991).

Grevemeyer J.-H., 'Afghanistan: das 'Neue Modell einer Revolution' und der dörfliche Widerstand' in *Revolution in Iran und Afghanistan*, Syndakat, Frankfurt am Main, 1980.

Halliday F., 'War and Revolution in Afghanistan', *New Left Review*, no. 119 (1980).

Harrison S., 'Afghanistan' in Kornbluh/Klare (eds), *Low Intensity Warfare*, Pantheon, New York, 1988.

Harrison Selig S., 'A breakthrough in Afghanistan?', *Foreign Policy*, no. 51 (1983).

———, 'Containment and the Soviet Union in Afghanistan' in T.L. Deibel/J.L. Gaddis (eds), *Containment: Concept and policy*, NDU, Washington, DC, 1986.

Hill J., 'Afghanistan in 1990: Year of the Mujahidin', *Armed Forces Journal International*, March 1989.

Ikram M.A., 'Liberation of Eastern Ningrahar', WUFA, Jan.-March 1989.

Iunin S., 'V poiskakh geroya', *Podvig*, no. 34 (1989).

Iurtaev V.I., 'Demokraticheskaya organizatsiya molodezhi Afganistana' in *Aprel'skaya Revolyutsiya 1978 g. v Afganistane, referatnyi sbornik*, INION/IV, Moscow, 1982.

'Kak prinimalos' reshenie', *Voenno-istoricheskii Zhurnal*, no. 7 (1991).

Karp C., 'Afghanistan: six years of Soviet occupation', US Dept. of State, Special Report, no. 135 (1985).

———, 'Afghanistan: eight years of Soviet occupation', *Department of State Bulletin*, March 1988.

Karpenko O., 'Iz afganskogo dnevnika', *Zvezda Vostoka*, 12/1987.

Keshtmand S.A., 'Uregulirovanie afganskoi problemy', *Partinaia Zhizn'*, no. 2 (1990).

Khakimdzhanov N.N., 'Kurs NDPA na rasshirenie sotsial'noi bazy aprelskoi revolyutsii', *Obshchestvennie Nauki v Uzbekistane*, 2 (1988).

Khalil A.J., 'My impressions of Afghanistan's visit', *Central Asia*, no. 13 (1983).

Khan A.H., 'The Militias in Afghanistan', *Central Asia*, no. 31 (winter 1992).

Khanif Sh., 'Afganskii dnevnik', *Pamir*, no. 12 (1989).

Kipp J.-C., 'Afghanistan: après la guerre', *Politique Internationale*, Aug. 1989.

Korgun V., 'Afganistan posle vyvoda sovetskikh voisk', *Vostok i Sovremennost'*, no. 1 (1990).

———, 'Est' li vikhod iz tupika?', *Aziya i Afrika Segodnia*, no. 6 (1992).

———, 'Natsional'noe primirenie i vnutripoliticheskaya situatsiya v 1988 g.', *Spetsial'nyi Byulleten' AN SSSR – IV*, no. 2 (1990).

———, 'The Afghan Revolution: a failed experiment' in D.F. Eickelman (ed.), *Russia's Muslim frontiers*, Indiana University Press, Bloomington, 1993.

Kornienko G.M., 'The Afghan endeavor: Perplexities of the military incursion and withdrawal', *Journal of South Asian and Middle Eastern Studies*, vol. XVII, n.o 2 (winter 1994).

Krasikov Yu., 'Internatsional'naya missiya sovetskogo voina', *Voennyi Vestnik*, no. 10 (1988).

Krivov S., 'Vooruzhennye sily v politicheskoi zhizni Afganistana', *Spetsial'nyi Byulleten'* IV AN SSSR, no. 2 (1990).

Kviatkovskii O., 'Komandirovka na voiny', *Prostor*, 2/1988.

Laurinchikas A., 'Zelenie kraski zhizni', *Nash Sovremennik*, 11 (1987).

Lifschultz L., 'Afghanistan: A voice from Moscow', *Monthly Review*, Sept. 1987, interview with N. Simoniya.

Lobato C., 'Civils et résistants dans la province d'Herat à l'automne 1989', *Afghanistan Info*, Nov. 1989.

———, 'Islam in Kabul', *Central Asian Survey*, vol. 4, no. 4 (1985).

———, 'Kabul 1980-1986: un Islam officiel pour légitimer le pouvoir communiste', *Central Asian Survey*, vol. 7, no. 2-3 (1988).

Loghinov A.V., 'Natsional'ny Vopros v Afganistane', *Rasy i Narody*, 2/1990.

Lyakhovskii A., 'Na afganskoi vizhzhennoi zemle', *Kommunist Vooruzhennikh Sil*, nos. 19, 20, 21, 22 (1990).

——— and Zabrodin V., 'Tainy afganskoi voiny', *Armiya*, 9 (1992).

Merimskii V.A., 'V boyakh s modzhakhedami', *Voenno-istoricheskii Zhurnal*, no. 8 (1994).

———, 'Voina po zakamu', *Voenno-istoricheskii Zhurnal*, no. 11 (1993).

———, 'Voina v Afganistane: zapiski uchastika', *Novaya i Noveyashaya Istoriya*, no. 3 (1995).

Michalski E. and Michalski K.J., 'Die revolutionär-demokratisch Umgestaltung der Agrärverhaltnisse und die Entwicklung der landwirtschaftlichen Produktion in Afghanistan', *Asien-Afrika-Lateinamerika*, vol. 13, no. 5 (1985).

Momand N.M., 'Afganistan: protsess revolyutsionnogo obnovleniya prodolzhaetsya', *Partiinaya Zhizn'*, 1/1987.

Mukherjee S., 'Evolution of the polity in Afghanistan during the laste decade' in V.D. Chopra (ed.), *Afghanistan: Geneva accords and after*, Patriot New Delhi, 1988.

Newman J., 'The future of Northern Afghanistan', *Asian Survey*, July 1988.

Nikitenko E.G./Pikov N.I., 'Razvenchannyi mif', *Voenno-Istoricheskii Zhurnal*, no. 2 (1995).

Nosatov V., 'Afganskii dnevnik', *Prostor*, no. 4 (1989).

———, 'Afganskii dnevnik', *Prostor*, no. 11 (1989).

———, 'V nachale deviatiletnei voiny', *Literaturnyi Kirgizistan*, no. 6, 1989.

Ol'shanskii D.V., 'Afganistan: sud'ba naroda, sud'ba obshchestva', *Sotsiologicheskie issledovaniya*, no. 5 (1988).

Olesen A., 'The Saur Revolution and the local response to it' in *Forschungen in und über Afghanistan*, S.W. Breckle and C.M. Naumann (eds), Bibliotheca Afghanica, Liestal, 1983.

Olimov M., 'Iz zapisok perevodchika', *Vostok*, no. 3 (1991).

Olinik A., 'Zarnitsy nad gindukushem', *Kommunist Vooruzhennykh sil*, no. 8 (1988).

Ovesen J., 'A local perspective on the incipent resistance in Afghanistan' in Huldt/Jansson (eds), *The tragedy of Afghanistan*, Croom Helm, London, 1988.

Pedersen G., 'Is there a future for the nomads of Afghanistan?', WUFA, vol. 3, no. 4 (1988).

Plastun V., 'Gorkii urok', *Aziya i Afrika Segodnia* part I, 1/93.

——, 'Gorkii urok', *Aziya i Afrika Segodnia* part II, 2/93.

——, 'NDPA: voprosy edinstva i soyuznikov na sovremennom etape revolyutsii', *Spetsial'nyi Byulleten' AN IV SSSR*, no. 6 (1987).

——, 'Pushtuny i ikh rol' v politicheskoi zhizni', *Aziya i Afrika Segodnya*, no. 11 (1995).

Podlesnyi A., 'Politika Natsional'nogo Primireniya i osobennosti ee provedeniya v yuzhnykh raionakh Afganistana', *Spetsial'nyi Byulleten' IV AN SSSR*, no. 2 (1990).

Prokhanov A., 'Afghanistan', *International Affairs*, Aug. 1988.

Puig J.J., 'La résistance afghane aujourd'hui', *Est et Ouest*, Jan. 1987.

——, 'Après le retrait soviétique en Afghanistan' in *Approches polemoligiques*, dir. D. Hermant, D. Bigo, FEDN 1991.

——, 'La Résistance afghane' in *Afghanistan. La colonisation impossible* CERF, 1984.

Rasul Amin A., 'Local organs of Soviet pattern in Afghanistan', WUFA, vol. 1, no. 4 (1986).

——, 'Stealthy sovietisation of Afghanistan', *Central Asian Survey*, vol. 3, no. 1 (1984).

Roy O., 'La politique de pacification sur le terrain' in A. Brigot and O. Roy, *La guerre d'Afghanistan*, La Documentation Française, 1985.

——, 'Le double code afghan', *Revue Française de Science Politique*, Dec. 1986.

——, 'The origins of the Afghan Communist Party', *Central Asian Survey*, vol. 7, no. 2/3 (1988).

Rubin B.R., 'Redistribution and the state in Afghanistan' in *The politics of social transformation in Afghanistan Iran and Pakistan*, Syracuse University Press, Syracuse, 1994.

Safronov V.G., 'Kak eto bylo', *Voenno-istoricheskii Zhurnal*, no. 5 (1990).

Samin A.Q., 'War impacts on Afghan agriculture', WUFA, April-June 1989.

Semenov Vs., 'Zemel'no-vodnaya reforma v Demokraticheskoi Res-

publike Afganistan', *Mirovaya Ekonomika i Mezhdunarodnye Otnosheniya,*
6/1983.

Shahrani M.N., 'Introduction. Marxist revolution and Islamic resistance'
in Canfield and Shahrani (eds), *Revolutions and rebellions in Afghanistan,*
International Studies Institute, Berkeley, 1984.

Sherbakov V., 'Po dolgu internatsionalistov', *Voennyi Vestnik,* 3 (1987):

Sigrist C., 'Die Mujahidin am Sheidenweg' in *Tritt Afghanistan aus dem
Schatten des Krieges am persischen Golf? – Konträre. Vorstellungen über die
friedliche Losung eines chronischen Bürgerkrieges: Materialien zum IAF-
Seminar vom 1.6.1991,* IAF, Bonn, 1991.

Steele J., 'Moscow's Kabul campaign', *Merip Reports,* July-Aug. 1986.

Tanin Z., 'To win the confidence of the masses', *World Marxist Review,*
1 (1984).

Taniwal H./Nuristani A.Y., 'Pashtun tribes and the Afghan Resistance',
WUFA, vol. 1, no. 1 (1985).

Traxler E., 'Aufbruch am Hindukusch', *Marxistische Blätter,* 2/1987.

Van Hollen E., 'Afghanistan 18 months of Soviet occupation', *Department
of State Bulletin,* no. 2055 (Oct. 1981).

———, 'Afghanistan 2 years of Soviet occupation', *Department of State
Bulletin,* vol. 82, no. 2060.

Vedad Kh., 'Rol DOMA v sotsial'no-politicheskoi zhizni RA 1978-1987
gg.' in *Respublika Afganistan,* Izdatelstvo Fan Uzbeskoi SSR, Tashkent,
1990.

'Voina est' voina, i russkikh mnogo', *Posev,* no. 3 (1983).

Zharov O., 'Sleptsy, navyazyvavshie sebya v povodiri', *Aziya i Afrika
Segodnia,* no. 12 (1992).

INDEX

Printed in the United States
3917